Manfred Kuhlmann

SOME OTHER GUYS

An anthology of 'Some Other Groups' that helped create the 1960's 'Mersey Sound'

A companion to Manfred's original book
'Beat Waves 'Cross The Mersey'
(ISBN 9781588502018)

© 2021 Veloce Enterprises Inc., San Antonio, TX 78230, USA

All rights reserved. This work may not be reproduced or transmitted in any form without the express written consent of the publisher
www.VelocePress.com

CONTENTS

ACKNOWLEDGEMENTS - Manfred Kuhlmann:	**Page** 2
PUBLISHER'S INTRODUCTION - Dave McClure & Manfred Kuhlmann:	**Page** 3
PUBLISHER'S COMMENTARY - Regarding copyright & fair use:	**Page** 4
AUTHOR'S FOREWORD - Manfred Kuhlmann:	**Page** 5
INSIDER'S FOREWORD - Dave Forshaw:	**Page** 7
MUSICIAN'S FOREWORD - Karl Terry:	**Page** 10
WHAT IS MERSEYBEAT? - Manfred Kuhlmann:	**Page** 11
GROUP STORIES:	**Page** 16
GROUP LINE-UPS:	**Page** 345
APPENDIX - The truth about the lost **ORIOLE** Cavern-recordings:	**Page** 372
SCRAPBOOK - A collection of images, tickets, handouts and photos from the era:	**Page** 377
INDEX - Group Stories, Line-Ups & Scrapbook images:	**Page** 431

AUTHOR'S ACKNOWLEDGEMENTS

This is always the important part, in which I do not know where to start and where to end, as there were so many people helping me in various respects that I really could fill pages with it.

Starting on the German side, the first to name is my wife, **Nelly Kuhlmann,** for her patience and comprehension.

Then there are my friends, **Armin Grants**, **Holger Roggemann** and **Gerry Nolan** – all from Bielefeld, **'Charly' Decker** (Berlin), **Alfred Hebing** (Essen), **Harald Mau** (Hamburg) and, not at last, **Ted 'King Size' Taylor** (Hamburg/Liverpool), for their tremendous support.

In Liverpool and the surrounding area, I received outstanding help from **Gina Hazlehurst**, **Arty** *'The Drummer'* **Davies**, **John Wishart**, **Paul Pilnick**, **Alan Stratton**, **Allen** *'Gaz'* **Gaskell**, **Allan Schroeder**, **Karl Terry**, **Ron Ellis**, **Alex Paton**, **Ian Hunter**, **Tony Aldridge**, **Geoff Taggart**, **Alan Watkinson**, **Dave Williams**, **Paul Hitchmough**, **Harry Prytherch**, **Peter Twist**, **Barry Cohen**, **Stephen Bailey** *(from the Beatles Shop)* and **Oliver Clay** *(Runcorn & Widnes Weekly News);* **Jaques Leblanc** *(Juke Box Magazine)* from Paris and, from overseas, **Pete Dunn**, **Freddie Ennis** and **Jose McLaughlin** (Australia) and my publisher, **Dave McClure,** from Texas.

Not to forget, of course, <u>**all the musicians**</u> who willingly gave me information, photos and images of their groups. It was a real pleasure to become acquainted and to spend time with all of you!

My very special thanks to both **Billy Geeleher** and young **Mike Jones,** for his tremendous help as, without him, this revised version of the book would not have been the same – in all honesty! Keep up your interest and good work, Mike!!!

Manfred Kuhlmann

PUBLISHER'S INTRODUCTION
(2021 Revised Edition of 'Some Other Guys')

The book that you now hold in your hands is the result of many years of additional research by Manfred since the first edition of 'Some Other Guys' was published in 2013. His research has unearthed an astonishing number of groups that were not included in the 2013 edition plus it expanded, and in some cases, corrected information related to some of the groups that were previously included. As I felt it was unnecessary to change the introduction pages, the only alteration is Manfred's foreword, and I encourage you to read it in its entirety. To cut to the chase, there are 50 new stories of groups that recorded, plus 35 new line ups. When added to the information in Manfred's companion publication, 'Beat Waves 'Cross The Mersey' (ISBN 9781588502018), this additional information brings the combined total to more than 825 groups that Manfred has researched and documented that were active on the Liverpool scene during the 1950's and 1960's. In addition, Manfred's recent research also unearthed information regarding the mysterious Cavern 'Oriole Recording Session' that took place in February 1964 which has never previously been documented to such a level of detail and that 'mystery' is unraveled in the appendix to the rear of this book.

Finally, once again both Manfred and myself extend our gratitude to Bill Harry creator and owner of the '*Mersey Beat*' newspaper who graciously allowed the use of a number of the images from that newspaper in the 2013 edition which are also reproduced in this revised version. As you page through this book, don't forget to thank another pioneer of the 'Mersey Sound' as, without Bill Harry and '*Mersey Beat*', many of these images would never have existed.

Thank you Bill!

Dave McClure & Manfred Kuhlmann

PUBLISHER'S COMMENTARY
Copyright and 'fair use'

Dave McClure (Liverpool 1962)

When I first reviewed the author's work with the consideration of publishing it, I was struck by the fact that it was a historically significant and extremely important document. However, I was also concerned. The reason for my concern was that I suspected it possibly included 'copyrighted' material and/or images.

My concern lay with the sources that had provided the material. Almost all of it came from the personal memorabilia collections and scrapbooks of the various groups and individuals that were featured in the book. Unfortunately, like most family photo albums, there was little or no data identifying who, what, when and where the material originated from. Consequently, I quickly arrived at the conclusion that researching ownership of 500 plus images and random 'scrapbook clippings' so that the appropriate credits could be established, would be a huge and probably impossible task.

I also concluded that even if we attempted to validate the owners, it would take more than a lifetime of digging and communicating, as most of the material was 45 years old (or older) and many of the images were obviously snapshots taken by friends, family, 'roadies' or other non-professionals. Some were publicity photos obviously taken by professional photographers, some of whom were no longer in business and may have been commissioned and paid for their services, by the groups. The real problem arose with the remaining images, how could we ever track down the owners of those images and, the answer was obvious, we likely could not.

Consequently, we are aware that this publication may unknowingly contain some material or images that may be subject to copyright. While every effort has been made to trace copyright holders of the material and images used in this book, we apologize for any omissions of the appropriate accreditation. However, as this is a digital publication, we can either apply the appropriate credit or withdraw the item immediately, upon notification of such. Even though the material or image may be subject to copyright, their use is possibly covered under section 107 of the US Copyright Act under the 'fair use' doctrine which allows limited use of copyrighted material without requiring permission from the rights holders as long as their inclusion adds significance and/or the material is the object of discussion within the story.

Finally, we ask that any copyright holders be commiserate to the intention of this book. It is meant to be a tribute to the individuals and the groups who contributed to what is possibly the most significant revolution in musical history in the 20th century and they deserve to have their story told. Therefore, we humbly request your unconditional approval for the unintentional use of any copyrighted material contained herein.

Dave McClure (info@VelocePress.com)

AUTHOR'S FOREWORD

**Manfred Kuhlmann and
"The Sound With the Pound"**

Before we get into the history of the 'Liverpool Sound' again, I'd like to take this opportunity to explain the story behind my books on the fabulous 1960's Liverpool Beat scene – and especially on this revised publication of "Some Other Guys".

Being from Bielefeld in Germany, I had been lucky enough to see a number of Liverpool groups in the local branch of the world famous 'Star-Club'. I was especially enthusiastic about those groups and naturally wanted to know more about them but it turned out that besides the groups that had international hits, information was difficult to find. Just for my own interest, I started to collect everything I could about those Merseybeat groups and that search continued for more than 20 years. At a certain point, my good friend and mentor - the legendary **Bob Wooler,** convinced me that I should publish a book containing the results of my archived research. This turned out to be easier said than done as, for many years, it proved impossible to find a suitable publisher. Even more unfortunately, **Bob Wooler** sadly died on February 8th 2002 so he never got to see the finished book. However, it was eventually published in 2009 using the title that Bob had proposed – "The Sound With The Pound". The book was well accepted on the scene, it generated many worldwide sales and also created a huge number of new contacts to musicians and tons of new information. It became apparent to me that everyone was taking my research at a serious level. . .

Based on the new information the book had generated, I felt that a revised version was necessary. I was in the process of negotiating with a Liverpool publishing company when I received an email from a former Liverpool musician, who was now living in San Antonio, Texas. Somehow he had got hold of a copy of my book and he expressed his appreciation for it but, at the same time, I felt he was disappointed that his group was not mentioned in it. I informed him about the latest developments and that I'd be happy to include his group in the revised version. During our friendly and interesting communication it turned out to that he was the owner of a Texas-based international publishing company. You can guess what is coming . . . ? Right, by far the best thing that could happen to me and my Merseybeat archives, **Dave McClure,** former member of the 1960's Liverpool group, the **Abstracts,** became my new publisher! This cooperation resulted in the 2012 publication of a completely updated edition, titled "Mersey Beat Waves", which contained significant additions to my original book. Due to copyright-complications, the book-title was changed to "Beat-Waves 'Cross The Mersey" after a few copies had been printed.

However, the sheer volume of information that I had obtained through those new contacts was such that it could not easily be included in "Beat-Waves 'Cross The Mersey". This finally led to the decision to produce a follow-up book – regardless of the fact that it would not be easy to attract as much reader interest without the popular names that were dealt with in my first book, names such as, the Beatles, the Searchers, Gerry & the Pacemakers, the Merseybeats, etc. But, as I never wasted much thought about becoming a bestselling author and only wanting to document this important era of musical history as completely as possible, I decided that there was no good reason for not writing another book. So, in 2013 a second book was published that, besides the Merseyside groups, also included a number of groups that did not come from Liverpool or its surroundings but became part of the scene through their frequent appearances. We chose the title, "Some Other Guys", as it hit the 'nail on the head' in various respects. It proved to be the right decision and both books were met with appreciation and international interest.

However, now being even more deeply connected to the scene, new contacts were made and information kept coming in. I kept Dave informed about these developments and, in 2019, he asked me if I would like to publish revised editions of my books. However, other than some corrections and additions at that time, there were actually no more than four or five new stories and a few additional line-ups. Giving consideration to the amount of work that would be involved in producing those revised publications, I asked him if he thought that he would sell more books because of four or five new stories. His response was: *"This has never been a matter of sales, but a matter of documenting the history of the era"*. He was so right with this comment and his reaction showed me that, in this respect, there was a kindred spirit between the two of us. Knowing that it would be unlikely that there will be another future revision, I started to go over the old ground again, diggin' here, there, everywhere – and each new piece of information proved that the task was worthwhile. The result of those additional two years research could never have been anticipated – almost 50 new stories of recording-artists and more than 30 new line-ups, besides all the other additional information that came to light in connection with the groups that had already been featured previously.

What you are now holding in your hands is the revised and significantly extended version of "Some Other Guys" – a real labour of love from both, the publisher and the author.

Bielefeld / Germany

February 2021

Manfred Kuhlmann

INSIDER'S FOREWORD

Dave Forshaw

It was a surprise when Manfred asked me to write this foreword for his latest book on the Merseyside groups/bands that recorded or played in the 60's and 70's and were never fully recognised for their music and talent at the time.

I can still remember his first telephone call in the mid-Eighties, requesting details and information about the various bands and members, and I was surprised that someone from Germany was so interested.

Then, when I read Manfred's first book, I was amazed at the amount of detail and information he had obtained and collated. I know now of various people who have read his book and had forgotten, but now suddenly remember, various detail(s) or even group members, which Manfred somehow had managed to discover.

It is now only right that, with this book, these additional groups should also be recognised for their input into the Merseybeat History.

Many of the groups who recorded never obtained the success or recognition they should have, maybe due to lack of publicity or promotion or the fact that there were no real recording facilities in Liverpool at that time, only for basic acetates.

I can think of at least three groups who, in my mind, would have made it if such facilities had been available plus. with modern publicity and promotion. they would have been a huge success.

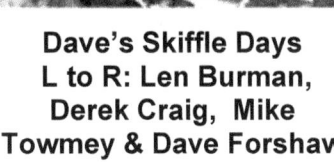

**Dave's Skiffle Days
L to R: Len Burman, Derek Craig, Mike Towmey & Dave Forshaw**

People never realised at the time the total number of groups which existed in the Merseyside area and the true amount of talent playing at that time. Plus, the large number of venues existing in the area offered groups the opportunity and experience to create their own style and brands of music. Venues which included dance halls, town halls, church halls, youth clubs, pubs and clubs, etc. – all booked live entertainment and this was predominantly groups.

Many of these venues were run by dance hall promoters, people who hired and promoted various venues and employed up to three or four bands per night, attracting dance and live music followers.

I was one of these promoters running various venues, including St. John's Hall in Bootle, Fazakerley Hall, the Church Institute in Ellesmere Port, Rainford Village Hall, Sampson & Barlow's (Walton & Bootle) plus Bootle YMCA.

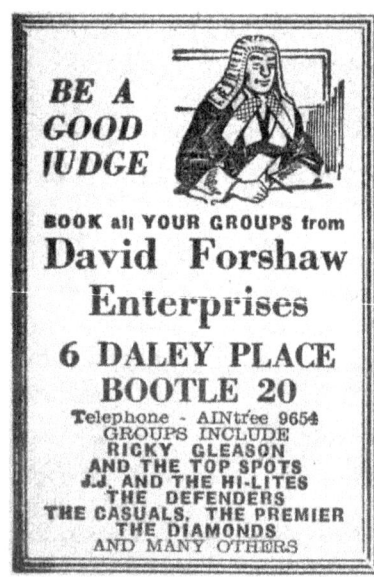

I first started promoting dances in 1957/8 and have, in my time, booked most of the Liverpool groups and bands, including the Beatles, who I first saw at Litherland Town Hall. That was on 27th December 1960 and I immediately went backstage after their show and booked them for a fee of £6-10 shillings and £7-10 shillings for the next two shows at St. John's Hall on the 6th January 1961. At all these venues, I also acted as the MC/compere, which I also did at various other venues in Liverpool, Warrington and on the Wirral.

Litherland Town Hall is recognised as the place the Beatles started after Germany but is also remembered by myself and many groups who played there for its unusual stage, which was sloped down towards the ballroom, with side doors cut at an angle to open onto the stage. Many musicians will recollect having to hammer nails in the floor or to put pieces of wood/cardboard in front of or under amplifiers and drums to stop them falling over or going forward while playing.

Litherland Town Hall, like most venues at that time (which included the Cavern), had no alcohol on sale. This meant that only tea, coffee or soft drinks were available to the audience. At many venues, jeans were not allowed, men had to wear a tie and you had to be at the venue by 9.30/10 pm to be allowed in.

I also booked many 'out-of-town' groups, such as the Rocking Vickers (Blackpool), the Thunderbeats (Preston), the Sabres (St. Helens), the Diplomats (Southport), Denny & the Witch Doctors (Yorkshire), Gerry Levene & the Avengers (Birmingham), plus many bands from the Wirral, Chester, Southport, St.Helens, Wigan, Warrington, Northwich and Wrexham areas played regularly.

In 1962, I took on my first group as a manager, which was the Memphis Three, followed by Ricky Gleason & the Topspots. I then opened my own theatrical agency, David Forshaw Enterprises, and represented, as a manager, the Defenders, J.J. & the Hi-Lites, the Lee Eddie Five, the Connoisseurs, the Premiers, Adam & the Sinners, the Renicks, the Pawns, the Topspots, the Twigg, Vikki & the Moonlighters, the Diamonds, the Casuals, the Mersey Gonks, the Four Musketeers, Sweet Illusion, the Soul Survivors etc., plus many others who I represented as an agent. This agency is still operating today.

I also sent groups to Germany, including Ricky Gleason & the Topspots, who went to the Star-Club in Hamburg. This was always an adventure! I remember having three groups getting ready to tour Germany and France when the agent booking them simply disappeared. Another group, the Defenders, were due to go to Biarritz but were cancelled by telegram three days prior to leaving.

> **DAVE FORSHAW ENTERPRISES**
>
> SOLE MANAGEMENT:
>
> THE TOP SPOTS (Oriole recording artistes)
>
> | THE DEFENDERS | THE MOTIFS |
> |---|---|
> | THE DIAMONDS | THE RENICKS |
> | THE PREMIERS | |
> | 4 TRAVELLERS | MEMPHIS 3 |
>
> 6 DALEY PLACE. BOOTLE 20.   AIN 9654
>
> Available Day and Night.

At that time, there were also the weddings and birthday parties, which offered further opportunities for groups to perform. On these nights, groups often had to play the whole evening, sometimes having to repeat songs, with just a short break during the night.

I also remember various groups being able to play two, three or more venues in a single night, having to arrive and set up at each booking. Can you see that happening today?

Those were the days my friend(s), I wish they'd never end . . . .

Litherland - Liverpool

June 2011

Dave Forshaw (Dance Promoter, Manager and Agent)

MUSICIAN'S FOREWORD

Karl Terry (1960's)

I have been active on the scene since the late Fifties, playing with quite a few of the original Merseybeat bands and I am still fronting my own group – Karl Terry & the Cruisers.

I first met Manfred at a gig I was playing in Liverpool in 1987 and was surprised that someone from Germany was so deeply interested in the history of Merseybeat.

His were not the usual questions about the Beatles etc., but he already knew a lot of the Merseybeat groups and their members.

I took a chance and asked if he could get me a gig in Germany and I have been playing there ever since with Manfred becoming a very close friend and my manager, recording with us the last Merseybeat LP on Vinyl, which he produced.

Over the years he asked me about so many groups whose names I could remember but not their details and I found it fascinating to see how he managed to find them in the end and even to make direct contact.

One must consider that in the Merseybeat days, hundreds of groups with thousands of musicians were active in Liverpool – the whole scene was 'vibing' and changing almost every day. Therefore, I can state that there was, and is, nobody who could know all of them.

Manfred is so thorough with his research, as proven in his original book, 'The Sound With The Pound', which is being re-published now as 'Beat Waves 'Cross The Mersey'.

Like that one, this new book is a must for everybody, who is interested in the true history of Merseybeat and the musicians who wrote that history.

This is not a book to flick through, you really have to read it and use it as a reference-book, as you will not find another one of its kind.

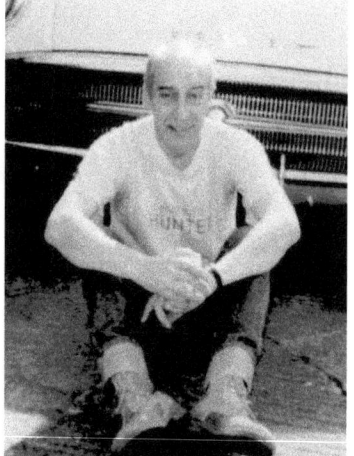

Karl Terry (today)

For all his research, Manfred made numerous visits to Liverpool and, through this, has become a German Scouser and, because of his merits in keeping our history, he has become a highly respected person on the scene and most of all one of us . . .

Old Swan - Liverpool, November 2011

Karl Terry (Karl Terry & the Cruisers)

WHAT IS MERSEYBEAT?

Listening to people talking about Merseybeat, it automatically gives the impression that this was a special and individual music style, such as Skiffle, Trad-Jazz or Folk-Blues for example. But is this really true? A Merseybeat pioneer once asked about it said: *"It's the American Rock 'n' Roll, only played worse!"*

This statement, of course, was more Scouse humour than serious, but it doesn't help to find the right answer. It might even be better to ask a musician from outside England for his opinion, as the expression Merseybeat became very popular in the international world of music in the first half of the Sixties.

Klaus Konopka, former bass guitarist with the 60's Rhythm & Blues group the **Highfields** from Bielefeld/Germany who, in the first half of the Sixties, often shared the stage with Liverpool groups at the local Star-Club and many other venues, gives his view as follows:

"The typical group consisted of four to five guys, who played lead guitar, rhythm guitar, bass guitar, drums and sometimes a front singer.

One guitarist tended to play a semi- or full resonator guitar, often a Gibson. The consistent beat in 4/4 rhythm was accentuated on the 2 and the 4 - known as Backbeat.

Just like Rock 'n' Roll and Rhythm & Blues, the Merseybeat was also mainly based on a 12-bar Blues pattern whereby, compared to the Rock 'n' Roll, the tempo was more moderate and the singing, supplied by almost all the group members, was in harmony, often orientated on the American all-girl groups and their vocal harmonies, amongst others.

John Schroeder

The solo guitarist, quite contrary to Rock 'n' Roll, played his melody part according to the harmony chords. Repeating the simplistic melodies and words frequently added to the impact on the audience.

The character of the kind of Merseysound that I consider typical is melancholic, due to the rough lead vocals and the consistent riffing of the rhythm guitar, as well as the idiosyncratic harmony singing. For me, the typical examples are the first two Beatles albums, as well as the Lennon/McCartney composition, "A World Without Love", by Peter & Gordon. Also consider "Needles and Pins" by the Searchers and also "Ferry Cross the Mersey" by Gerry & the Pacemakers . . ."

For the examples given, he is probably right in his judgement, but it is not really sufficient, taking into account that there were so many different sounding groups whose music was, and still is, classified as Merseybeat.

Let's have a look at the classic compilations, "This Is Merseybeat" Vol. 1 and Vol. 2, which **John Schroeder** produced for the Oriole label in 1963.

There you have the Country-influenced Rockabilly of **Sonny Webb & the Cascades**, the Rock 'n' Roll of **Rory Storm & the Hurricanes** and **Faron's Flamingos**, the **Everly Brothers** sound of **Del Renas**, the Rhythm & Blues of **Ian & the Zodiacs** and the **Nomads**, the Soul influence with **Derry Wilkie & the Pressmen**, the **Merseybeats**' ballad and the more commercial sounding Beat of **Mark Peters & the Silhouettes** or the superb **Earl Preston & the TTs**. So what was typically Merseybeat in this?

The Nomads

Left: Mark Peters

The Merseybeats

Right: Earl Preston

Going a step further, how can you identify that Merseybeat sound, if the following popular Merseybeat groups are compared musically?

>> the **Beatles** to **King Size Taylor & the Dominoes**,
>> the **Swinging Blue Jeans** to the **Undertakers**,
>> the **Dennisons** to the **Kirkbys**,
>> the **Escorts** to the **Mojos**,
>> the **Searchers** to the **Roadrunners**,
>> the **Remo Four** to **Gerry & the Pacemakers**
>> the **Chants** to the **Hideaways**,
>> the **Merseybeats** to the **Big Three**
>> the **Fourmost** to **Billy J. Kramer & the Dakotas**

There is one thing that all these groups had in common compared to earlier popular sounds: the drums were much more in the foreground and it was this which gave their music the fantastic drive – the Beat!

The Chants

Far Right: The Clayton Squares

But was this really making an individual sound? So where were the other similarities, the typical Merseybeat characteristics?

Bands that were influenced by the music of the American all-girl groups often sang the verses and choruses in close harmony, but that too was not applicable to all of them.

How does the unadulterated Rock 'n' Roll of **Karl Terry & the Cruisers**, the swinging Blues of the **Michael Allen Group** or the raw Blues of the **Prowlers**, the Country sound of **Johnny Sandon**, the Mod sound of the **Clayton Squares** or the jazzy Beat of **Them Grimbles** fit into that picture? And why does a mainstream pop singer such as **Cilla Black** belong to the Merseybeat?

Questions, questions and more questions, to which only one answer can be correct Merseybeat was not the name for a sound, but the expression stands for the scene as an integral whole.

And here we have finally arrived at the most important thing of all – the Merseybeat scene. It might well be that there were other British groups playing in that style before any of the Liverpool groups, maybe in London, Birmingham, Manchester or Newcastle, but that does not matter.

The first big scene was in Liverpool, with its numerous groups, pushing the Beat out into the world and so, at the same time, ending the musical predominance of Rock 'n' Roll cover-softeners such as **Cliff Richard** (compare his "Lucky Lips" to the original by **Ruth Brown**), **Ricky Valance** or **Craig Douglas**.

Young musicians, initially in Europe and ultimately, throughout the world, were influenced by the Merseybeat groups in their sound and many also in their choice of their names.

Germany alone, for example, in addition to the recording groups, the **Merseyblues** (ME Records) from Bielefeld and the **Mersey Kings** (Scherer) from Heidelberg, produced the **Mersey Counts** (Friedrichsdorf), the **Mersey Group** (Saarland), the **Mersey Sounds** (Clausthal-Zellerfeld), the **Merseys** (Reutlingen before 1966), the **Merseyshakes** (from the Hanover area) and, from Berlin, the **Mersey Teens.** Even in the late Nineties, there was a revival group calling themselves the **Merseyville Spyders**.

Other international recording groups were the **Merseyboys** from the USA, the **Merseybeats** and **Les Merseys** (both from Canada), the **Mersey Moptops** (Japan), **Les Mersey-Rockers** (France/Switzerland) and the **Merseymen** (New Zealand).

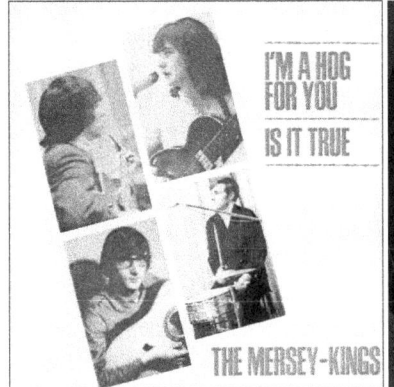

Mersey-Kings (Germany!)   **Merseymen (New Zealand!)**   **Merseyblues (Germany!)**

Merseybeats (Canada!)

God only knows how many beat groups worldwide used 'Mersey' in their names but this, of course, underlines the significance and the influence of Liverpool's Merseybeat scene.

From approximately 1964 onwards, the expression Merseybeat was replaced by the general term, Beat, but Liverpool, or the Liverpool Sound, was still a mark of quality. This can be seen from the fact that many groups were still announced as being from Liverpool, although some of them had probably never set foot in British harbour city.

Furthermore the record companies still misused that name, mainly for compilation albums on which Liverpool groups were featured in a minor way or, sometimes, not at all.

The Danish Metronome label had two singles with the title, 'News From Liverpool', one by the **Mike Cotton Sound** and the other by **Brian Diamond & the Cutters** - both from London!

There is the classic French album, "The Best Of The Liverpool Sound" (Columbia 1964), with 11 groups, of which only **Gerry & the Pacemakers** and perhaps the **Jynx** came from Merseyside. Amongst the other featured groups were the **Dave Clark Five**, **Chris Farlowe & the Thunderbirds**, **Deke Arlon & the Off-Beats** and **Mike Sheridan & the Nightriders**.

Brian Diamond (London!)

The British Embassy long-player "Liverpool Beat" (1964), of which two volumes were also released by CBS in Argentina, does not include one Liverpool artist.

The German Fontana label, on its compilation, "Liverpool Beat" (1964), also included groups such as the **Pretty Things**, **Troy Dante & the Infernos** and **Davy Jones & the Blue Sounds** in addition to five Merseyside outfits

Also in Germany, the Ariola label had an album series called "Liverpool Beat", of which only half a long-player was by a Liverpool group – **King Size Taylor & the Dominoes**, coupled with the **Bobby Patrick Big Six** from Scotland on the other side.

Another, allegedly live recording from the 'Kaskade Beat-Club' in Cologne by the **Soundriders**, is considered to have been by a Merseybeat group, but the musicians behind this obviously fictitious group name have never been identified.

"Liverpool Beat" Ariola (Germany!)

The other albums in this line are by the German groups, **Rattles** (Hamburg), **Mike Warner & the New Stars** from Bielefeld (with the participation of **King Size Taylor**), the **Mustangs** (Münster), the **German Blue Flames** (Gelsenkirchen) and the **Kettles** (Kassel). Also, the Indo Rock group, **Tielman Brothers,** from Holland, and **Mike Rat & the Runaways**, a Spanish group with the German singer, **Mike Kogel**, soon to become **Los Bravos** of "Black Is Black" fame.

Another obscure association with Liverpool was used by the small independent German label, 'Storz Records'. They released a series of 45's called 'Liverpool Beat-Club', in which only one British group was featured – the **Mad Classix** from Coventry. All the other groups were from Germany and included the **Strangers** (Hamburg), the **Silhouettes** (Koblenz), the **Sharks** (Hanover) and the **Pipelines** (Bremen).

The only real Liverpool group under contract with Storz was the **Mersey Five** (see **Gerry Bach & the Beathovens** story) but, funnily enough, their two singles on that label were not featured in that series, although they were released at the same time as the others. Does that make any sense?

But the worst, in this respect, was the German Columbia label. On their sampler, "Liverpool Hop" (1965), the **Black Knights,** the **Blackwells** and **Gerry & the Pacemakers** were the only Liverpudlians out of 16 groups, which included **Johnny Kidd & the Pirates**, the **Downliners Sect Christian's Crusaders**, the **LeRoys**, the **Federals**, and even **Gene Vincent & the Shouts.**

The same is valid for their other two compilations, "Liverpool" and "Liverpool '65", on which only **Gerry & the Pacemakers** and the **Swinging Blue Jeans** came from that city, while other songs were mainly from the **Dave Clark Five**, **Mike Rabin & the Demons**, **Peter & Gordon**, **Georgie Fame & the Blue Flames**, the **Zephyrs**, the **Naturals**, and even **Manfred Mann**.

The final attempt in this direction came from the British Decca in 1975, with a double album called "Merseybeat At Liverpool" with only the **Mojos** and **Big Three** from the Mersey along with 14 (!) other artists – among them groups such as the **Rockin' Berries**, the **Strangers**, the **Mountain Kings**, the **Cavern Four** and the **Blue Stars**, all hailing from Birmingham's Brumbeat scene. With exception of the **Rockin' Berries**, the other groups named had already been featured on a Decca compilation, called "Brumbeat" in 1964. These, of course, were misleadingly packaged but, when it came down to sales figures, there were no scruples anymore. *'From Liverpool'* was still an attractive brand and so easy to sell . . .

THE ABSTRACTS

For a number of reasons this group never got the recognition it deserved in the history of Merseybeat. One of those reasons was that more than one third of their bookings were outside of the greater Liverpool area. However, the main reason was most probably their name, even if this sounds a bit paradoxical, the name **Abstracts** was simply used by too many groups on the scene at that time - to the confusion of the local music newspapers.

There were the **Abstracts** from Birkenhead, who later became the **Michael Allen Group**. Then there were the **Abstracts** from Speke, that later continued as the **Excerts** and then the **Knights** from Garston added to the confusion when they changed their name to the **Abstrax** for a short time. There was also a short-lived group called the **Abstract Minds!**

However, the **Abstracts** in this story came from the Waterloo/Crosby area and evolved from an association between two friends, **Peter Darwent** (g/voc & t/bass) and **Dave 'Mac' McClure** (g/voc). Their first public appearance was at St. Marys Church Hall on Saturday, August 11th 1962 and, by that time, **Ray Pate** (g) had been added to the line-up. A little later they were joined by **Dave Lawton** on washboard, and they became a fairly typical skiffle line up of that time. However, in October 1963, **Dave Lawton** replaced his washboard with a set of drums and around that same time, **Peter 'Gilly' Gillham** joined as their lead vocalist. Finally, in March 1964, **Ray Pate** was replaced by **Paul Richards** as their lead guitarist and the **Abstracts** had morphed into a true Merseybeat group. Due to the previously mentioned confusion arising from the multiple use of the **Abstracts** name, the group had it officially registered in April 1964 and, from then on, the **Abstracts** appeared in the following line-up:

Peter 'Gilly' Gillham	(voc)
Paul Richards	(lg/voc)
Dave 'Mac' McClure	(rg/voc)
Peter Darwent	(bg/voc)
David Lawton	(dr)

Dave McClure had previously played in a guitar/vocal duo in the style of the **Everly Brothers** together with **Jeff Hill** under the name of **Jeff & Dave** in the late fifties.

Paul Richards, who was the last one to join, had formerly played with the **Henchmen** and the **Orbit Five**. All the other group members were newcomers to the scene.

Interestingly, **Paul Darwent,** brother of the bass guitarist, together with **John Liptrot** and **Bryan 'Chorley' Lowes,** acted as 'Roadies' for the entire time that the group was together.

Peter Gillham's singing voice was similar to that of **Eric Burdon** and accordingly, the **Abstracts**' programme included a few **Animals** numbers such as "We've Gotta Get Out of This Place" and "House of the Rising Sun", as well as similar types of R&B songs.

On the other hand the group also played a lot of Rock 'n' Roll and Beat numbers including "Glad All Over", "Lucille", "Love Potion # 9", "Long Tall Sally", "Twist and Shout" and even the comedy number, "Short Shorts", a somewhat risqué part of their live performances!

In an 1964 article, The 'Crosby Herald' newspaper described their music quite accurately as *'Dave Clark crossed with Muddy Waters and more power added'*.

The Abstracts - L to R: Pete Darwent, Dave Lawton, 'Gilly' Gillham, 'Mac' McClure & Paul Richards, Victoria Street, Liverpool - 1964

L to R: Pete Darwent, Paul Richards, 'Mac' McClure, Dave Lawton & 'Gilly' Gillham (1964)

In 1964, the **Abstracts** recorded a demo with the Merseybeat standard, "Some Other Guy", at the Crosby Labour Club and this shows them to be a really good, driving Beat group.

For personal reasons, none of the members had aspirations of achieving musical fame or stardom - they even turned down an offer to go to Germany. Also, in 1965, they turned down the opportunity to become the new backing group for **Mark Peters** who had just separated from the **Method**. The **Abstracts** were only interested in playing music and entertaining the audience for the sheer fun of doing it and anyone that ever saw this group live will certainly remember them and their ability to interact with the audience.

Besides playing the usual clubs in the Liverpool city centre such as the 'Black Cat', the 'Peppermint Lounge', 'Mardi Gras' and 'Cavern', they also played many of the area's dance halls such as St Lukes, Alexander Hall, St. Marys and the Winter Gardens. They also made many appearances in nearby cities including Southport ('Klik-Klik'), Wigan ('Sportsman'), Warrington ('Heaven & Hell'), Bolton ('Beachcomber'), Oswestry (Victoria Rooms), Keswick (Pavilion Ballroom), Leigh (Casino) and Wrexham (Horns Hotel).

(December 18th. 1964)

They played the 'Plaza' in St. Helens on a regular basis and the club owner, **Harry Bostock**, was so enthusiastic about the **Abstracts** he was absolutely convinced that they would make the big time. Therefore, he arranged for a professional recording of a few of their live-sessions in 1965, of which extracts were most probably cut in acetates for better storage. The group members recently tried in vain to track him and the recordings down but their efforts have proved unsuccessful – so far!

(October 3rd. 1965)

Unfortunately, that is why it is not known which songs were on the recordings, but it is quite possible that the **Paul Richards** originals, "Lazing In the Haze" and "(Do the) Jam Buttie", were among them.

The **Abstracts** continued to play the club circuit in the northwest and became one of the most requested groups at the 'Orrell Park Ballroom' and the 'Grave', a Liverpool venue that was very popular for its all-nighters.

In April 1966, **Dave Lawton** left the group – he was unable to continue drumming due to arthritis in his knees. His replacement, **Dell Robinson**, was a former member of the **Deans**, who had recently disbanded.

He played his first gig with the **Abstracts** on April 15th 1966 at the Orrell Park Ballroom without having had a previous practice session with the group.

This really great drummer stayed with the **Abstracts** until September 1966 and then re-joined his old comrades from the **Deans** in a group called **Solomon's Mines**. Unfortunately, he did not stay for too long and he left them and quit the music business. What a loss of talent . . .

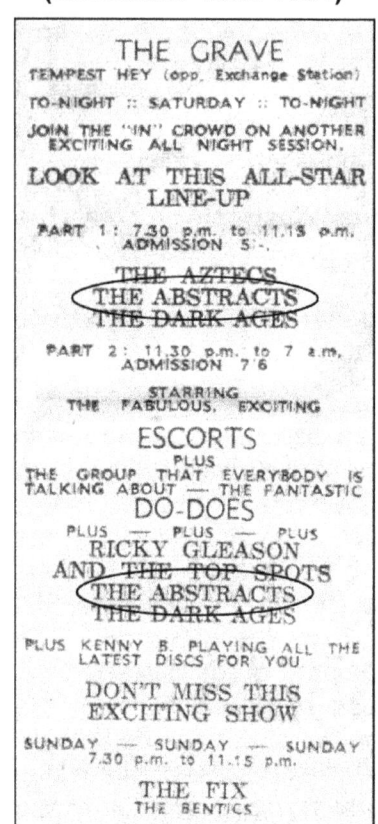

(May 21st. 1966)

L to R: Pete Darwent, 'Gilly' Gillham, Dell Robinson, 'Mac' McClure & Paul Richards (1966)

In September 1966, the **Abstracts** were re-joined by their original drummer, **Dave Lawton** who, through medication and treatment, was able to play drums again. A few weeks before he came back to the group, singer **Peter 'Gilly' Gillham** had left and quit showbiz.

The **Abstracts** continued as a four-piece, with the three guitarists sharing the vocals.

As the scene changed over the years, the **Abstracts** added more **Beach Boys** and Tamla Motown numbers to their set and also played the clubs of the so-called cabaret scene, such as the famous 'Garrick' in Leigh, where they appeared quite regularly supporting some of the major 60's artists during their one week appearances at the club.

The **Abstracts** final appearance was at **Paul Richards's** wedding in September 1968. It is known that **Peter Darwent** and **Paul Richards** continued to play for charity events on the local scene for some time after that.

In 1978, **Dave McClure** emigrated to the USA and, in 1989, **David Lawton** also became a full time resident of the United States.

Discography

Some Other Guy   **UK - demo / 1964**

In addition, it is known that **Harry Bostock**, the owner of the Plaza Ballroom in St. Helens made professional recordings of a few live sessions of the **Abstracts**, from which extracts were possibly cut in acetate. Unfortunately, it could not be established which songs were on those recordings, but it is likely that the two groups' originals **"Lazing In the Haze (of the Golden Sun I Love)"** and **"(Do the) Jam Buttie"** were among them.

> *"I'm sure that none of the 60's Liverpool groups gave any consideration to the fact that they were making musical history. It's somewhat unfortunate that they were all part of an era that turned out to be one of the greatest musical revolutions of all time, but failed to realize it . . "*
>
> **Dave McClure / The Abstracts**

Above comment taken from the book:

"The Abstracts - A 1960's Liverpool Group That Time Almost Forgot"

VelocePress - B&W Edition: ISBN 9781588501646 or Color Edition: 9781588501462

STEVE ALDO

Edward Alban Jean-Pierre Bedford was born on October 4th, 1945 in Toxteth, Liverpool into a very musical family. An early influence was one of his aunts who, whenever she took care of him as a young child, used to sing and dance for him. Later on he would stand outside the local clubs and listen to the music of the bands.

At 11 years of age, he took part in a talent-competition at the Rialto Ballroom in Liverpool where he performed the **Sammy Davis Jr.** number, "Because of you". His first club experience came a little later on when he sang the song, "Sixteen candles" at the Holyoake Hall in Liverpool, backed by **Bob Evans & the Five Shillings**.

At 13 years of age, he was part of the 'Backyard Kids' show at the Pavilion in Lodge Lane, singing "Short Fat Fanny" and one year later, during a holiday with the 'York House' boys-club on the Isle of Man, he won every talent-competition he entered and ended up staying there for a few more weeks, singing with the **Ivy Benson Big Band** at the 'Villa Marina'.

Back in Liverpool he guested with the **Casuals** at the 'White House' in Duke Street, where he met up for the first time with the guitarists, **Walter Quarles** and **George Dixon** and their drummer **Norman Frazer**, who later on would cross his path again. After that great experience, he quite often sang with **Howie Casey & the Seniors***.

Steve Aldo

The Liverpool manager, **Joe Flannery** became aware of this young talented singer and wanted to take him under his wings, he also suggested a name-change into **Aldo Stevens**. Unfortunately, the planned management arrangement did not work out but that is how **Eddie Bedford** became **Steve Aldo**. With this new stage-name, he continued guesting with various groups before he joined the **Challengers**, the former backing-group of **Tommy Quickly**, and, from then on, appeared as **Steve Aldo & the Challengers***. The group became very popular on the Merseybeat-scene and, in 1963, went to Hamburg in Germany to play the famous 'Star-Club' for a few weeks.

During that time, a complete live-set of **Steve Aldo & the Challengers** was recorded for an album, most probably by Ariola. Unfortunately, the album was never released. While still in Hamburg, **Steve Aldo** fell out with the **Challengers** drummer and, due to this disagreement, the group returned to Liverpool without him. However, **Steve Aldo** remained in Hamburg and joined **King Size Taylor & the Dominoes*** as an additional singer. **King Size Taylor & the Dominoes**, at that time, were recorded by Polydor for another album that very likely featured **Steve Aldo** singing on some of the tracks. Unfortunately, once again, that album never saw the light of day but some of the songs were released on various sampler albums and, for those releases, the pseudonym of **Boots Wellington & his Rubber Band** was used.

Steve Aldo then returned to Liverpool and joined the **Nocturns*** but this did not last for too long as, in February 1964, he became the singer with a new group that was formed by **Brian Griffiths** of the **Big Three** and **Ron Parry**, former drummer of **Joe Brown & the Bruvvers** plus **Vinnie Parker** and **Francis Galloway**. This group was the **Griff Parry Five*** who were signed to Decca and, according to an article in the 'Mersey Beat' newspaper, recorded the songs, "Don't make my Baby blue" (probably an original), "Irresistible you" and the **Crests**-success, "Sixteen candles", obviously a favourite of **Steve Aldo**. For unknown reasons, none of these recordings were ever released. **Brian Griffiths**, **Ron Parry** and **Vinnie Parker** (p/org) soon left to join **Johnny Gustafson** in his new group, called the **Johnny Gus Set.*** This left **Steve Aldo** and **Francis Galloway** (bg/sax) who had already played together in Hamburg in

The Griff Parry Five

the line-up of **King Size Taylor & the Dominoes.** They obviously got on well together and decided to form a new group and they recruited a guitarist, whose name, in spite of intensive research, could not be established. The new line-up now appeared under the name of the **Steve Aldo Quintet** and their manager became **Spencer Loyd Mason** who, among others, already had the **Mojos*** under his wings. Through his connections with Decca, he managed to get **Steve Aldo** signed to that label but, obviously, as solo-artist. However, the **Steve Aldo Quintet** at that time consisted of the following musicians:

Steve Aldo	(voc)
???	(g/bg)
Spike Jones	(org)
Fran Galloway	(bg/sax)
Brian Low	(dr)

The former groups of **Spike Jones** and **Brian Low** are, unfortunately, unknown.

Still in 1964, **Steve Aldo** recorded a great version of **Marvin Gaye's** "Can I get a witness", coupled with **Jimmy Reed's** all-time Blues classic, "Baby, what you want me to do". The single was only released under the name of **Steve Aldo** and, therefore, it is not known if this fantastic recording was made by the complete **Steve Aldo Quintet** or if there was a backing group arranged by Decca. Unfortunately, the **Steve Aldo Quintet** disbanded when **Steve Aldo** left to join up with **Howie Casey** in the **Krew***, with whom he went to France. Of the other members, it is only known that, at a later date, **Fran Galloway** went on to play in various groups in Italy, amongst them **I Baronetti** and the **Four Kents**.

During his time with the **Krew** in France, **Steve Aldo** was on the same bill with French idol, **Johnny Hallyday,** at an evening show on the 'Palladium' in Paris. **Johnny Hallyday** was so impressed by **Steve Aldo's** singing that he arranged for him to go solo and even put a new backing-group together for him, which obviously did not have a name. **Steve Aldo,** with that group, became resident at the 'Kir Samba' in St. Germain, Paris. At the end of 1965, **Steve Aldo** returned to UK and, initially, he was based in London where he was backed by the Essex band, the **Fairies**. **Tony Stratton-Smith** contracted him as a support-act for the final **Beatles*** tour in England which did not bring him the long deserved breakthrough but did result in a recording contract with Parlophone.

In 1966, the single, "Everybody has to cry", was released - another brilliant record that was coupled with "You're absolutely right", which the singer himself always considered as his best number. On this record, **Steve Aldo** was backed by Parlophone's studio big-band. Like it's forerunner, this record also did not become a chart-success but today both of his singles are favourites with the so-called 'Northern Soul' scene and the prices asked for original pressings of those records are ridiculous. But this, of course, did not help **Steve Aldo** at that time so he left London and returned to Liverpool and became a member of the **Fyx**.

After that, for a short time he was backed by the **Munchkins** but, in 1967, he was a member of the **Incrowd** (another story in this book), this group included **Walter Quarles** and **George Dixon** from the **Casuals**, and, at one point, had also included **Fran Galloway** from the **Steve Aldo Quintet**. With the **Incrowd,** he recorded the songs, "I can make love to you", "Love ain't love", "Thank you Darling" and "You're my Pigeon", for the Deram label but, these again remained unreleased. At that same time, **Steve Aldo** also sang with the house-band of the Wooky Hollow Club but got back with the **Incrowd** for the next Deram recording-session. This time

the single, "Where in the world", was released but **Steve Aldo's** lead-vocals are only featured on the B-side, "I can love you too". The record did not make any impact in England but it was well received in the Netherlands.

It was not too long after this release that the **Incrowd** fell apart and **Steve Aldo** became a bar-manager in London. After that, he earned his money as a 'singing bartender' on the cruise-ships before he became the manager of a Yate's wine-bar in Liverpool. At that time, he was still singing now and then – among others with the **A-Team**, but he never seriously tried a comeback.

Steve Aldo, a great stage-personality with a most impressive bluesy voice simply faded from the scene without having had the recognition and the success he truly deserved. In later years, already wheelchair bound, he dedicated his life to public reading until he died in 2017.

Steve Aldo & the Incrowd

Discography

Steve Aldo:

Can I get a witness / Baby what you want me to do　　UK- Decca F.12041 / 1964

Everybody has to cry / You're absolutely right　　　　UK- Parlophone R 5432 / 1966

With the **Incrowd**:

Where in the world / I can love you too　　　　　　UK- Deram DM 272 / 1969

(On this Deram single **Steve Aldo**'s lead vocals were only featured on the B-side.)

Besides this, there were the Hamburg recordings with **King Size Taylor & the Dominoes** under the name of **Boots Wellington & his Rubber Band** on the German Polydor label. For these recordings please see the story of **King Size Taylor & the Dominoes***.

Unreleased recordings:

In 1963, **Steve Aldo & the Challengers** were recorded live at the 'Star-Club' in Hamburg, probably by Ariola for an album, that in the end was never released and therefore it is not known how many or which songs were recorded.

In 1964, he recorded together with the **Griff Parry Five,** for the English Decca label the songs, "**Make my Baby blue**", "**Irresistible you**" and "**Sixteen candles**", that were never released.

In 1968, together with the **Incrowd,** he recorded the numbers, "**I can make love to you**", "**Love ain't love**", "**Thank you Darling**" and "**You're my pigeon**" for Deram. Of those recordings, at least the first two named, featured **Steve Aldo** as lead-vocalist. None of the numbers were ever released.

*The stories of these groups can be followed in 'Beat Waves 'Cross The Mersey' (*VelocePress ISBN 978-1-58850-201-8*).

THE APPROACHERS

This Rhythm & Blues-type group was formed in the early 1960's and hailed from the Liverpool district of West Derby. They had taken their name from a pub on Queens Drive, called 'The Western Approaches'.

There is very little known about the early days of the **Approachers** as they mainly played the mining venues and night-clubs around St. Helens and Wigan - in a line-up with:

Barry Williams	(voc)
Peter Randles	(lg)
Ken Beattie	(rg)
Dave Kitching	(bg)
Steve Hale	(dr)

None of the musicians had ever appeared on the scene before and therefore, it could be taken for granted that, all of them were newcomers. As they already were all well into their twenties at that time, and they all had jobs, there was never a thought wasted on becoming professionals which is why they only performed live at the weekends.

Their bookings, at that time, were handled by **Glady Morais**, probably the father of well-known drummer **Trevor Morais** and he wanted some sort of a demo from the group. So in 1964, the **Approachers** finally decided to record an acetate at the Kensington studio of **Percy Phillips**. Of that session, it is only known that on the a-side was a version of the **Rufus Thomas** classic, "Walking the dog". It is not certain if **Peter Randles** was still playing the lead-guitar on that recording as, around that time, he left and was replaced by **Brian Harper**, whose former group is not known. **Peter Randles** became a member of the **Henchmen** but then moved away from Liverpool, he later emigrated to Australia.

Tommy Flude

Towards the end of 1965, **Brian Harper** left and disappeared from the scene. He was not replaced and, from then on, **Ken Beattie** was doing all the guitar-work. In early 1966, **Barry Williams** was the next to leave and, at first, the other members shared the vocals.

Soon after **Barry Williams** left, the **Approachers** were joined by a very young **Tommy Flude** as bluesharp-player. He came from the just disbanded **Deans**, where he had played bass-guitar but had also done a lot of harmony-singing. So naturally, the development was that **Tommy Flude**, besides playing the harp, also became the lead-vocalist of the **Approachers**. The management of the group now was 'Maghull Promotions', who got them regular bookings at the Westhougton 'Casino' or the 'Hole In The Ground' in Horwich, as well as other clubs in places like Bolton, Rochdale and Wigan but rarely in Liverpool.

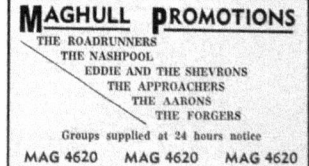

The **Approachers** then added an organ-player to their line-up, whose name sadly is lost and it is only remembered that he came from the Manchester-area. The group now played heavily organ influenced R&B in the style of **Zoot Money**, **Graham Bond** and **Georgie Fame**.

With their new sound, they decided that they needed a new name and so the **Approachers** became the **Krunjing Nabs**. How wrong can a decision be . . . . ! As this silly name did not mean anything to anybody, it is delivered in different spellings and even **Bob Wooler** on his poster for the '21 Beat Spectacular' at the Grafton Rooms on 13th May 1966, put them down as *'Kringin' Nabs'*. But that was not really important anymore, as the group very soon called it a day.

Steve Hale disappeared from the scene and **Tommy Flude** teamed up with his old mates from the **Deans**, once again, in the re-formed **Solomon's Mines**, but that's another story in this book.

Ken Beattie and **Dave Kitching** obviously re-united with **Barry Williams** and teamed up with **Roy Ellis (dr)** and **Robert Luke (rg/voc)** from the also just disbanded **Defiants**. This five-piece group then appeared as the **Defiants** but occasionally also used the **Approachers** name at some of their gigs. The group then took a new name, calling themselves the **Bent Sect** and had at least one appearance at the 'Cavern'. It is not known for how long they were together or what happened to the former original **Approachers** musicians after that.

Robert Luke, together with **Les Thompson** from his old band, re-formed the **Defiants** with new members. They became **This End** and moved to Nottingham, where they changed their name again – this time to the **Exitement**. By that time, they had developed into a successful professional group that toured the European continent intensively. In 1969, **Robert Luke** was a member of **Zelda Plum** that became very popular all over the North of England. Of **Roy Ellis** it is known that he had a very short spell with the **Earthlings** before he quit showbiz.

Discography :

as **The Approachers** :

Walking the dog / ??? 　　　　　　　　　　　UK- Phillips Kensington acetate / 1964

THE AZTECS

The foundation of this group, and the way they all came together, was very typical of Liverpool's group-scene at that time.

In late 1963, three pupils of the Holt High School in Childwall, who all played the guitar, decided to form a group. **Billy Hargreaves**, who took over the bass-guitar, knew someone from his boy-scout group who could play the drums. So the **Aztecs** started to rehearse as an instrumental group in the style of the **Shadows** and **Ventures** but soon realized that they needed to add some vocals and, once again, it was the bass-guitarist who came up with the solution – his next door neighbour was a good singer – and so the **Aztecs** were complete in a line-up with:

Pete O'Connell	(voc)
Billy Ford	(lg)
Phil 'Jack' Frost	(rg)
Billy Hargreaves	(bg)
Les Calder	(dr)

They rehearsed in the attic of a newspaper shop in Wavertree that was owned by **Billy Ford's** father. All the members were of a very young age and all of them were newcomers to the Merseybeat-scene that was 'exploding' at the time and already had begun to conquer the world. In order to jump onto that train, the **Aztecs** did not waste any time, and, after their first few gigs, they went into the Kensington studio of **Percy Phillips** in early 1964 to record a one-sided acetate. What is incomprehensible about this recording is that, although the **Aztecs** had a good singer, they decided on an instrumental. Furthermore, instrumentals had become somewhat outdated by 1964.

Regardless, **Billy Hargreaves** insists that they recorded "Saturday Night At The Duck Pond", a theme from 'Swan Lake', a rocking version of which had been a 1963 success for the **Cougars** from London. Shortly after this recording, the **Aztecs** were joined by **Ritchie Rutledge** as additional rhythm-guitarist, who was also a good singer. He formerly had played with the **Drumbeats** and the **Detonators**.

When **Billy Ford** decided to leave to resume his scholarly studies, **Alan Hanson**, a former member of **J & the Juniors**, became the new lead-guitarist. Additionally, the group was joined by **Pete Byrne**, an excellent organist. Being a seven-piece group, the **Aztecs** decided that they needed a manager and this position was filled by **Robert Ramsey**, the former drummer of the **Chessmen**. A little later, **Phil Frost** left the group and disappeared from the scene.

The **Aztecs** now became quite popular on the scene and played all the major Liverpool clubs. Their first gig at the 'Cavern' was on Tuesday the 8th December 1964 and, between 1965 and February 1966, they are documented as having fifteen more appearances at that venue.

At some later stage, the **Aztecs** were joined by **Dave Croft** as a new drummer, who came from the **Cliftons**. Unfortunately, the **Aztecs** broke up when **Pete O'Connell** decided to join the **Signs***.

Ritchie Rutledge left to join the Cryin' Shames*, while Pete Byrne at first became a member of the Inmates from Norris Green and then teamed up again with Ritchie Rutledge in his new group, who then used the name of Paul & Ritchie & the Cryin' Shames. After that, Ritchie Rutledge joined the Hideaways*, who then changed their name into Confucius. In 1972, he was a short-time member of the Swinging Blue Jeans* and then went on to play with Blackwater Park and the Grimms. Of Pete Byrne it is known that in 1968 he was a member of the Mumbles.

The remaining three members of the Aztecs, namely Billy Hargreaves, Alan Hanson and Dave Croft, teamed up with John Gobin and Alan Martin in Becket's Kin, whereby Dave Croft soon went on to join the Thoughts*. Still in 1966, Becket's Kin changed their name into the New Denims. Billy Hargreaves then left and joined the Mistake, who soon changed their name into the Curiosity Shoppe* who also appeared as Napoleon due to contractual reasons whenever they played gigs in London. After that, he quit the music business and went back to a normal day job.

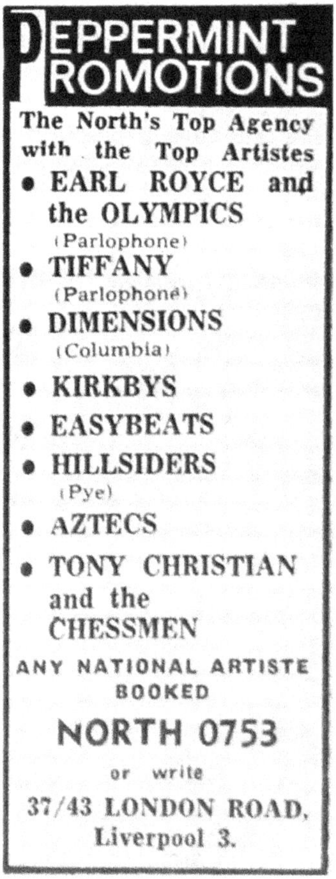

PEPPERMINT PROMOTIONS

The North's Top Agency with the Top Artistes
- EARL ROYCE and the OLYMPICS (Parlophone)
- TIFFANY (Parlophone)
- DIMENSIONS (Columbia)
- KIRKBYS
- EASYBEATS
- HILLSIDERS (Pye)
- AZTECS
- TONY CHRISTIAN and the CHESSMEN

ANY NATIONAL ARTISTE BOOKED

NORTH 0753

or write

37/43 LONDON ROAD, Liverpool 3.

Discography:

"Saturday Nite At The Duck Pond"   UK-Phillips Kensington one sided acetate / 1964

*The stories of these groups can be followed in 'Beat Waves 'Cross the Mersey' (*VelocePress ISBN 978-1-58850-201-8*).

GERRY BACH & THE BEATHOVENS

This is a very interesting and, in some ways, typical story that, unfortunately, came to light a little bit late, but luckily not too late.

The Beathovens, as they were called from the beginning, were formed in the Liverpool area of West Derby in 1960 by **Keith Dodd**, **Rod Long** and **Graham Beasley**, together with **Vincent Romnez**, who was of Spanish origin. After some rehearsals, they started to gig around in the local pubs and social-clubs. They were soon joined by **Gerry Hale** as their vocalist, who also used the stage name, **Gerry Temple,** he had previously sung with the **Mystery Five**.

He now adopted **Gerry Bach** as his new stage name and the group accordingly became **Gerry Bach & the Beathovens** – in the line-up with:

Gerry Bach	(voc)
Keith Dodd	(lg)
Rod Long	(rg/voc)
Graham Beasley	(bg/voc)
Charlie Evans	(dr/voc)

Charles Richard Evans was a former member of the **Mustangs** from West Derby.

The music of **Gerry Bach & the Beathovens** was oriented around American Rock 'n' Roll and they gave it that typical Mersey touch.

Gerry Bach & the Beathovens - L to R: Rod Long, Charlie Evans, Keith Dodd, Graham Beasley, Gerry Bach (Front)

As their musical quality was very good, they soon became popular on the scene and had appearances at all the major venues in the Liverpool area. Amongst them were the 'Cavern', the 'Iron Door', the 'Holyoake' in Smithdown Road, 'Samson & Barlows' (that later became the 'Peppermint Lounge') and 'Blair Hall'.

In spite of this success, in 1962 **Gerry Bach** decided to join the **City Kings** and he changed his name yet again – this time into **Gerry De Ville** and his new group, of course, became **Gerry De Ville & the City Kings**, but that is another story.

It is also said that **Jimmy Stevens** (voc/p) joined the **Beathovens** as a replacement for **Gerry Bach**. While this is not absolutely correct, it is a fact that **Jimmy Stevens**, who normally performed as a solo-act, appeared with the group on many occasions but without ever becoming a steady member. He, by the way, was a talented songwriter and amongst others wrote the song, "Baby That's It", which the **Young Ones** released on record.

L to R: Rod Long, Graham Beasley, Jimmy Stevens, Keith Dodd & Charlie Evans

He later went down to London and, in 1966, a solo single by him was released on Fontana with his compositions, "I Love You/Wharf 130". In the following years, he became a successful singer/songwriter and often worked with the **Bee Gees.** Because of that association, he lived and worked in the USA for a number of years and, in 1973, he had a solo album released in the US with the title, "Paid My Dues" (RSO Polydor RS1-872). Sometime in the late Nineties, he returned to Merseyside and, since then, he has been playing the pubs again as a solo-performer - under the name of **Jimmy Summertime**.

But back to the **Beathovens**, who besides their appearances with **Jimmy Stevens,** continued as a quartet with all members sharing the vocals after **Gerry Bach** had left.

In 1963, **Rod Long** and **Keith Dodd** left at the same time and there was a rumour that they were both going to join the **Crescendos**, a Canadian group that had a long residency in Liverpool and later recorded as the **5 A.M. Event**. For some reason, this did not work out and **Rod Long** joined **Alby & the Sorrals**, played with the **Young Ones** and, later, with the **Coins**.

Keith Dodd became a member of **Ricky Gleason & the Topspots**, he continued on with the **Topspots** after **Ricky Gleason** left and, after that, he played with the **Principals**.

The new lead guitarist for the **Beathovens** was **Pete Campbell**, who came from **Karl Terry & the Cruisers**, and the rhythm guitar was taken over by a certain **Ray**, whose surname cannot be recalled.

Graham Beasley left and quit the music business and he was replaced by **Gerard Anthony Gilbertson**, also known as **Tony Nelson**, as their new lead singer and rhythm guitarist. **Tony Nelson** was a former member of **Mike Savage & the Wildcats**, who became **Sonny Webb & the Cascades** a little later on. At this point, **Ray** switched to bass and the group changed their name to the **Mersey Four**.

In late 1963, **Pete Campbell** left and, for a short time, played with the **Fontanas**. After that, together with **Bob Montgomery** of **Derry Wilkie & the Others**, he formed the backing group for Oldham singer, **Tony Prince.** This new group, under the name of the **Tony Prince Combo,** was also joined by **Tony Nelson** and **Charlie Evans** who, in the meantime, had adopted the stage name of **Carl Riche**.

The **Tony Prince Combo** went down to Bristol where they were joined by a sax player called **Gary Clampett.** They became really successful on the Southern UK scene and also played a lot in London. This ultimately resulted in **Tony Prince** starting a very successful career in London as a disc-jockey for various radio-stations and quitting the live-music business.

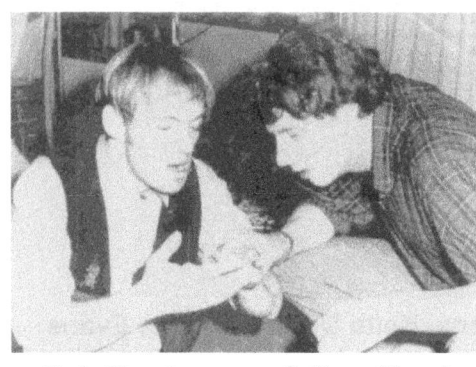

Bob Montgomery & Don Alcyd (Mersey Five)

However, the group stayed together, changed their name to the **Mersey Five** and accepted a long engagement in Munich in Germany. **Gary Clampett** got tired of playing those long hours and returned to England while the others remained in Germany. Although they were now a four-piece, they continued as the **Mersey Five**, they simply used an inflatable rubber 'man' as their 'fifth member'.

They had a really long residency in Germany and, in 1964, recorded two great singles for the Storz label from Osterode, but this is a different story . . .

For the complete story of the **Mersey Five** please see the book *"Beat Waves 'Cross The Mersey"* ISBN 1588502015 or 9781588502018.

Discography

Gerry Bach & the Beathovens never had a record released and as far as it is known, there were also no acetates cut by the group. However, they later evolved into the **Mersey Five** and recorded in Germany only.

Jimmy Stevens – solo :

I love you / Wharf 130   UK-Fontana TF ?? / 1966

THE BANSHEES

It was in January 1960 that three 15-year old pupils from the Maghull Grammar School decided to form a Beat group.

All three of them played guitar and the group had a name before they even found a suitable drummer - they called themselves the . . . **Rolling Stones**!

When, in April 1960, they were joined by the badly-needed drummer, they looked for another name but not because of **Mick Jagger's Rolling Stones** as, at that time, they didn't even exist!

The reason for the change was simply because the four Maghull teenagers thought that **Rolling Stones** sounded too much like a Skiffle group and that they would not become famous with a name like that . . .

Anyway, they became the **Strangers** and played their first local dances under this name until they found out that there was already a much more established group of the same name playing in Liverpool. So they became the **Dynamos** for a short time and then, finally, the **Banshees** – still in the same line-up with:

Dave Walker	(voc/rg)
Rod Flanagan	(lg/voc)
Roger Cooper	(bg/voc)
Rob Allin	(dr)

Now that the problem with the right name was sorted out, the **Banshees** concentrated on pushing their career and attempting to break into the increasingly competitive world of the Mersey group scene – and with some success, playing the usual circle of Liverpool dance halls for promoters such as **Bob Wooler**, **Brian Kelly**, **Dave Forshaw** and **Doug Martin**, to name just a few.

In addition, the group broadened their range of venues by obtaining work outside of Liverpool. They became something like the resident band at the 'Flamingo' in Warrington and also appeared regularly at places that included the 'Casino Ballroom' in Leigh, the 'Helena House' in St. Helens, as well as various clubs in Maghull and Southport.

In early 1962, the **Banshees** became a five-piece when they were joined by another school friend, **Jim Stead,** on piano and clavioline, some sort of an embryonic synthesizer. This addition helped expand the appeal of the group and increased their growing success.

The Banshees (1961) - L to R: Rod Flanagan Dave Walker, Rob Allin & Roger Cooper

With this line-up, the group went into the Eroica studios in Eccles and recorded a demo with "It'll Be Me" and "Halfway to Paradise" which, unfortunately, did not lead to a recording contract.

Jim Stead

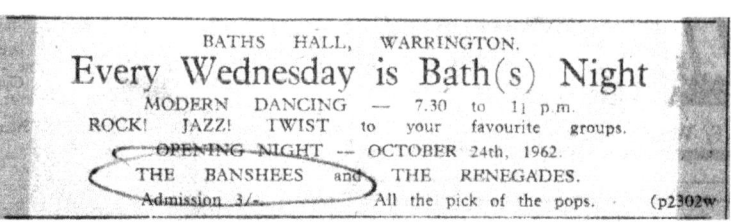

BATHS HALL, WARRINGTON.
Every Wednesday is Bath(s) Night
MODERN DANCING — 7.30 to 11 p.m.
ROCK! JAZZ! TWIST to your favourite groups.
OPENING NIGHT — OCTOBER 24th, 1962
THE BANSHEES and THE RENEGADES.
Admission 3/- All the pick of the pops. (p2302w)

BEATLAND PROMOTIONS
present their
2nd TEENBEAT SHOW
SATURDAY, 25th NOVEMBER, 1962
MAGHULL INSTITUTE
Jive! Twist! Locomote!
with
* TWO STAR GROUPS *
THE BANSHEES   Featuring
Fabulous New Sound   DEE YOUNG AND
(Resident Group)   THE PONTIACS
TICKETS 3/6 (any unsold tickets will be available at the door)
8 to 11-30 p.m.   Doors open 7-30 p.m.   Top Pop Discs

DANCING
HELENA HOUSE BALLROOM
BALDWIN STREET, ST. HELENS
Tel. 6286.

Manager: Sylvester Burrows,
F.D.T.A., M.I.S.T.D.

MONDAY, 1st Ooctober — Johnny Knight and the Crusaders, plus The Dixieband. Adm. 2/6. 8 to 11.
TUESDAY, 2nd October — Old Time Dancing, The Les Greenough Orchestra. Adm. 2/6. 8 to 11.
WEDNESDAY, 3rd October — New Mid-Week Special Beat Night. Presenting the fabulous Banshees. Non-stop Dancing, 8 to 11. Adm 2/6.
THURSDAY, 4th October—Rock Night with the Chequers (instead of Friday for this week only). Adm 2/6. 8 to 11.
FRIDAY, 5th October — Lancashire Championships. See separate announcement.
SATURDAY, 6th October — Night of the Week. Adm. 3/6. 8.15 to 11.15

TRY HELENA HOUSE BALLROOM FOR A REAL GOOD TIME—
39gr—tfo

Members' Notice.
Flamingo
BEWSEY STREET, WARRINGTON.
EVERY SUNDAY. 8—11 p.m. JIVE, TWIST, LOCOMOTE.
To our Resident Group the fabulous
BANSHEES,
plus Guest Groups.
BALLROOM NOW AVAILABLE FOR PRIVATE BOOKINGS. (1465w)

CASINO BALLROOM
LEIGH
FOR ONE NIGHT ONLY
THE BANSHEES
WITH THE NEW IRRESISTIBLE SOUND
Plus
THE FABULOUS BEAT BOYS
Plus
TOP POP RECORDS
7.30—10.30.   No Extra Charge, 2/6

By the end of 1962, school examination commitments and musical differences led to the break-up of the **Banshees**.

Rod Flanagan disappeared from the scene for a while and **Roger Cooper** became a member of the **Futurists** from Maghull. He later trained as a fighter pilot with the Royal Air Force and was tragically killed when his plane crashed into a lake in North Wales in 1965.

Dave Walker, Rob Allin and Jim Stead stayed together and, in January 1963, were joined by Dave Kent (lg) from the Kingpins and Bob Hewlett (bg) from the Futurists, as well as the 16-year old songstress, Doreen Savage, of whom Dave Walker says that ". . .she could sing the songs of Brenda Lee better than Brenda Lee."

Dave Kent & Doreen Savage

This new outfit continued as the Galaxies and sometimes was billed as the Galaxies with Doreen. They were handled by Birchall Promotions from Southport who got them a lot of bookings. But, despite this, it was a short-lived venture and the Galaxies disbanded after a few months.

Dave Walker became a member of the Clansmen and remained with them until they disbanded in 1966. After that, he teamed up again with Rod Flanagan in a cabaret group, called the First Edition.

Rob Allin and Jim Stead both joined other groups, the names of which are not known. Dave Kent initially formed a new group with Doreen Savage which was short-lived and of which it is only known that a certain Hank was on bass guitar and the drummer was called Colin. Unfortunately, both of their surnames, as well as the group's name are not known.

Dave Kent and Doreen Savage then continued on as a duo before Doreen went solo on the cabaret scene. Initially, Dave Kent became a member of the Corvettes and then he joined the Mersey Gamblers, who soon evolved into the second take of the Connoisseurs.

```
        BIRCHALL  PROMOTIONS
                    for
   Rock Group, Jazz Bands, Dance Bands, Comperes,
              Entertainments, etc., etc.
                   'Phone:-
   SOUTHPORT 57298           BURSCOUGH 2388
     Promotion through the whole range of Entertainment
   Sole Agents for
        ★  THE FABULOUS GEMS
              Rock & Twist Unit
        ★  THE GALAXIES with DOREEN
           A new All Star Group with a Sensational Girl
           Vocalist incorporating former members of
                    THE BANSHEES
```

Sometime in the Nineties, Dave Kent was a member of the revival group, Sounds Sixties, and later played with the newly formed Ian & the Zodiacs for a short time.

Bob Hewlett was last heard of playing bass guitar in the Chants backing group who, by that time, were no longer the Harlems.

Discography

It'll Be Me / Halfway to Paradise   UK- Eroica acetate / 1962

(Photos of the Banshees and Jim Stead provided by Ken Flanagan)

THE BLUE SOUNDS

The foundation-stone for this group from the Sefton Park area of Liverpool was laid when the very young **Mick Pappas** started to play drums 'just for fun' with his older cousin, **Yanni Tsamplacos** (g), both of Greek origin. Sometime later, they were joined by **David Edwards** (voc/bg) and, when a second guitarist, **Mike Mizzelas,** joined them, they had obviously become considerably more serious about their music. Still without a name, they soon had their one and only live appearance at the 'Mousetrap' in Everton, which was owned by another cousin of Mick and Yanni. Unfortunately, due to disagreements about the type of music they wanted to play, **Mick Pappas** and **Mike Mizzelas** left, while **Yanni Tsamplacos** and **David Edwards** continued on with **Michael Barron** as their new drummer and this trio was the embryonic beginning of the **Seftons***.

After that break up, **Mike Mizzelas** disappeared from the scene, but **Mick Pappas,** who wanted to play in a more 'bluesy' style group, got together with **Michael Wallis,** his schoolmate from the Liverpool Institute, and they placed an advert in a newspaper that they were looking for a guitarist. They found one, **Alan???** who came from Anfield, and the trio started to rehearse in the basement of **Mick Pappas** parental home in Toxteth. They soon came to the realisation that for their type of music they needed a second guitarist. It was the mother of **Mick Pappas** who proved to have a practical mind and came up with a solution by the name of **Eddie Berry** (see the note at the end of the story) and so, finally the **Blue Sounds** had become a quartet in a line-up with:

The Blue Sounds
L to R: Alan ?, Mick Pappas, Eddy Berry
(Photo by Michael Wallis)

Alan	(voc/lg)
Eddie Berry	(rg/voc)
Michael Wallis	(bg/voc)
Mick Pappas	(dr)

Their musical style was orientated toward American Country Blues by the likes of **Woody Guthrie** and **Muddy Waters** but the **Beatles** also had some influence. After intensive rehearsals, the **Blue Sounds** started to play the local youth-clubs and church-halls as the majority of the members were too young to perform on the usual club-circuit. 'Hope Hall' was one such place where they appeared on a regular basis.

After they had been very successful at the 'Woolton Music-Festival' in 1964, it was arranged for them to take part in the 'Battle of the Bands' competition at 'Renshaw Hall'. The **Blue Sounds** placed third and were presented with a so-called recording deal. While this sounded like a major award, in fact they could only record one (!) number in the Unicord studio of **Charlie Weston** in Moorfields. For that recording, the musicians picked the **Larry Williams** classic, "Slow Down", as the **Beatles** version of that song was very popular at that time. It is sad that the **Blue Sounds** were not given the chance to record a second number. They only received a minimal amount of that one-sided acetate and these were shared among the members.

It was towards the end of 1964 or in early 1965 that **Eddie Berry** decided to concentrate on his academic studies and gave up music. As the **Blue Sounds** could not find a suitable replacement for him, they disbanded very soon after his departure. The lead guitarist, **Alan,** disappeared from the scene while **Michael Wallis** and **Mick Pappas** continued on together and joined a Garston group called the **Lawrence James Federation**. After approximately one year, **Mick Pappas** was contacted by **Kenny Parry** of the just disbanded **Modes** as he was looking for a really qualified drummer for his new group. **Mick Pappas** agreed and became a member of the **Rigg** (another story in this book). Later on, he led his own group called **Pappas** and then became a member of the **Good Earth Bluesband** where he played right into the Seventies. **Michael Wallis** stayed with the **Lawrence James Federation** until they group broke up sometime in 1966. As far as it is known, he quit the music business after that.

> *We had been practising in the cellar of my house in Liverpool 8, Toxteth, for several weeks and we had worked on the same maybe six songs at each practise.*
>
> *One evening (after school), my mother came into the cellar with a young man, older than us and he had a guitar with him. We talked and practised a few songs we all knew and some that he introduced and he, Eddie, agreed to join us.*
>
> *Later that evening, I asked my mother how she knew Eddie and she told me that she didn't but she was so tired of hearing our same few songs being blasted out endlessly that when she saw him walking in our street carrying a guitar, she did not hesitate to invite him down. She must have been pulling her hair out!*
>
> *Toxteth at that time was a 'lively' place and you never really know how to judge people.*
>
> *It was about a month later when Eddie told me how apprehensive of accepting the 'older woman's' invitation to go into her house and even more so when she asked him to go down into the cellar. He was really worried, fearing drugs and the worst until he heard us playing.*
>
> *He was either very brave or not averse to experiencing what he thought might happen...*
>
> **Mick Pappas / The Blue Sounds**

Discography:

Slow Down　　　　　　　　　　　　　　　　　　　　one-sided Unicord-acetate / 1964

*The story of this group can be followed in 'Beat Waves 'Cross The Mersey' (*VelocePress* ISBN 978-1-58850-201-8).

BOBBY & THE BACHELORS

This group, originally formed in the early Sixties under the name the **Bachelors**, came from West Kirby at the outer end of the Wirral peninsula, situated at the mouth of the River Dee where it exits into the Irish Sea, facing the northern end of North Wales.

Because the Irish vocal-trio with the name of the **Bachelors** became very popular in 1963 with their hit-singles, "Charmaine" and "Diane", the West Kirby group added their singer's name, who hailed from Bebington on the Wirral, and they became **Bobby & the Bachelors**. Other than this, there is almost no information available about their early days – only that their original drummer was **Malcolm Roback**, who left the group sometime in 1962 and then disappeared from the scene. Also, from the end of 1963 through January 1964, **Bobby & the Bachelors** temporarily became a sextet when they were joined by songstress **Sue White** as an additional member.

They played locally for most of the time of their existence and so the Liverpool music-press did not pay them much attention. This is not really surprising as it was quite a distance from West Kirby to Liverpool's city-centre and, in those days, many of the younger aged groups, due to lack of alternatives, were dependent upon public transportation.

However, **Bobby & the Bachelors** somehow made their way into the Liverpool scene and they must have had quite a good quality sound, as from the 3rd September 1963 until the 31st October 1964, they are documented as having a total of seventeen appearances at the 'Cavern', where they became firm favourites with the audience. That probably was the reason why they were chosen by **Bob Wooler** to be part of an Oriole recording session at the Cavern – in a line-up with:

Bobby Dalton	(voc)
Mike Godwin	(lg)
Mike Barrie	(rg)
Ian Gordon	(bg)
Pete Davies	(dr)

Here it should be noted that a confusion of the assignments of the guitars to the musicians is possible as it is only known for sure that **Bobby Dalton** was the singer and that **Pete Davies** was their new drummer. **Pete Davies** was formerly a short-time member of **Gus & the Thundercaps***, who, about that same time, changed their name to **Gus Travis & the Midnighters*** and, after that, possibly sometime in 1960 or 1961, he had played with the **Morockans** (another story in this book).

Regardless, **Bobby & the Bachelors** were selected to be featured on the planned Volume 3 of the legendary Oriole albums 'This Is Merseybeat'. It was on Friday the 21st February 1964 that they were recorded at the Cavern by producer **John Schroeder** with the Oriole mobile recording unit. A Canadian Broadcasting Corporation film team was also at the Cavern at the same time recording film footage for a documentary with the unconfirmed title, 'All Abroad'. Sadly, it could not be established how many or which numbers were recorded by **Bobby & the Bachelors** in that session as the album was never released.

After this recording session, **Bobby & the Bachelors** kept on playing the scene on both sides of the River Mersey and it is documented that through the end of October 1964 they had an additional eight bookings at the 'Cavern'. They also participated in the 'Rael Brook Beat Contest', made it into the finals, but unfortunately did not win. As the music-press did not pay much attention to the group, there is nothing known about any changes in their line-up or if any other recordings were made by **Bobby & the Bachelors** who apparently disbanded towards the end of 1964.

None of the musicians appeared on the scene again, which could mean that they all quit showbiz, but it's not possible to be absolutely sure.

Discography:

On Friday the 21st of February 1964 Bobby & the Bachelors were recorded by Oriole for the planned 3rd Volume of their legendary albums, 'This Is Merseybeat', which sadly was never released and so, it is not known, how many or which numbers were recorded. For details regarding the Oriole session see the appendix at the end of this book.

*The stories of these groups can be followed in 'Beat Waves 'Cross The Mersey' (*VelocePress* ISBN 978-1-58850-201-8).

THE BO-WEEVILS

With this story, a confusion from my original book will be corrected – a confusion that can be blamed on the fact that there were two totally different Merseyside groups with the same name, both of them performing during the same time-frame.

The **Bo-Weevils** featured in my original book were a folk-blues-band from the Wirral with **Gordon Varley Robinson** (12-string-g), **Harry ???** (g/harp), **Martin Craig** (g/voc) and **Lynnette Carwood** (voc/perc) but as it came to light at a later date, this was <u>not</u> the group that recorded the songs listed in their discography.

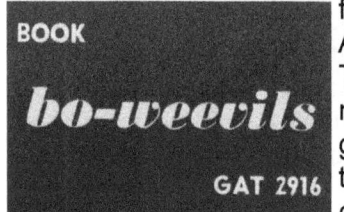

The **Bo-Weevils** recording group came from the South of Liverpool, where they were formed in 1963 by three musicians from Speke, one from Allerton, a singer from Toxteth and a drummer from Huyton. Their manager was **Tommy Gaul** from Gateacre, who owned a motorbike business in Garston, which was fortunate for the group as they could use his van to transport their equipment to their gigs. The **Bo-Weevils** were a real earthy Blues-group and consisted of:

Jimmy Mack	(voc/harp)
Edward Smith	(lg/voc)
Dave Bennett	(rg)
Peter McCoubrey	(g)
Tommy Spencer	(bg)
Ken Folksman	(dr)

According to some sources the group's leader **Edward 'Ted' Smith** was sometimes referred to by the nickname 'Bo'. It is very probable that all of them had played in other groups previously. However, it is known that the youngest member, drummer **Ken Folksman**, who was just fifteen at the time, was a former member of the **Almanax**, who as a group, were a still-born-child with only one public appearance and, after that, he had been a member of the **Climaks**. The **Bo-Weevils** musical style was heavily American Delta-Blues influenced, artists such as **Slim Harpo**, **Arthur Gunter**, **Lightnin' Slim** or **Silas Hogan**, just to name a few.

It was in late 1963 or early 1964, that the **Bo-Weevils** went into **Percy Phillips's** studio in Kensington to record a demo on acetate. It's no surprise that for the recoding they choose two Delta-Blues classics. One was "I'm A Lover Not A Fighter", a song that was written by Excello-producer **Joseph Denton Miller** for **Lazy Lester**,

Ken Folksman

who had success with it in 1958. The other song was the **Huddie Ledbetter** (better known as **Leadbelly**) composition "Keep Your Hands Off Her". A remarkable fact is that "I'm A Lover, Not A Fighter" was recorded by the **Bo-Weevils** almost a year before the **Kinks** had a major hit with that same song in late 1964.

On their weekend-bookings, the group was always joined by **Geoff Russell**, who was serving in the RAF and so could only make it on weekends. A great singer, who played guitar and also played piano, if there was one available at their gigs. **Geoff Russell** had formerly gigged with the **Nashpool Four***.

Geoff Russell

The group became quite popular in the Northern Blues-scene and, according to an article in the *Liverpool Weekly News,* there was a fan-club founded for them in March 1964. The **Bo-Weevils** had regular appearances at the 'Sink Club' ('Rumblin Tum') in Hardman Street as well as clubs such as 'Maggie May's', the 'Winter Gardens' in Waterloo and the lesser known 'Norton Club'. They also had regular repeat performances at the 'Peppermint Lounge', 'Hope Hall' and the 'Cazzie'. Some of their bookings even took them out of town to places such as Warrington, Carlisle or even into Lincolnshire.

It was sometime in 1964, that **Ken Folksman** left to join the **Modes**. After that, he was a member of the **Verbs** and the **Admins** that, with him as a member, evolved into the **Poke**. Later, he played in groups such as **Peyton Place**, the **S.O.S. (Sounds of Style)** and **Ray Peters & the Raytones**, who were resident at the 'Grafton Ballroom'. His replacement in the **Bo-Weevils** was **Steve Doyle** from Woolton, whose former group is sadly, not known. The **Bo-Weevils** kept on playing for another year and then simply disappeared from the scene.

LIVERPOOLS NEW BEAT CLUB
TO-NIGHT FRIDAY:
NEW RECORDING ARTIST
DENNY SEYTON AND THE SABRES
PLUS THE BO-WEEVILS
SATURDAY SPECIAL!!
THE KARACTERS
PLUS THE NASHPOOL FOUR
PLUS THE CAVE DWELLERS
SUNDAY BE EARLY.
THE NIGHT WALKERS
PLUS THE BLUE BEATS
MAUREEN GAULTON
21 AIGBURTH RD., L'POOL 17

THE PEPPERMINT LOUNGE
FRASER STREET, LIVERPOOL
TO-NIGHT FRIDAY
TO-NIGHT FRIDAY
THE VALKYRIES
THE FALONS
THE ELEKTONES
TO-MORROW SATURDAY
TO-MORROW SATURDAY
DENNY SEYTON & THE SABRES
THE 4 DIMENSIONS WITH
TIFFANY
THE CHESSMEN
SUNDAY
SUNDAY
THE BLACKWELLS
THE BO-WEEVILS
THE VIKINGS

After the original group had 'officially' disbanded, there was one more documented appearance by the **Bo-Weevils** at an engagement-party on the Royal Iris in late summer of 1965. However, this was more of a session group with **Dave Bennett** and **Geoff Russell** being the only original members as the also nominated, **Jimmy Mack,** did not show up. This line-up was completed by an unknown but great lead-guitarist and a 'not so great' drummer who, most of the time, was replaced by a guest that had been invited to the party. That 'guest' drummer turned out to be **Pete Wiggins**, the former drummer for the **Mafia** who, at that time, was a member of the **Profiles***.

Edward 'Ted' Smith later emigrated to Australia and **Dave Bennett** moved to Weston-super-Mare in Somerset, where he is still living today. It is known that in 1966, **Geoff Russell** was a member of the **Rigg** (another story in this book) before he quit playing and, in the Seventies, emigrated to South Africa, where he lived for 25 years.

When he returned to Merseyside, he settled in Southport and sometimes went to the 'Merseycats' session-nights to sing on stage again. On some of those 'Merseycats' appearances, he was backed by **Karl Terry & the Cruisers**. He never joined a group again but through his association with 'Merseycats' he eventually got back into the music-scene. In 2004, he moved to Hailsham in East-Sussex, got into Country music under the name of **Cowboy Geoff** and, as a DJ, he hosts a C&W-show on the local radio station.

Discography:

I'm A Lover, Not A Fighter / Keep Your Hands Off Her   UK - Phillips Kensington acetate / 1963/64

*The stories of these groups can be followed in 'Beat Waves 'Cross The Mersey' (*VelocePress ISBN 978-1-58850-201-8*).

THE BROTHERS GRIMM

Here we are going to take a risk again that this group should not be featured in this book, as it proved to be impossible to find out the place of origin of the **Brothers Grimm**.

There were groups with that name tracked down in Somerset, Kent and Cumbria, but none of them had anything in common with the outfit in this story.

The group apparently started as **Mel & the Brothers Grimm**, with the coloured singer, **Melvyn Simpson,** sometime in the first half of the Sixties.

They most probably hailed from somewhere in Lancashire, where they appeared quite regularly at the 'Palais' in Bolton, the Mecca Carlton in Rochdale and the 'Palais' in Bury, often supporting acts from Liverpool and Manchester (see the comment of **Keith Hubbard** at the end of this story).

The **Brothers Grimm**, sometimes still appearing as **Mel & the Brothers Grimm** in early 1965, included the following musicians:

Melvyn Simpson	(voc)
Richard Morgan	(g/voc)
Michael Higgins	(g/voc)
Andrew Grocott	(bg)
Ivon Brace	(dr)

It should be noted that the allocation of the instruments is not certain to be 100 % accurate.

They were signed to Decca and, in August 1965, the **Brothers Grimm** had their first single out with the **Bobby Darin** song, "Lost Love". Contrary to their live-appearances this record was really soft and harmless. The A-side reminded one of the style of the **Walker Brothers**.

While "Lost Love" was a boring production, the flipside, "Make It or Break It", was much better, even though it was also a ballad but done in a 'Merseybeatish' style with nice vocal harmonies.

All in all, it was not an exciting record and, therefore, it is hard to understand why it was re-released by Decca in October of the same year with the same catalogue-number but under the name of **Barry & Tony,** as neither name ever appeared in the line-up of the group.

In the meantime, the **Brothers Grimm** were signed by the independent and later very successful music-publisher, **Hal Shaper**, who apparently was also associated with the Regent Sound Studios in London.

Hal Shaper got them signed to Ember and, in October 1965, at the same time of the above mentioned Decca re-release, the **Brothers Grimm** released their second single with "A Man Needs Love", which again was closer to the **Walker Brothers** territory than Beat, but was better than their debut.

"A Man Needs Love" was penned by **George Fishoff** and **Tony Powers**, who also wrote the hits "98.6" for **Keith** and "Lazy Day" for **Spanky & Our Gang**.

The B-side "Looky Looky" is much more interesting as it was a good rocking number, written by **Nick Ashford** and **Valerie Simpson** and was previously recorded in the USA by the all-girl group **The Kittens**.

This single of the **Brothers Grimm** was also issued in USA on Mercury and in Italy on Vedette.

"Looky Looky" later became a 'Northern Soul' favourite and is an expensive collector's item today but, in 1965, it did not help the **Brothers Grimm** achieve any sort of a major breakthrough.

It was their final record and there is nothing known about any tours in Europe or elsewhere.

Towards the end of the Sixties, the group and the members simply disappeared from the scene and nothing further was heard of them.

Discography

Lost Love / Make It Or Break It	UK - Decca F. 12224 / 1965
A Man Needs Love / Looky Looky	UK - Ember EMB 222 / 1965

(Please note that, still in 1965, the first single was re-released on Decca under the artists' name of **Barry & Tony** with the same catalogue-number)

Keith Hubbard, gutiartist of **Ian & the Rebels** recalls a joint-appearance with the **Brothers Grimm** as follows:

"In 1964, Dave Forshaw gave us a booking at the 'Palais' in Bury, one of the old style ballrooms. On the arrival at the gig we were overwhelmed with the sight of our name brandished on a billboard, which ran across the entire front of the building.

It read :   ***From Liverpool, the fantastic IAN & THE REBELS***

   plus** (in very small print)* ***THE BROTHERS GRIMM.

The Brothers Grimm arrived, fully equipped with Vox-amps and a P.A. that we had not seen until this day. They were told to set up in the front part of the stage and to make sure all their gear was cleared before the main-act – us! – went on stage.

The Brothers Grimm opened the night – they were a real knockout!

Picture the scene, the audience had just enjoyed a great band and the expectation was absolutely high and we had to follow them. Guess, whose faces were now grim?

CADILLAC & THE PLAYBOYS

Geoff Taggart, guitarist with the late Fifties St. Helens Rock 'n' Roll group, the **Zephyrs**, remembers that, for months, when his group was playing locally, a young man turned up regularly, joined the group on stage for one song and then disappeared again.

The Hot Rods

The number he sang was always the **Vince Taylor** song, "Brand New Cadillac", and as nobody knew his name, they simply called him 'Cadillac'.

This young man was none other than **Mike Barnes**, who apparently liked the name that was given to him and so called himself **Mike Cadillac** when he decided to join the local **Hot Rods** as an additional singer.

Roy Lenard, the rhythm guitarist was the first to leave the **Hot Rods** and when the original singer, **'Donny'**, also left a little later, the group changed its name to **Mike Cadillac & the Playboys** and now appeared in the following line-up:

Mike Cadillac	(voc)
Stuart Fahey	(lg/voc)
Alan Watkinson	(rg/voc)
Malcolm Darwin	(bg)
George Pickup	(dr/voc)

George Pickup sometimes called himself **George Adams** and this name was also on his bass-drum.

As St. Helens is approximately half way between Liverpool and Manchester, **Mike Cadillac & the Playboys**, in addition to playing at the local St. Helens venues such as the Co-op Ballroom and the Plaza, also performed on both the Liverpool and Manchester scenes. In the beginning, it was predominantly in Liverpool where they appeared regularly at the Iron Door, but they also played the other Merseyside clubs.

Malcolm Darwin left and was replaced by **Kevin Lang**, who, by the way, was the brother of **Bob Lang**, the bass-guitarist of **Wayne Fontana & the Mindbenders**.

In 1963, the group who, by that time, had dropped the 'Mike' from their name, had a session with a certain 'Matthew' in

Huddersfield, in whose studio they recorded some demos on acetate and, of which, it is only known that their original, "Little Boy Lost" and "The Muffin-Man" were amongst them.

Cadillac & the Playboys became very popular throughout Lancashire and were able to make a good living out of their many engagements but nothing is known about any other recordings.

When **Kevin Lang** left to join **Neil Landon & the Burnettes**, the group continued on as a quartet and **Alan Watkinson** took over the bass guitar.

In 1965, some of the musicians wanted to turn professional and that was the reason **George Pickup** left. He sadly died of MS in the Seventies.

His replacement in **Cadillac & the Playboys** was **Mel Preston**, the former drummer with the **Classics** who, prior to joining **Cadillac & the Playboys,** had played with **Lee Castle & the Barons** from Liverpool.

Then **Mike Cadillac** decided to leave and the group was joined by **John Denson** (key/voc), whose real name is **John Olive** and who also was a former member of the **Classics**.

As a result of this, the group initially dropped the 'Cadillac' from their name and continued as the **Playboys**.

This was probably the time when their new management signed them for a six-week tour in Romania, together with **Carol Kay** and **Bobby Shafto** as additional singers.

In Romania, the **Playboys** recorded a 10-inch album with 8 songs for Electrecord which featured the two additional singers with three songs each. This album, simply called The Playboys, included mainly standards such as "Sweet Little Sixteen", "Boys" and "Zip-a-Dee-Doo-Da". The most outstanding tracks were the Soul rocker, "I Do Just What I Want" and the **Phil Upchurch** instrumental, "You Can't Sit Down", (both without the participation of the guest singers). On their return, they were joined by **Les Stocks** from the **Classics** as their new lead singer. He also played the rhythm guitar and, prior to joining the **Playboys,** he had been a member of the **Downbeats**, who had a long and successful residency in Paris/France.

The Playboys with Carol Kay and Bobby Shafto in Romania

There were already too many groups using the **Playboys** name and so the St. Helens group thought it better to change their name again and as the group's management was now in Manchester, they decided to continue as the **Manchester Playboys** in the following line-up:

Les Stocks	(voc/rg)
Stuart Fahey	(lg/tr/voc)
John Denson	(key/voc)
Alan Watkinson	(bg/voc)
Mel Preston	(dr)

Bobby Graham, an ex-member of **Joe Brown & the Bruvvers**, was a studio drummer at that time and amongst many other big hits, he can be heard on the **Kinks** success, "You Really Got Me". In addition, he was the British producer for the big French Barclay recording company and, when he became aware of the **Manchester Playboys,** he invited them to London for test recordings.

The result was that he took over their management and the group was signed to Barclay. The EP, "Wooly Bully", was released in France and apparently sold quite well as the **Manchester Playboys** went over there for a long and very successful tour.

When they came back to England, they became the backing group for **Lorraine Gray**, a popular Manchester songstress who already had recorded with her former group, **Lorraine Gray & the Chaperons**. They adopted the name **Lorraine Gray & the Manchester Playboys**, but this co-operation did not last too long as **Les Stocks** and **Lorraine Gray** emigrated to Australia, where they later got married to each other. This resulted in various changes in the line-up of the **Manchester Playboys**.

Kerry Burke from the **Denims** came in as the new front man and a saxophone player, **Malcolm Tag-Randall**, who had formerly played with **Beau Brummell & the Noblemen**, was added to the line-up.

Lorraine Gray and The Manchester Playboys

John Denson left to join **Wayne Fontana & the Opposition** and, at this time, bandleader, **Stuart Fahey,** decided to concentrate on playing trumpet. The group now was in need of a new lead guitarist and so **Jimmy Warhurst**, who had formerly played with the **Meteors** and the **Hobo Flats**, joined them. This was the line-up that recorded the single, "I Feel So Good", for the English market in 1966, which was released on Fontana and was licensed by Barclay.

This recording featured **Alan Hawkshaw** on keyboards, although he did not stay with the group.

It was also around that time that the **Manchester Playboys** recorded an EP for the British Avenue label, again produced by **Bobby Graham**. As the group did not have a contract with Avenue, they received a one-time fee for that recording.

'Avenue' was one of the 'cheapos' that released a lot of EPs with cover versions of current hits but, unfortunately, they never identified the artists and so it was not helpful for the **Manchester Playboys** at all. Through intensive enquiries it was established that they recorded the **Eddie Floyd** success, "Knock On Wood", **Manfred Mann's** "Ha, Ha Said the Clown", **Georgie Fame's** "Because I Love You", the **Monkees** "A Little Bit Me, a Little Bit You", the **Seekers** number, "Georgie Girl" and another Soul classic with "You've Got What It Takes.

Mel Preston left to join the **Kaytones** and his place was taken by **Peter Simensky**, who was also a former member of the **Meteors** and the **Hobo Flats**.

The **Manchester Playboys** toured Germany where they played the 'Storyville' clubs in Duisburg, as well as in Cologne and Frankfurt where they also backed the

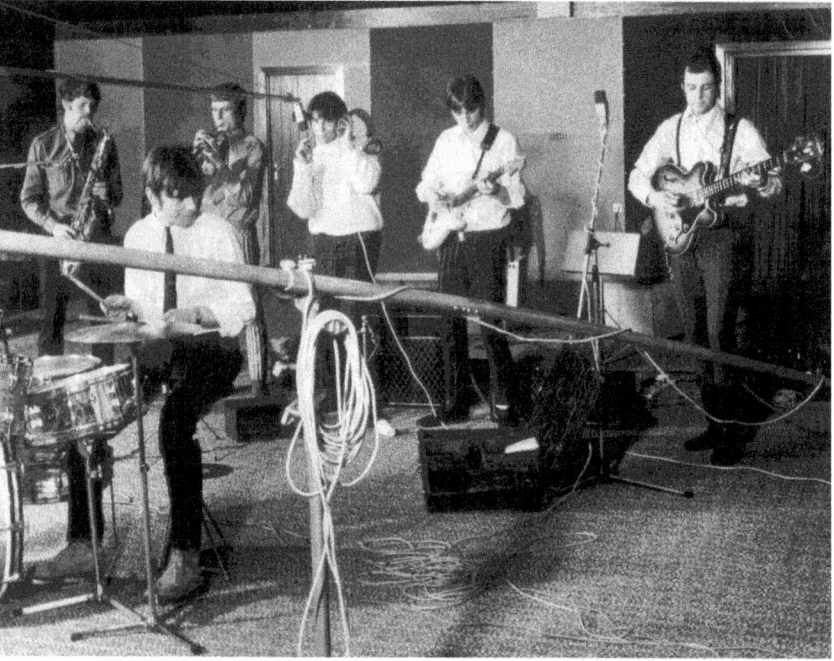

The Manchester Playboys at Avenue Studios

Liverpool vocal group, the **Chants**. In addition, they were booked to appear at the famous 'Star Club' for the complete month of June in 1967 and, during this engagement, they also played at the 'Savoy' in Hanover and the 'Liverpool Hoop' in Berlin.

In Berlin they were taken into the Hansa studios and recorded the single, "Huff Puff", for the German market which, contrary to what could be assumed from the title, was not an instrumental. "Huff Puff", as well as its B-side, "I'm Left Alone", were both **Alan Watkinson** and **Peter Simensky** compositions.

The Manchester Playboys backing the Chants at the 'Storyville' Germany

At the 'Star Club' in Hamburg they shared the bill with the **Remo Four** and the **Birds & Bees** and became friendly with **Graham Slater**, the keyboard player with the latter group, who joined the **Manchester Playboys** when they returned to England.

In late 1967, they went back to Hamburg where they played the equally famous 'Top Ten' for a full month, together with the **Floribunda Rose**, a London group that included two South Africans. Two of their members later made it big – **John Kongos**, who started a successful solo career and **Henry Spinetti**, who later became a studio and session drummer and can be heard on records by **Eric Clapton**, **Bob Dylan**, **George Harrison**, **Pete Townshend** and many other well-known artists.

Back to the **Manchester Playboys**, who kept on playing as professionals throughout England until they broke up in late 1969 or early 1970. Prior to that break up, there had been more personnel changes in the group and the final line-up consisted of **Kerry Burke** (voc), **Ken Anders** (g/voc), **Alan Watkinson** (bg/voc) and **Peter Simensky** (dr).

Peter Simensky is still active on the scene as a songwriter and drummer with a group called **Treetown**. Of **Alan Watkinson** it is known that he later played with **Petrus Boonkamp** and then also joined the **Kaytones** from St. Helens who, in the 70s, recorded an album in Germany under the name of **Smiffy**. After that, he was part of a duo called **Rack 'n' Ruin** and today plays on a semi-pro basis with the **Newton Sound** from Newton-le-Willows near St. Helens, where he originally hails from. Group founder and leader **Stuart Fahey** sadly died a few years ago.

**The Manchester Playboys
(Final line up)**

Discography

as **"Cadillac & the Playboys"**:

There was never an official record released by **Cadillac & the Playboys**, but at a recording session for Decca in 1963, a few songs were recorded, but not released. Therefore, it is only known that their original **"Little Boy Lost"** and **"The Muffin-Man"** were amongst them.

as **"The Playboys"**:

LP "The Playboys"   ROM – Electrecord EDD 1115 / 1966

- Sweet Little Sixteen / Zip-a-Dee-Doo-Da / You Can't Sit Down / Boys /   Baby, Don't Go / I Do Just What I Want / I Saw Her Standing There / I'm Going To Be Strong

as **"The Manchester Playboys**:

I Feel So Good / I Close My Eyes   UK– Fontana TF 745 / 1966

Different French release:

EP   "Wooly Bully"   F - Barclay 70852 / 1966

- Wooly Bully / Lipstick Traces / And I Do What I Want / Tell Me What You're Going To Do

Different German release:

Huff Puff / I'm Left Alone   G – Hansa 14041 / 1967

In addition, in 1966, the **Manchester Playboys** recorded the following EP for the cheap label **Avenue Records**, on which the artists were not named on the label or sleeve:

Ha, Ha, Said the Clown / Because I Love You / A Little Bit Me, a Little Bit You /Georgie Girl / Knock On Wood / You Got What It Takes   UK- Avenue AVE 39 / 1967

WAYNE CALVERT & THE CIMARRONS

Initially, they were the **Cimarrons**, sometimes also named **Cy & the Cimarrons**, with **Thomas Thornton** alias **Cy Tucker** (voc/rg), **Paul Doyle** (lg), **Terry Dowding** (bg) and **Gordon Templeton** (dr), who sometimes were joined by **Tommy O'Brian** as an additional singer. **Gordon Templeton** was a former member of **Terry & the Teen Aces**, a forerunner group of **Karl Terry & the Cruisers.**

Their manager was **Vic Railton**, who also managed **Earl Preston & the TTs** which included his brother **Lance Railton** on lead guitar.

Describing the story of this early Liverpool group offers the chance to show how people, group connections and developments worked together in those days, if we follow the tracks of a musician named **Alan Greer**.

In 1959, **Alan Greer** joined his first group, which was the Tuebrook outfit, **Danny Havoc & the Dakotas**, consisting of **Wally Staines** alias **Danny Havoc** (voc), **Alan Greer** (lg/voc), **Mick** (rg), whose surname no one can recall, **Johnny Brodigan** (bg) and **Frankie Smith** (dr).

When **Danny Havoc** left to join the **Hi-Cats**, soon to become the **Secrets**, the Liverpool **Dakotas** broke up and **Alan Greer** and **Johnny Brodigan,** together with **Ricky Dobie** (voc) and an unknown drummer, formed **Mr. X & the Masks**, who played regularly at Hambleton Hall in Huyton. This group was then joined by **Les Cave** on drums and **Danny Dring** as their new bass guitarist. A little later, they changed their name to the **Renegades** and were sometimes joined by **Chris Prescott** on rhythm guitar, who also sporadically appeared with the **Cimarrons**.

When, in 1961, **Cy Tucker** left the **Cimarrons** to become a member of **Earl Preston & the TTs**, the **Cimarrons** were in need of a new singer and it was **Lance Railton** who recommended **Alan Greer** to his brother.

Soon after **Alan Greer** joined, **Terry Dowding** left, as did **Gordon Templeton**, who rejoined his old comrades in **Karl Terry & the Cruisers**.

Alan Greer, following a suggestion of **Vic Railton** and **Bob Wooler,** adopted the stage name of **Wayne Calvert** and, together with **Paul Doyle,** they recruited new members for the group that, as **Wayne Calvert & the Cimarrons,** played their first gig for promoter **Dave Forshaw** at St. Johns Hall in Bootle in a line-up with:

Wayne Calvert	(voc/rg)
Paul Doyle	(lg/voc)
Charlie Smullan	(bg)
Tommy Hart	(dr)

The music of **Wayne Calvert & the Cimarrons** was based on the Rock 'n' Roll of **Chuck Berry**, **Bill Haley**, **Carl Perkins** and the likes.

Still, in 1961, they went into the Phillips recording studio in Kensington and recorded an acetate together with part-time singer **Tommy O'Brian**. The songs on that acetate were **Hank Thompson's** success "Drop Me Gently" and "I Will".

In 1962, the group went on a two-month tour of France and, especially for that tour, the female singer, **Carol Laine,** was added to the line-up. **Carol Laine** may have been the Carol of **Carol & the Corvettes**, but that is not known for certain.

On their return, **Wayne Calvert & the Cimarrons** took up a residency at the 'Beat Route' coffee club in Smithdown Road, but they also played regularly at many of the other local clubs, including the 'Jive Hive' in Crosby, the 'Civil Service Club' (Lower Castle Street), the 'Mandolin' in Toxteth, the 'Peppermint Lounge', the Hoylake YMCA, the 'Ivamar Club' in Skelmersdale, St. Barnabus Hall and the 'High Park Club' in Southport.

Wayne Calvert & the Cimarrons became very popular on Merseyside but never played too far outside Liverpool and they did not record again. Accordingly, they never made the breakthrough that they doubtlessly deserved.

In late 1963, **Alan Greer** decided to go back to sea and **Cy Tucker** returned to the **Cimarrons** as his replacement. The group continued on under the name of **Cy Tucker & the Friars**, but that is another story.

Wayne Calvert

With regard to the tight connection between the named groups, it is interesting to note that **Charlie Smullan** and **Tommy Hart** later joined **Earl Preston's** new group, the **Realms**, and they were replaced in the **Friars** by **Danny Dring** and **Les Cave**, the former members of **Mr. X & the Masks** and the **Renegades**, respectively.

It was only in 1967 that **Alan Greer** got back into the scene as a member of the **Plainsmen**, a Country & Western outfit from Birkenhead. After that, he played Jazz in the **Alan Thompson Trio** and then joined the **Ryles Brothers**, the backing group of **Solomon King**. In 1969, he played with **Me & Them**, who were, at that time, the backing group for **Chris Andrews** but who had previously recorded for PYE in their own right.

In 1972, **Alan Greer** formed the **Lettermen**, who recorded a great and much sought after album on the Stag label. At the same time, he was also a member of **Mother Redcap**. He then joined the **Vince Earl Attraction** and toured Spain with a group called **Sideshow**.

From 1980 until 1983, he was a member of **Cy Tucker & the Friars** (!!!) and, in 1985, he played with **Thin On Top** and, after that, with **Yue Who** (**Ozzie Yue** of the **Hideaways**), **ELO-Experience** and the **Cunard Yanks** before he quit show business and opened a music store.

Discography

Drop Me Gently / I Will   UK - Phillips acetate / 1961

THE CAREFREES

Well, it can be argued whether the story of this Liverpool group should be included here or not, as it could not be ascertained if it was really a steady group making live appearances or just a recording session line-up.

The fact is that the author never came across their name on the bills of the appropriate clubs and venues and therefore it is most probable that this mixed sextet was only called together for recording sessions. And, as the Oriole label is involved here, it may have been the producer, **John Schroeder,** who was behind it. However, this is only an assumption.

On the other hand, it has to be considered that the line-up was stable throughout the group's existence and so it cannot really be described as just a session group. However, the **Carefrees** came together in 1963 and consisted of:

Lyn Cornell	(voc)
Betty Prescott	(voc)
Barbara Kay	(voc)
Don Riddell	(lg/voc)
John Evans	(bg/voc)
John Stevens	(dr/voc)

Barbara Kay was a former singer with the **Oscar Rabin Band** and, after that, had various solo singles released on the Embassy label under the name of **Kay Barry**.

Lyn Cornell was a former member of the successful Liverpool all-girl vocal outfit, the **Vernon's Girls** and, from 1960 up to 1962, had had no less than eight solo releases on Decca, of which, "Never On Sunday" (1961), was the most successful though the most interesting was her final single, "Sally Go Round the Roses", from 1963.

It is interesting in this context to know that she was married to session drummer, **Andy White**, notable for replacing **Ringo Starr** on one take of the first **Beatles'** single, "Love Me Do".

Betty Prescott was also a former member of **Vernon's Girls** and after that had been with one of its offshoots - the **Breakaways**, also a very successful female vocal trio.

Don Riddell, **John Evans** and **John Stevens** were all former members of the **Don Ridell Four**, however, it is not known why the fourth member of that same group, **Len Starkey**, was left behind on this project.

The **Don Riddell Four** were something like a **Four Freshmen/Lettermen** type group with influences of Jazz and Rock in their music. They had an interesting record, "Casablanca", released on Decca shortly before they became part of the **Carefrees**. Furthermore, it is said that they backed **Helen Shapiro** on a nationwide tour.

The end of 1963 saw the first single release of the **Carefrees** with the song, "We Love You Beatles", which peaked at # 39 of the British charts and so was the only **Beatles** novelty that ever reached the Top 40. This song was based on "I Love You Conrad" from the 'Bye Bye Birdie' musical, changed into simple sing-a-long lyrics and pepped up with a good drive and the typical 'yeah-yeah-sound' as can be heard on the **Beatles** success, "She Loves You".

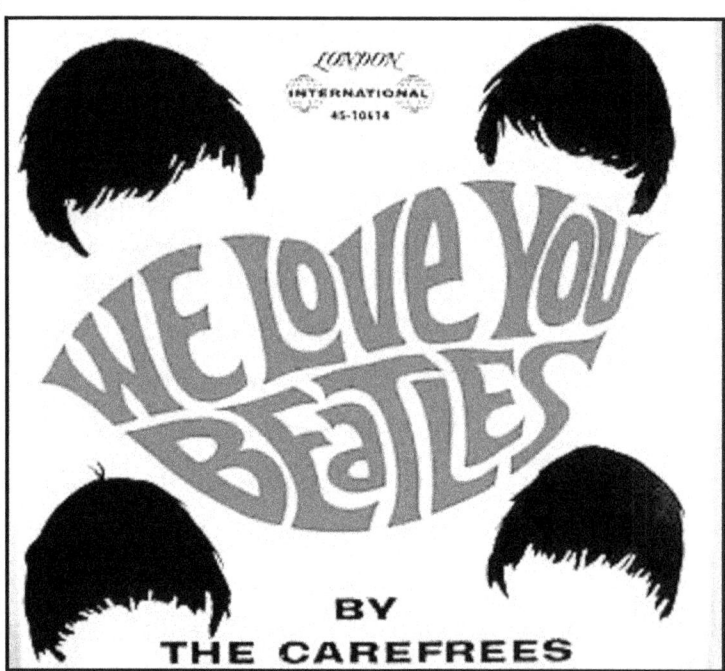

The follow-up was the **Johnny Burke** song, "Aren't You Glad You're You", a Jazz-Blues-Traditional sound put into a modern catchy style. It was not successful at all in England and did not come close to entering the charts.

Both records were also released on the American London International label and "We Love You Beatles" climbed up to No. 19 and remained there for five weeks on the US Billboard. Following this and still, in 1964, a complete album was released in the USA with the title, "We Love You All".

Besides the singles tracks, this album contained typical Beat numbers of that time, such as "All My Loving", "Glad All Over" and "Needles and Pins", but more commercially produced than the originals.

After 1964, nothing more was heard of the **Carefrees,** but it is known that **Betty Prescott** re-joined the **Breakaways**.

Lyn Cornell later may also have been a member of the **Breakaways** for some time but then sang with the **Ladybirds** (another offshoot of **Vernon's Girls**), the **Chucks** and the **Raindrops**.

In the 70's, she was part of the very successful duo, **Pearls,** who had a Top-10 hit with "Guilty" and achieved further international chart success with songs such as "You Came, You Saw, You Conquered" and "Dr. Love".

Don Riddell, **John Evans** and **John Stevens** with a fourth member, (**Len Starkey**?), were said to have re-formed as the **Don Riddell Four** again later. . .

Discography

We Love You Beatles / Demon Lover   UK- Oriole CB 1916 / 1963
                                               (US- London International 10614)

Aren't You Glad You're You / Paddy Whack   UK- Oriole CB 1931 / 1964
                                                      (US- London International 10615)

"WE LOVE YOU ALL"   US- London Intern. PS 379 / 1964

- **We Love You Beatles / The Paddy Whack / All My Loving / Glad All Over /
  Needles and Pins / I Only Want To Be With You / Everything I Do Is Wrong /
  Aren't You Glad You're You / You Were Made For Me / Hot Blooded Lover /
  Demon Lover / Won't You Be My True Love / Tell Me Something I Don't Know**

The Don Riddell Four :

Casablanca / The Four Corners of the World   UK – Decca F. 11651 / 1963

TONY CARLTON & THE MERSEYBOYS

This was a Southport group and their history goes back as far as 1959 when the **Clubmen** were formed by **Alex Paton** (dr), together with **Derek Henderson** (lg), **Billy Abbott** (rg) and **Joey Porter** (bg).

All of the members were newcomers to the scene with the exception of **Billy Abbott** who had previously played with the **Berry Pickers**. This initial line-up did not last long and, in 1960, the complete group changed with the exception of **Alex Paton**.

The new members were **Pete James** (voc), **Eric Wright** (g/voc), **Ian Sheldon** (g) and **Ray Marshall** (g/voc), who came from **Little Gene & the Outlaws**, formerly known as the **Berry Pickers**. At that time, the **Clubmen** changed their name to the **Toledos**.

When **Ray Marshall** left and **Ian Sheldon** also dropped out, the others continued on as the **Toledo Four**, together with **Tony Jones** as their new lead guitarist.

But this line-up was still unstable so **Tony Jones** was replaced by **Freddie Seal**, whose place, a little later, was taken by **Russel Peart**, while **Bim McBain** came in when **Pete James** left to join the **Take Five**, a forerunner group of **Timebox**.

After that, **Pete James** formed the **Rondels** together with his sister **Stella James** and, in the late Sixties, he was the leader of the **Peter James Bluesband**.

Billy Abbott returned to the group and took the place of **Bim McBain** as bass guitarist.

It was probably this line-up of the **Toledo Four** that, slowly but surely, established a very good name on the local scene.

Billy Abbott left again when **Ray Marshall** returned in 1964.

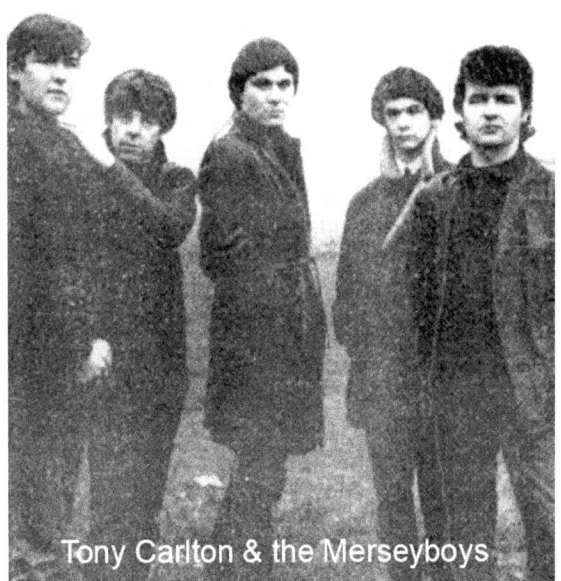

Tony Carlton & the Merseyboys

At this point, the **Toledo Four** took on the name of the **Mersey Four** and turned professional. A little later, they were joined by singer, **Anthony Mathieson**, who came from the **Citadels** from Litherland and who had adopted the stage name **Tony Carlton**.

Initially, the group continued as **Tony Carlton & the Mersey Four** but then changed it to **Tony Carlton & the Merseyboys** – in a line-up with

Tony Carlton	(voc)
Russel Peart	(lg)
Eric Wright	(rg/voc)
Ray Marshall	(bg/voc)
Alex Paton	(dr)

They soon became very popular on the scene and, in 1965, accepted an offer to tour the south of Germany. During that tour, they had a long engagement at the well known Habana-Bar in Munich, where they went down very well.

One night, while they were performing at the Habana-Bar, they were approached by an individual that offered them six hundred German Marks if they made a record for him. The group, of course, accepted and went into a studio in Schwabing the next day to record **Gene Chandler**'s "Duke of Earl" and **Bo Diddley**'s "Roadrunner" as a demo disc.

During a conversation with their 'employer', whose name unfortunately nobody can recall, it turned out he was a manager and record distributor who also had connections with a Liverpool group based in Sweden. From this fact, it can be assumed that it was **Jo May**, who around that same time, had taken over the management of the **Cherry Stones** from Sweden, a group that included Liverpool musicians.

If indeed it was **Jo May**, it is more than probable that this recording of **Tony Carlton & the Merseyboys** was for his own independent label, JMP Records, on which the **Cherry Stones** also recorded in 1966 before they became the **Kinetic** and went to France. However, there is no real evidence to support this association and no further details are known.

Nevertheless, **Tony Carlton & the Merseyboys** returned to Southport and continued to play the normal Merseyside club circuit until **Ray Marshall** left to join the **Big Three**.

The group probably broke up at this time but was re-formed in 1966 by **Alex Paton** and **Russel Peart**, together with the returning **Ray Marshall** (bg/voc), **Graham Powell** (key/voc) and **John Surguy** (sax). They continued on the scene as the **Merseyboys** and went over to Germany again. This time they played the Hamburg scene, which included gigs at the 'Big Apple' and 'Crazy Horse'. In addition, they also went down to Frankfurt for a long engagement at the famous 'K 52'.

When they returned to Southport, some of the members wanted to change back to performing on a semi-pro basis but, unfortunately, the decision was not unanimous. So **John Surguy** went on to play with **Rhythm & Blues Incorporated** and the recording groups **Pete Kelly's Solution, Jasmin T** and **Inner Sleeve**. All three of these groups had evolved (in some form) from **Rhythm & Blues Incorporated.**

Russel Peart got a job as pilot in the Royal Air Force and quit the music business, while **Graham Powell** also disappeared from the scene.

Alex Paton and **Ray Marshall**, together with **Dougie Appleton** (voc/lg), continued as a trio for a short time, using the name of the **Merseyboys** again.

When they split up, **Alex Paton** formed another group with **Mick Hardy** (voc), **John Fanklin** (lg) and **Ian Robinson** (bg). They called themselves the **Mersey Four** (again) and it is interesting to know that **Mick Hardy** was none other than **Little Gene** of Southport's pioneer group, **Little Gene & the Outlaws**.

When this group disbanded, **Alex Paton** teamed up with **Alan Woodcock** (key/voc) and **Peter Hulme** (lg/voc) from Southport's **Blue Chips**. Together with **Ernie Moreton** on bass guitar, they performed under the name of the **Mersey Four** (yet again!), but they did not stay together for very long.

Alex Paton then became a member of the **Principles** from Southport and, after that, he gigged around as resident drummer for many years, including two seasons on the famous Mersey ferry boat, the 'Royal Iris'.

In the Eighties, **Alex Paton** jumped onto the musical bandwagon once again when he became a member of **Gerry De Ville & the City Kings**, after that he quit the music business.

Discography

as "Tony Carlton & the Merseyboys":

Duke of Earl / Roadrunner   G – JMP (?) demo-disc / 1965

(This demo was definitely recorded in a studio in Munich-Schwabing but the JMP-label is only an assumption – even if a very strong possibility. For details see story.)

THE CASUALS

No, this is not the "Jesamine" hit-group and there is also no connection to the Southport group of the same name, which evolved into the third **All Stars** backing group for **Lee Curtis,** or to the outfit from Brownlow Hill that became the **In Crowd**.

This story is about the **Casuals** from the Liverpool district of Bootle, where they were formed in the early 1960's. After their first gigs at local venues, **Dave Forshaw** booked them to appear on the 'Litherland Town Hall', where they went down very well – so well in fact, that they became part of the 'David Forshaw Enterprises' stable, which of course secured them regular bookings all over the scene.

In 1963, the original bass-guitarist, whose name is sadly not known, left the **Casuals** and, from then on, they appeared in the following line-up:

Terry Lloyd	(voc)
Malcolm Miller	(lg)
Alan Jones	(rg)
Gordon Loughlin	(bg)
Peter Hepworth	(dr)

L to R: Malcolm Miller, Terry Lloyd, Peter Hepworth, Alan Jones, Gordon Loughlin

Gordon Loughlin was a former member of a group called **Peter & the Boys**, who were resident at the 'Harland & Wolff Social Club' in Bootle.

The **Casuals** mainly played **Chuck Berry**, **Arthur Alexander** and **Carl Perkins** music, and now, besides playing the church-halls such as 'St. Christopher's', they also appeared at the popular Liverpool clubs including the 'Peppermint Lounge', the 'Iron Door', the 'Sink' and the 'Cavern' and they even travelled to Ellesmere Port in Cheshire where they regularly performed at the 'Civic Hall' and the 'Show Club'.

They developed a special stage-act with the musicians wearing blonde wigs and they would jump around in the style of **Freddie & the Dreamers** with their guitars kept under control. It must have looked fairly crazy but it was obviously entertaining and their music was excellent.

In 1964, they took part in *'The People National Talent Competition'* held at the 'Floral Pavilion' in New Brighton. The **Casuals** came in first out of twelve groups, probably not at least because of their stage-show but also because **Terry Lloyd** had a great day, finishing their set while sitting on the stage and singing a fantastic "You better move on". The first prize was a week's holiday at the Butlin's holiday-camp in Pwllheli in Wales. However, what should have been a lovely holiday was nothing more than another talent competition held in Butlin's South Camp, which ultimately turned out to be a sort of a disaster – for details read the tale as told by **Gordon Loughlin** in his own words at the end of this story.

Anyway, back in Liverpool, the **Casuals** went into **Percy Phillips** studio in Kensington and made an acetate with a great version of **Chuck Berry's** "No particular place to go" and **Arthur Alexander's** classic "You'd better move on". However, this demo-record did not bring any greater success for the **Casuals** and unfortunately, towards the end of 1964 they disbanded. The reasons for the break up are not entirely clear but it could have been because **Malcolm Miller** emigrated to Australia. **Peter Hepworth** then joined the **Dions*** and after that became a member of **Vikki & the Moonlighters**.

Gordon Loughlin at first joined the **Harmonies**, which was the resident band at the ODVA (Orrell District Veterans Association) but in October 1964 got the offer to join the **T.T.'s**, that had just recruited **Karl Terry*** as their new singer. A little later, **Gordon Loughlin** and other remaining members of **Karl Terry & the T.T.'s** got together with remaining members of the **Clayton Squares*** and continued as the **T-Squares** and, in 1966, they toured Germany as the **Clayton Squares** once again. But this development can be followed in the story of **Earl Preston & the T.T.'s***.

When the **T-Squares** disbanded after their German tour, **Gordon Loughlin,** for a short time, was a member of **Liverpool Scene** but then joined the **Renicks**, that a little later were also joined by **Ricky Gleason** from the **Rebels** as vocalist and, from then onwards, went out as **Ricky Gleason & the Topspots*** once again. From there, **Gordon Loughlin** became a member of the cabaret-band **Natural Gas**, he then joined the Folk-Rock band **Mr. Blundell's Arms** and, after that, played with the **Old Peculiar Band**.

He is still active today in a group called **Fast Track** that, besides him, also includes the former **Notions*** drummer **Dave Armstrong**.

Discography :

No particular place to go / You'd better move on   **UK- Phillips Kensington acetate / 1964**

Casuals-Tale

We entered "The People National Talent Competition" at the Floral Pavillion and on our arrival found out that we were on the final spot, which gave us plenty of time to get well oiled (with ale).
When our turn came we burst out as the curtains opened and gave it all we had got – balls and all! Terry sat on the stage on "You better move on" – the rest was full on.

Anyway we won and as we made our way off stage, past the grimaces of the other contestants and dodging the occasional fag-packet, we told ourselves that the best wine had been saved till the last.

We pondered the prospect before us and the first prize was a week's holiday at Butlin's holiday-camp in Pwllheli. On arrival there we were shown to our chalets hut with 1 and 2 bunk beds and ablutions at the end of the block. We found that we were entered for a further heat of the competition but nobody had told us that before!!! So our long suffering manager Dave George had to drive back to Liverpool to fetch our gear. We found that the contestants on the Empire Theatre in the south-camp were comedians, child singers, etc. – good family entertainment - and we were the only Beat-group.

So when we leaped out, good as it was, we just about cleared the place. The compere felt so sorry for us that he suggested we played the staff-canteen at 1 pound each per night and all the ale that we could drink. So a churn of bitter was placed on the bar each night for us.

Somehow we had taken to walking around in our bare feet – I mean we thought we were on holiday, even if it was May in Great Britain. I remember the floor of the canteen being all wet with spilt beer as we danced in our bare feet during our performance.

We all agreed that the second prize on that competition must have been a two-weeks holiday at Pwllhelli.

Gordon Loughlin / The Casuals

*The stories of these groups can be followed in 'Beat Waves 'Cross The Mersey' (*VelocePress*) ISBN 978-1-58850-201-8).

THE CENSORS

The lifeline of this group was an extremely 'hard nut' and, even after writing this story, it cannot be stated that it was finally cracked.

The Censors

Despite the most extensive research over the years and even personal visits to their booking-address and the addresses of their fan-club secretaries, these efforts failed to yield any significant information about the group.

In addition, repeated calls to various shows on Radio Merseyside and searching internet-platforms, as well as asking those individuals that were part of the scene at that time, did not bring any totally verifiable results. There was only a recording and a promo-sheet with the Christian-names of the musicians that had surfaced and, as it ultimately turned out, they were from different times and did not really fit together. Even more unfortunately, information unearthed at a later date did not help unravel the mystery and so, this write-up is based more on probability taking into account all the information that was provided from various sources. So here we go:

The **Censors,** as they were most probably named from the beginning, were formed as a four-piece group in the Liverpool area of Anfield sometime in 1964. They appeared regularly on the Beat sessions at the 'Locarno' dance-hall on West Derby Road and also took part in the 'Northern Sound 65' Beat-contest, but did not get into the finals which was won by the **Tabs**. The **Censors,** for sure, were one of the softer commercial groups and obviously included Country music in their repertoire as, in 1965, they were repeatedly part of the "Country & Western Big Night Out" river cruises on the 'Royal Iris' – in a line-up with:

Bill Wookey	(lg/voc)
Dave ???	(rg)
Charles 'Chas' Williams	(bg/voc)
'Gilly'	(voc/dr)

Their lead-vocalist was the drummer, **'Gilly'**, whose nickname was derived from his surname which is sadly, not known. It is rumoured that it could have been **Colin Gilmour**, a former member of Litherland's **Ramrods**, one of the very rare lead vocalist drummers, but that is not guaranteed.

In 1965, the **Censors** became the resident group at the 'Sefton Park Club', where they regularly backed a girl-singer called **Gloria**, whose full name is also not known. Around that same time, an organist was added to the group but, once again, only the Christian name, **'Pete'**, is known. In this line-up, but without **Gloria**, the **Censors** went into the Unicord-studio of **Charlie Weston** and recorded a demonstration disc single with two group-originals. The A-side "I'm Going" is an up-tempo song with an interesting guitar-solo. In the opening, it is somewhat reminiscent of a harmless version of "Boppin' The Blues", while the B-side "Memories" is a melodic, more organ dominated ballad. It must have been shortly after this recording that **Bill Wookey** left the **Censors** and was replaced by **Johnny Roue** on lead-guitar, whose former group is not known. This is the line-up shown on the previously mentioned promo-sheet.

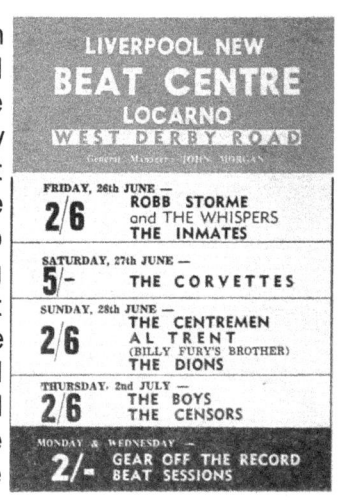

The **Censors** kept playing the Liverpool-scene and, after they broke up sometime in 1967, **Charles Williams** and **Johnny Roue** teamed up with **Terry Youds** (org), who was either the brother or cousin of the **Censors'** fan-club secretary and, together with drummer, **Tony Spencer,** formed the **Spencer Williams Sound**. **Tony Spencer** was a former member of the **Aljitones** and **Kathy & the Kadettes**. Together, with two occasionally changing girl-singers, the **Spencer Williams Sound** had a number of successful years on the cabaret-scene.

At some stage, **Bill Wookey** of the original **Censors** took over again from **John Roue** and **Tony Spencer** was replaced by **Billy Bryden**, a former member of the **Five Aces** and **Carol & the Memories**. That then was the reason for the group to change their name into the **New Pickwick Sound**, after the public house 'Pickwicks' where the group had a residency at that time. None of the other members of the **Censors** appeared on the scene again.

Discography

I'm Going / Memories   UK- Unicord (without number) / 1965

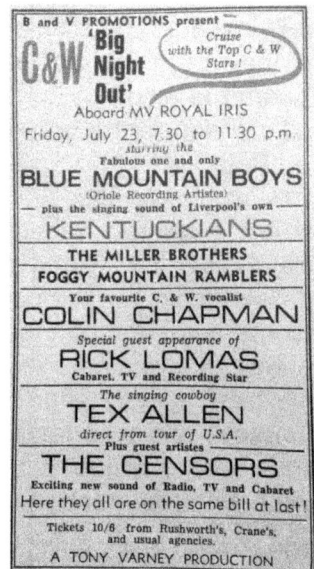

With The Compliments Of

DAVE CHAS GILLY JOHNNY PETE

THE CENSORS

—— FAN CLUB ——

Miss G. YOUDS,
73, Selborne Street,
Liverpool, 8.

Mrs. M. GRIMES,
49, Bourne Street,
Liverpool, 6.

—— STUDIO ——
39a, St. Anne Street,
Liverpool, 1.
For Bookings Ring ANField 3090.

(ASHLEY PHOTOS)

CHRIS & THE AUTOCRATS

St. Helens, situated halfway between Liverpool and Manchester, part of Lancashire in the 1960's and now part of Merseyside, had a really lively and interesting music-scene in the Sixties.

For some reasons, the groups from St. Helens tended to become more part of the Liverpool music scene than Manchester, for example the **Blackwells***, the **Incas***, **Cadillac & the Playboys** and **Ray Malcolm & the Sunsets** were all Liverpool 'regulars'. (The last two groups mentioned also have stories in this book).

This association with Liverpool also applies to **Chris & the Autocrats**, a group that was formed in the early Sixties in St. Helens by brothers **Chris** and **John Richmond** and in 1963 consisted of:

Chris Richmond	(voc)
Gerald 'Ged' Knight	(lg/voc)
Dave Banks	(rg/voc)
John Yates	(bg)
John Richmond	(dr)

It is not known if any of the members had played in any other groups as **Chris & the Autocrats** never really made the headlines and the Liverpool music-press did not pay much attention to them.

Their manager was a certain **Thomas Kilgannon,** and it was him, who arranged for the group to take part in a band-competition in aid of Oxfam at the 'Cavern' in Liverpool. **Chris & the Autocrats** did not win but came a close second to the **Connoisseurs** in a heat of 18 groups and so they did not go to the finals in London.

But in the end, it was much more important for their career that they obviously left a very positive impression on **Bob Wooler**, the Cavern's DJ and booking-manager, as he was the one who chose the groups to be part of an Oriole recording session at the 'Cavern' for the planned third volume of their album-series, "This Is Merseybeat". This session took place between the 17th and the 22nd of February 1964 and **Chris & the Autocrats** were among the groups that were recorded by A&R man **John Schroeder**. As this album was never released, it could not be established how many or which songs were recorded by **Chris & the Autocrats.** This must have been a big disappointment for them as the record would have meant a huge boost to their career. Surprisingly,

Chris & the Autocrats L to R: Chris Richmond, Dave Banks, John Yates, John Richmond, Gerald 'Ged' Knight

after that recording-session, there is only one more appearance of **Chris & the Autocrats** documented at the 'Cavern' – on 13th November 1964.

In the interim, the group had recorded an EP on acetate in their own right. Unfortunately, it is not known at which studio that recording was made. The outstanding song on that EP is a really good rocking "Don't start running away", which was probably an original of the group. The other songs were the **Peter & Gordon** success "World without love", **Bobby Day's** "Rockin' Robin" and the **Rufus Thomas** classic "Walking the dog".

As it seems, **Chris & the Autocrats** kept playing the local scene in St. Helens and places like Whiston, Prescot, Keswick, Newton-le-Willows and Barrow for a few years. Their last documented appearance dates from 28th June 1967, when they played on a Royal Iris Mersey River cruise for the Whiston Hospital staff-dance. After that, nothing was heard of **Chris & the Autocrats** and none of the musicians appeared on the scene again.

Discography:

World without love / Don't start running away /

Rockin' Robin / Walking the dog   **UK- acetate EP / 1964**

Sometime between the 17th and 22nd of February 1964 Chris & the Autocrats were recorded by Oriole for the planned 3rd volume of their legendary albums 'This Is Merseybeat', which sadly was never released and so it is not known, how many or which numbers were recorded. For details regarding the Oriole session see the appendix at the end of this book.

*The stories of these groups can be followed in 'Beat Waves 'Cross The Mersey' (*VelocePress* ISBN 978-1-58850-201-8).

THE CITY BEATS

In 1960, **Billy Roberts,** who had played with the Liverpool Rock 'n' Roll group, **Don Bosco & the Gauchos** from 1958 to 1959, formed his own group together with **Arthur Owen** (g), **Jimmy Moran** (rg) and **Ken Duggan** (bg). That group was called the **Apaches** however, for unknown reasons, they only ever rehearsed together and never performed in public.

Jimmy Moran went on to play with the **Martinis** and **Lee Castle & the Barons** and, in later years, formed the C&W group, **Idle Hours**, who were successful on the C&W scene for many years.

Arthur Owen and **Ken Duggan** continued to play together and became founding members of the embryonic **Mafia-Group**. **Arthur Owen** continued to play in the **Mafia-Group** until they broke up in 1964.

In 1961, **Billy Roberts** decided to give it another try and he formed a new group with the name of the **City Beats** with the following line-up:

Billy Roberts	(lg)
Wally McCrystal	(rg)
Paul Eker	(bg)
Danny Bell	(dr)

This Wavertree outfit was a real instrumental group in the style of the **Shadows** or the **Virtues** but, from time to time, they were also joined by **Wes Paul Gerrard** as their singer, although he never became a steady member.

Prior to **Danny Bell** joining, **Ritchie Galvin**, a former member of the **Galvanisers**, was their drummer. He went on to play with groups including **Earl Preston & the T.T.s**, **Earl Preston's Realms** and **Gerry DeVille & the City-Kings**.

The City Beats at Blackpool

In the beginning, the **City Beats** mainly played the local social clubs such as the 'Norton Street Social Club', the 'N.U.R. Club' or the 'Lomond', where they always went down well. In 1962, they took part in the 'Frankie Vaughan Talent Competition', sponsored by the Liverpool Echo newspaper. This competition was held over a one week period at the Crane Hall in Liverpool and the final round was held at the south Pier Theatre in Blackpool.

For this competition, the **City Beats** played the instrumentals "Never on Sunday", "Lover's guitar" and "El Cumbachero" so well that they reached third place and won a recording contract. It is not known whether this was a contract for a guaranteed release with an established record company or just for a recording test. It is also possible that it was nothing more than an opportunity to cut an acetate in some recording studio.

Whatever, it is doubtful that the **City Beats** made use of it, as not long after the competition **Billy Roberts** and **Danny Bell** were asked to join the **Crusaders** – and they accepted. This, of course, was the end of the **City Beats** who disbanded shortly after their major success.

Paul Eker became a member of the **Profiles** and **Wally McCrystal** played with some other groups on the Liverpool scene, but then he quit the music business.

The **Crusaders** very soon changed their name into the **Kruzads** and as such appeared in a line-up with:

Ken 'Dixie' Dean	(voc/g)
Billy Roberts	(lg/voc)
Eddie Hill	(bg/voc)
Danny Bell	(dr)

Dixie Dean had previously played with the **Mars Bars** and the **Gerry Marsden Skiffle Group**, while **Eddie Hill** was a former member of the **Texans** and the **Easybeats**.

Gordon Brown of the 'Mersey Sounds' agency became their manager and it was him who arranged for the **Kruzads** to play the 'Star-Club' in Hamburg. According to **Dixie Dean,** it was during their stay in Germany that they recorded the **Rolling Stones** ballad, "Tell me", and **Arthur Alexander's** "You better move on" for the German Polydor label, but this record was apparently never released.

Britain's Most Progressive Agency

MERSEY SOUNDS LIMITED

87 LORD STREET, LIVERPOOL 2

Tel. CEN 3671, CEN 0272 (STD code 051)

FOR MERSEYSIDE'S MOST PROMISING GROUPS.

ANY NATIONAL ARTISTES BOOKED

DON'T DELAY !
BOOK TO-DAY !

**The original line-up of the Kruzads at the Orrell Park Ballroom (1963)
L to R: Billy Roberts, Danny Bell, Dixie Dean, Eddie Hill**

Back in Liverpool, the **Kruzads** were hailed as *'Liverpool's answer to the Rolling Stones'* and, in fact, there were similarities. The group became very popular throughout the northwest but, in spite of their excellent musical quality and their hard driving Beat, they never released any records or managed to achieve nationwide fame.

Dixie Dean moved to London as a session musician and from 1972 until 1974 he was a member of **McGuinness Flint**. He was replaced in the **Kruzads** by **Mal Jefferson** (voc/harp), a former member of **Buddy Dean & the Teachers** and the **Mastersounds**.

Later, in 1964, **Eddie Hill** also left the group, he was replaced by **Arthur Megginson**, who came from the **Clayton Squares**. **Arthur Megginson** did not stay for too long, and his place was taken by the returning **Paul Eker**. This meant that, in 1964, the former **City Beats** were almost completely reunited again under the name of the **Kruzads**.

Later in that year, **Chris Finley,** who had previously played with the **Runaways,** was added on keyboards. This line-up of the **Kruzads** lasted until early 1966 when the group disbanded.

Chris Finley joined the **Masterminds**, who became the **Fruit Eating Bears**. After that, he was a member of **Confucius**, a group that had evolved from the **Hideaways**. Later, he played with the new **Merseybeats** and **Herman's Hermits**.

Paul Eker joined the **Nashpool**, that with him developed into the **Bones Of Men**, while **Danny Bell** disappeared from the scene. This really marked the definitive end of the **City Beats**.

However, still in 1966, **Billy Roberts** re-formed the **Kruzads** with completely different musicians but that is a different story . . .

The 1966 Kruzads L to R: (Back) Jimmy Ikonomidis, John Thompson, Joey Maher, & Paul Hitchmough - (Front) Billy Roberts & Steve Barton

For the complete story of the **Kruzads** please see the book *"Mersey Beat Waves" – ISBN 1588502015 or 9781588502018*.

<u>Discography</u>

The **Citybeats** won a recording contract in 1962 when they placed third in the big 'Frankie Vaughan Talent Competition'. However, it is unlikely that they received any benefit from that success, as they broke up soon after the competition.

THE CLANSMEN

To avoid any confusion, it should be pointed out right away that the **Paul Dean** who had a short spell with this group was not the London singer/pianist, **Paul Beuselinck**, who also adopted the stage name **Paul Dean** and was the leader of **Paul Dean & the Dreamers**, recorded as **Paul Dean & the Soul Savages** and **Paul Dean & the Thoughts** and later became a popular actor under the name of **Paul Nicholas**.

Having made this clear, we can proceed with the history of the **Clansmen**, who were formed in Burscough, near Southport, in 1962 and in the original line-up consisted of

David Rosbotham	(voc/lg)
Edgar Walsh	(rg/voc)
Ian Collier	(p/voc)
Ray Bradshaw	(bg)
Eric Iddon	(dr)

This line-up achieved some local success and continued to gain momentum throughout 1962.

In March 1963, **Edgar Walsh** left the group and was replaced by **Dave Walker**, who was a former member of the **Banshees**, who were also quite popular and who had changed their name to the **Galaxies** shortly before he left them.

The two Daves shared the lead vocals and guitar duties until late 1963, when **Ray Bradshaw** also decided to leave. **David Rosbotham**, who in the interim, had been using the name **Dave Rossi**, took over on bass guitar.

The **Clansmen** were heavily Rock and Blues influenced and continued as a quartet with **David Walker** now playing the lead guitar and his father **Charles Walker** took over their management – apparently a very successful arrangement as this line-up achieved a lot of attention and a large following throughout the northwest of England. They were regular attractions at the 'Empress Ballroom' in Wigan (later to become the 'Wigan Casino') and the 'Floral Hall' in Morecambe and Southport, often appearing on the same bill with many top names of the day, such as, the **Pretty Things**, the **Moody Blues** and **Cliff Bennett & the Rebel Rousers**.

The **Clansmen** were signed to the Southport agency 'Birchall Promotions' and in 1964 recorded an acetate at Deroy studios in Hest Bank/Lancaster, containing the two self-penned numbers "Long, lonely time" and "Were you with him?".

BIRCHALL PROMOTIONS
(*The "Personal Touch" Agency*)
51 SEFTON STREET, SOUTHPORT
Southport 57298 & Burscough 2388

Sole representation for—
THE CLANSMEN   **THE DIPLOMATS**
(solid "rock" merchants)   (you name it!)

also booking for
MANY LEADING MERSEYSIDE GROUPS

If its Entertainment, — we promote it !

This very interesting disc was brought to the attention of the Liverpool songwriter and talent scout, **Ralph Bowdler** who, at that time, was attempting to obtain a recording contract for the Liverpool born singer, **Daryl Philip Core**, who had adopted the stage-name of **Paul Dean**.

Ralph was impressed by the **Clansmen** and suggested that, in return for a possible recording contract, they should act as **Paul Dean's** backing group.

Daryl Phillip Core, in spite of his interest in the local Merseybeat scene as the former manager of the **Dions** and the **Black Velvets**, was a trained opera singer and, accordingly, the suggestion of a co-operation was met with a mixed reaction by the **Clansmen** after meeting **Paul Dean** and hearing his singing. Some of the group members were not convinced of the compatibility of their widely contrasting styles, but the possibility of a contract temporarily helped them to put some of these misgivings aside.

Southport United Commercial Travellers' Association
PRESENT AT THE
FLORAL HALL, SOUTHPORT
Gerry and The Pacemakers
The Big Three
THE TEENBEATS   THE CLANSMEN
The Diplomats
On WEDNESDAY, 8th MAY, 1963
8-0 P.M. TO MIDNIGHT
Tickets 6/-
Available from H. P. RADIO, Ormskirk and Southport, also SCOTTS CAMERA CENTRE, Chapel Street.
At the Door, 7/6. No Money Refunded.   Free Late Transport
All proceeds to U.C.T.A. Charities

So the **Clansmen** continued to perform in their own right with occasional engagements earmarked to include **Paul Dean** on a few numbers.

A campaign was launched to publicise **Paul Dean & the Clansmen** in local newspapers and music magazines but, as time went on, it became increasingly obvious to the group members and a considerable number of their fans that this arrangement was just not working out.

Before their ways separated, **Paul Dean & the Clansmen** cut two demos of songs written by **Ralph Bowdler** in **Brian Kelly**'s Lambda recording studios in Crosby. Unfortunately, no one can recall the titles, which is no great loss, as it was not the right kind of music for the **Clansmen** anyway.

The Clansmen

PAUL DEAN
and the
CLANSMEN
Enq.: C. H. WALKER
Tel.: Burscough 2388.

Ralph Bowdler's efforts finally resulted in a deal with PYE for **Paul Dean**, but not for the **Clansmen**.

Paul Dean then adopted the stage name **David Garrick** and 1965 saw his first record with a dramatic ballad called "Go", an adaption of the Italian song "O mio Seniori". The record flopped as did the similarly styled follow-up "One little smile".

John Schroeder was his producer and the PYE team obviously tried to market **David Garrick** as a sort of opera singer with the visual image of a pop-star – probably based on the model of the successful US group **Jay & the Americans**, but that did not work out as they did not choose the right material and the arrangements were badly missing the much needed drive.

They tried to correct this and so picked the **Rolling Stones** number "Lady Jane" for the next release and this climbed the charts up to number 28 and brought a national breakthrough for **David Garrick**. This was followed by the simple pop song, "Dear Mrs. Applebee", which got to number 22 in the British charts and became a big hit throughout Europe. Of course, the singer continued with unpretentious pop-songs, but failed to match the success of his previous releases.

It is said that on the first records he was backed by the **Iveys** from Swansea, but perhaps, with the exception of "Lady Jane", that is hard to believe. On the other hand, it is certain that the **Iveys** backed him on a tour of Germany in 1968 where an album was recorded live at the 'Blow Up' in Munich under the name of **David Garrick & the Dandy** - in a line-up with the Liverpool guitarist, **Tom Evans** (formerly of the **Calderstones**), **Pete Ham** (g/key), **Ron Griffiths** (bg) and **Mike Gibbins** (dr), one year later this line–up became the hit group **Badfinger**.

David Garrick spent a few years in Germany where he successfully released more lightweight pop and even some really atrocious songs in the German language.

In the Seventies, he is thought to have gone back to opera singing and nothing further was heard of him on the scene until he tried a comeback in the Nineties, at one time impersonating **James Brown**. Needless to say, this did not work out. He often appeared in the usual Oldies package shows later but without any outstanding success.

Back to the **Clansmen** who of course, continued under their old name when **Paul Dean** became **David Garrick**. Birchall Promotions recommended them as *'solid Rock merchants'*, which apparently was an accurate description.

They went into the Lambda studios again and recorded further demos with the songs "You'd better move on" and "Youngblood" as well as "Route 66", "Some other guy" and "Walking the dog". The **Clansmen** kept busy playing the clubs until late 1966 and then called it a day.

In 1968, **Dave Walker** was a member of the cabaret group **First Edition** and of **Dave Rossi** it is also known that he continued on the scene but, unfortunately, no further details could be ascertained. All the other members disappeared from the scene . . .

Discography

as **"The Clansmen"**:

Long lonely time / Were you with him	UK – Deroy-acetate / 1964
You'd better move on / Youngblood	UK – Lambda acetate / 1965
Route 66 / Some other guy / Walking the dog	UK – Lambda acetate / 1965

as **"Paul Dean & the Clansmen"**:

Here it is only known that they recorded two demos with **Ralph Bowdler** originals in the Lambda studios in Crosby, but nobody can remember the titles anymore because nobody kept the acetates as it wasn't the right kind of music for the **Clansmen** anyway.

THE CLASSICS

The story of this really good and very interesting group starts in July 1961 in St. Helens, when the former **Fireflites** drummer, **Mel Gallagher**, better known as **Mel Preston**, joined the **Zephyrs**.

This very popular group disbanded when, after some internal problems, **Mel Preston** and **Les Stocks**, the rhythm guitarist of the **Zephyrs**, decided to form a new group under the name of the **Classics** in the following line-up:

Les Stocks	(voc/rg)
Johnny Olive	(lg/voc)
Stan Gibbons	(bg/voc)
Mel Preston	(dr)

The Zephyrs - L to R: Les Stocks, Geoff Taggart, Mel Preston, Ray Malcolm & Johnny Olive

In this context, it is interesting to note that the other members of the **Zephyrs** became **Ray Malcolm & the Sunsets**, another story in this book, which also includes the **Zephyrs** story.

Johnny Olive was also a former member of the **Zephyrs** but had already left almost a year before the split, while **Stan Gibbons** was a newcomer to the scene.

The **Classics** soon became popular on the local scene and also had a lot of gigs in the clubs of nearby Liverpool and Manchester.

In order to accelerate their career, they needed a demo and so they went into the Welsby Sound studios in Rainhill and recorded an acetate with the **Majors** song "A little bit now" and "I love you Betty" in 1963. The B-side was an adaptation of a song originally known as "I love you Eddie" by the **Crystals**.

This very interesting acetate of the **Classics** did not result in a recording contract and so the group just kept gigging on the scene.

Sometime in 1963, **Mel Preston** left to join **Lee Castle & the Barons** from Liverpool, who a little later recorded for Parlophone.

He was replaced by **Bob O'Hanlon** from Liverpool, who came from **Mark Peters & the Silhouettes**, prior to that he had played with both **Frank Knight & the Barons**, which later evolved into **Lee Castle & the Barons.**

The **Classics** played a summer season at Morecambe Floral Hall and, after that, **Bob O'Hanlon** returned to **Mark Peters & the Silhouettes**.

Mel Preston returned to the **Classics** as his replacement but he did not stay for too long and became a member of **Cadillac & the Playboys** from St. Helens, but that is another story in this book.

The **Classics** recruited another Liverpool drummer. Unfortunately, no one can recall his name.

In this line-up, the **Classics** accepted an offer to work in France for **Jean Besnard**, a Corsican who ran a small hotel in Fontenay-St. Pére, which was not open to the public but housed two groups - the **Downbeats** and of course the **Classics**.

Due to problems about money with their agent, **Johnny Olive** and the Liverpool drummer returned home, while **Les Stocks** and **Stan Gibbons** joined the **Downbeats**, a Lancashire group who had a long and very successful residency in France (they also have their own story in this book).

Johnny Olive who, in the meantime, had changed his name to **John Denson**, initially joined the **Rats,** he then became a member of **Cadillac & the Playboys**, who shortened their name to the **Playboys.** Ultimately, after a tour in Romania they changed it to the **Manchester Playboys**. After that, he joined **Wayne Fontana & the Opposition** and then a Jazz and Rhythm & Blues trio called **Crocus Bowl**, that, from September 1966 onwards, was the resident band at the 'Drokiweeny' in Manchester. After that, **Johnny Olive** (alias **John Denson)** quit the music-business.

In 1965, **Les Stocks** also returned from France and became a member of the **Manchester Playboys**. Therefore, this group now consisted of three fifths of the former **Classics**, but as already mentioned, this story can be followed under **Cadillac & the Playboys**.

Les Stocks later married the Manchester recording star **Lorraine Gray** and they emigrated to Australia. As far as it is known, they are still living there.

Mel Preston continued to play with the **Manchester Playboys** for some time but then joined the **Kaytones** from St. Helens, where he met up again with former members of the **Zephyrs**.

After his return from France, **Stan Gibbons** worked as musician on various cruise-ships and, after that, played sessions and residencies in the London clubs until he quit showbiz in 1982.

Discography

A little bit now / I love you Betty   **UK- Welsby Sound -acetate / 1963**

THE CORSAIRS

This interesting group was formed sometime in the early Sixties in Huyton by **Phil Boardman**, **Ray Dale** and **Colin Sayers** together with a bass-guitarist, called '**Dave**'. After some rehearsals, they began to play the local youth clubs and pubs.

The **Corsairs**, as they were named from the beginning, soon became popular and they also started to play the major Beat clubs and halls in and around Liverpool.

In late 1963, the group was joined by **William Carruthers**, who had become a popular singer under the name **Clay Ellis** and who was the former leader of **Clay Ellis & the Raiders**.

Of course, the group now took advantage of the singer's popularity and adopted the name **Clay Ellis & the Corsairs**. This connection only lasted for a few months and then **Clay Ellis** became '**Mr. Lee**' and formed a new group under the name of **Mr. Lee & Co.**

It was probably around the same time that the lead guitarist, **Phil Boardman,** left to join the **Thoughts** and the original bass-guitarist also left.

The **Corsairs** then continued in a line-up with:

Tony Coates	(voc/lg)
Ray Dale	(rg/voc)
Pete Bowden	(bg/voc)
Colin Sayers	(dr)

Tony Coates had previously played with the **Hungry I's**, who probably hailed from Walton, while **Pete Bowden** came from the **Katz**.

The **Corsairs** were a very good Beat group, and they became really popular throughout Merseyside.

In 1966, **Tony Coates** joined the **Squad**, formerly known as the **Riot Squad**, who had amalgamated with singer **Mark Peters** as **Mark Peters & the Method** and had toured France with him as their lead singer. This is another story that can be followed in this book under the **Riot Squad**.

The Corsairs (1964)

From 1967 until 1969, **Tony Coates** was a member of **Ian & the Zodiacs** and after that played with the **HiFis** in Germany.

Bill Ennis became the new singer and guitarist with the **Corsairs.** He had formerly had the same position in the **Riot Squad** and **Mark Peters & the Method**.

In 1967, the **Corsairs** went into a Liverpool studio and recorded an interesting acetate with the songs "Pay you back with interest" and "Going to shut your mouth". At that time, **Ray Dale** had already left the **Corsairs** who continued to play the regional club circuit as a trio until 1968, at which time they split-up.

After the split-up, **Colin Sayers** joined **Hank Walters & the Dusty Road Ramblers**, Liverpool's legendary Country & Western group.

Bill Ennis and **Pete Bowden** teamed up in a group with **Tony Coates** again - the **Steve Alan Set** that, in 1969, changed their name to **Paper Chase**, but this development can also be followed in the story of the **Riot Squad**.

Paper Chase disbanded when **Tony Coates** and drummer, **Derek Cashin,** of that group teamed up with **Roger Craig** (key) and **Tony Crane** from the **Merseybeats** in a group under the name of the **New Merseybeats** that also recorded under the name of **Crane** on the Buk Label.

At the same time, **Bill Ennis** and **Pete Bowden,** together with a new drummer, continued as the **Steve Alan Set** for quite a few years. However, it seems both of them quit showbiz after that.

After **'Crane'**, **Tony Coates**, **Derek Cashin** and **Roger Craig** were members of **Liverpool Express** who, under the leadership of **Billy Kinsley** (ex **Merseybeats**), had a string of international hits through the Seventies.

In 1980, **Tony Coates** played in Liverpool comedian **Billy Shine's** group and later he became a member of the **Vince Earl Attraction**, where he still plays today, even if not on a regular basis.

Discography

Pay you back with interest / Going to shut your mouth   UK - ? ? ?   acetate / 1967

THE COUNTDOWNS

This is one of the Merseybeat groups whose early days are unclear as little or no information could be found about them. They never made the headlines although they are remembered as being a really polished group that was around for a long time.

Formed in Speke in the early Sixties, the **Countdowns** as they were probably named from the beginning, started to play the local pubs and clubs, including the 'Speke Labour Club' and some of the venues in the Southern part of Liverpool, such as the 'Wilson Hall' in Garston. It was sometime in 1963 that they also began to play the popular clubs in Liverpool city-centre – in the following line-up:

Billy Quirk	(voc/lg)
Alan Stuckley	(rg)
Ken Owen	(bg/voc)
Phil Nickelson	(dr)

Billy Quirk was a former member of the **Cheetahs** from Widnes and it is said that he was also possibly involved with the Country group the **Alaskans** from Ellesmere Port. As none of the other members of the **Countdowns** had appeared on the scene previously, it is likely that this was their first group.

Their live-programme was mainly based on American Rock & Roll and Rhythm & Blues numbers and, sometime in 1963, they recorded an acetate with the songs "Shake Sherry" and "School Days" but it is not known in which studio that recording took place.

The **Countdowns** were now performing at all of the major Liverpool clubs such as the 'Peppermint Lounge', 'Iron Door' and the 'Downbeat'. However, over the years, there are only four documented appearances at the 'Cavern' – Sunday the 29th September 1963 (with the **Mojos*** and **Vic & the Spidermen***), Sunday 14th June 1964 (with the **Mike Cottton Sound**, the **Koobas*** & the **Jensons**) Friday 30th October 1964 (with the **Ian & the Zodiacs***, the **Georgians** & **Uzz Strangers**) and Thursday 4th August 1966 (with the **Cryin' Shames***).

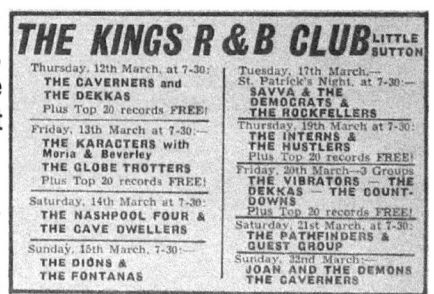

In 1966, **Alan Stuckley** left the group and disappeared from the scene. His replacement was **Dave Ferguson**, who had formerly played with the **Bumblies**, the **Politicians** and the **Fontanas**.

The **Countdowns** now put more value on close harmony-singing but were still a real Beat-group. They appeared regularly in places such as the 'Orrell Park Ballroom' and 'Blair Hall' but also kept on playing the clubs in Liverpool.

Towards the end of 1967, **Dave Ferguson** quit the music-business but the **Countdowns** kept on playing. Unfortunately, the name of their new rhythm-guitarist is not known. As the music-press did not pay too much attention to the group, there was nothing heard of them for quite some time, from which it could be concluded that they had disbanded, as the music, the business, and the groups had changed drastically by 1968.

L to R: Ken Owen (bg/voc), Billy Quirk (lg), Phil Nicholson (dr), Dave Ferguson (rg)

However, on Saturday the 31st May 1969 and Saturday the 26th July 1969 a group with the name of **Frankie & the Countdowns** appeared again at the 'Cavern'. Now, this of course could have been another outfit but it is highly probable that it was the group from Speke. It could not be found out, who the mysterious Frankie was but perhaps he was the replacement for **Dave Ferguson?** The story of the **Countdowns** leaves a lot of questionmarks behind but it also leaves a very interesting acetate, that hopefully one day will turn up again somewhere.

Discography

Shake Sherry / School Days   UK – (?) acetate / 1963

*The stories of these groups can be followed in 'Beat Waves 'Cross The Mersey' (*VelocePress ISBN 978-1-58850-201-8*).

THE DALEKS

This group, of course, has got nothing in common with the belligerent race, created by writer **Terry Nation** and designed by **Raymond Cusick** for a series in the ever popular British science fiction television series, *"Dr . Who"*, broadcast in weekly parts from December 1963 through February 1964. The only connection might be that they most probably 'lifted' the group's name from that series.

Regardless, this group was formed in Liverpool in the early Sixties, originally under the name of the **Breakaways**, though it is not known from which part of the harbour city they hailed from. Actually, very little is known about them anyway, as the local music press never paid much attention to them and consequently they failed to make any headlines.

The **Breakaways** were just one of a few hundred groups in Liverpool that played the usual club circuit, in a line-up with:

Graham Mallanphy	(lg/voc)
Kenny Hobson	(rg/voc)
Ronnie Tinsley	(bg/voc)
Jimmy McNaught	(dr/voc)

It seems **Jimmy McNaught** was their lead singer and they created somewhat of an individual sound, integrating a blend of folk music and Beat.

When **Vicki Haseman** (later **Vicki Brown**), **Margot Quantrell** and **Betty Prescott** broke away from **Vernon's Girls** they formed a new vocal trio also named the **Breakaways.** The trio was signed to the PYE label and, in early 1964, they started to cut records under that name, so the Merseybeat group changed its name to the **Daleks**.

Soon after the name change, the **Daleks** played in a club in Crosby and they were spotted by a talent scout from Fontana, who was especially interested in their original numbers. They recorded a demo and, a few weeks later, the **Daleks** were invited down to London for test recordings.

This should have been followed by an official single, but nothing further was heard about this and nothing shows up in the UK Fontana catalogue – but that does not necessarily mean that nothing was released – maybe it was just released in other countries such as France or Italy.

After that, nothing more was heard of the **Daleks** and only **Jim McNaught** appeared again on the Liverpool scene when, in late 1964, he was the vocalist with the **Vabers**. Unfortunately, what happened to the other members could not be established, but of course there is the possibility that they remained in London and continued there on the music scene as many other Liverpool musicians did . . . .

Discography

In Spring 1964, the **Daleks** recorded a demo with original numbers for a talent scout from Fontana and following this demo they went down to London for test recordings, from that an official single should have been released on the Fontana label. Unfortunately, it has proved impossible (so far) to uncover any details about the various recordings as no direct contact could be made . . .

THE DEANS

This interesting story starts in the early 60's, with a group formed by some very young students of the Florence Melly Senior Boys' School in the Liverpool area of Walton.

This six-piece group, who did not have a name, only played at the school and, in the end, only three of them stayed on the band scene. Together with a friend from Norris Green who they had met at a youth night at St. Aidans and who ultimately became their bass guitarist, they now continued as a four-piece.

Still without a name, they rehearsed every day after school at the Essoldo Bingo club and as a repayment, they played some songs during the intervals at the Thursday, Friday and Saturday bingo sessions which, of course, was really good practice for them.

As the drummer only played the bongos, the club manager, a certain Mr. Dean, arranged for the group to get a full drum set from the bingo club.

When the group was offered their first 'real' booking, a charity event at Walton Hospital, they were in need of a name and decided on the **Deans**, after the helpful club manager.

As such, they appeared in the following line-up:

Eddie Williams (voc/lg)
Jimmy Humphreys (rg/voc)
Tommy Flude (bg/voc)
Dell Robinson (dr)

The Deans L to R: Jimmy Humphreys, Eddie Williams, Dell Robinson & Tommy Flude

They were a typical Merseybeat band, playing songs such as "Some other guy", "Walking the dog", "Long tall Sally" and "Roll over Beethoven".

Tommy Flude's father took over their management and, after playing the usual gigs in the local Conservative and Labour clubs, he came up with their first gig at the 'Cavern'.

On 15 February 1964, the **Deans** played a lunchtime session together with the **Panthers** (soon to become the **Kirkbys**) and the **Escorts**.

The Deans at the Cavern

They apparently went down well as **Bob Wooler** rebooked them for another lunchtime session on 2 May where they appeared together with a number of established groups including **Chick Graham & the Coasters**, **Earl Preston's Realms** and the **Hideaways**.

Between their two Cavern bookings, the **Deans** had already played gigs in other well known venues, including the 'Moulin Rouge' in Formby, Warrington's 'Parr Hall', the 'Plaza' in St. Helens and the 'Orrell Park Ballroom', which of course helped their popularity on the Merseybeat scene.

Norris Green Social Club - L to R: Tommy Flude, Dell Robinson, Jimmy Humphreys & Eddie Williams & Eddie Williams

Out of the blue and still in 1964, the **Deans** were called to audition at the Adelphi Hotel for a part in the legendary music film 'Ferry Cross The Mersey' with **Gerry & the Pacemakers** in the main role. They had a successful audition and so it was clear that they would have a part in that film, but a few weeks later they got a telephone call informing them that because of the length of the film, two groups had to be dropped – and one of the unlucky ones was the **Deans**.

Now, having had the smell of success, the group wanted to pursue their career and the next logical step was a demo record to send out to promoters and recording companies. So the **Deans** went into **Percy Phillips**' studios in Kensington and recorded the **Little Richard** number "Long tall Sally" and the **Tommy Flude** original "Let's walk".

This was a very interesting acetate that, unfortunately, did not result in a recording contract.

The **Deans** continued to perform successfully throughout Lancashire but due to work and other commitments they disbanded sometime in early 1966.

Tommy Flude became a member of the **Approachers**, who a little later changed their name to the **Krunjing Nabs** – for heaven's sake why did they pick that name?

A few months later, **Dell Robinson** joined the **Abstracts** from Crosby, while **Jimmy Humphreys** started jamming with a group whose singer he knew from school. That singer was **Allan Devon** and the group was **Solomon's Mines**, another story in this book.

Eventually, **Jimmy Humphreys** joined that group and then, one by one, each of the original members left and they were replaced by **Eddie Williams**, **Tommy Flude** and finally **Dell Robinson**.

So it can be said that the complete line-up of the **Deans**, together with **Allan Devon** as their vocalist, continued under the name **Solomon's Mines.**

In late 1966, **Dell Robinson** quit the music business and was replaced on drums by **John Sorsky**.

In that line-up, **Solomon's Mines** played successfully on the scene and, still in 1967, they took part in the nationwide 'Search For Sound' contest and made it to the finals in London.

It was probably in late 1968 that they finally broke up. Of **Jimmy Humphreys** it is known that he emigrated to Canada where he continued to play solo in the clubs.

Tommy Flude later played with a cabaret band called **Grand Prix** but, after that, got back into Rock 'n' Roll as a member of the **Rockets** and the **Sensations**.

Eddie Williams joined a group called **Charlie Boy**, who became very successful. They also appeared on the British TV talent show 'Opportunity Knocks', made it to the finals and won. He later emigrated to the United States, where he got married.

Discography

The Deans:

Long tall Sally / Let's walk   UK - Kensington acetate / 1964

THE DEFIANTS

In the embryonic days of its formation, there were a number of teenagers from the Huyton/Rainhill area making plans about forming a group. It is known that, beside the drummer **Roy Little,** there was also **Ritchie Campion**, who already had an electric-guitar and **Bryan Scott**, who later went on to form his own group, of which the name is not known. Such evolvement takes time and it is natural that various individuals are coming and going. Finally, by mid-1963, the members had been solidified and they decided to call their group the **Defiants** – in a line-up with:

Robert Luke	(voc/rg)
John Gerrard	(lg)
Les Thompson	(bg)
Roy Ellis	(dr)

They were fortunate enough to have access to a room to rehearse in that was conveniently located in a transport-cafe in Tarbock Road, which was owned by the father of **Rob Luke.** In September 1963, the **Defiants** had their first public appearance at the nearby 'Cronton Youth Club' with a repertoire that included the **Surfaris'** instrumental "Wipe out" as well as the **Rolling Stones** first record, "Come on". **Stuart Morton** took over their management and things worked out well for them – so well that one newspaper carried a headline calling them 'The Pioneers of the Huyton Sound', whatever that was!

The group travelled quite a lot for their bookings, playing many of the Liverpool clubs such as the 'Peppermint Lounge', the 'Bears Paw', the 'Temple Bar' and of course the 'Cavern', but also the 'Boathouse' in Runcorn, the 'Garrick' in Leigh, the 'Pink Elephant' in Wigan, the 'Winter Gardens' in Morecambe, the 'Royal Lido' in LLandudno and the 'Beachcomber' clubs in West-Houghton and Bolton. This was quite an achievement for a group of young musicians that mostly performed at weekends.

In late 1965, due to differences over musical direction, the **Defiants** broke up and **Rob Luke** and **Roy Little** together with **Derek Cleary** (voc/lg), from the **Inmates**, and his then girlfriend and later wife, **Sheila McVeigh** (bg), teamed up and continued under the name of the **Defiance**. As such, they often played on the same bill with the **Approachers** at the 'Casino' in West Houghton and other clubs in the Manchester area.

When the **Approachers** disbanded in mid-1966, the remaining members asked **Rob Luke** and **Roy Little** to join them, which they did. This new line-up at first sometimes appeared as the **Approachers** and at other times as the **Defiants** until the musicians decided on a new name – the **Bent Sect**. But this also did not last too long as the group broke up towards the end of 1966.

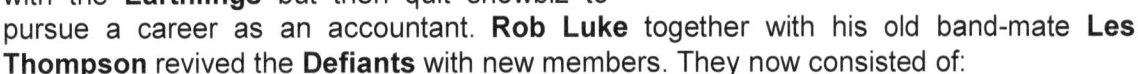

After the break up, **Roy Little** had a short spell with the **Earthlings** but then quit showbiz to pursue a career as an accountant. **Rob Luke** together with his old band-mate **Les Thompson** revived the **Defiants** with new members. They now consisted of:

Rob Luke	(voc/rg)
Warren Simpson	(lg/voc)
Les Thompson	(bg)
Reg Coulsting	(dr)

THE DEFIANTS

Warren Simpson was a former member of the **Cobbles** from Huyton, the former group of **Reg Coulsting** is not known.

This line-up then went into the private studio of a friend in Leasowe and recorded the demo "Land of thousand dances", coupled with the group's original "I want you" for Radio Caroline but, sadly, this was not followed by an official release. Soon after this recording, **Reg Coulsting** was replaced by **John Hazelhurst** on drums and, after some deliberation, the group changed its name to **This End**. Once again, they performed at all the local venues until they were persuaded to move to Nottingham under the professional management of Banner Productions. After some time in Nottingham, **Warren Simpson** decided he wanted to return home and so the group continued on as a trio.

One night, they played a gig with the **Small Faces** and, in a conversation with **Steve Marriott**, he stated that he really liked the group but that they should get a keyboard-player. This was discussed with their agency who found them a keyboard-player from Dunstable, by the name of **Mick Burgess**.

At this stage, the group adopted a new name yet again and became the **Exitement**. They were sent on an extended tour of Europe, for more than half a year, performing in Belgium, France, Switzerland and Germany. One night at the Hotel 'Zum Hirschen' in Zurich, they were contacted by **Brian 'Cass' Cassar**, formerly of **Cass & the Cassanovas**, who now lived in Frankfurt/Germany and, with his band, **Casey Jones & the Governors,** had released a number of singles and albums that had done well in the charts all over Europe. He even had his own TV-show in Frankfurt called 'Beat Beat Beat' which was similar to the British TV-show 'Ready, Steady, Go'. He asked the **Exitement** to become his new backing-band as the **Governors** were returning to England. Unfortunately, circumstances led to a misunderstanding and so this never happened. On their way back to England their van suffered a major breakdown and as they were unable to afford the repair or a replacement the **Exitement** made the decision to call it a day. Ultimately, all the members returned to the UK.

In 1969, **Les Thompson** contacted **Rob Luke** to see if he wanted to play again. He jumped at the chance and along with **John Kenyon** on drums the trio **Zelda Plum** was formed. They became really successful playing the clubs on Merseyside and further afield. In addition, a one hour-show of **Zelda Plum** was recorded live at the Cavern in late 1970. The future looked bright but then **Rob Luke's** health started to decline and he decided to leave. **John Kenyon** joined a local group called **Gravy Train** and **Les Thompson** emigrated to New Zealand with his young family.

In 2010 **Les Thompson** returned to England with the sole intention to reform **Zelda Plum** with **Rob Luke** and **John Kenyon**. Unfortunately, **John Kenyon** had medical issues and was unable to join them. **Les Thompson** and **Rob Luke** found another drummer and a vocalist but the camaraderie was not the same and the project failed before their first public appearance. Consequently, **Les Thompson** returned to New Zealand and **Rob Luke** quit the music-scene.

Discography

<u>as the **Defiants**</u>:
Land of thousand dances / I want you　　　　　　　　UK –　demo unreleased / 1967

THE DELEMERES

No, this was definitely not a Liverpool or Merseyside group, but it played a substantial role in the Merseybeat scene.

Formed in Newcastle by **Dave Shipley** in or around 1959, the **Delemeres**, as they were named right from the beginning, consisted of four Geordies and one Scot.

After gigging around their hometown for some time, they went into the Morton Studios in Newcastle and cut an acetate with the **Majors** song, "What in the world" and "Hully Gully Baby", which they used as a demo disc. Through that, they got an engagement to play the big 'Palais de Dance' in Edinburgh in 1961, where they apparently went down very well. The manager of that hall, which was part of the Mecca Dance Hall chain, was **Gordon Knowles**, who hailed from Liverpool. He arranged for the **Delemeres** to get a steady engagement at the 'Locarno' dance hall in Liverpool, which was part of the Mecca chain and where the group had to play four nights a week, which of course was almost a residency and meant that they would be well paid.

In September 1962, the **Delemeres** went to Liverpool in a line-up with:

Dave Shipley	(voc/lg)
Colin Wemyess	(rg/voc)
Gordon Railton	(p/voc)
Dave McGibbon	(bg/voc)
Gerry Ellis	(dr/voc)

Dave McGibbon hailed from Edinburgh and all the other members came from Newcastle.

The big advantage for the **Delemeres** was certainly the fact that they were all good singers and so, they did a lot of close harmony work, as well as some instrumentals. As the Locarno was a real dance hall, the group also had to play a lot of the current Top 10 numbers, which was no problem for them as they were all accomplished musicians.

Gerry Ellis did not want to settle down in Liverpool and soon returned to Newcastle. He was replaced by **Mike Wakefield**, a really great drummer from Blythe. In 1963, **Colin Wemyess** also left to get married (in Liverpool) and quit the music business.

His replacement, suggested by **Gordon Knowles**, was none other than the 'Sheik Of Shake' **Karl Terry** himself, a real Merseybeat original who had previously played with the **Gamblers Skiffle Group, Terry Connor & the Teen-Aces** and had just disbanded his popular group **Karl Terry & the Cruisers** and who had played with **Group One** for a very short time.

From this moment on, more Rock 'n' Roll and Rhythm & Blues numbers were added to the **Delemeres** programme, who appeared at all the major venues in Liverpool whenever they were not contractually bound to perform at the Locarno. Venues such as the 'Iron Door', the 'Cavern' and the 'Peppermint Lounge', where they also became very popular with the audience.

The Delemeres at the Cavern

Still in 1963, the group went into the Deroy Studio in Hest Bank in Lancaster and recorded the group's original, "See you on Saturday night", and an interesting arrangement of the **George Gershwin** classic, "Summertime".

This acetate was used as demo again but, unfortunately, it did not lead to a major recording contract.

In early 1964, the **Delemeres** took part at the Walls/Mecca Beat Contest and in April of that same year they travelled to Manchester for the semi-finals, where they placed second to **Herman's Hermits**.

In July 1964, the **Delemeres** got another engagement from Mecca and left the Locarno to go to Glasgow, where they became the resident group at the 'Dennison Ballroom'.

Karl Terry apparently became homesick and returned to Liverpool later on in the year, where he continued to play with a number of different groups including **Karl Terry the T.T.s** and the **Clayton Squares.** He also had a short spell with **Rory Storm & the Hurricanes**

and with **Capricorn** before he re-formed **Karl Terry & the Cruisers** again. He, of course, is still going strong on the scene and continues to tour the European continent.

His replacement in the **Delemeres** was **Harry Przyzinski**, a musician of Polish origin.

However, he did not stay for too long and left the group after the big 'Geordie-Beat-Tour', that toured throughout England with a number of well-known groups.

The **Delemeres** remained in Glasgow and continued as a quartet but they returned to Newcastle in the middle of 1965, where they disbanded a few months later.

Dave Shipley went on to play with the **Vance Clayton Trio**, a very successful club band who played throughout England.

Mike Wakefield joined a big band from Edinburgh but later returned to Newcastle where he played with a local group.

Gordon Railton became a part-time member of various Blues bands and **Dave McGibbon** quit the music business after the **Delemeres** split.

Discography

What in the world / Hully Gully Baby	UK – Morton acetate / 1961
See you on Saturday night / Summertime	UK – Deroy-acetate / 1963

THE DETROITS

This group hailed from Birkenhead in the Metropolitan Borough of Wirral opposite Liverpool on the other side of the River Mersey and was formed sometime in 1963. Accordingly, it was a little bit too late for the pure US Rock & Roll influence and, therefore, from the very beginning, they were a sort of commercial Beat-band and called themselves **Dee-Dee & the Detroits**. **Dee-Dee** was a girl singer, whose real name was sadly lost with the passing of time.

Their first appearances were at local youth and social-clubs and they had somewhat of a residency at the British Legion club in Birkenhead. After approximately one year, **Dee-Dee** decided that showbiz was not right for her, especially as she did not see a career for herself. The Detroits continued, soon found the right singer for their group and now appeared in the following line-up:

Phil Munro	(voc)
Peter Birch	(lg)
John Birch	(bg)
Eddie Bravender	(dr)

None of the musicians had previously played in another group and **Phil Munro** was also a newcomer to the scene. He loved Rhythm & Blues and influenced the programme of the **Detroits** that, from now on, became more of a hard rocking group. They played the usual Beat-clubs on the Wirral, like the 'Majestic' in Birkenhead, the 'Hole In The Floor' in Seacombe or the 'Kraal' and 'Tower Ballroom' in New Brighton. Besides this, they continued to play regularly at the British Legion in Birkenhead. Their manager at that time was **William Crabtree**. They only occasionally performed in the clubs on the other side of the River Mersey – mostly in the downtown Liverpool clubs, where they mainly appeared at the 'Temple Bar' in Dale Street, the 'Iron Door' and the 'Mardi Gras'.

In the second half of 1965, the **Detroits** were joined by **Freddie Davis** as rhythm-guitarist and, soon after that, went into the Unicord studio in Moorfields and recorded the **Phil Munro** composition "Hey Girl" – a somewhat 'soul style' number. This probably was an acetate with the cover-version of a nice ballad on the b-side, the title of which sadly could not be recalled and, unfortunately, no copies of the recording have survived. **Tony Varney**, possibly an A&R-man with the Unicord-label, had formed his own agency called 'Grove Entertainments' and he took the **Detroits** under his wings.

● Wirral group THE DETROITS recorded a number "Hey Girls" written by their lead vocalist PHIL MUNRO at Unicord last week. The group are handled by agent TONY VARNEY, who recently left Unicord to set up his own agency Grove Entertainments together with the manager of Southport's Klic Klic Klub.

Freddie Davis, who hailed from Moreton in Merseyside, tended to bring some comedy into the act of the **Detroits** – too much comedy for the others and, so after 3-4 months, he was asked to leave. He later became a professional comedian and had some appearances on British TV.

The **Detroits** continued quite successfully on the scene for another year but then **Peter Birch** became seriously ill and had to undergo major surgery. As it was clear that after that he would no longer be able to play the guitar, the group disbanded totally. **John Birch** and **Eddie Bravender** quit the music-business, while **Phil Munro** became the new lead-vocalist with the **Prowlers**.

After that, **Phil Munro** never joined a group again but appeared as guest-vocalist with various bands on Merseyside and he is still occasionally doing that to this day, from his new home in Herefordshire, close to the South Wales border.

Discography:

Hey Girl / A ballad cover-version   **UK- Unicord acetate / 1965**

THE DIPLOMATS

It was in the Autumn of 1960 that **Kevin Finlayson**, **Dave Tollins** and **Keith Bottomley** formed a Rock group in Southport.

One night, **Keith Bottomley** brought another friend around to a rehearsal – **Quentin Hegarty**, who had already played with a Skiffle group at Southport Art College. He joined and this new group, apparently still without a name, played a few gigs at the local youth clubs.

At one of these performances, the promoter **Ronnie Fearn** introduced them to **Barry Walmsley** who, at that time, was playing with the **Hot Strings**. He joined the group but, then, **Keith Bottomley** left.

The group now needed a name and the musicians decided on the **Diplomats** and, as such, they appeared in the following line-up:

Quentin Hegarty	(voc/rg)
Barry Walmsley	(lg/voc)
Dave Tollins	(bg/voc)
Kevin Finlayson	(dr/voc)

The Diplomats - 1962

The **Diplomats** now started to play the local clubs and were signed by **Mike Birchall** (Birchall Promotions) and, through his agency, they got more gigs, in bigger and better venues. Places such as the Floral Hall, the 'Kingsway' and Cambridge Hall where they often appeared alongside groups from nearby Liverpool and were musically influenced by them – and so they evolved into a real Beat group.

Soon they were topping the bills at the 'Django Club' (Queen's Hotel), the 'Palace' in Birkdale and the 'Derby' in Burscough. They got a lot of bookings throughout the northwest and the north Midlands, appearing at many of the popular venues including the Floral Hall in Morecambe, the Belle Vue in Manchester, the Wigan Empire and the Leigh Casino, as well as at the clubs in Liverpool, such as the 'Odd Spot'.

In 1963, they had an audition for ABC television but things were going too slowly for them. Therefore, when they became the resident group at a new Southport club in Eastbank Street called the 'Rave'l', and the owner, **Philip Mardon,** offered to pay them for a recording if they changed their name to the **Ravells**, the musicians accepted.

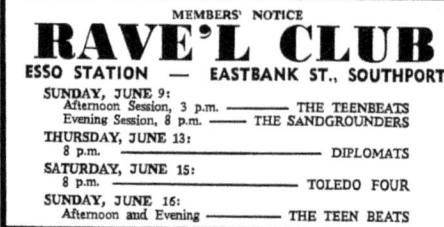

The Diplomats - L to R: Dave Tollins, Kevin Finlayson & Quentin Hegarty

So, in August 1963, they went into **Percy Phillips**' studio in Kensington, where they recorded the original "She said that . . ", written by a local lad called **Howard Clarke**. On the B-side of this acetate was the classic instrumental "Begin the Beguine", played in typical **Shadows** style.

Percy Phillips and Barry Walmsley at the Kensington Recording Studio

With this demo, the **Ravells** went down to London and tried to get signed to a major record company. The successful DJ and agent **Murray Cash** became interested in the group and got them a booking at the famous '2 i's' coffee bar, but the **Ravells** did not manage to get a recording contract.

Disillusioned, they returned to Southport where they kept on playing as the **Ravells** for some time but then they changed their name back into the **Diplomats**.

In the spring of 1964, after an argument about their musical direction and future, the musicians decided to go their separate ways.

Quentin Hegarty left the area and joined the Army, while **Dave Tollins** and **Kevin Finlayson** jammed around with various local groups.

Barry Walmsley joined **Rhythm & Blues Inc.** He then had a short stint with the **Big Three** before returning to his old group **Rhythm & Blues Inc.** – that by then had evolved into **Pete Kelly's Soulution**. After that, he played with **Jasmin T** and then **Inner Sleeve**, both of these groups having evolved from **Pete Kelly's Soulution**.

In 2007, the **Diplomats** were reunited for one last time on **Kevin Finlayson's** birthday – it was definitely the last time as, sadly, **Dave Tollins** died the following year.

Barry Walmsley together with his brother, **Don Walmsley,** still perform under the name of the **Walmsley Brothers** and they are occasionally joined on stage by **Quentin Hegarty**.

Discography

as **"The Ravells"**:

She said that . . . / Begin the Beguine　　　　　　　　　　UK - Kensington acetate / 1963

Queen's Hotel
CLUB DJANGO
TO-MORROW (THURS.), JANUARY 2 at 8 p.m.
THE RAVELS

"The Liverpool Beat-scene erupted and we were thrown shoulder to shoulder to these very competent and exciting bands, which shook us out of our small town comfort zone. We started to play the sort of music they did, which made us develop a sharper edge . . ."

Quentin Hegarty / The Diplomats

THE DOMINANT FOUR

To correct a very common error, it should to be noted, that there was absolutely no connection between this group and **Rhet Stephens & the Senators**, as is so often stated. This Widnes group never had a member called **Rhet Stephens** and never backed anybody of that name.

David Marsh and **Malcolm Penney** formed the **Senators** as an instrumental group in the very early Sixties, playing locally and becoming very popular in their hometown and the areas of Runcorn, Frodsham, Helsby and Ellesmere Port, where they appeared regularly in the local clubs including the 'La Scala' in Runcorn, the 'Queens Hall' and the 'Navy Club' in Widnes.

In August 1962, the group took part in the *'Widnes/Runcorn Popularity Poll'*, organised by the 'Mersey Beat' newspaper and Nems, where they placed fifth.

A little later their original drummer **Robert Abram** quit the music business and was replaced by **Frank Houghton**. Then **Ted Batty** joined the group as their lead singer and shortly after that, they changed their name to **Ricky & the Senators**.

Frank Houghton did no stay for too long and later appeared as a member of **Vic Takes Four**, another Widnes recording group whose story can be followed in this book.

With a new drummer, the former **Senators** finally changed their name to **Ricky & the Dominant Four** and by then they had become a real Rhythm & Blues group with the following line-up:

Ricky Lincoln	(voc)
Dave Marsh	(lg/voc)
Malcolm Penney	(rg/voc)
Alan French	(bg)
Chris James	(dr)

Ricky Lincoln, of course, was the stage name for **Edward 'Ted' Batty**.

Cliff Hayes, who was writing for a local newspaper, became their manager and got them signed to Liverpool's 'Northern Variety Agency' (N.V.A.) with the result that **Ricky & the Domiant Four** now regularly appeared in the Liverpool clubs, including the 'Grafton', the 'Locarno', the 'Peppermint Lounge' and the 'Iron Door'.

Best Wishes Paul Francis

Ted Batty, for unknown reasons, left the **Dominant Four** and his replacement was **Ronnie Ince**, the vocalist who used the stage name **Paul Francis**, a former member of the **Cheetahs**.

Chris James left and joined the **Wanderers**, formerly known as **Geoff Stacey & the Wanderers**, another story in this book. **Barry Eaton** replaced him as the new drummer for **Ricky & the Dominant Four**.

In the Autumn of 1963, this line-up travelled to London and made a test recording for Decca at the Regent Sound Studios. They recorded two original numbers, "In time to come " and "A time for love" by the Liverpool songwriter **Ralph Bowdler.** They also recorded two instrumentals "Blue star" and "Whispering", that were possibly originals by the group.

Unfortunately, these songs were only released on acetate and were never released commercially.

During their stay in London, they had appearances at the 'Fifty-Club' and the famous '2 i's Coffee Bar'.

Ted Batty, alias **Ricky Lincoln**, returned to the group and **Paul Francis** left and joined the **Wanderers** from Widnes, that later became the **Merchants**.

In December 1963 **Ricky & the Dominant Four**, together with the **Landsliders** from Chester, auditioned for the 'Star-Club' Hamburg at the Rialto Ballroom. They were successful at that audition and were contracted to play Germany in May 1964.

```
TOWER BALLROOM      WHIT
       NEW BRIGHTON   MONDAY
WHIT "BEAT" SHOW     JUNE 3rd
Merseyside Sounds    7-30—11-30

DERRY WILKIE AND THE PRESSMEN
RORY STORM AND THE HURRICANES
Ian & the Zodiacs  The Nomads  The Renegades
PAUL FRANCIS & THE DOMINANT FOUR
Admission (at door 5/-)       Licensed Bars
```

Meanwhile, the **Dominant Four** continued gigging on the northern club circuit and, amongst others, on 23 February 1964 they played the 'Cavern' together with **Alexis Korner's Blues Inc.**

Around that same time they also appeared regularly at the Plaza Ballroom in St. Helens, where they became very popular with the audience and often topped the bill. Other venues were the 'Heaven & Hell' and 'Parr-Hall' in Warrington, the 'Klik Klik' in Southport, the 'Casino' in Leigh, 'Monaco Ballroom' in Hindley, 'River Park' in Chester, as well as some of the Manchester-clubs.

One night before their planned departure to the 'Star Club', the **Dominant Four** played a club in Runcorn and during this gig the musicians had a big falling out, with the result that the group disbanded that same night. Consequently, they did not go to Germany and never got back together again, what an inglorious end to a really good Rhythm & Blues group . . .

Dave Marsh and **Alan French** quit the music business, while **Mal Penney** joined a group called **Styx** and after became a solo-performer in the local pubs.

Of **Ted Batty** it is known that he joined the **Cast** and later had short stints with other local groups before he got married and emigrated to Ireland, where he got into the Country-scene as a singer with groups such as **Blue Ridge Country** and the **Kentucky Gamblers**. The last that was heard of him was that he and his wife were working together as a cabaret duo, calling themselves **Split The Difference**.

Barry Eaton continued to play the drums professionally and later was a member of the legendary hit group **Ivy League**.

Finally, to prevent any confusion, it should be pointed out that the group always used the name of **Ricky & the Dominant Four**, although the advertisements in general were only for the **Dominant Four**. The only exception was during the period when **Ted Batty**, alias **Ricky Lincoln**, temporarily left and was replaced by **Paul Francis**. For that short period of time the group was occasionally announced as **The Dominant Four with Paul Francis.**

Discography

In time to come / A time for love / Blue Star / Whispering   UK- Regent Sound Acetate / 1963

THE DOWNBEATS

Not much is really known about the early days of this very interesting group – not even exactly where they came from.

It could be that this was the same **Downbeats** that were handled by the agent **Norman Hurst** from Lark Lane in Liverpool, but this is not a proven certainty.

```
THE BLACK KNIGHTS
NORMAN HURST    DOMINATORS
LAR 5574        DOWNBEATS
                STEREOS
ALSO AVAILABLE
SEPTEMBER ONWARDS  THE ROADRUNNERS
```

Regardless, in 1963 they toured the European continent and as far as could be ascertained they did not take part in the Merseybeat scene after that. From Scandinavia via Germany they went to France, where they settled down in Paris in the Autumn of 1963.

In November of the same year, the **Downbeats** were the backing group for the French singer **Moustique** at the big festival 'Idoles 64' at the 'Européen' club – in a line-up with:

Bobby Day	(voc)
Mike Bamford	(lg/voc)
? ? ?	(rg)
Sam Ian Percival	(bg)
Malcolm Olroyd	(dr/voc)

'Moustique'

Mike Bamford is sometimes identified as **Michael Bamforth** and the name of the original rhythm guitarist is not known.

Initially, the **Downbeats** continued as the backing group for **Moustique** but from 1964 onwards they also performed in their own right – as such, their first booking was at the famous 'Golf Drouot'.

They very soon became the No. 1 British group in the Paris region. They were based in Fontenay-Saint-Père, just west of Paris, and they were managed by **Jean Besnard**.

The **Downbeats** had so many bookings in the capital of France that they rarely performed outside Paris. However, one such booking was the 'West Side' in Lyon, where they also went down very well.

In April 1964, they were chosen to back **Moustique** on his second EP "Joy Joy Joy" on the Barclay subsidiary label 'Golf Drouot'. A great record which, besides the main track also included interesting versions of **Eddie Cochran**'s "Cut across Shorty", the **Ronnie Hawkins** number "Baby Jean" and **Ritchie Valens**' popular ballad "Donna".

After a show in Caen, **Bobby Day** was involved in a car crash and injured so badly that he decided to return to England and the rhythm guitarist apparently went with him. The **Classics** from St. Helens, who were under the same management, also had a residency in Paris at the same time and the lead guitarist and drummer of the **Classics** decided to go back to England with **Bobby Day** and the rhythm guitarist from the **Downbeats.** So the singer and rhythm guitarist from the **Classics** teamed up with the remaining members of the **Downbeats** and continued under that name in the following line-up:

Leslie Stocks	(voc/g)
Mike Bamford	(lg/voc)
Stanley Gibbons	(rg/voc)
Sam Ian Percival	(bg)
Malcolm Olroyd	(dr/voc)

Prior to joining the **Classics, Les Stocks** was a member of the **Zephyrs** from St. Helens.

Together with **Moustique**, this new line-up was the supporting group for **Little Richard** during his appearance at the world-famous 'Olympia' from the 1 to 3 June.

One month later, they backed the female vocalist duo **Les Jumelles** on their EP "Um Um Um Um Um" on the Windsor label which, amongst others, also including the French version of "Surfin' safari".

The Downbeats with the female duo 'Les Jumelles'

It must also have been around that time that the **Downbeats** went into the IRS studio in Paris and, in their own right, recorded the classics, "I Can Tell", "More Than I Can Say", "Shakin' All Over" and "Reeling and Rockin'". Sadly nothing was released, but it was cut on an acetate-EP at Pyral in Créteil.

In August, they replaced the English **Krew-Kats** as the backing group for **Billy Bridge**, later known as **Billy Swan** of "I can help" fame, at his show at the Casino in Deauville. It was most probably at this show where the **Downbeats** were spotted by producer **Gérard Cote** and signed to the Philips label.

It only took a few days until their first solo EP was released under the title "On Est Cinq Copains", which included the great French (!) versions of the **Mojos** success "Everything's alright", the two **Merseybeats** hits' "Don't turn around" as "Adieu tu pars" and "I think of you" as "Je pense a vous", as well as the **Carl Mann** standard "Pretend" as "Imaginez". From that EP the two French versions of the **Merseybeats** songs were coupled out as a single.

In addition, with the support of their 'ever growing' French fan club, a short film of them together with **Les Jumelles** was produced at the 'Golf Drouot' by 'L'Office de Documentation du Film'.

A second **Downbeats** EP followed with the title "Dans La Rue", which was the French version of the **Newbeats** number "Pink Dally Rue", it also included "Je le vois" ("I can tell"), "Clary" and "A demain soir", which was the **Geoff Stephens** song "Tomorrow night".

In this context, it is an interesting fact that around the same time **Eden Kane** released "Tomorrow night" on Fontana in England. On that recording he was backed by the **Downbeats**, but in spite of the same name these two groups had nothing in common. What a coincidence . . .

The new **Downbeats** EP sold so well that all four songs were issued again on two singles.

In December 1964, the group was invited to appear on the **Petula Clark** TV show 'Hello Paris' to present their really popular "Dans la rue" number. However, they appeared without **Les Stocks**, who in the meantime had gone back to England. A little later **Les Stocks** joined the **Playboys**, a group that had evolved from the St. Helens group **Cadillac & the Playboys**, but that is another story in this book.

The **Downbeats** continued as a four-piece and in January 1965 they packed the 'Golf Drouot' for one week and the audience was enthusiastic about this real Beat show, which included songs such as "Little Queenie", "Wondrous place", "Shakin' all over", "What'd I say", "Hippy Hippy Shake" and of course all their recorded songs.

One month later, the **Downbeats** returned to the 'Olympia' as a support group for the **Chuck Berry** show.

Unfortunately, in spite of their really successful live appearances they did not have any other records released.

It was probably sometimes in late 1965 or early 1966 that they disbanded totally. **Stan Gibbons** continued as a musician, playing on cruise-ships and later in the clubs in London until he retired in 1982. Unfortunately, what happened to all the other **Downbeats** members is not known.

After his time with the **Playboys** or the **Manchester Playboys**, as they were re-named later, **Les Stocks** married the Manchester recording songstress **Lorraine Grey** and with her emigrated to Australia, where he is still living.

Discography

The Downbeats:

Je pense a vous / Adieu tu pars	F – Philips 373.393 / 1964
A demain soir / Clary	F – Philips 373.499 / 1964
Dans la rue / Je le vois	F – Philips 373.500 / 1964
EP "**On Est Cinq Copains**"	F – Philips 434.932 / 1964

- **Everything's alright / Adieu tu pars** (Don't turn around) / **Je pense a vous** (I think of you) / **Imaginez** (Pretend)

EP "**Dans La Rue**" F – Philips 434.990 / 1964

- **Dans la rue** (Pink Dally Rue) / **Je le vois** (I can tell) / **Clary** (Kathy) /
  A demain soir (Tomorrow night)

Unreleased tracks:

I Can Tell / More Thank I Can Say / Shakin' All Over /

Reelin' and Rockin' F – Disques IRS (Pyral) acetate EP / 1964

As the backing-group for **Moustique**:

EP "**Joy Joy Joy**" F – Golf Drouot / 1964
- **Joy, joy joy / Ne me fait plus souffrier** (Cut across Shorty) / **Baby Jean / Donna**

As the backing-group for **Les Jumelles**: F – Windsor / 1964

EP "**Um Um Um Um Um**"
- **Um um um um um / Le roi de la guitare / Surfin' safari / C'est toi que je vois**

DUKE DUVAL'S ROCKERS

As this is, in all probability, the story of the very first Rock 'n' Roll-group in Liverpool, it is appropriate to start with a Skiffle-group called the **Black Denim Boys** that was formed in Speke sometime around the end of 1954.

Their first documented appearance was in 1955 at the Dunlop factory in Speke, performing in the employee cafeteria during their lunchtime-break. This was arranged by the father of guitarist, **Alan Rotheram**, who worked in the factory. This first, probably unpaid gig, was followed by a number of bookings at many of the Liverpool and Warrington clubs. At this time, the **Black Denim Boys** consisted of the following musicians:

Vince Kenny	(voc)
Alan Rotheram	(g)
Norman Stevens	(g)
Melvin	(sax)
Bob Pierson	(t-bass)
Mickey Garner	(wb)
Phil Dougan	(dr)

Speke "Skiffle"

OPINIONS may differ as to exactly what is 'skiffle, but there was no apparent diversion of opinion among the youthful rhythm enthusiasts at Speke as to the merits of the 'Black Denim Boys Skiffle Group' (seen here on the stage at the Speke factory) when they performed recently during meal breaks in the canteen.

With some improvised and some conventional instruments plus a good deal of talent and tremendous enthusiasm, these boys—the youngest was 14 and the oldest 17—put on a show which many a veteran combination might envy. A large audience rewarded their efforts with a great ovation.

In June 1957, the group was engaged to play the 'Skyline Club' at the large American USAF base at Burtonwood in Warrington and they subsequently appeared there on a regular basis. They also went into the studio of **Percy Phillips** and recorded a single-sided acetate of the **Bob Pierson** composition, "Has anybody heard". Sadly, the only copy of it disappeared but it should have been quite a rocking number.

In the interim, another guitarist was added to the above line-up by the name of **Terry Dowker** but then **Vince Kenny** and **Mickey Garner** left the group towards the end of 1957 to join the Royal Navy. Consequently, the **Black Denim Boys** disbanded, and the members all went their separate ways.

Terry Dowker teamed up with drummer, **Ken Furlong,** and **Derek Roley** (bg) to form a new group that, a little later, was also joined by **Norman Stevens**. They initially used the name the **Duke Duval Rhythm Group**, whereby it was the drummer **Ken Furlong** that had adopted the stage-name of **Duke Duval**. Unfortunately, **Terry Dowker** had a motorcycle accident and had to spend some time in the hospital, so he was replaced by **Alan Rotheram**, another former member of the **Black Denim Boys**, whose nickname was 'Speedy Gonzales' - for whatever reasons! When **Terry Dowker** returned, **Alan Rotheram** stayed with the group as an additional guitarist and so all three former guitarists of the **Black Denim Boys** became the backbone for that new group. Finally, a vocalist, **Arthur Lea** (stage name **Lee Vincent**) was added to **Duke Duval's Rockers** as they were now called, who appeared as a sextet with:

Arthur Lea	(voc)
Terry Dowker	(lg)
Alan Rotheram	(rg/lg)
Norman Stevens	(rg)
Derek Roley	(bg)
Duke Duval	(dr)

They had now become a real Rock 'n' Roll band and became somewhat of the resident group at the 'Skyline-Club' and the 'NCO' (Officer's Mess) at the Burtonwood airbase. They also appeared at venues in Speke and other nearby locales including Garston and Aigburth, and they often appeared at the 'Merrifield Club' in Old Swan.

In February 1958, **Duke Duval's Rockers** played the Cavern for the first time (unbilled) on a night with **Mr. Acker Bilk** and his **Paramount Jazz-Band**. They were booked as a Skiffle-group but, during their stage-performance, also switched to playing Rock 'n' Roll numbers. While this was really disliked by the club's management, it went down well with the audience and, in the end, it was the reason for them getting additional gigs there.

Ellesmere Port

Most of the time they were not billed, as the owner of the Cavern, **Alan Sytner**, saw the Cavern as a Jazz club and he wanted to keep it that way. Accordingly, Rock 'n' Roll groups were not among his favourites, to say the least. The chances for **Duke Duval's Rockers** improved when on October 3rd 1959 **Ray McFall** took ownership of the 'Cavern' and, on Wednesday the 5th of October 1960, they were on the same bill with **Gerry & the Pacemakers*** and, a little later, on the 14th of December with the **John Barry Seven** and another Liverpool Rock 'n' Roll-band – **Cass & the Cassanovas***. It was also **Ray McFall** who booked **Duke Duval's Rockers** to play the first 'Beat-Cruise' on the famous 'Royal Iris' and they were also the very first group to play at 'Hope Hall'.

In the meantime, the group had been joined by a very talented young man – singer and guitarist, **Richard John Harrickey** who, in the press, had already been described as 'Merseyside's Elvis Presley'. He became the additional lead vocalist and changed his name to **Johnny Moreno** at that time. He was only 13 years of age and had previously played with **J.H. & the Cool Cats.**

Holyoake Hall 1960
L to R: Alan Rotheram (g), Terry Dowker (g), Duke Duval (dr), Johnny Moreno (v), Derek Roley (bg), Arthur Lea (v) (used stage name Lee Vincent), Norman Stevens (g)

Besides this, **John White,** a saxophone-player was added and **Duke Duval's Rockers** now played at venues as far afield as Blackpool and Ellesmere Port but also appeared regularly at the well-known Liverpool venues, such as the 'Montrose', the 'Rialto Ballroom', the 'Casbah' and the 'Wooky Hollow', as well as on the Wirral at the 'Majestic' in Birkenhead and the 'Tower Ballroom' in New Brighton.

One Saturday night when they played at the 'Holyoake Hall', they were approached by a very tall guy who asked if he could sing a couple of numbers with them. They agreed and when he got on stage, he went wild singing and dancing around the stage. A great stage-personality and a fantastic singer - all the girls were screaming for him. This guy was **Ronald Woodbridge** – 'Big Ron', the former singer of **John McNally's** Skiffle group, which had evolved into the **Searchers***. From that night on, he became the regular singer with **Duke Duval's Rockers** who, because of his height, nicknamed him 'Loftus'. With this new addition, they had become something like a Rock 'n' Roll Big-Band - now with nine members including three outstanding singers. This line up was also ideal for backing solo-singers, and so **Duke Duval's Rockers** occasionally backed **Freddie Starr** (then billed as '**Freddie the Teddy**'), **Derry Wilkie**, **Johnny Gentle** and the Jazz-singer, **Jill Martin**.

Early in 1961, **Terry Dowker** left the group and joined **Nick Olson & the Four Aces**, who were resident at the 'RAF Club' in Bold Street. His departure was followed by **Alan Rotheram** also leaving in September of that same year. **Alan Rotheram** then played with an American orchestra at the Royal Court for some time. After that, he recorded with the **Derek Hilton Trio** at the Grenada TV studios in Manchester for the TV-series 'The Odd Man'. He then got married and moved to the Midlands, where he kept on playing in bands – the last being the **Savoy Swing Band**, of which he was a member until 2007.

In early 1963, **Ron Woodbridge** accepted an offer as a full-time vocalist with the Mecca Dancehall Company which was a great opportunity for a professional career. For a few years he toured nationwide as the singer with the **Nat Allen Orchestra** and, with them, he also had a long engagement at the 'Palais

Ron Woodbridge

De Dance Ballroom' in Edinburgh. Tired of steadily touring, **Ron Woodbridge** decided to settle down in the Scottish capital where he kept on singing. The almost six-foot-tall man adopted the stage-name of **Shorty Rogers** (must have been that typical Scouse humour) and formed his own band under the name of the **Giants**. As far as it is known, **'Big Ron' Woddbridge** is still active these days as **Shorty Rogers**.

But now back to **Duke Duval's Rockers** that in a two-year period had shrunk from nine members to a quartet as **Arthur Lea** and **John White** had also left one after the other and both of them had disappeared from the scene. They now had the typical line-up for a Merseybeat group – two guitars, bass and drums – with **Ken Furlong, Derek Roley, Norman Stevens** and good vocals with **Johnny Moreno,** now playing guitar in addition to vocals.

L to R: Les Carlin, Ken Furlong, Johnny Moreno, Norman Stevens

When **Derek Roley** left, **Johnny Moreno** switched to the bass-guitar. **Les Cotgreave** (voc/g), who called himself **Les Carlin**, a great singer and stage personality, came in as a new member. He had previously performed as a solo singer and, as such, had appeared on TV and had also auditioned to sing with the **John Barry Seven**.

Duke Duval's Rockers continued to be successful on the scene and, in 1963, became the resident group at the Empress-Ballroom in New Brighton. Later that same year, **Johnny Moreno** was contacted by **Ron Woodbridge,** as the **Nat Allen Orchestra** was resident at the 'Locarno' in Liverpool and they were looking for a bass-guitarist who could also sing. **Johnny Moreno** got the job and was contracted to the Mecca organisation. He was replaced in **Duke Duval's Rockers** by **Graham Dixon** (bg/voc).

Johnny Moreno toured throughout Britain with that orchestra until **Nat Allen** died in 1966 and the orchestra was disbanded. Some of the younger members formed a new band under the leadership of **Johnny Moreno**, called the **Ricky Allen Set**. When this group split in 1967, **Johnny Moreno,** who now called himself **Ricky Allen**, became a member of **Johnny Duncan & the Blue Grass Boys** where he played well into the Seventies. He then reformed the **Ricky Allen Band** and later was signed up by 'First Leisure' for bookings at various venues in Blackpool with the **Ricky Allen Trio**. Following this, **Ricky Allen** started a successful career as a solo performer, did some TV work in Bristol and finally retired from the music scene in 2007.

With slightly changing line-ups, but under the leadership of **Ken Furlong** together with **Norman Stevens** and **Graham Dixon**, the group kept on playing the Empress Ballroom until 1969. Although they no longer used the old band-name, *'Duke Duval'* still adorned the bass-drum. What happened to **Les Carlin** is not known - only the sad fact that he died in 2003. **Ken Furlong** became a member of the **Lockerby Trio**, playing Jazz into the Eighties and **Graham Dixon** disappeared from the scene. **Norman Stevens** continued playing in various groups, including the **Karl Martyn Sound** and **Patches**. He is still active on the scene as a member of the **Remnants.**

Discography:

The Black Denim Boys:

Has Anybody Heard   UK- Phillips Kensington acetate   / 1957

Duke Duval's Rockers never made a studio recording and there is also no evidence that a live appearance was ever recorded.

Duke Duval's Rockers in the beginning had very little amplification-equipment. After I had joined, I purchased valve amplifier chassis and adapted them for the guitars – larger amp and loudspeaker for the bass-guitar. Terry and myself together (the technical guys of the group) built all the cabinets and fitted 'Goodmans' loudspeakers inside them.

At this time, I was employed in an electronics company. We needed a tremolo unit and could not afford one. I wrote to the manufacturer, Selmer, told them I had one of their units, which was faulty and could they send me a circuit diagram of the unit!! They did!! I built one using an 'Oxo'-tin (!) as a chassis and it worked well. Terry then built one for himself. Those amps were probably some of the best in Liverpool at that time – used by Duke Duval's group.

Alan Rotheram / Black Denim Boys and **Duke Duval's Rockers**

---

*The stories of these groups can be followed in 'Beat Waves 'Cross The Mersey' (*VelocePress *ISBN 978-1-58850-201-8).*

THE EASY THREE

It was already 1964 when three youngsters from the Anfield area of Liverpool formed a group that they called the **Easy Three**. Unfortunately, it was just too late to jump on the Merseybeat train that was already on its way to conquering the music-world. However, the aim of these young musicians was not necessarily to become famous, they just wanted to enjoy making good music and that's what they ended up doing. The **Easy Three** consisted of the following musicians:

>   **Billy Manville**   (lg/voc)
>   **Phil Loughren**   (bg/voc)
>   **Keith Robinson**   (dr)

L to R: Billy Manville and Keith Robinson with Phil Loughren (inset)

After a period of intensive rehearsals, they started to play the youth-clubs in their local area. Their music did not follow any particular direction they just played the hit numbers of that time. As they became more experienced, they played the nearby pubs such as the 'Richmond', where they appeared quite regularly, and the 'Sandon'.

Towards the end of 1965, they went into the **Percy Phillips** studio in Kensington and recorded "Hang On Sloopy" which, at that time, was a worldwide hit-success for the great American group, the **McCoys,** from Union City, Indiana. On their acetate, "Hang on Sloopy" was coupled with the **Drifters** classic, "Under the Boardwalk" but, of course, more in the style of the **Rolling Stones** version, who had covered the song on their second album. This acetate showed the musical ability of the **Easy Three**, who used the record for promotion – and it worked! Soon they were playing many of the well-known Liverpool Beat-clubs such as the 'Cavern', the 'Blue Angel', the 'Mardi Gras', the 'Victoriana' and 'Dino's'.

Frank Delaney of 'Apendstane Promotions' took the **Easy Three** under his wings and also got them bookings outside of Liverpool, such as the 'Embassy Club' in Prescot and the 'Night Spot' in Warrington, which was **Shane Fenton's** club. Sometime in or around 1968, the **Easy Three** disbanded and, through their agency, **Billy Manville** and **Keith Robinson** got an engagement to play at a bar in Palm Beach in Florida for a period of time. After they returned to the UK, they received an offer to become the backing-band for **Vocal Perfection**, which soon became the **Real Thing**. As a result of this offer, they got together again with **Phil Loughren**, who switched to guitar as **Joe Gamble,** who came from the **Gambols,** was added to their line-up as their bass guitarist. Being a four-piece they could no longer use their old name and so they became the **Formula**. On occasions, it is known that **Alan Fisher** substituted for **Joe Gamble**. At that time, this combination of **Vocal Perfection** and **Formula** often performed at 'Reeces Ballroom' in Liverpool as well as the local night clubs and university dances.

After a while **Phil Loughren** left and **Joe Gamble** returned to the **Gambols**. The new members were **Gerry Allen** on guitar and his brother, **Dave Allen,** on bass-guitar. But this did not last for long and **Formula** ultimately disbanded in 1970. For a number of years, **Keith Robinson** was a resident drummer at various clubs before he joined the group **Salamander** from Runcorn, an off-shoot of **Sonny Kaye & the Reds***. Initially, **Billy Manville** became a solo-artist in Liverpool's Country-scene and later he joined the **Bar Room Boys**. Of **Phil Loughren,** it is known that he continued to play in bands and, at one time, he was a member of the **A-Team** that became very successful locally.

Discography:

as the **Easy Three**:

Hang on Sloopy / Under the boardwalk   **UK- Phillips Kensington acetate / 1965**

*The story of this group can be followed in 'Beat Waves 'Cross The Mersey' (*VelocePress ISBN 978-1-58850-201-8*).

THE FAIRYTALE

Short but impressive, that's how the career of this group could be described. They hailed from Warrington near Liverpool where they were formed as a five-piece under the name of **Fairytales** towards the end of 1966 and, accordingly, their music was no longer classic Merseybeat but more psychedelic sound based, which was popular at that time.

Their original singer was **John Ryan**, who left the group in the middle of 1967. A little later, **John Ryan** was one of the founding members of the recording-group, **Smiley,** together with **Robert Garner**, who also hailed from Warrington where he had started his career as the bass-guitarist for the **Brokers** in 1963. In the interim, **Robert (Bob) Garner** had played in well-known groups such as the **Merseybeats**, **Lee Curtis & the All-Stars** and the international hit-group, the **Creation**, to name just a few. After **John Ryan** left the **Fairytales,** the vocals were shared by the remaining members and they continued as a four-piece in the following line-up:

John Weston	(lg/voc)
Malcolm Rabbitt	(org/voc)
Kenneth Penketh	(bg/voc)
William Fagg	(dr)

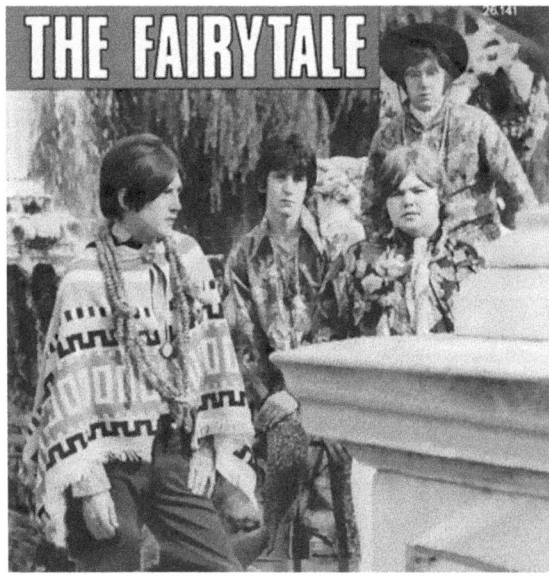

L to R: Kenneth Penketh, John Weston, Billy Fagg, Mal Rabbitt

All the musicians were of a very young age (between 15 and 17) and were newcomers to the scene. **William Fagg** is sometimes reported as **Billy Fogg**. In addition, **John Weston** and **Malcolm Rabbitt** were very talented songwriters and wrote all the material for the band.

Somehow, **Mark Wildey**, producer of the **Don Arden** music organization, became aware of this promising new group and, in August 1967, took them into the Decca studio to record the originals, "Guess I Was Dreaming" and "Run And Hide". For the release of their first single, the group dropped the 's' from the end of their name. "Guess I Was Dreaming" was a psychedelic pop-song while "Run And Hide" was a catchy Sixties' style number with a foot stomping beat and a really good chorus. The record sold quite well but failed to make the charts although it brought the **Fairytale** their first TV-appearance. As a result, they had suddenly become so popular within the greater Merseyside area that more than 1000 people came to their live-appearance at the 'Odeon' in Warrington.

A second single quickly followed, again with two group-originals but "Lovely People" was a flop. For the US-market the American London label put the A-sides of both records on one single but, unfortunately, this did not dramatically improve sales. However, **Paul Revere & the Raiders** saw the potential of "Guess I Was Dreaming" and released it as a single in the same year. Decca obviously had lost interest in the **Fairytale** and did not extend their contract which could have been the reason for the group calling it a day in early 1968.

Kenneth Penketh went to London and disappeared from the scene, while **William Fagg** followed **John Ryan** to the group **Smiley**. **John Weston** concentrated on song writing and, amongst others, **Mighty Joe Young** and the group, **Pesky Gee** (forerunner of **Black Widow**), released records featuring his compositions. **Mal Rabbitt** wrote both songs for the only single of the **Curiosity Shoppe** and, in 1968, he released a solo single on Parlophone with "Why Won't The Sun Shine On Me", which, with a different B-side, was also released in the United States on the Red Lite label. There is nothing known about any of the former **Fairytale** members ever playing in other groups at a later date.

Although all their records did not make a real impact at the time they were released, today they are expensive collector's items.

Discography :

Guess I Was Dreaming / Run And Hide	UK- Decca F 12644 / 1967
Lovely People (Like You And Me) /	
Listen To Mary Cry	UK- Decca F 12665 / 1967

Different US-release :

Lovely People / Guess I Was Dreaming	US- London 20032 / 1967

Malcolm Rabbit – solo :

Why Won't The Sun Shine On Me / Sarah	UK- Parlophone R 5720 / 1968

Different US- release :

Why Won't The Sun Shine On Me /	
All I Want Is My Baby	US- Red Lite RL 101 / 1968

THE FIRECRESTS

This was certainly one of the pioneering groups of the Mersey music scene. Formed at a Birkenhead school in 1957, the musical style of this vocal/instrumental/harmony group focused on the American Doo Wop sound. This style and sound was just starting to gain popularity in England at that time and so the group soon became an attraction on the Wirral.

The **Firecrests**, as they were named from the beginning, at that time consisted of:

        Chris Morris   (voc/g/p)
        Dave Williams   (voc/g)
        Barry Ezzra   (voc/g)
        Gavin Melville   (voc)
        Brian Wrench   (voc)

Occasionally, the group was also joined by **Brian Allen** as an additional singer.

Dave Williams was a very active guitarist and, besides the **Firecrests**, he also played in a un-named Rockabilly trio together with **Ian 'Goz' Boyle** (bass) and **Vic Hubbert** (dr). He was also a member of the **Del Rio Mountain Boys**, a local Skiffle group.

Back to the **Firecrests** who, in as early as 1957, went into Allansons Radio & Recording shop in Birkenhead and recorded "Let's have a party", **Buddy Holly's** "That'll be the day", the **Del-Vikings** success "Come go with me" and the **Moonglows** number "I knew from the start". These songs were released on two acetates.

Of course, these recordings did not help the group make a breakthrough but they are an interesting piece of Merseyside's musical history.

In 2005, the songs "Come go with me" and "That'll be the day" were released on the CD "Unearthed Merseybeat" Vol. 3 (Viper CD 032).

It was probably in 1959 that the **Firecrests** disbanded totally.

The Firecrests

The Jetblacks

Dave Williams, together with his Rockabilly comrades **Ian Boyle** and **Vic Hubbard**, plus **Ken Price** (voc) and **Phil Rodgers** (rg), formed the **Jetblacks**, which was the forerunner of the group **Dale Roberts & the Jaywalkers**.

After that, **Dave Williams** played with **Group One** and the **Four Originals**, who are still going on the scene (another story in this book).

Barry Ezzra joined **Vince Earl & the Zeros** and after that he became a member of both **Steve Day & the Drifters**, which later evolved into the **Rainchecks**.

While **Gavin Neville**, **Brian Wrench** and **Brian Allen** disappeared from the scene, **Chris Morris** went down to London. He was spotted singing at the '2 i's Coffee-Bar' by **Larry Parnes**, who took him under his wing, gave him the stage name **Lance Fortune** and got him a recording contract with PYE.

In 1960, **Lance Fortune** had an international hit with his first record "Be mine", which was also covered by numerous international artists in various languages.

"Be mine" reached No. 5 in the British charts and became a real classic, while the follow-up "All on my own" stopped at no. 26. His other singles "I wonder" (1960) and "Who's gonna tell me" (1961) were not that successful.

Obviously disillusioned, he gave up singing for a while and got involved with a live club in Plymouth, where among many other groups **Dave Lee & the Staggerlees** from Cornwall appeared quite often.

However, in the interim, **Lance Fortune's** recording of "Be mine" had become a huge hit in Germany and because of this he was offered a gig at the famous 'Top Ten' club in Hamburg. As he needed a backing group he asked **Dave Lee & the Staggerlees** to accompany him.

Upon their return **Dave Lee & the Staggerlees** settled down in Sheffield and were signed by Oriole and (without **Lance Fortune**) they recorded "Dance, dance, dance" and "Love me" (September 1963).

Sometime later, but still in 1963, the group's bass guitarist was replaced by **Lance Fortune** who now became a steady member of **Dave Lee & the Staggerlees.** The group recorded two nice Beat singles "Sweet and lovely" and "Forever and always" (February 1964). The B-side of that second single, "Forever and always", was co-written by **Chris Morris** (alias **Lance Fortune**).

LANCE FORTUNE
Exclusive PYE Recording Artist

The group at that time often appeared at the major venues in Manchester and Liverpool.

In order to prevent any confusion, it should be pointed out here that the original lead singer **Dave Lee** was the stage name used by **David Penrase**, who left the group in summer of 1964 and later became a successful photographer. However, **Lance Fortune** was also both bass guitarist and vocalist for **Dave Lee & the Staggerlees,** but he never adopted the stage name of **Dave Lee.**

After **David Penrase** left, the group shortened their name to the **Staggerlees** and ultimately became a trio with **Lance Fortune** (voc/bg), **Anthony Grigg** (lg/voc) and **Bill Covington** (dr/voc). Apparently they were really successful on the British cabaret scene for quite some time although they didn't release any more records.

The **Staggerlees** trio was still performing through the mid Seventies but, unfortunately, it is not known when they finally split, or what happened to **Lance Fortune** after that.

Discography

The Firecrests:

That'll be the day / Let's have a party	UK - Master-Sound-System-acetate / 1957
Come go with me / I knew from the start	UK - Master-Sound-System-acetate / 1957

Lance Fortune:

Be mine / Action	UK - PYE 7N 15240 / 1960
All on my own / This love I have for you	UK - PYE 7N 15260 / 1960
I wonder / Will you still be my girl	UK - PYE 7N 15297 / 1960
Who's gonna tell me / Love is the sweetest thing	UK - PYE 7N 15347 / 1961

Dave Lee & the Staggerlees (feat. Lance Fortune):

Dance, dance, dance / Love me	UK - Oriole CB 1864 / 1963
Sweet and lovely / Forever and always	UK - Oriole CB 1907 / 1964

THE 5 A.M. EVENT

This is definitely not a Liverpool group as the musicians actually hailed from the Osborne Village district of Winnipeg in Canada, where they were formed by **Terry Loeb** and **Vance Masters** in 1962. However, the reason their story is included here results from the fact, that they lived in Liverpool for almost two years and during this time became a significant part of the Merseybeat-scene.

In their hometown they were a top-group, having residencies at the 'Cellar' and the 'Twilight Zone' clubs and having a patron in **Doc Steen** of the CKRC Radio, who let them rehearse in the basement of his station, promoted their shows and broadcast their performances.

It was in July 1965 that the **Crescendos**, as they originally were called, travelled from Canada to Liverpool and started to play the local venues. They very soon became popular with the audiences on Merseyside in a line-up with:

Glenn MacRae	(voc/harp/sax)
Terry Loeb	(lg/voc)
Dennis Penner	(bg/voc)
Vance Masters	(dr/voc)

Apparently, it was their first group for all of the members. **Vance Masters**' real name is **Vance Schmidt**, from which can be concluded, that he had German ancestors.

In December 1965 **Dennis Penner** became homesick and left the group to return to Canada.

The Crescendos

Initially, it was rumored that **Rod Long** a former member of **Gerry Bach & the Beathovens** would join them, but in the end it was Liverpudlian **Stuart McKiernan**, who became their new bass guitarist. The spelling of his surname was also reported as McKernan, his former group is not known.

At an appearance at the 'Cavern' it was this line-up of the **Crescendoes** that caught the attention of **Searchers** drummer **Chris Curtis**, who at that time was also working as a producer for the PYE record-company.

He got them signed and it was probably him, who convinced them to change the name as there were already too many groups called **Crescendos** at that time.

Accordingly the Canadian/Liverpool outfit became the **5 A.M. Event** and in early 1966 **Chris Curtis** produced the single "Hungry" with them for the PYE label.

"Hungry", a pepped up cover of the **Paul Revere & the Raiders** hit-success, coupled with an interesting version of "I Wash My Hands In Muddy Water", was an outstanding record with great guitar-work, powerful drums and excellent vocal harmony.

It identified the **5 A.M. Event** as a top Beat/R&B-group, but unfortunately, it did not make the charts and so did not help the group make any sort of a breakthrough.

During their time in London (for the Pye recording session) they accepted a few local gigs. It was probably at one of these gigs that **Kit Lambert** saw them and was so impressed with their drummer **Vance Masters** he convinced him to join the **Fruit Eating Bears**, the backing-group of the **Merseys**.

The **5 A.M. Event** at that time were the resident group at the famous 'Blue Angel' in Liverpool and they were joined by **Pete Clarke** as their new drummer. **Pete Clarke** had previously played with **Vince & the Volcanoes**, **Groups Inc.**, the **Escorts**, the **Krew** and **Them Grimbles**. He did not stay with them for too long, he re-joined the **Escorts** when **Vance Masters** returned to the group.

The **5 A.M. Event** did not do any more recordings, but they kept playing the Liverpool circuit until they went back to Canada in early 1967.

The Crescendos at the Blue Angel

Back in Canada, they were re-joined by **Dennis Penner** and continued as the **Crescendos** until they disbanded when **Glenn MacRae** and **Vance Masters** both left in late 1967 to get married.

5 A.M. Event - L to R: Stuart McKiernan, Terry Loeb, Glenn MacRae & Vance Masters

Glenn MacRae became the manager of a local music-store and quit the music-business, while **Vance Masters** and **Terry Loeb** went on to play with local groups that included the **Exiled** and the **Clayton Squares** (no, not that Liverpool group).

5 A.M. Event (Both photos)

In 1968 **Vance Masters** joined the recording-group the **Fifth** and after that played with **Brother** and **Diane Heatherington & the Merry-Go-Round**, before he became very successful as singer/songwriter.

In 1977 he played with **Burton Cummings** from the internationally known **Guess Who** and towards the end of that year they jointly revived **Guess Who**.

From 1992 until 2002 **Vance Masters** was a member of the Country Rock-band **Guns 4 Hire** and after that he continued to play locally.

All the other members of the **Crescendos** disappeared from the scene.

In 1968, **Stuart McKiernan** appeared on the Liverpool scene once again as member of a very interesting group, called **Amos Bonny & Friends**. Besides him and singer **Amos Bonny** (ex **T.T.s**) the group also featured well known Merseybeat-musicians, including **Jose McLaughlin** (p – ex **Timebeats** and **Modern Blues Quartet**), **Paul Pilnick** (g – ex **Vince & Volcanoes** and **Lee Curtis & the All Stars**) and **Phil Chittick** (dr – ex **Johnny Ringo & the Colts**).

In 1970, when **Amos Bonny** was replaced by **Mike Byrne** (ex **Thunderbirds** and **Them Grimbles**), this group in the same line-up continued on as the **Mike Byrne Band**.

It is believed that sometime after this **Stuart McKiernan** moved to Twickenham.

Discography

as "The 5 A.M. Event" :

Hungry / I Wash My Hands In Muddy Water   UK – PYE 7 N 17154 / 1966

THE FIVE TRIBUTES

To write down the story of this group from the Childwall - Wavertree area of Liverpool, it is best to start with **Graham Andrews**, a pupil of the Bluecoat school, who could play the drums. For a Christmas concert at the school, someone came up with the idea of putting a band together. It turned out that two of the pupils already played in an established group called the **Citrons** and they were both willing to be part of the Christmas jam band, along with **Graham Andrews** and two others. The Christmas concert went down well and **Graham Andrews** obviously did a good job, as following this, he helped out on drums at a few live-gigs of the **Citrons** but never became a steady member. However, one of the members of the **Citrons** had some friends who were in the process of forming a band and they were in need of a drummer. He recommended **Graham Andrews**, they approached him and, after their first rehearsal, he completed the line-up of the **Tributes**, that in February 1964, had their first public appearance at the 'Vernon Johnson School of Dance' in Allerton Road - in a line-up with:

Keith Billows	(voc)
Eddie Nugent	(lg/voc)
Trevor Roberts	(rg/voc)
Ian Taylor	(bg)
Graham Andrews	(dr)

All of them were newcomers to the scene and their biggest influence was the music of **Buddy Holly**. Initially, the **Tributes** played the local pubs and social-clubs but soon became somewhat of a resident group at the 'Shipperies' pub in Edge Lane.

Trevor Roberts' family hailed from Lincoln and, during a holiday there, he spoke to a local agent, who organised a week-long series of bookings for the **Tributes**, which brought the musicians a lot of experience. Upon their return to Liverpool, they started to play at the downtown clubs, such as the 'Mouse Trap' and the 'Temple Bar'.

To take the next step forward, the **Tributes** went into **Charlie Weston's** Unicord studio in Moorfields and recorded a great E.P. on acetate with the **Eddie Nugent** instrumental, "Spanish Eagle", a version of **George Gershwin's** classic, "Summertime" and two additional group-originals called "You'll always be my girl" and "I can't help myself", which is a great number. It can be said that musically the **Tributes** had become a Rhythm & Blues band. Only 25 copies of this record were made and they were used by their agent **Tony Varney** as demos for other promoters.

Following that E.P., the **Tributes** now played at all the main Liverpool venues such as the 'Downbeat' the 'Grafton', the 'Peppermint Lounge' and the 'Mardi Gras''. However, in 1965, soon after the recording, **Ian Taylor** left the **Tributes** to get married to a girl that he had met during their time in Lincoln. He moved to Lincoln and was replaced by **Alan Jones**.

The Temple Group Agency
(AN ARTIST FOR EVERY OCCASION)

You've Seen the Rest!
NOW BOOK THE BEST
SOLE REPRESENTATION OF

The Blue Mountain Boy's (Oriole) - The Cobbles
The 5 Tributes - Johnny Ringo's Colts - The Halo's
The Anzaks - Them Grimbles - The Croupiers
Hank Walter's Dusty Road Ramblers (Decca)
The 4 Countdowns (E.M.I.) - T.L.'s Bluesicians
Baby Jane & The Syndicate (Bristol) (Pye)

At the most reasonable fees on Merseyside

Ring Tony Varney CEN 3168
After 9 p.m. AIN 3968

Then the musicians discovered that there was already a group from the Wirral originally known as the **Flints** that had been playing on the scene for two years using the name of the **Tributes**. Consequently, they changed their name into the **Five Tributes** and on 10th December 1965, had their first appearance at the 'Cavern' under this new name.

The Five Tributes - L to R: Alan Jones, Graham Andrews, Eddie Nugent, Keith Billows, Trevor Roberts

Gigs followed at the 'Grave', 'Dino's' and the 'Orrell Park Ballroom'. The **Five Tributes** played the 'Blue Angel' and they also made regular appearances at the 'Silver Blades Ice Rink' on Prescot Road.

When the group was joined by **Sammy Rothwell** on organ, for a short time, contrary to their new name, they were a six-piece. However, that changed again when **Trevor Roberts** left the group to become a member of the **Hookers,** shortly followed by **Eddie Nugent** who teamed up with him as a duo, unfortunately, the name of that duo cannot be recalled.

The Five Tributes - L to R: Eddie Nugent (?), Alan Jones, Keith Billows, Graham Andrews, Sam Rothwell

The Mistake - (as a 4-piece) L to R: Alan Jones, Graham Andrews, Sam Rothwell, Keith Billows

For a short time, the group appeared as a four-piece and, at that point, changed their name to the **Mistake**. **Alan Jones** obviously was not happy with the changes and soon left the group. Shortly after that, **Keith Billows** also decided to leave and he teamed up with remaining members of the just disbanded **Lay-Bys** from Huyton and they formed a new group under the name of **Keith's Kind**. The remaining members of the **Mistake** were joined by **Harry Shaw** (voc/harp) and **Mick Rowley** (lg), who both came from the above mentioned **Lay-Bys**. The new bass-guitarist, **Billy Hargreaves,** came from the just disbanded **Aztecs** (another story in this book).

After those changes, the **Mistake** in early 1966 appeared in the following line-up:

Harry Shaw	(voc/harp)
Mick Rowley	(lg)
Sammy Rothwell	(org/voc)
Billy Hargreaves	(bg)
Graham Andrews	(dr)

The **Mistake** went into a studio again, this time to **Percy Phillips** in Kensington, and recorded an interesting version of **Marvin Gaye's** "Ain't that peculiar", coupled with a group original titled "Image". The recording was funded by **Jim McCulloch**, the owner of the 'Tavern' in New Brighton who, as it seems, was something like their manager at that time. This acetate was sent to the major record-companies but it did not bring the recording-contract it was hoped for.

The **Mistake** kept playing the Liverpool scene where they became regulars at the 'Cavern' through 1966 and into 1967. They were also regulars at the 'Klic Klic' club in Southport and even had an agent in Blackpool, who supplied them with plenty of bookings in and around that locale. However, in August 1967, **Graham Andrews** made the decision to concentrate on his job and quit the group and the last original member of the **Tributes** had gone. The **Mistake** obviously had severe problems finding a suitable replacement and, so, **Graham Andrews** stood in again at various gigs until they were joined by **Billy Geeleher**, an experienced drummer, who formerly had played with the **Modes**, the **Calderstones***, the **Dions*** and the **Times.** This resulted in another name change and the **Mistake** became the **Curiosity Shoppe*.**

All that is left to say is that **Graham Andrews** became a sea-going electrical engineer on the P&O Ferries between Liverpool and Belfast and so was unable to join another group. In 1981, his job took him to Bahrain and, later on, he lived for a few years in Abu Dhabi. Here he became friendly with a local group and occasionally stood in as their drummer. On his return to Liverpool, he got in touch again with **Sammy Rothwell** and they both decided to form a new group but that never materialized due to **Sammy Rothwell's** declining health.

Discography:

as **The Tributes:**

Spanish Eagle / I can't help myself

Summertime / You'll always be my girl   UK- Unicord acetate EP / 1965

as **The Mistake:**

Ain't that peculiar / Image   UK- Phillips Kensington acetate / 1966

*The stories of these groups can be followed in 'Beat Waves 'Cross The Mersey' (*VelocePress ISBN 978-1-58850-201-8*).

FOCAL POINT

Formed in summer 1967, this group is not really part of the Merseybeat wave, but was still a Liverpool recording group of the 60's and, therefore, their story is featured here.

It all started sometime in 1966 when **Dave Rhodes**, at that time, the lead guitarist with the **Maraccas,** decided to write songs together with **Paul Tennant**.

Paul Tennant had also been active as a guitarist on the Liverpool scene since the early Sixties. Unfortunately, the names of the groups he had played with are not known.

Dave Rhodes left the **Maraccas** and they both formed a group called **Obsession** and they began playing the Liverpool clubs. This did not last too long and the song-writing duo went on to form the **Big Lox Blues Band**, which also was quite short-lived.

After that, **Paul Tennant** joined the **Almost Blues**, but also kept on writing together with **Dave Rhodes**.

In early 1967, the song-writing duo went down to London and somehow managed to meet with **Paul McCartney**. Apparently, they were able to convince him regarding the quality of their songs and so he put them in touch with **Terry Doran**, another Liverpudlian who, at that time, was in charge of Apple Records. He listened to their songs and took the duo to the Central Sound studio to record four of their songs on acetate, namely "Except me", Miss Sinclair's courtship", "Reflections" and "Hassle Castle".

These acetates were taken to **John Lennon** and **Brian Epstein**, who also liked them and a five year publishing deal was signed with Apple.

Brian Epstein suggested that Dave and Paul should form a group and, at the same time, also came up with an idea for their name.

The songwriters went back to Liverpool and formed **Focal Point**, which then consisted of:

Paul Tennant	(voc/rg)
Dave Rhodes	(lg/voc)
Tim Wells	(key/voc)
Dave Slater	(bg/voc)
Ted Hesketh	(dr)

Tim Wells and **Dave Slater** were former members of a group called the **Top**, while **Ted Hesketh** had played together with **Dave Rhodes** in the **Maraccas**.

Unfortunately, although **Brian Epstein** had intended to become their manager he died unexpectedly. So **Terry Doran** and **Lionel Morton** of the **Four Pennies** became the joint management team of **Focal Point.** The group moved down to London but also toured the north of England quite regularly, appearing with well-known artists including **Stevie Winwood, Peter Frampton, Chris Farlowe** and the **New Yardbirds**, soon to become **Led Zeppelin**.

Although **Focal Point** kept recording for Apple, they were also signed to Deram and Liverpudlian **Wayne Bickerton**, who had played with groups including the **Bobby Bell Rockers, Steve & the Syndicate** and the **Pete Best Four**, became their producer.

They recorded four Rhodes/Tennant numbers on the Deram label: "Love you forever", Sycamore Sid", "Never, never" and "Girl on the corner", of which the first two were chosen to be released on a single in 1968. The record did not sell too badly but it failed to get into the charts.

The psychedelic song "Never, never" was then recorded by the **Alan Price Set** but it was not released, because at the last minute, **Alan Price** and Decca chose "Simon Smith and his amazing dancing bear" instead.

Around that time, **Focal Point** were also backing **Jackie Lomax** at Apple on the rehearsals for his album, which must have been "Is this what you want". The sessions were recorded but when the album was finally released, **Focal Point** were not part of it.

The group returned to Liverpool and split up in the second half of 1969 without having recorded again. However, a CD was recently issued that includes their complete recordings for Apple and the two Deram single tracks (for details see discography).

Paul Tennant, **Tim Wells** and **Dave Slater** formed a publishing company called Focal Point Music which is still going today. Unfortunately, **Paul Tennant** sadly died in March 2010, aged 64.

Dave Rhodes moved to Morpeth, where he is working as a lecturer in mental nursing facility and of **Ted Hesketh** it is known that he kept on playing, having been a member of the newly formed **Merseybeats**, who also performed as **Tony Crane & the Merseybeats**, from 1979 until he emigrated to Canda in 1983.

After moving to Canada he played with various local groups in Toronto before he joined the **James Anthony Band**, a Blues/Rock outfit, where he played until 2008.

Focal Point - L to R: (Back) Tim Wells, Dave Slater, Dave Rhodes (Front) Ted Hesketh & Paul Tennant

Discography

Love you forever / Sycamore Sid   UK- Deram DM 186 / 1968

Unreleased tracks:

From 1967 until 1968 **Focal Point** recorded the following Rhodes/Tennant originals, which were not released:

Except me / Miss Sinclair's courtship / Reflections / Hassle Castle / Never, never / Lonely woman / Far away from forever / Tales from the GPO files / McKinley Morgan the deep sea diver / Falling out of friends / Girl on the corner / Goodbye forever / This time she's leaving

(All these songs, plus some alternate versions from the 'Apple' acetates and the two Deram single tracks were released on the 2009 Kissing Spell label CD **"First Bite Of The Apple"** (KSCD 953).

THE FOUR GENTS & BERNADETTE

This group was formed in Dingle, Liverpool in the second half of 1963 – a little too late to catch the already international high-speed Liverpool Beat-train. This was probably the reason that their repertoire consisted of different musical styles including Merseybeat, Country & Western, **Shadows** type instrumentals, ballads and popular tunes of the day which they called the 'Sophisticated Mersey Sound'. According to a newspaper-article in 'Liverpool Weekly News' of the 24th October 1963, the secret to their success was in their *'quickness to recognize exactly what their audience wants and the ability to alter their programme accordingly'*. This strategy, of course, made the group less dependent upon bookings at the Beat clubs......but was it the right strategy for greater success?

Whatever, the founding member of the **Four Gents** was lead-guitarist, **Tony Bell**, who previously had played with **Tony Crane** and **Billy Kinsley** in a guitar-trio (without a name), which was the beginning of the embryonic **Mavericks** who then, of course, became the **Merseybeats***. The **Four Gents** practised at the Dingle 'South Hill Hotel', whose manager, **John Shinner**, was the father of their drummer, **Ian Shinner,** and he also took over the group's management. Besides the usual Beat clubs such as the 'Iron Door', 'Peppermint Lounge' and the 'Cazzie', the group regularly appeared at the night-club 'Talk Of The Town', which was the former 'Top Hat' that ultimately became the 'Starline Club', a real institution in Liverpool's cabaret-scene.

It was probably around that time that three of the group-members changed their names and so the original bass-guitarist, **John Jenkins,** became **Johnny Reslo**, drummer, **Ian Shinner** became, **Ian 'Snowy' White** and finally **Tony Bell** called himself **Tony Barrow**.

John Jenkins obviously was not too happy with the music they played and left in early 1964 to join the **Citadels** and after that was a member of the **Soul Seekers.**

In March 1964, the **Four Gents** were looking for a female singer and through a newspaper advertisement they found the ideal candidate in **Bernadette O'Toole**.

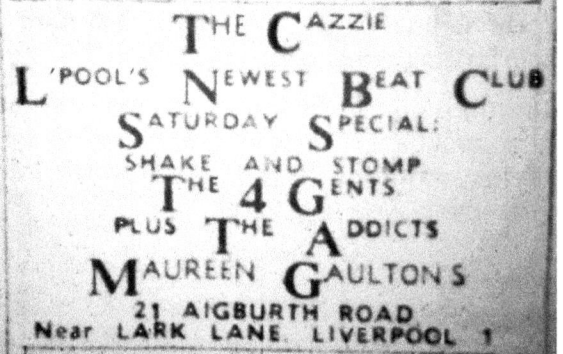

They changed their name into the **Four Gents & Bernadette** and now appeared in the following line-up:

Bernadette O'Toole	(voc)
Tony Barrow	(voc/lg)
Dave Murdoch	(rg)
Paul Edgar	(bg)
Ian White	(dr)

The former group of **Paul Edgar** is not known and nothing is known about **Bernadette O'Toole** but it is assumed that she had sung in cabaret previously. It is confirmed that on Monday, 27th July 1964 the **Four Gents & Bernadette** went into the **Percy Phillips** recording studio in Kensington and cut a demo-disc – probably with four tracks but it was not possible to ascertain which songs they played at that session.

Four Gents & Bernadette, often advertised as **Bernadette & the Four Gents**, now appeared quite regularly at the Beat-sessions held at the 'Locarno' and the 'Beat-Ville' shows at the 'Wintergardens' in Garston. According to their management, the group also had offers to play in France, Germany and Italy but that could have only been for the American or British military-bases in those countries as for sure there was little or no demand for their musical style on the normal club-circuit. However, it is not known if **Bernadette & the Four Gents** ever went to Europe and towards the end of 1964 and into early 1965 information about the group became very sporadic which was probably due to the fact that they had concentrated more on their cabaret-act at that time.

It was sometime in early 1965 that the group disbanded and **Tony Bell** then became a member of the **Mike Crombie Combo**, which was the resident band at the 'Starline Club' which besides himself on vocals and lead-guitar consisted of **Frank McTigue** from the **Easybeats*** (bg), **Mike Swift** (voc/rg) and **John Crombie** (dr). In this line-up they played at that club throughout 1965 and into 1966. **Tony Bell** was last heard of as being part of the resident duo at the 'Aldonian Club' in the mid-Seventies. **Bernadette O'Toole** very likely continued singing on the cabaret-scene for some period of time but none of the other members of the **Four Gents** appeared on the scene again. However, it is known that sometime later **Ian ('Snowy' White) Shinner** was a compere at the 'RAF Club' in Kirby.

Discography:

It is only known for a fact that **Bernadette & the Four Gents** recorded a demo-acetate at the **Percy Phillips** studio in Kensington on the 27th July 1964 but sadly, it proved impossible to find out which numbers they recorded.

*The stories of these groups can be followed in 'Beat Waves 'Cross The Mersey' (*VelocePress* ISBN 978-1-58850-201-8).

THE FOUR MUSKETEERS

Okay, this group did not record in the Sixties but it is included here because their story contains so much interesting information about other Liverpool recording groups that it simply could not be left out.

The best way to start is with the **Statesmen**, who were formed in the West Derby area in the very late Fifties or very early Sixties.

In their original line-up, they consisted of **Len Bowers** (voc/lg), **Vic Brunskill** (rg), **Les Coe** (bg) and **John Banks** (dr).

The Statesmen

They soon established a good name for themselves but approximately six months after their formation, the line-up started to change. **Vic Brunskill** left, he later became a member of **T.L.s Bluesicians**, where he switched from guitar to drums. He was replaced in the **Statesmen** by **Dave Elias**, who came from the **Merseybeats**.

Around the same time, **John Banks** left to join the **Merseybeats** and his place was taken by **Frank Sloane**, who came from the **Merseybeats** – so the two groups just swapped drummers. **Frank Sloane** did not stay for too long and went on to form the **Nocturns**, together with former members of **Alby & the Sorrals**.

At that time, the **Statesmen** found out that there was a recording group with the same name and so they became the **Diplomats.** However, as there were a number of other groups around using that name, they changed it again to the **Four Musketeers,** in a line-up with:

Len Bowers	(voc/lg)
Dave Elias	(rg/voc)
Les Coe	(bg)
Gordon 'Snowy' Fleet	(dr)

Unfortunately, it is not known whether **'Snowy' Fleet** had played in another group previously or if he was a newcomer to the scene.

The **Four Musketeers** joined the stable of **Dave Forshaw Enterprises**, who really kept them busy on the scene, playing all the important venues on Merseyside.

In spite of their success, the group did not continue for too long and disbanded totally when **Dave Elias** left to follow **Frank Sloane** to the **Nocturns**, where he switched to piano.

After that, **Dave Elias** went down to London where he played with the **Beat-Chicks**. He then returned to Liverpool and teamed up with **Keith Draper** (ex **Alby & the Sorrals** and **Nocturns**) in a cabaret duo called the **Jade Brothers**.

Len Bowers joined **Sounds plus One**, another West Derby group, before he continued on Liverpool's Country scene as a member of the very popular and successful **Kentuckians**.

Apparently, **Les Coe** quit the music business or, at least, he never appeared on the scene again.

'Snowy' Fleet played with the **Mojos** before he emigrated to Australia where he was a founding member of the internationally successful group **The Easybeats**, who had major chart successes with classics such as "Friday on my mind", "Hello, how are you", "Good times" and "(*Show me the way to*) St. Louis".

THE FOUR ORIGINALS

This was a group from the Wirral, where it was formed in October 1964. To describe the group's development, it is best if we follow the musical journey of guitarist, **Dave Williams**. It begins in 1957 when he was a member of the **Firecrests** but, around that same time, he was also a member of **The Del Rio Mountain Boys** Skiffle group. After that, he played with the **Jetblacks**, from which the popular Merseybeat group **Dale Roberts & the Jaywalkers** evolved, where he also played until they disbanded in 1962.

He then joined **Group One**, where he played until that outfit split up in mid '64. Without a group, he contacted his old comrade **George Roberts** (alias **Dale Roberts**) and they both decided to form a new group, the **Four Originals**, who started off with the following line-up:

George Roberts	(voc/g)
Dave Williams	(lg/voc)
Phil Howard	(bg/voc)
John Nugent	(dr)

The Four Originals (1964)

The name of the group was chosen because all the members were already 'originals', having been on the scene since the early days of Merseybeat.

George Roberts was actually **Dale Roberts** of **Dale Roberts & the Jaywalkers** but he had taken a break to get married. **Phil Howard** came from the **Defenders** and drummer, **John Nugent** was a former member of the **Lee Eddie Five**.

The **Four Originals** were more of a commercial Beat group and, as such, they did not really take part in the Liverpool club scene, instead they played the dance halls on the Wirral.

This absence from the Liverpool scene, coupled with the fact that the group occasionally appeared as **Dale Roberts & the Jaywalkers,** was the reason the **Four Originals** were easily overlooked in the evolution of Merseybeat.

The **Four Originals** kept themselves very busy on the scene, playing their mixture of Beat and Pop, without ever becoming a true cabaret group.

In 1966, the group recorded the **Lovin' Spoonful** hit "Daydream" and **Herman's Hermits**' "You won't be leaving" along with some other numbers. They were not released at the time but they were included on the CD "Unearthed Merseybeat" Vol.3 (Viper 032) in 2005.

In spite of the fact that the **Four Originals** never released an official record and never made major headlines, they had a long and successful existence and there were no changes in the line-up until 1973 when **John Nugent** left the group and disappeared from the scene.

His replacement was **Colin Middlebrough**, another experienced Liverpool musician having played with the **All Blacks Skiffle Group** and the **Kansas City Five** in the Sixties and prior to joining the **Four Originals,** he had been a member of a C & W group called the **Westerners**.

Phil Howard sadly died in May 2005 and his place in the group was taken by **Derek Green** (voc/bg), who had played with the **Del Renas** and the **Motifs** in the Sixties.

When **George Roberts** also died in January 2007, his replacement was **Terry Fisher** (rg), also a Sixties member of the **Del Renas** and the **Motifs**.

In this line-up, the **Four Originals** are still going successfully on the scene, joined now by **Phil Howard's** daughter, **Catherine Howard,** as their vocalist.

Discography

Daydream / You won't be leaving   UK -   Acetate (?) / 1966

THE GEORGIANS

This very interesting group had its place of origin in the Liverpool district of Childwall where it was formed by three young boys who were also school-mates at the Quarry Bank High School in Allerton that later became famous for being the birthplace of the **Quarrymen** Skiffle group and, of course, their development into the **Beatles**. All three had also started to play guitars and, in 1962, they decided to form a group under the name of the **Georgians** in the following line-up:

Tim Dugdill	(voc/rg/harp)
Lawrence 'Lol' Ashley	(lg)
Geoff Jones	(bg)
Mike Sloan	(dr)

All of the members were newcomers to the scene and accordingly did not have any experience. The three guitarists originally wanted to be a sort of a **Shadows** style band but very soon discovered their love of American Rhythm & Blues which changed their musical direction. **Mike Sloan** was not a school-mate but a childhood friend of **Tim Dugdill** – and he was the younger brother of **Frank Sloan**, who at that time played drums in the **Merseybeats***.

L to R: Tim Dugdill, Geoff Jones, Mike Sloan, Lol Ashley

Like all the other groups, the **Georgians** started to play at local youth-clubs and schools. They went down well, especially at the Quarry Bank school, where they built up a great following and soon had a fan-club. The **Georgians** then also appeared at clubs such as 'St. Barnabus Hall' in Allerton, before they made their way into the city-centre where, through the support of Bob Wooler, they played quite regularly at the 'Cavern' – at first the lunchtime-sessions but soon also in the evenings.

As it seems, all the members were in a hurry to accelerate their musical career and so sometime, toward the end of 1963, they went into the Kensington studios of **Percy Phillips** and recorded the R&B-classics "I got my mojo working" and "Hoochie Coochie Man" on acetate.

In 1964, **Roger Lewis** a sax-player was added to the line-up of the **Georgians** that had already established themselves as a R&B-group on the scene and so, besides their continuing gigs at the 'Cavern' and 'Hope Hall', they got many bookings at the 'Mardi Gras' which, at that time, became the 'in-place' for American R&B and Soul-music.

Mike Sloan soon left the group and became a member of the **Feelgoods**. His replacement was **Roger Bioletti**, whose former group is, sadly, not known. It was probably this line-up that was spotted by the vice-president of the American Mercury label on his trip to Liverpool - successful producer, **Shelby Singleton,** and in a newspaper-article it said, *'He put an encouraging interest in a little known group, called the Georgians, who played at the Cavern'.* Unfortunately, this was not followed by any recordings.

Then **Geoff Jones** received an offer to play with the **Clayton Squares*** and also left. He at first was replaced by **Lewis Collins**, the former drummer of the **Renegades*** and, for a short time, of the **Kansas City Five***. In the interim, he had played the bass-guitar with the **Eyes*** in Germany and it was this instrument he played in the **Georgians.** He obviously did not stay too long with the group, as he accepted an offer to become a member of the **Mojos***. After that, he played with the **Robb Storme Group** and, later, he became a successful actor, probably best known for being *'Bodie'* in the crime/action series *'The Professionals'*.

****
● When SHELBY SINGLETON, vice president of America's Mercury Records was in Liverpool he made a visit to the Mardi Gras, The Cavern, The Peppermint Lounge and The Hope Hall. "I am particularly impressed by THE GEORGIANS," he told me, as he watched them perform on stage at the Cavern. "They've definitely got something different. Although they're still rough at the edges, in a couple of months time they should be a powerful outfit and I'd like to record them for the American market."
****

The **Georgians** did not recruit another bass-player but **Lawrence Ashley** switched from lead guitar to bass and **Tim Dugdill** took over the lead-guitar position.

L to R: Lewis Collins, Tim Dugdill, Roger Bioletti, Lol Ashley, Roger Lewis

Their long time roadie **Brian Farrell** was added to the band line-up as lead-vocalist. He had a fantastic gravely Soul-voice and, through his influence, the music of the **Georgians** moved very much towards Soul. Around that time, their line up may have also included **Rod Stanson** on organ, who came from the **Cobbles,** but this was only a very short-lived project that came to an end when **Tim Dugdill** joined the **Kinsleys*** with whom he also toured Germany.

Roger Lewis followed **Mike Sloan** to the **Feelgoods** but later moved to the South of England and there he likely continued in the music-business but no further details are known. **Brian Farrell** and **Rod Stanson** became members of **Fringe Benefit**, that soon changed the name into **Colonel Bagshot's Incredible Bucket Band** but that is part of the story of the **Cordes***.

When the **Kinsleys** broke up at the end of 1965, **Tim Dugdill** teamed up with his old mates **Lawrence Ashley** and **Roger Bioletti** again and they performed as a trio under the name of **Terence, Anton & Brown**. Sometime in 1968, they changed their name into **Fresh Garbage**, after a song they played that was on the first **Spirit** album.

HOPE HALL	
GOES	
BEAT	
5 Nights Weekly	
at 8 p.m.	
Thurs. Nov. 21st	'The Roadrunners'
Fri. Nov. 22nd	'The Georgians'
Sat. Nov. 23rd	'The Four Strangers'
Sun. Nov. 24th	'The Roadrunners'
Wed. Nov. 27th	'The Huntsmen'
Thurs. Nov. 28th	'The Roadrunners'
Fri. Nov. 29th	'The Satanists'
Sat. Nov. 30th	'The Georgians'
Sun. Dec. 1st	'The Roadrunners'
Wed. Dec. 4th	'The Huntsmen'
Thurs. Dec. 5th	'The Roadrunners'

LICENSED BAR

DO NOT MISS
"FAREWELL TO
  THE ROADRUNNERS"
TUESDAY, DECEMBER 17th
ON STAGE

ENQUIRIES
CHIldwall 4694.

FAN CLUB
LARk Lane 5986.

This group did not last for very long, **Lawrence Ashley** quit the music business and **Tim Dugdill** became a member of **Familiarity Breed** before he also quit the music business. **Roger Bioletti** also stopped playing and died way too young - at the age of 50. In 2007, **Tim Dugdill** travelled over the ocean to play one more time together with **Lewis Collins** – in a session on the 40th birthday of Lewis' wife in Los Angeles.

Discography

I got my mojo working / Hoochie Coochie Man   UK- Phillips Kensington acetate / 1963

> *Early influences on our music were Muddy Waters, Howlin' Wolf, Buddy Guy, Sonny Boy Williamson and Chuck Berry – all of whom we were to play with as support band later. What a privilege!*
>
> **Tim Dugdill / The Georgians**

*The stories of these groups can be followed in 'Beat Waves 'Cross The Mersey' (*VelocePress ISBN 978-1-58850-201-8*).

THE GIBSON JAMES BAND

Of course, it could be argued that the story of this group should not be featured in this book as it was not a group from the Sixties. But you can imagine that there is a special reason for its inclusion, which is explained in the author's note at the end of this story.

In 1978, there was the sampler-album titled, **'Mersey Survivors',** released on the little known Raw-label, featuring well-known Liverpool groups from the Sixties with new recordings and a spoken introduction by the great and legendary 'Cavern' compere, **Bob Wooler**. The groups featured on the album were **Faron's Flamingos***, the **Dimensions**, **Karl Terry & the Cruisers***, the **Pawns***, the **Renegades***, **Groups Inc.*** - and the **Gibson James Band**.

Nobody had ever seen the **Gibson James Band** advertised for any live-appearances because that name was only used for this recording. It was actually a trio that normally went under the name of **Red Fire** on the Seventies-scene and it was comprised of the following Merseybeat veterans:

L to R: Arty Davis, Pete Jones, James Majors

Pete Jones (voc/lg)

James Majors (voc/bg)

Arthur 'Arty' Davies (dr)

In the Sixties, **Pete Jones** had played with the **Crosbys**, the **Renegades***, **Groups Inc.***, the **New Avengers** and the **Dresdens**. When he got married, he originally quit the music-business but was back in the Seventies in a cabaret-duo with **Chris Graham** under the name of **Alias Smith & Jones**. This was before he became a member of the newly formed **Faron's Flamingos**, where he played a few years but then revived the duo, **Alias Smith & Jones** together with **James Majors**, who was his brother-in-law.

James Majors had played in the Country-group the **Northwesterners** and, after that, was a member of **New Pence** before he teamed up with **Pete Jones** in the duo, **Alias Smith & Jones** that later, with the addition of **Arty Davies,** became the trio, **Red Fire**.

Arty Davies started off as a bass-guitarist in the **Rapides** but then switched to the drums in his main group, the **Pressure Points**. After that, he sat in with the **Toreadors**, played with the **Pastel Shades** and **Korner Kafe**, as well as many other groups before he joined **Red Fire**.

Why **Red Fire** recorded under the name of the **Gibson James Band**, no one could really explain but the name was picked in the studio – pieced together from the fact that **James Majors** played a **Gibson** 'Les Paul' guitar - it was just a last minute decision. On that recording of the **Barrett & Strong** classic, "Money", the trio was joined by the bass-guitarist and the sax-player of **Karl Terry & the Cruisers***, while **James Majors** played rhythm-guitar. So it can be said that this was just a recording-session jam band.

Here it should be mentioned that there was a peculiarity about this group as **Arty Davies** was struck down with polio when he was still a child and, accordingly, he was using a wheel-chair, as did **James Majors**, who had suffered an un-repairable spinal injury. However, after the recording, the trio continued to play the clubs on Merseyside under the name of **Red Fire** for approximately two more years. After that, **Arty Davies** went on to play with various groups, amongst them the re-formed **Four Just Men*** and **Faron's Flamingos**. He then played with the **Tempos** and nowadays he is a member of a group called **Knight Crew**. **Pete Jones** and **James Majors** continued as a duo again under the name of **Alias Smith & Jones** until **Pete Jones** suffered a stroke and had to give up playing. **James Majors** sadly died in 2018.

Discography:

as Gibson James Band on compilation-album

Money on **'Mersey Survivors'** UK-Raw RWLP 104 / 1978

Author's note :

The 'Mersey Survivors' album became a classic for Merseybeat collectors and others who were interested in the Liverpool Beat-scene. As people knew that I was familiar with Merseybeat history, they often asked me about the Gibson James Band, as it was a mystery to them. With the exception of that band, all the other groups from that album were featured in my books and so finally I thought, if the Gibson James Band, although not a Sixties-group was good enough for the producer and especially for Bob Wooler to be featured on that album, they should be good enough to be featured in my book and, with that, the numerous questions about this group would finally be answered.

I also like to take this opportunity to thank Arty Davies for his tremendous support on compiling the group-stories for my books. He has always helped me with information and direct contacts to the musicians. Without his kind help, my books probably would not have been the same.

---

*The stories of these groups can be followed in 'Beat Waves 'Cross The Mersey' (*VelocePress* ISBN 978-1-58850-201-8*).

THE GLOBETROTTERS

This group, which is always identified as being from Rock Ferry, came into life when the Birkenhead group, the **Strollers,** broke up in late 1962 or early 1963. **Billy Maybury** and **Geoffrey Lawlan,** former members of the **Strollers**, along with other local musicians and under the management of **George Parker,** continued as the **Page-Boys,** which in 1963 consisted of:

Geoffrey Lawlan	(voc/rg)
Dave Owens	(lg/voc)
Stan Ferguson	(bg/voc)
Billy Maybury	(dr)

It was confirmed that this was the first band of **Stan Ferguson**, but it is not known if **Dave Owens** had played in another group previously.

While the business-card of their management recommended them for parties, dances and club-appearances, a newspaper-advert identified them as Rhythm & Blues group. Regardless, the **Page-Boys** started to play the local venues on the Wirral such as the 'King Edward Hall', 'St. Luke's' in Tranmere and they also built up a large following at the 'Anglican Youth Centre' in Woodchurch.

The next step for the group was the popular Beat-clubs such as the 'Majestic', the 'Hole In The Floor', the 'Cubik' and the 'Witch's Cauldron' but it seems it took the **Page-Boys** quite a while before they also played the Liverpool venues and their only documented appearance on the 'Cavern' was Wednesday, the 5th February 1964.

Soon after this, the group changed its name into the **Globetrotters** and their management was taken over by **Bill Ross**. Sometime in mid-1964, the **Globetrotters** went into the **Percy Phillips** studio in Kensington and recorded an acetate with the **Bob B. Soxx** success "Zip-A-Dee-Doo-Da" and a group original, that was written by **Geoff Lawlan** but, unfortunately, no one can recall the title. Although they had become quite popular, for unknown reasons, the **Globetrotters** called it a day towards the end of 1964.

Billy Maybury became a member of the Shake-Spears and Stan Ferguson joined the short-lived Set-Up, which consisted of a mixture of Liverpool and London musicians and, after that, he also became a member of the Shake-Spears. However, Dave Owens disappeared from the scene while Geoffrey Lawlan joined a group called the Tagg. When the Tagg broke up in early 1966, Al Stone from that group and Geoffrey Lawlan teamed up with Billy Maybury again and, together with Steve Crombie (sax) and the keyboarder Peter Forsett, they formed the Fynke. Before joining the Tagg, Al Stone had played with the Deerstalkers and most probably was the one and the same former leader of Al Stone & the Earthquakes.

The Fynke in that line-up turned professional and appeared regularly in Matlock, Derbyshire – so regularly that they ultimately decided to live there for 12 months. Sometime in 1968, they broke up and none of them appeared in other groups again which could mean, that they all went back to normal day jobs.

TOP RANK DANCING

MAJESTIC
BALLROOM
Conway St., BIRKENHEAD
*
Your Programme for the next TWO WEEKS

Thursday, February 28th—
GERRY AND THE PACEMAKERS
(Hear Gerry sing "How Do You Do It"— The day prior to release)
THE UNDERTAKERS
(Direct from Hamburg)
THE GLOBE TROTTERS

Friday, March 1st—
FARON'S FLAMINGO'S; LEE SHONDELL AND THE BOYS.

Saturday, March 2nd—
THE FOUR MOSTS; THE MERSEY BEATS; DEE AND THE DYNAMITES; THE PANTHERS; DELL AND THE DELTONES.

Sunday, March 3rd—
JOHNNIE SANDON AND THE REMO 4; KEN DALLAS AND THE SILHOUETTES.

Alan Finnigan Pete Fenton Ray Hilton

To prevent any confusion, it should be pointed out that after the original Globetrotters disbanded in late 1964, there was still a group performing on the Wirral under that same name but there is absolutely no connection between the two groups. The Wirral based Globetrotters consisted of Alan Finnigan (voc/perc), Ray Hilton (g), Ted Hayes (bg) and Peter Fenlon (dr). Ray Hilton was a former member of Rhythm Amalgamated and Peter Fenlon had previously played with the Breakdowns, and, at a later stage, he appeared again as a member of the Minits before joining the Vampires.

Discography:

Zip-A-Dee-Doo-Da / (unknown group original) **UK- Phillips Kensington acetate / 1964**

THE HARLEMS

This is a very interesting story which, in its origin and development, is very closely connected to **Vince & the Volcanoes**, one of the early Liverpool groups, whose story is also featured in this book.

The first line-up of the **Harlems** in 1963 consisted of **Vinnie Ismail**, alias **Vinnie Tow** (lg/voc), **Rob Eccles** (bg/voc) and **Dave Preston** (dr). All three were former members of the recently disbanded **Vince & the Volcanoes.**

Dave Preston had a short stint with **Sonny Webb & the Cascades**, before joining with his old comrades again in the **Harlems**, the backing group for the **Chants**, Liverpool's most successful coloured vocal group.

Dave Preston did not stay with the **Harlems** for too long and went on to play with the **Secrets** and the **Kinsleys**. After that he was a member of the **Creation** who had some major international hits in the second half of the Sixties, including "Painter man" and "Tom Tom". In late 1963, the **Harlems** continued with the following line-up:

Vinnie Ismail	(lg/voc)
Bob Gilmore	(rg/voc)
Rob Eccles	(bg)
John Bedson	(dr)

Bob Gilmore and **John Bedson** both came from the **Challengers** and, before that, **John Bedson** had played with the **Four Clefs** and the short-lived **Roadrunners**, who were not the same as the Liverpool recording group of the same name.

In early 1964, **Vinnie Ismail** left the **Harlems** to work with a group called the **Dakotas**, which was not the group of the same name that backed **Billy J. Kramer**.

The new lead guitarist was **Brendon McCormack**, a former member of the **Memphis Three** and **Rikki & the Red Streaks**.

The **Harlems** had bookings in their own right but also continued to back the **Chants** at their live appearances throughout England

The Harlems at the Cavern

and on their tours in Germany and Ireland. What is not so sure is whether they also backed them on their tours in Germany or if studio musicians were used. However, it is known that the **Harlems** were featured on the **Chants** recording of "Sweet was the wine" in September 1964.

Brendon McCormack apparently left shortly after this, while **Vinnie Ismail** returned to the group.

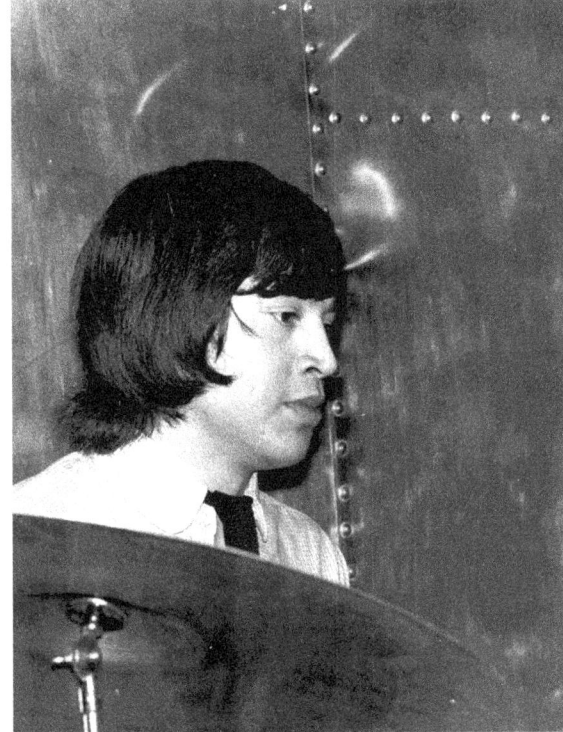

Johnny Sze at the 'Top Ten' club

The next to leave was **Bob Gilmore**, who was replaced by **Frank Bradshaw** and when **John Bedson** left shortly afterwards, the **Harlems** split up, which also meant that their co-operation with the **Chants** came to an end.

Bob Gilmore and **John Bedson** later played together again in the **Myths**.

In December 1964, the **Harlems** came back to life with their founders **Vinnie Ismail** (lg/voc) and **Rob Eccles** (bg/voc), together with a new drummer **Johnny Sze**, a long-time friend, who had formerly played with the **Satanists**, the **St. Louis Checks** and the **Memphis Rhythm & Blues Combo**.

This line-up went over to the Star-Club in Hamburg as the backing group for the great Liverpool songstress, **Beryl Marsden** – as such, they sometimes also appeared as the **Blue Boys**.

This association only lasted for a few bookings and when **Beryl Marsden** returned to Liverpool, the **Harlems** continued to play in Hamburg at the famous 'Top Ten' and other clubs until they split up in Spring 1965 when **Robb Eccles** went back to Liverpool to join **Henry's Handful**.

Vinnie Ismail remained in Hamburg and played with the **Top Ten All Stars** for a while but then also returned to Liverpool and became a member of **Henry's Handful**.

Johnny Sze also remained in Hamburg and gigged around with some bands but without becoming a member of any. He then went to Sweden, where he joined the **Cherry Stones** who became the **Kinetic** in 1967 and had a long and very successful residency in France.

Now this normally would have been the end of the **Harlems** story but, in the late Sixties, **Vinnie Ismail** went on to join the **Detours**, a Liverpool group that was active down in London. From there, he became a member of the **Valentinos**, another coloured vocal group hailing from Liverpool and consisting of **Ramon 'Sugar' Dean**, **Tony Fayle**, **Barry Phylburne** and **Lawrence Areety**.

Vinnie Ismail took the place of **Tony Fayle**, who had left the group and sadly died in the 70s. **Vinnie Ismail** was the only member who played an instrument and most probably there was also a bass guitarist and a drummer backing the **Valentinos** but their names are not known.

The Valentinos

In 1970, the group was joined by **Billy Good** (bg) and **Alan Sef** (dr), who came from the recently disbanded **Shufflers Sound**.

Billy Good did not stay for too long and, a little later, joined the newly formed **Lee Curtis & the All-Stars**. Today he is a member of the **Undertakers**. His replacement in the **Valentinos** was most probably **Barry Young**.

It did not take too long until the **Valentinos** disbanded, but **'Sugar' Dean**, **Lawrence Areety** and **Barry Phylburne**, together with **Vinnie Ismail**, re-formed the group in the mid-Seventies under the name of the **Harlems**.

This time they had **Roy Steadman** (bg) and **Kenny Guy** (dr) backing them. **Kenny Guy** was a former member of the **Bonnevilles**, the **Kingbees**, the **Detours** and **Karl Terry & the Cruisers**.

The Harlems

The **Harlems** became very popular once again, particularly on the London scene and under the wings of **Mickey Hayes**, recorded some tracks for Polydor. Unfortunately, they were never released.

Vinnie Ismail left the group, later on he also played with **Karl Terry & the Cruisers** but sadly died in the late Eighties.

The **Harlems** were joined by **Michael Chang** and, in addition to this, **Kenny Guy** was replaced on drums.

This most probably was the line-up that recorded the single, "It takes a fool like me", for **Dick James**' DJM label in 1977. For this **Mitch Hiller** production the group's name was shortened to **Harlem**. Unfortunately, the record was unsuccessful and so the **Harlems** did not record again and broke up in the late Seventies or very early Eighties.

Ramon 'Sugar' Dean and **Lawrence Areety** still perform as solo artists and ex-drummer **Kenny Guy** later played with **Kenny Johnson & Northwind** and is still active on the Country scene.

With this, the second life of the **Harlems** came to an end . . .

Discography

as backing group for **"The Chants"**:

Sweet was the wine / One star	UK- PYE 7N 15691 / 1964

(it could well be possible that the **Harlems** backed the **Chants** also on their other Pye records, but this is not proven.)

as **"Harlem"**:

It takes a fool like me / There I go	UK- DJM DJS 10748 / 1970

THE HERALDS

"Three boys and a girl from the Walton area of Liverpool are making sure that the devil doesn't have all the good tunes".

Based on this opening statement – and what a statement! - from an article in the Liverpool Echo of the 14th April 1967, it can be immediately concluded that the content was about a so-called Gospel Beat-group. In fact, it was about the **Heralds**, which was a very common name for groups in that very special field of music. From other similar stories, it is known, that these types of groups normally grew out of Church communities or even out of Church choirs. However, the **Heralds** from Walton where different, as all of the members were also members of the Salvation Army. In the beginning, the group was a loose connection of young musicians with various changing members or guest-musicians until, in 1964, a steady four-piece line-up emerged and from then onwards appeared under the name of the **Heralds** with:

Gordon Lorenz	(voc/lg)
Gillian Twist	(voc/g/bj)
Geoff Kendall	(bg/voc)
Robert Johnson	(dr/voc)

THE HERALDS

The group worked on a semi-professional basis and, somehow, in addition to their jobs as a shipping-clerk, Inland Revenue tax-officer, salesmen and student of dentistry they found the time to play their music in prisons, youth-clubs, churches, coffee-bars and halls throughout the country. However, their music did not conform to modern arrangements of traditional church-hymns, psalms or sermons. Some of their songs were written by **Gordon Lorenz**, but most of their repertoire featured well known pop numbers from the hit-parade with the **Heralds'** own lyrics added to them. Maybe that was the reason for them being so successful on the scene.

In 1966, the popular evangelist, Dr. Eric Hutchins and his team, took over the 'Liverpool Empire Theatre' for a complete month to promote their 'Merseyside Evangelistic Crusade' and he booked the **Heralds** to play there. During this event, the group also provided the backing for the well-known American gospel singer, **Betty Lou Mills**.

Because of their somewhat unusual style of music, the **Heralds** never made the headlines but, during a weekend-engagement in Birmingham in 1967, an enthusiastic promoter paid for recording time at the local professional studio of Hollick & Taylor. The result of that session was an interesting single with three of the **Heralds'** own compositions, namely "You Say That No One Loves You", "Seeking an Answer" and "Take My Hand, Precious Lord".

This private single did not have a catalogue-number and was mainly sold at the live-appearances of the **Heralds**. Unfortunately, it is sadly not known how long they continued to play on the scene or what happened to the members after the group finally disbanded.

Discography

You Say That No One Loves You / Seeking an Answer /
Take My Hand, Precious Lord   UK- Hollick & Taylor (no number) / **1967**

"Beat music with a religious meaning is our way of bringing home the Gospel to the young people".

Gordon Lorenz / The Heralds - (Liverpool Echo interview, April 1967)

THE HUNTSMEN

In the very early Sixties, two neighbourhood kids, **John Michael Hacket** and **John Kinrade** from Alverstone Road decided to form a group, which ultimately turned out to be the embryonic **Escorts** but they did not have a name at that time. For some unknown reason, it did not work out and **Mike Hacket**, the drummer, left after a few weeks and **John Kinrade** became a member of a group that adopted the name of the **Escorts.**

Shortly after leaving, **Mike Hacket** was in Hessy's music-shop in downtown Liverpool and spotted an advertising-card that said a little known group from the Dovecot/Knotty Ash area of Liverpool was looking for a drummer. He got in touch with them and became a member of **Archie & the Atoms**. Unfortunately, the name of the original **Archie & the Atoms** drummer is not known. Soon after he joined **Archie & the Atoms,** the singer **Archie Moore**, for unknown reasons, decided to leave and disappeared from the scene. Accordingly, the group had to change their name and so **Archie & the Atoms** became the **Huntsmen** in 1962 – in a line up with:

Joe Burns	(voc/lg)
Neil 'Gus' Garland	(rg/voc)
Tommy Kain	(bg/voc)
Mike Hackett	(dr/voc)

The group played a mixture of Rock'n'Roll and Rhythm & Blues and became firm favourites with the local audience. They also started to play the major venues in Liverpool, such as the 'Peppermint Lounge', the 'Downbeat' and the 'Paladin'. They became the resident band at 'Hope Hall' and put on their own shows regularly at the 'Knotty-Ash Village Hall'. Outside of Liverpool city-centre, they had bookings at 'St. John's Hall' in Bootle, the 'Orrell Park Ballroom' and 'St. Luke's Hall' in Crosby and on the Wirral.

In 1963, the **Huntsmen** went into the Kensington-studio of **Percy Phillips** and recorded a three-track demo on acetate. Of that acetate, only their version of "Right string Baby but the wrong yo-yo" is known.

One of their best remembered appearances was at the 'Gala Ballroom' in Norwich, billed as 'Mersey Sound Comes South'. This big ballroom was completely sold out approximately ten minutes after the doors were opened. The **Huntsmen** kept on playing successfully and, in 1964, were joined by **Ray Rees** on saxophone as an additional member. This, of course, resulted in a change in their sound but the **Huntsmen** did not exist for too long after that. In middle of 1964, they called it a day as they were all too involved with their day jobs.

Shortly after the **Huntsmen** broke up, **Tommy Kain** sadly committed suicide. **Joe Burns** became a butcher and **Neil Garland** a photocopier salesman. **Mike Hackett** worked for the 'Liverpool Echo' but he continued to play on the scene under the name of **Mike Stacey** and, as such, became a member of the **Vibrators** from the Wirral – together with **Ray Rees**, who had also joined them around that same time. However, **Mike Hackett**, alias **Mike Stacey,** did not stay for too long and then gave up playing. It is not known for how long **Ray Rees** kept playing with the **Vibrators** or what happened to him after that.

Discography

Right String But The Wrong Yo-Yo / + 2 others   UK- Phillips Kensington acetate / 1963

IAN & THE REBELS

It was in 1963 that three youngsters formed a trio under the name of the **Nightriders** at the St. Anne's Youth Club in Ormskirk – on the outskirts of Liverpool.

The Nightriders

They almost exclusively played at this club, where they supported other Liverpool groups.

Roy Smith, **Keith Hubbard** and **Chris Kenny** basically played **Shadows** music and the only vocal number that is remembered was "My Bonnie".

In 1964, they became a five-piece and the name of the group was changed to **Ian & the Rebels** – they now consisted of the following line-up:

Ian Gregson	(voc)
Keith Hubbard	(lg/voc)
Roy Smith	(rg/voc)
Derek Brough	(bg)
Chris Kenny	(dr)

All group members were newcomers on the scene but very soon started to make regular appearances at the well-known venues including the 'Cavern', the Orrell Park Ballroom and St. John's Hall. Besides this they also played the venues in nearby Southport.

Ian & the Rebels became very popular locally and really started to build up a good name for themselves, with many bookings throughout Merseyside.

In 1964, before the group had made any real progress, **Ian Gregson** took a job as a sales representative. Unfortunately, as the job required an extensive amount of travel he decided to leave the group and quit the music business.

Initially, there was no replacement for him and the **Rebels** continued as a four piece with **Roy Smith** taking over the lead vocals.

Ian and the Rebels

Also in 1964, they made their first recording with the original "Only time can tell", written by **Derek Crumbleholme**, at that time bass guitarist with the **Jokers**. The recording was made on an acetate at the Deroy Studios in Hest Bank, Lancaster.

After that the group found a new singer in **Derek Banks**, better known as **Ricky Gleason** of **Ricky Gleason & the Topspots** fame.

The Rebels continued quite successfully on the scene but at the end of 1965 **Ricky Gleason** left because of problems with their management. He became a member of the **Renicks** and after that he quit singing for more than 40 years.

Besides him **Derek Brough** also left the group in 1964 and disappeared from the scene.

The new members of the **Rebels** were **Alan Grundy** (voc), formerly known as **J.J.** of **J.J. & the Hi-Lites**, who evolved into the **Mersey Monsters** and **Kelvin Harrison** on bass guitar, who also came from the **Mersey Monsters** and prior to that he had played with **Tommy & the Satellites** and **Ricky Gleason & the Topspots**.

In 1966, drummer **Chris Kenny** had to leave due to illness and his replacement was **Roy David**, who came from the **St. Louis Checks**. In this line-up, the **Rebels** continued until 1967 and then disbanded totally without having recorded any more songs.

Of **Roy David** it is known that he joined the **Richmond**, while **Kelvin Harrison** emigrated to Canada and **Alan Grundy** emigrated to Australia. **Keith Hubbard** and **Roy Smith** gigged around the local clubs but without joining another group.

In 1969, **Keith Hubbard** secured a part in the Rock musical 'Hair', touring throughout the UK until May 1971.

After his return to Merseyside, he contacted his old comrades **Roy Smith** and **Chris Kenny**, who in the meantime had recovered from his illness. Together with bassist **Ray Chapman**, the three original members of the **Rebels** formed a group under the name of **Caliban**.

They successfully toured Denmark and regularly appeared at the Liverpool venues including the 'Victoriana' and the 'Cavern', where they were the last group ever to play, when this famous club was finally closed down on 27 May 1973. **Caliban** continued successfully on the scene until 1975 and then broke up.

Keith Hubbard played with the hit-group **Chicory Tip** for some time and then returned to **Caliban**, who had re-formed in the meantime and which in various line-ups existed until 1981.

After that **Keith Hubbard** formed the group **Shooter**, which is still going strong on the scene. In addition, he is also a member of the newly re-formed **Ricky Gleason & the Topspots**, together with former **Rebels** members **Kelvin Harrison** and, of course, **Ricky Gleason**.

The line-up also includes, **Tommy Limb** and **Keith Dodd** of the 60's line-up of **Ricky Gleason & the Topspots**.

It appears that all the other members of the **Nightriders** or the **Rebels** quit showbiz.

Discography

as "The Rebels":

Only time can tell	UK – Deroy acetate / 1964

THE INFORMERS

Another phenomenon that grew up at the side of Liverpool's commercial Merseybeat was the so-called 'Gospel-Beat Scene'. Young committed Christians, infected by the beat, formed groups within their church-communities and started to play traditional church hymns in typical beat-rhythm and, through that, shared their faith with others in a modern way. One such group was the **Informers** who were founded in 1963 in the old 'Brethren Chapel' in Mill Lane, the West Derby district of Liverpool, originally called 'Olive Hall'. The group from the beginning consisted of the following musicians:

Phil Young	(lg/voc)
Maurice Lee	(rg/voc)
Harry Reynolds	(bg)
Lew Eccleshall	(dr)

All members were newcomers to the scene and, at first, they rehearsed in the lead-guitarist parent's house but, on occasions, they were also allowed to use an old converted room above their church, which was used by the youth of the church and surrounding neighbourhood as a coffee-bar. In addition, a friend from Anfield, a skilled electrical engineer, had built their amplifiers and speaker cabinets at a very inexpensive cost. In their early days, the **Informers** were also supported by **Tom Cooper**, the organist of 'St. Leonard's' church in Bootle, home of the **Crossbeats**, who were certainly the most successful group of the Gospel-Beat scene, which was thriving on Merseyside at that time.

The **Informers** started to play the usual youth-clubs and coffee-bars of the scene – such as the 'Drawbridge' in Birkenhead, the 'Maranatha Coffee Bar' in Liverpool and they were also featured in the popular 'Children's Christian Crusade', run by evangelist **Ralph Chambers** at his 'Number One Gospel Disco'. **The Informers** improved their musicianship, gained experience, built up a good name for themselves and soon had bookings all over the North of England such as the 'Mustard Seed' in Sheffield, the 'Fishnet' in Stourbridge, the 'Session' in Chester and the legendary 'Catacombs' in Manchester, a very popular Christian venue that attracted large crowds of young people at that time. The group-members had also started to write their own religious songs, which would turn out to be advantageous for them a little later on.

In the interim, **Harry Reynolds** had left the group, got married and moved to Bristol. His replacement in the **Informers** was **Bill Scowcroft**, also a newcomer to the scene. Their ever increasing catalogue of songs at that time included well-known Christian songs and cover-versions of other Christian bands but also quite a few of their own compositions.

However, **Bill Scowcroft** left the group in 1969 and he was replaced by **Derek Christoffer**, who was already known by the band-members as the former bass-guitarist of another Christian group called **His Servants**.

The **Informers** continued successfully on the scene and took part in a major Christian concert, the 'Beat Capital 70' in Liverpool's 'Philharmonic Hall' alongside other acts like the **Crossbeats**, **Time Ltd.** and **Trinity Folk.** After that concert, the **Informers** finally went into the studios of **Charly Weston** in Moorfields to make a recording on the CAM-label. For that

recording, they chose their own compositions "Jennifer" and "Looking". Both songs were written years previously and, over the time, had become favourites with the audiences. "Jennifer" on the A-side was a fairly upbeat song with interesting changes in the tempo and "Looking" was a gentler, rhythmical track. Both were 'Merseybeatish' sounding songs with great singing, featuring **Phil Young** on lead-vocals and a very strong support by **Maurice Lee**. There were only 99 copies made of this record (100 copies or more were subject to tax in those days)

"The Informers" a gospel beat group from Liverpool who entertained teenagers at St. Philip's Hall, Common Road, on Friday. They are (left to right) Phil Young, Lou Eccleston, Maurice Lee and Harry Reynolds.

and, in no way could that recording ever have become a commercial success – especially not as the sales-price was set at 48 Pence.

The **Informers** continued in that line-up until the mid-Seventies and then they added two girls to their act with **Shirley Ward** (voc/g) and **Anne Fullerton** (voc). This did not last for too long and, when **Shirley Ward** left, the group changed its name to **Sound Advice**. In the mid-Eighties, **Derek Christoffer** left and later on became a member of a gospel-group (probably from Maghull) called the **Believers**. At that time, **Phil Young** took over the bass-guitar and **Sound Advice** continued as a quartet. In order to be accepted by commercial Merseyside booking-agents, the band-members had decided to add commercial songs to their programme and the agreement reached between the agents and the band was that the musicians were allowed to play the first set of every gig using their Gospel material, whilst any subsequent sets would be of wider known commercial songs. As such, **Sound Advice** continued to play the scene until they finally disbanded in the early Nineties.

Discography:

The Informers:

Jennifer / Looking   UK-Cam 300 / 1971

> *"It must be said that the creation of such a 'modern' band in the early Sixties was quite revolutionary and it was never supported 100 % by the elders of the church.*
>
> *Some of them frowned upon the Merseybeat music-scene as they believed 'the drums were of the devil'*
>
> **Lew Eccleshall / The Informers**

THE IN CROWD

This is the group that is very often described by other Merseybeat musicians as the best vocal harmony outfit that ever came out of Liverpool. Even if the **In Crowd** never made it big, in their hometown they became a real legend.

Their story goes back to 1958 when the **Casuals** were formed in the Brownlow Hill area of Liverpool by **Walter Quarles** (lg/voc), **George Dixon** (voc/bg) and **Norman Frazer** (dr/voc).

It is said that **Colin Areety** (voc) was also a temporary member of the **Casuals**. If so, this would have been his first group, he then joined the **Conquests**.

The **Casuals** became the resident group at the White House in Duke Street, where they played every weekend, from Friday to Monday.

When they broke up, **George Dixon** and **Walter Quarles** formed the **Takarady Allstars**, who, in 1960, changed their name to the **In Crowd** and consisted of:

George Dixon	(voc/bg)
Walter Quarles	(lg/voc)
Gerry Stewart	(sax)
Dave Stead	(dr/voc)

Gerry Stewart and **Dave Stead** were both former members of the **Black Cats** or **Benny & the Black Cats**, as they were originally known.

The In Crowd

The **In Crowd** were the resident group at the Masonic pub on Renshaw street. In addition, they frequently played at the very popular downtown Locarno Ballroom. As a result, they soon caught the attention and admiration of the Liverpool musicians because of their perfectionism.

In early 1962, the **In Crowd** also obtained an engagement to play the American military bases in Greece and Turkey!

The group apparently broke up in early 1964 when **Gerry Stewart** left to join the **Mastersounds**, who soon changed their name to the **Bluesville Bats**. After that, he was also a member of the **Faces**, an offshoot of the **Bluesville Bats**. He later emigrated to Canada, where he is still living.

Walter Quarles formed the **Walter Quarles Combo**, which also may have included **George Dixon**, but that could not be confirmed.

However, the **In Crowd** came back to life in 1965 when **George Dixon** and **Walter Quarles** re-formed the group together with **Tony Fayle** (voc) and **John Carney** (dr). **John Carney** was very soon replaced by **Little Tony Adams** on drums, who was also an extremely good singer.

Steve Aldo (aka Edward Bedford)

It was probably in 1967 that **Tony Fayle** left to join the **Valentinos**, another great coloured harmony group from Liverpool. His replacement was **Eddie Bedford** (sometimes reported as **Eddie Berrisford**), who had adopted the stage name **Steve Aldo.** He was a former member of the **Challengers**. He also had a short stint with **King Size Taylor & the Dominoes** (in Hamburg). After he returned to Liverpool, he was a member of the **Nocturns**, the **Griff Parry Five**, the **Steve Aldo Quartet**, the **Krew** and the **Fix**.

The group was signed to the Deram label and their only record, "Where In The World", was released in 1969. It is not known if **Steve Aldo** was the singer on that record as he left the **In Crowd** in 1969.

His replacement was **Tommy Brown**, who was the predecessor of **Tony Fayle** in the **Valentinos** and who, in the meantime, had sung with the **Almost Blues**. Furthermore, **Colin Areety** joined them as an additional vocalist, he had previously sung with the **Almost Blues**, the **Dennisons**, the **Fix** and the **Michael Henri Group**. A little later, **George Dixon** decided to take a break from the music business and he was replaced by **Tony Lawrence**.

This line-up of the **In Crowd** apparently stayed together until late 1971 and then disbanded. **Colin Areety** started a successful solo career and, in 1972 and 1973, had four singles out on the RCA and Deram labels of which "Holy cow" was his best and most successful record. His backing group on "Holy Cow" was the **Olympic Runners.**

In 1971, **George Dixon** stepped back into the music scene as a member of **Just Us**, a group that, in addition to his former drummer **Dave Stead,** also included **Kenny Ross** and **Willy Wenton**. This group was successful on the local scene until it spit up in the middle of the Seventies.

Discography

There was never any official record released by the **In Crowd**, but according to a statement by **George Dixon**, there were recordings made in about 1967, when **Steve Aldo** was with them. Unfortunately, no further details could be found and no official releases are known.

The In Crowd

Where in the world / I can love you too	UK—Deram DM 272 / 1969

Colin Areety – solo

Dancing child / All for you	UK – RCA 2078 / 1971
Poco Joe / To give all your love away	UK – Deram DM 360 / 1972
Holy cow / I can't do it for you	UK – Deram DM 370 / 1972
(If loving you is wrong) I don't want to be right / One night affair	UK – Deram DM 383 / 1973

'J' & THE JUNIORS

Sometimes presented with the wrong spelling of **Jay & the Juniors**, this group was formed in late 1962 in the Everton area of Liverpool. As it seems, the driving force behind the formation was **Alf Snape**, who became the manager of the group and was also the father of **Jimmy Snape** the lead vocalist. In January 1963, **'J' & the Juniors** started to play the local clubs in a line-up with:

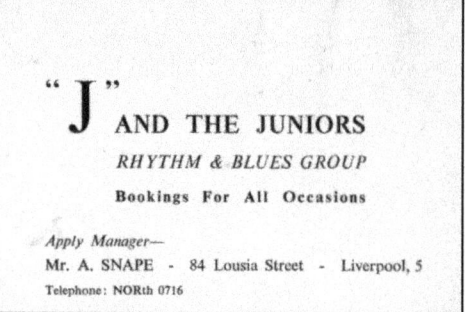

'J' Jimmy Snape	(voc)
Alan Hanson	(lg)
Tommy Lovell	(rg)
Ted Barry	(bg)
Frank Corke	(dr)

With the exception of **Tommy Lovell**, who was 20, all the other members were only 16 years old and, most probably, all newcomers to the scene. Regardless, **'J' & the Juniors** did not waste any time and, it was probably towards the end of 1963 that they went into the Kensington studio of **Percy Phillips** to record a one-sided acetate with the song "Mister Moonlight" that, shortly before, had been released by the **Merseybeats** on the B-side of their single, "I think of you". This acetate was probably

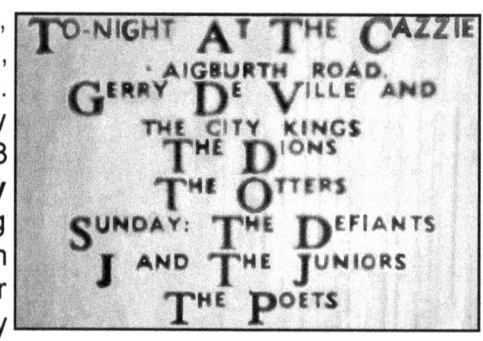

used as a demo to get them bookings and it obviously worked, as the group soon started to perform at some of the major Liverpool venues.

In early 1964, **Frank Corke** temporarily left **'J' & the Juniors** when he replaced **Robert Ninnim**, who did not want to go to London with his group the **Easybeats**. So, **Frank Corke** went to London in his place and it was most probably during their extended stay in London that they recorded as the **Dealers** for the Ponte & Oates agency. However, when the **Easybeats** returned to Liverpool in May 1964, **Robert Ninnim** took his old place in the **Easybeats** and **Frank Corke** returned to **'J' & the Juniors** who, in the interim, had probably gigged with a stand-in drummer, but this could not be confirmed.

In June 1964, **'J' & the Juniors** had their first appearance at the 'Cavern' but, as it seems the group did not exist for too long after that, as also in 1964 **Alan Hanson** left to become a member of the **Aztecs** and later he played with **Becket's Kin**. Furthermore, it appears that **Frank Corke** also returned to the **Easybeats** sometime in 1964, where he played until that group broke up in 1968. **Jimmy Snape**, **Tommy Lovell** and **Ted Barry** disappeared from the scene and so it can be said that **'J' & the Juniors** only had a short career but left behind an interesting acetate, that hopefully will be dug out by one of the reissue-labels someday.

Discography:

Mister Moonlight　　　　　　　　UK- one-sided Phillips, Kensington acetate / 1963

THE JACOBEATS

It was 1957 and **Joe O'Shaugnessy** was playing guitar and banjo together with his older brother **Maurice O'Shaugnessy** in the **Cavendish Skifflers**, a group that had already played the 'Cavern' a few times.

They had taken the name from the road where they lived in Crosby and a neighbour **Malcolm Nixon**, who lived across the road and was also learning to play the guitar, would always go over and listen to them practising.

When the Skiffle days came to an end, **Joe O'Shaugnessy**, together with work colleagues from the Bootle tax office, formed a Rock 'n' Roll group and in 1962 (that neighbour) **Malcolm Nixon** was asked to join.

Beside **Joe O'Shaugnessy** and **Malcolm Nixon** the group consisted of **Alan Price** (bg) and **Bruce Cherry** (dr).

On their first public appearance at a wedding reception in a church hall in Waterloo, a friend of **Malcolm Nixon** stood in for the **Alan Price** and stayed with the group.

Very soon after that, **Bruce Cherry** was also replaced and the four-piece group now continued as the **Jacobeats** in a line-up with:

Joe O'Shaughnessy	(voc/rg)
Malcolm Nixon	(voc/lg)
Chris Horne	(bg/voc)
Dave Harrison	(dr)

The Jacobeats at the Cavern

Dave Harrison originally hailed from a place called Peaceheaven, near Brighton in the south of England and, through his job as a slot machine engineer, he had ended up in Liverpool. He apparently had played in groups in the Brighton scene previously but, unfortunately, no further details are known.

The **Jacobeats** now played covers of the popular Rock 'n' Roll and Rhythm & Blues numbers such as "Little Queenie", "Hoochie Coochie Man", "Can I get a witness", "Pretend" and "The fool", mixed with topical pop and beat numbers. They soon started to play the club circuit in Liverpool, appearing at the 'Downbeat', 'Cavern' and 'Mardi Gras', as well as the 'Jive Hive' in Crosby and places in nearby Southport.

Occasionally, they also played at Country & Western clubs under the name of the **Arkansas Travellers**, where **Joe O'Shaugnessy** then switched from guitar to banjo.

Peter G. Denton, a Londoner, who had relocated to Liverpool, signed the **Jacobeats** to his management stable, in addition to the **Reasons** from Widnes (?) and the **Trolls** from the Old Swan area.

At an appearance at the Formby Ice Rink, he arranged a full live set of the **Jacobeats** to be recorded by a mobile unit. Four songs of this were cut onto an acetate at the Lambda studios in Crosby.

With the exception of the **Tommy Tucker** song, "Hi-heel sneakers" and **Rufus Thomas**' classic "Walking the dog", the other two songs on this acetate cannot be recalled.

As **Dave Harrison** regularly travelled to Brighton to visit his parents, he contacted some of the local clubs there and the **Jacobeats**' 'Cavern'-connection proved to be useful in getting some gigs, which were also quite well paid.

On their first trip to Brighton, the group played on the bill with the **Unit Four plus Two**, who had just had a big hit with "Concrete and clay". The **Jacobeats** went down well and subsequently took regular weekend trips to play in Brighton.

In August 1964, their manager, **Peter Denton,** recruited two 'extra' members for the group, a female vocalist **Carmen De Sousa** and a Blues singer and harmonica player called **'Mitch'**.

At one of their gigs that included the additional members, **Peter Denton** brought along an individual who offered the group a contract to play the famous 'Star-Club' in Hamburg. However, as none of the musicians wanted to leave their jobs, they declined the offer, much to the annoyance of **Peter Denton** who, from that time on, lost interest in the **Jacobeats** and did very little to promote them.

The Jacobeats with 'Mitch" and Carmen De Sousa

Chris Horne decided to leave as he wanted to go to sea and he later emigrated to South Africa, where he is still living with his family.

His replacement was a certain **'Steve'**, whose surname is not known and, for a short time, **Brian Crummey** joined as an additional singer and guitarist. **Brian Crummey** by the way is the brother of **Searchers** drummer **Chris Curtis**.

At this time, the **Jacobeats** appeared regularly at the 'Cherry Tree' in Runcorn, the 'Fareways' in Wrexham and they also became the resident group at the Park Hotel in Netherton.

In 1965, **Dave Harrison** had to leave the group for job related reasons and **Martin Sawyer** joined as the new drummer for the **Jacobeats**.

This line-up continued until May 1966 and broke up when **Joe O'Shaughnessy** and **Malcolm Nixon** both left to get married.

The Jacobeats at the Cherry Tree (Runcorn)

The Jacobeats (Sturlas Store Dance 1964)

In 1990, **Joe O'Shaugnessy** emigrated to Northern Ireland, where he is still living and until 2008 he played the local pubs as part of a duo, as well as performing solo.

In 1969, **Malcolm Nixon** teamed up again with **Dave Harrison**, who had returned to Liverpool. They initially performed as a duo, then added a bass guitarist and as a trio became resident at the 'Nile' club in Liverpool.

When **Malcolm Nixon** moved to Hindley, he became a member of the resident group at the 'Miners Club' in Leigh. In this band he met up with **Terry Knowles** and they decided to continue as a duo on the cabaret scene under the name of the **Malter Brothers**. They became very popular on the northern scene and at one point they were awarded the 'Best Comedy Duo' in Manchester.

The **Malter Brothers** played the cabaret scene until 1990 and called it a day when, as a result of an accident, **Terry Knowles** had to quit. **Malcolm Nixon** then continued on as a solo performer for a couple of years.

It is known, that in 1969, **Dave Harrison** became associated with remaining members of the **Kirkbys** or **23rd Turnoff**, as they were called at that time. This new group, under the name the **Clique,** successfully played the northwest circuit for some time, before evolving into the recording-group **Rockin' Horse**. Although not included on their records, **Dave Harrison** also played with **Rockin' Horse** when they backed **Chuck Berry** on his 1970 British tour and TV appearances.

After that, **Dave Harrison** continued to play with pick-up groups, but sadly died in 2002.

Discography

Hi-Heel sneakers / Walking the dog + 2   UK – Lambda acetate / 1964

(A full live set of the **Jacobeats** was recorded at the Formby Ice Rink in 1964, of which four songs were cut on an acetate. Unfortunately, two of the songs on this acetate are not known).

THE ROGER JAMES FOUR

This story is in some way is the continuation of the 'lifeline' of the **Prestons.** (For the complete story of the **Prestons** please see the book *"Mersey Beat Waves" - ISBN 1588502015 or 9781588502018).*

To follow the highly interesting story of this group, it might be the best to document the path of group leader **Roger Scarrott**, who adopted the stage name **Roger James**.

He had started his career as a solo singer/guitarist and songwriter and was signed to the **Reg Calvert** management stable in the early Sixties.

In 1962, his manager put him together with singer **Danny Storm's** backing group, where he played lead guitar on the chart success "Honest I do" in the same year.

Roger James became a steady member of **Danny Storm & the Strollers** but, in 1962, he parted from them and became **Robby Hood** of **Robby Hood & the Merrymen**, who played a 3-month season at the famous 'Top Ten' Club in Hamburg. Besides himself, **Robby Hood & the Merrymen** consisted of **Pete Mist** (bg) and **Tony Burnette** (dr) of the **Strollers**, the future **Fortunes** member, **Glen Dale** (voc) and **Roy Young**, who remained in Germany as the resident keyboarder at the 'Top Ten'. In addition, he often played with **Tony Sheridan** and later formed the **Roy Young Band**.

Robby Hood & the Merrymen

After his return to England, **Roger James** first worked as a DJ but then had a short stint with **Eddie King & the Chequers** from the Hayes, Middlesex area of London, before he became a member of the **Johnny Woolaston Band**, which was resident at the Top Rank Ballroom in Preston, Lancashire.

During his stay there, he met some local musicians and, with them, he formed the **Prestons**, who went down to London for a recording session with **Joe Meek**. All the songs recorded were **Roger James** originals but, unfortunately, none of them were ever released.

The **Prestons** became very popular in their hometown as well as in Liverpool and the surrounding area. In addition, they often accepted bookings down in London.

It was at one of these London gigs at the Dorchester Hotel in 1964 that **Roger James** decided to part from his old mates, who then immediately disbanded.

Roger James formed a new line-up and they initially continued under the name of the **Prestons** and when, still in 1964, they got an offer to record with the female vocalist **Beverly Jones**, they also used that name for the recording. Accordingly, the single "Heat wave", coupled with the **Roger James** original "Hear you talking" on the Parlophone label was credited to **Beverly Jones & the Prestons**. This record, made under the guidance of **Hollies** producer **Ron Richards**, sold quite well but did not get near the charts.

Apparently, it was right after this that the group changed their name and became the **Roger James Four** – in a line-up with

Roger James	(voc/lg)
Paul Edmonds-Riley	(org/p/voc)
Bill Stanley	(bg/voc)
Howard Tibble	(dr/voc)

Beverly Jones

The Roger James Four

Paul Edmonds-Riley, **Bill Stanley** and **Howard Tibble** were former members of **Pat Richards & the Diamonds** who had appeared on the same bill as the **Prestons** at the Dorchester Hotel. **Harry Stanley**, the father of the bass guitarist, became their manager.

The group played throughout England and their manager not only booked them into the top clubs in the north but also introduced them to the well-known producer, **Norrie Paramor**, who was very impressed with them and secured a recording contract with Columbia.

1965 saw their first single released as the **Roger James Four** with "A letter from Kathy", a nice ballad, which was coupled with the much better Merseybeat number "Leave me alone".

Both songs were written by **Roger James** and the record sold very well, not the least due to the promotion it received at Butlin's Holiday Camp in Bognor Regis, where the group played the full summer season.

Their follow-up single in 1966, the **Roger James** original, "Better than here", also had a great song "You're gonna come home cryin' " on the B-side.

In 1967, **Roger James** accepted an offer to do session work for **P. J. Proby** and played lead guitar in his band at a show at the 'Wooky Hollow Club' in Liverpool.

Also in 1967, when female vocalist **Clare Torry** recorded some of her original numbers, she was backed by the **Roger James Four.** The song, "The music attracts me", was released as a single on Fontana in the same year but the group was not given any credit on it, and only **Reg Tilsley**, who was responsible for the brass/orchestral arrangement, was credited. **Clare Torry** later became popular when she sang on the **Pink Floyd** success "Dark side of the moon".

In addition to this, the **Roger James Four** recorded various songs for HMV, but none of them were ever released on record.

In spite of this, the **Roger James Four** apparently existed very well in the professional music business until **Paul Edmonds-Riley** left to join a group called **Harlem Shuffle**. He later emigrated to France, where he is still living today.

The group continued as a trio and accordingly had to change their name – they became the **Hobby Shop**.

It took until 1968 before their next record was released with "Why must it be this way", which had a more of a psychedelic sound. Again, it was a very good record, but it had no chart success.

Howard Tibble left the **Hobby Shop** and joined **Noell Doren's** resident 10-piece band at the Galtymore Irish Pub in Cricklewood, London where he played for 10 years. He then formed a 'hard rock' group called **Max** together with their singer **Max Sinclair** and his old mate **Bill Stanley**, but that this did not last for too long.

Howard Tibble was spotted by **Dave Travis**, who got him into the **Rockerbilly Killers**, who toured throughout Europe, backing a lot of the 50's Rockabilly stars. **Howard Tibble** was then asked to play a session with **Shakin' Stevens** and he got a steady job in Shaky's group, where he is still playing.

But, back to 1969, when the **Hobby Shop** broke up, **Roger James** went solo for some time and was signed to the NEMS label, where he released two interesting singles with "Faces and places" and "If I didn't have you". After that, he became a radio presenter and did a lot of session work for producers such as **Tim Rice** and **Les Reed**.

In 1973, **Les Reed** also produced the **Roger James** solo album "Riding Free" on Chapter One (CHS 807), from which the songs "The return/Lauretta", "Gold/Something's wonderful" and "Riding free/Lauretta" were coupled out as singles.

When these did not become hits **Roger James** teamed up with **Bill Stanley** again and they were joined by **Doug Perry** (rg/voc) and **Terry Doe** (dr/voc). Being a four-piece they could have switched back to their old name, but decided on the **Roger James Group**.

In 1974, they were featured on the Country sampler "Up Country", which was released on the BBC label (Rec 179), with the songs "She's leaving me again", "I wonder if she'll sometimes think of me", "It took someone like you" (all written by **Roger James**) and the **Johnny Tillotson** number "Out of my mind over you".

Obviously, from these sessions the single "The little orphan boy/She's leaving me again" was also released on BBC Records, but it was probably not too long after that the **Roger James Group** broke up.

Bill Stanley went to play with **Noell Doren's Band**, where he met up with **Howard Tibble** again. **Roger James** and **Doug Perry** also had a stint with them.

Bill Stanley was then a member of **Max**, a group that had evolved from the Irish band and also included **Howard Tibble** (see above).

Doug Perry became the main booking agent for the **Joe Loss Orchestra** but also kept on playing at the same time. He sadly died of a heart attack a few years ago.

Bill Stanley later continued working with **Roger James** and then joined a Country outfit called **Christine & the Cachina Band**. He stayed with that group for some years and they played throughout England and ended up in Dubai. After that, he became a member of **Noel Dillon & the Foster Boys**, another Country group that also toured the USA.

He then stopped playing in groups but he still works with **Roger James** sometimes, who continues to be successful on the scene as a solo performer.

Discography

Beverly Jones & the Prestons:

Heat Wave / Hear you talking	UK-Parlophone R 5189 / 1964

The Roger James Four:

Letter from Kathy / Leave me alone	UK - Columbia DB 7556 / 1965
Better than here / You're gonna come home cryin'	UK - Columbia DB 7829 / 1966

as backing-group for **Clare Torry** (not named on the label):

The music attracts me	UK-Fontana 267738 TF / 1967

The Hobby Shop:

Why must it be this way / Talk to me	UK - Columbia DB 8395 / 1968

Roger James – solo:

If I didn't have you / I know it's love	UK – Nems 56-3719 / 1969
Faces and places / If you try	UK - Nems 56-3972 / 1969

(for further solo recordings by **Roger James** or the **Roger James Group** – see text)

Unreleased tracks as **The Roger James Four**:

That's When It Hurts Me / Not Another Day / I Owe It All To You / Don't You Care / Dum Diddy Dum / Don't You Worry / La La La	Various acetates / all 1964

THE JENSONS

Two boy-scout friends from the Litherland-Bootle area of Liverpool formed this group in 1962. The **Jensons**, as they were named from the start, played a mixture of Beat and Blues.

Their first booking was for a wedding reception party in Bootle but, as they gained more experience, they appeared regularly at the local youth-clubs and in places such as 'St. John's Hall' in Bootle, the 'Winter Gardens' in Waterloo, the 'Orrell Park Ballroom' and the 'Jive Hive' (St. Luke's) in Crosby, where they were spotted by **Dave Forshaw**, who became their booking-agent, along with **Doug Martin** of 'Ivamar Promotions'.

Original Lineup - L to R: Alan Jones, Tommy Gordon, Pat Martin, Larry?

In their original line-up, the group consisted of **Tommy Gordon** (voc/rg), **Larry ???** (lg), **Alan Jones** (bg) and **Patrick Martin** (dr), whereby only of **Alan Jones** is it known that he formerly had played with the **Mikados**. A great boost for this young group was when promoter **Brian Kelly** engaged them to play at 'Litherland Town Hall' on the same bill with American Blues star **Sonny Boy Williamson**. The lead guitarist **Larry**, whose surname was sadly lost with the passing of time, was replaced by **John Jones** after approximately six months and, soon after this, **Tommy Gordon** put the guitar aside and stepped in front as their vocalist. **John Bancroft** came in as new rhythm guitarist, he had formerly been a member of the **Tuxedos** from Crosby, **Rikki & the Red Streaks**, the **Memphis Three** and the **Black Velvets**. At that time, another memorable gig came up for the **Jensons** when they appeared on the same bill with **Jerry Lee Lewis** at the 'Heaven & Hell' club in Warrington.

John Bancroft did not stay for too long, he joined the re-formed **Memphis Three** and then switched to organ and played with the **Soul Seekers** before he finally became a member of **Chapter Six**. Shortly after their new rhythm guitarist **John Edwards** joined them, **Tommy Gordon** left and, a little later, formed a new group under the name of the **Exit**. Following all these changes, the **Jensons** now appeared in the following line-up:

John Jones	(lg/voc)
John Edwards	(rg/voc)
Alan Jones	(bg/voc)
Patrick Martin	(dr/voc)

'Maggie May's'
L to R: Pat Martin, Alan Jones, John Jones, John Edwards

The former groups of **John Jones** and **John Edwards** are not known and as there was no lead-singer, all the members now shared the vocals.

The **Jensons** became quite popular and accordingly they also started to play regularly at the well-known clubs in Liverpool's city-centre, such as the 'Cavern', the 'Iron Door', the 'Mardi Gras', the 'Peppermint Lounge', the 'Temple Bar' and the 'Blue Angel'. **Dave Forshaw** got them many bookings that stretched as far as from the 'Klic-Klic' in Southport to 'Quantways' in Chester and even some venues in Wales.

It was only logical that the next step would be to make a recording and so, in early 1965, the **Jensons** booked into the Cavern Artist studio and recorded the songs "Gin House" and "See See Rider" on acetate. Unfortunately, this interesting recording did not help the **Jensons** as they disbanded totally in May 1965 when, at first, **Alan Jones** decided to join the **Exit** and he very soon was followed to that same group by **John Edwards**. After that, both were members of the **J.B. Almont Scene** that soon changed its name into the **Whole Scene**.

What happened to **John Jones** is sadly not known but it can be taken for sure that he kept active on the scene. **Patrick Martin,** at that time, joined the **Mersey Gonks** that, after a name-change to the **Pitiful** in the second half of the Sixties, developed into **Chapter Six**, where he met up with **Alan Jones** again, who came from the recently disbanded **Exit**. When **Chapter Six** broke up in the early Seventies, **Patrick Martin** played in a cabaret-trio called **Chapter Three**, where he met up again with **John Edwards,** his old comrade from the **Jensons**. After that, **Alan Jones** was a member of **Silverwing**, another cabaret-trio that had evolved from **Chapter Six**.

Discography:

Gin House / See See Rider   UK-   Cavern Artists acetate / 1965

THE KARACTERS

Four friends from Birkenhead who, after they went swimming at the 'Derby Pool' swimming-baths in Wallasey, would go to the 'Kraal' coffee-club on the Mersey riverfront in New Brighton to watch the live-performances of the **Pressmen**. These performances fuelled their musical enthusiasm and they became more and more obsessed about forming a group themselves. That was in 1960, but unfortunately none of them could play an instrument except **John Ellison** who could play some piano, so it was not off to a promising start.

The boys held on to their dream, learned to play their instruments, rehearsed and, finally in July 1961, had their debut-appearance as **Jenny & the Tall Boys** at the 'Kraal' club fronted by vocalist **Jenny Ellison**, who was the sister of **John Ellison**. The group was going quite well and they had built up a following on the scene until, for unknown reasons in March 1963, **Jenny Ellison** decided to leave them. However, as the **Tall Boys** did not want to call it quits, they asked two of their loyal female followers if they wanted to join as singers. They did, and accordingly, one month later, it was time for a name-change as with two attractive girl vocalists now fronting the group, there was no way to go on as the **Tall Boys**. So they became the **Karacters** in the line-up with:

Beverly Frazer	(voc)
Myra Grayson	(voc)
John Ellison	(lg/voc)
Ray Hughes	(rg)
Peter Byrom	(bg)
Keith Murray	(dr)

MYRA GRAYSON and BEVERLEY FRAZER of THE KARACTERS

The voices of **Myra Grayson** and **Beverley Frazer** who, by the way was the daughter of English diving-pioneer and recipient of the Victoria Cross, Sir Edward Frazer, harmonized from the very first moment and so, other than lacking the stage experience, there were absolutely no problems. The **Karacters** also took a chance on their sound being different to other groups and concentrated on the **Phil Spector** sounds of the **Crystals**, the **Ronettes** and **Bob B. Soxx & the Blue Jeans**, and also on material of the **Chiffons** and even the **Everly Brothers**. They soon became an attraction on the scene and were performing as many as five nights a week in places such as the 'Savoy' in Waterloo, the 'Casino Ballroom' in Leigh, the 'Empress' in Wigan, the 'Plaza' in St. Helens and the 'Kings R&B Club' in Little Sutton. Also, in the city-centre of Liverpool they were a high demand group with appearances at all the popular venues such as the 'Cavern', the 'Teenbeat' and they were also regulars at the 'Iron Door' and the

'Peppermint Lounge'. Another distinctive feature of the **Karacters** was that they travelled to their gigs in a 1932 Rolls Royce hearse, which they had converted in something like a van. This had a certain style and later on it was copied by other Merseybeat groups for publicity reasons.

In early 1964, the **Karacters** did some home-recordings of the titles, "Why do lovers break each other's hearts" and "Then he kissed me", obviously, they were cut in acetate. Both numbers show clearly the quality and the harmony of the group. **George Blood** of the 'Peppermint Lounge' wanted them to become professionals and offered to be their manager. This was rejected by the musicians, who preferred to remain semi-professional just gigging around the scene in Liverpool and Lancashire. Unfortunately, it was not long after that they disbanded because the majority of them had full-time jobs and they did not see any great chance for a showbiz career. It also appears that **John Ellison** had left sometime previous as a, then current, newspaper-article about the group only mentioned the other three musicians and the female singers.

The Karacters are a group who have something special to attract the male element in audiences—two beautiful girl vocalists. Yes, Keith Murray, Peter Byrom and Ray Hugh provide the musical backing and the attraction to girls— but the boys are delighted when 16-years-old Myra Grayson and 17-years-old Beverley Fraser take the stage.

Regardless, on the 27th June 1964, the **Karacters** held their farewell performance at the 'Aldershot High School'. That was the end of the group and none of the members ever appeared on the scene again.

Of **John Ellison** it is known that he went to live in Menorca in Spain while **Ray Hughes** moved to Milton Keynes and **Peter Byrom** emigrated to Vancouver, Canada, where he lived for many years before returning to the Wirral. What happened to **Keith Murray** is, unfortunately, not known. **Beverley Frazer** and **Myra Grayson** never got up to sing on stage again and, sadly, **Beverley Frazer** died quite some time ago. In the end, it can be said that, despite the fact that the **Karacters** were part of the Merseybeat scene for just a little more than a year, their career was really intensive and they left behind a positive and lasting impression.

THE KARACTERS' HEARSE
IS FOR SALE
GENUINE 1932 ROLLS ROYCE IN PERFECT CONDITION.
IDEAL GROUP BUS.
Enquiries: J. M. ELLISON, ESQ.
22 GROVELAND ROAD, WALLASEY

Discography:

Why do lovers break each other's hearts / Then he kissed me   UK-acetate / 1964

THE KESTRALS – THE SABRES

It was around 1959 when three young school-mates from Liverpool's Kensington area decided to make music together, which for sure was not Rock & Roll at that time, as their line-up would not support that style of playing and so their music was heavily influenced by the **Shadows** and the **Ventures**. Anyway, after intensive rehearsals, they started to play at school-parties and local youth-clubs. For these public appearances, they needed a name and decided on the **Kestrals** – in the following line-up:

Ronnie Davies	(lg/acc)
Jim Whitfield	(rg)
Alan Menzies	(dr)

It is a mystery what was behind their idea to go into the nearby studio of **Percy Phillips** to record an acetate in 1961 – they just did it. For that acetate, they had chosen two instrumental numbers one of them called "Kestral" was written by **Ronnie Davies** and played by him on the accordion (!) while the title on the other side, no one can remember but most probably it was a **Shadows** instrumental, which for sure was not easy without a bass-guitar and no

possibilities for an overdub. *(See Alan Menzies comment at the end of the story).* After that recording 'adventure', the **Kestrals** kept on playing the schools and youth clubs as they were still too young to appear at the usual pubs and clubs of that time.

The reason for **Alan Menzies** leaving in 1961 is not known as he kept on playing in various groups, among them **Jan & the Vendettas**, **Chris & the Quiet Ones**, **Rhythm & Blues Inc.***, the **Tabs*** and the **Bootles**. His movements can best be followed in the **Rhythm & Blues Inc.** story. **Alan Menzies** is still active on the scene today as the drummer of the '**No Name – The Band**'.

THE SABRES

Ronnie Davies and **Jim Whitfield** found another drummer and also added the long needed bass-guitarist to their new group that now appeared under the name of the **Sabres** in the line-up with:

Ronnie Davies	(lg)
Jim Whitfield	(rg)
John Adams	(bg)
Les Reynolds	(dr)

Both new members were obviously newcomers to the scene – at least there is nothing known about any former groups that they had played with.

When **Ronnie Davies** left the group and emigrated to Canada, **Jim Whitfield** switched to lead-guitar and **Ritchie Bennett** joined them as their new rhythm-guitarist and the **Sabres** kept on performing as an instrumental group for another year. All attempts of **John Adams** to get the other members to add vocal-numbers sadly proved to be fruitless and so he left the **Sabres** and, together with his friend **John Stretch** on drums, formed his own group called the **Kingpins**. After that, he was a member of the **Homeless Bones**.

For a short time, the **Sabres** kept on playing under that name but, it is not known who the new bass-guitarist was. It was probably in early 1963 that **Les Reynolds** also left to join the **Defenders*** and the **Sabres,** as such, came to an end. **Jim Whitfield** and **Ritchie Bennett** went on to form the **Four X's** that then became the **Concords***, but that is another story.

Discography:

as the **Kestrals**:

Kestral / guitar-instrumental   **UK- Phillips Kensington acetate / 1961**

> "I might have only been 13 when I recorded at Percy Phillips' with two guys I went to school with – Ronnie Davies and Jimmy Whitfield. Ronnie played guitar and accordion, odd mix I know.
> We went in the studio on a Saturday afternoon around 2ish – it was good weather as we walked from Jimmy's house as he lived further up Kensington. We recorded two instrumentals, one on the accordion, which I think Ronnie had written. The band was called the Kestrals and so he called it "Kestral". The other one was on guitars but I can't remember that one, very likely it was a Shadows or Ventures number – it was around 1961 – oh, I nearly forgot, no bass-guitar so it can't have been very good. I never got a copy as I couldn't afford it."
>
> **Alan Menzies / The Kestrals**

*The stories of these groups can be followed in 'Beat Waves 'Cross The Mersey' (*VelocePress* ISBN 978-1-58850-201-8).

THE KONDA GROUP

To give the complete history of this band, it is only right to start with two different groups that were both formed in or around 1962/1963 and, at that time, were absolutely independent from each other.

The first group was called the **Swaydes** and can be placed as being from the Everton area as the majority of the members came from there, together with a sax-player from Fazakerley and a rhythm guitarist from Norris Green. They played the local clubs in the following line-up:

Fred Losh	(voc)
Dougie McArd	(lg)
Arthur Jones	(rg/voc)
Colin Maude	(sax)
Tony Jones	(bg)
Roger Jones	(dr)

The bass-guitarist and the drummer were brothers. **Colin Maude** was also a very good pianist and, as such, had previously played in a Liverpool night-club, which is thought to have been either the 'Pink Parrot' or the 'Blue Angel'.

The second group was the **Condors** who came from the Seaforth/Old Roan area of Liverpool and quickly started to build up a name for themselves in their original line-up with:

Glenn Kelly	(voc/rg)
Michael Flanagan	(lg/voc)
Ronnie McCann	(rg)
Bobby McCann	(bg/voc)
David Mann	(dr)

Ronnie McCann was the cousin of **Bobby McCann** and, as far as it is known, for all of the members it was their first group.

Both groups kept playing on the scene for approximately a year but, in 1964, **Glenn Kelly** left the **Condors** to join the **Principals** from Netherton as their lead-vocalist, where his brother **Ronnie Kelly** was already playing bass-guitar. The **Condors,** at first, carried on as a four-piece but, as **Glenn Kelly** had not only been their rhythm-guitarist but also their main singer, they advertised for a replacement vocalist and among the applicants were **Fred Losh** and **Colin Maude** of the **Swaydes**. Both musicians were accepted and joined the **Condors**.

Ronny Mann, the drummer's father, who was also a musician and trumpet player with the resident trio at the 'Star Of The Sea' club, took over the management of the **Condors**. When a few months later, **Ronnie McCann** left the group and disappeared from the scene, his place was taken over by **Arthur Jones** from the **Swaydes**, who was also a good singer. The group now consisted of 50% former **Swaydes** and 50 % former **Condors** members and that, most probably, was the reason for changing the name to the **Konda Group** in 1965 – with the following musicians:

Fred Losh	(voc)
Mick Flanagan	(lg/voc)
Arthur Jones	(rg/voc)
Colin Maude	(t-sax/p)
Bobby McCann	(bg/voc)
David Mann	(dr)

With four good singers in the group, they also featured songs by the **Beach Boys**, **Drifters** and other similar styled numbers in their repertoire.

John Seddon, who was possibly a partner or had some connections with **Ian Comish** of 'Maghull Promotions', became their booking agent and, in early 1966, he secured an audition with Polydor for the **Konda Group.** For that audition, the group went to London and besides cover-versions of the **Gene McDaniels** success, "The Point Of No Return", the **Beach Boys** number "Help Me Rhonda" and the **Drifters'** "I'll Take You Where The Music's Playing", they recorded three of the group's own compositions, "Don't Take Your Heart From Me", "I Know I'm Good For You" and "You Don't Know What Love Is For". Sadly, none of these recordings were ever released.

John Seddon had some experience in the recording field as he had already released the LP, "Ee-Aye-Addio", after Liverpool FC's cup win in 1964 and that LP had been a commercial success for him. Two years later in 1966, Liverpool FC won the League Championship and Everton FC the FA Cup and so he asked the **Konda Group** to come up with some appropriate songs to celebrate the event.

The musicians were not enthusiastic but agreed purely as a favour for their booking-agent. For the A-side **Bobby McCann** wrote new lyrics to the **Beach Boys** success "Barbara Ann". The title for that was "Roarin' and Scorin'" and, for the B-side, **Arthur Jones** wrote "The Toast Of Merseyside", a Country sounding number about football that, in parts of its melody, is somewhat reminiscent of "Heartaches By The Number". These two numbers were recorded in a studio in London and with the title, "Mersey Boot", were released on Major Records. As the members of the **Konda Group** were not really happy to be associated with this recording, they were not credited on the record sleeve and on the label, their identity took the form of four dashes and a question-mark. For a promotion photograph the musicians hid their faces behind the promo-posters. **Ronnie McCann** was totally unhappy with the whole development and left the group soon after the recording even before the single became available on the market. His replacement in the **Konda Group** was **Kevin Murphy**, who formerly had played with the **Movement** from Litherland. The single, "Roarin' and Scorin'", was

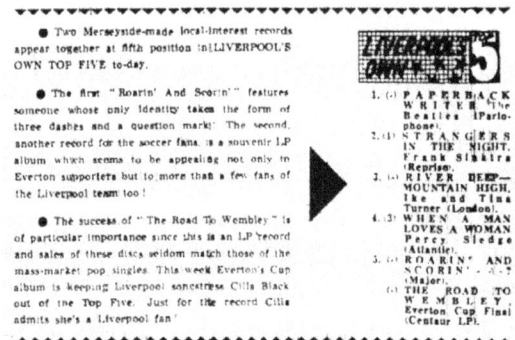

moderately successful and climbed to No. 5 in the Mersey-charts but that, of course, did not help the popularity of the **Konda Group** at all.

The **Konda Group** now concentrated more on the Stax-Soul style of music and, therefore, **Arthur Jones** switched to organ and **Ken Kilby**, a baritone sax player, was added to their line-up. They now often supported many of the top 60's Soul-acts, playing throughout the Northwest but also kept appearing in the local venues, including the 'Downbeat', the 'Peppermint Lounge', the 'Orrell Park Ballroom', the 'Floral Hall' in Southport, 'Quantways' in Chester and, on a couple of occasions the 'Cavern'.

In 1968, **Ian Comish** had worked out a contract for the **Konda Group** to appear in Italy for an extended time but, for that, the musicians had to enter into a professional contract. **Kevin Murphy**, who occasionally had stood in with **Gerry De Ville & the City-Kings*** decided to leave for family reasons. His replacement was **Joe O'Connor**, a former member of the **Lay-Bys** and **Keith's Kind** from Huyton. It is also said that he was a short-time member of the **Connoisseurs*** but, that could not be confirmed. **David Mann** (whose father **Ronny Mann** had been the group's manager up to this point) did not want to go to Italy and so he left the group. He later moved to Southport, where he joined a local group. His replacement in the **Konda Group** was **Roger Jones**, another former member of the **Swaydes**. When **Mick Flanagan,** the last original member of the **Condors** left and quit the music-business, he was not replaced in the group, which continued as a six-piece again. In this line-up, the **Konda Group** went to Italy where they had a long residency at the 'Bang Bang Club' in Milano – a funny name, most probably taken from the 1966 **Sonny & Cher** hit of which an Italian version by the great Beat group, **I Corvi** was very popular in Italy around that same time. The initial agreement for the **Konda Group** was to fulfil the residency, return home to the UK for the Christmas holidays and then back to Italy in the New Year of 1969. Unfortunately, as a result of a dispute with the Musicians Union, they were unable to return for their second residency in Italy.

However, when **John Seddon** was offered the possibility for **King Size Taylor** to play some dates in Japan, he asked the **Konda Group** if they would be willing to act as his backing-band. They agreed but, in the end, the Japan opportunity failed to materialise. This obviously was the beginning of the end of the **Konda Group's** professional career and they disbanded sometime in 1969.

All the members initially disappeared from the scene and only of **Kevin Murphy**, who had left earlier, is it known that he kept on playing on the semi-pro basis with the **Concords** from Manchester until 1985. After that, he was a member of various groups, including the **Hazbeans** and the **Cyndicate**, as well as the successful Liverpool group, **Shooter**, for two years. In 2010, he joined the newly-formed **Bumblies**. In the Eighties, **David Mann** teamed up again with **Glenn Kelly** and his brother **Ronnie Kelly** in a trio called **Second Chance** that kept on playing on the scene right into the Nineties. **Colin Maude** sadly died in the 80's followed by **Fred Losh** sometime in the 90's.

Discography:

The Point Of No Return / Help Me Rhonda / I'll Take You Where The Music's Playing / Don't Take Your Heart From Me / I Know I'm Good For You / You Don't Know What Love Is For UK- Polydor (unreleased) / 1966

Un-credited as artists:

Roarin' and Scorin' / The Toast Of Merseyside   UK- Major Records MAJ 1 / 1966

*The stories of these groups can be followed in 'Beat Waves 'Cross The Mersey' (*VelocePress ISBN 978-1-58850-201-8*).

THE L.S.D.

Firstly, it should be pointed out that the name of this group was not associated with the hallucinogenic drug - which was not readily available at that time anyway - **L.S.D.** was an acronym of the initials of the founding members: L for Les, S for Skipsy and D for Derek.

Now that that has been cleared up, we can follow the story of this group, formed as a trio (without a drummer) in Bebington on the Wirral in the early Sixties.

The **L.S.D.**, as they were named right from the beginning, later recruited a drummer and played a mixture of Beat and Rhythm & Blues and their original line-up consisted of **Les Taylor** (lg/voc), **Phil Skipsy** (rg/voc), **Derek Taylor** (bg) and that drummer, whose name no one can recall and who was very soon replaced by **Phil Hughes**.

It was probably still in 1963 that **Les Taylor** accepted an offer to join the **Hillsiders** and **Phil Skipsy** got married and quit the music scene.

Derek Taylor and **Phil Hughes** then formed a new group under the old name (which now stood for the abbreviations used for English currency – pounds, shillings and pence).

The **L.S.D.** consisted of a line-up with:

Terry Moran	(voc/lg)
Charles Harris	(rg/voc)
Derek Taylor	(bg)
Phil Hughes	(dr)

The group now had gigs from as far away as Wales up to Southport, where they very often appeared at the famous 'Kingsway Casino'.

As their new singer, **Terry Moran** also acted in 'Coronation Street' at that time, he was very popular and so the group was offered a tour of the west coast of Scotland in 1964, which was very successful.

On their return, the **L.S.D.** went into **Charlie Weston**'s Cam studio in Moorfields and recorded an interesting, slowed down version of **Neil Sedaka**'s "Oh Carol", as well as an up-tempo, Country influenced "I washed my hands in muddy water".

An acetate was cut of these two numbers that the group used as a demo, which very clearly showed the great singing ability of **Terry Moran**.

The group started to play more frequently in downtown Liverpool, including 'Hope Hall' and the 'Blue Angel' but they never really made much progress. In fact, it took them until the end of 1966 to play the 'Cavern' for the first time.

In 1968, **Phil Hughes** split from the **L.S.D.** to become a freelancing musician and the others continued with **Alan Belsher** as their new drummer for another year but then disbanded totally.

Terry Moran concentrated on acting, while **Derek Taylor** became a DJ before he emigrated to Canada, where he is still living.

It is known that **Charles Harris** joined a Soul band called **Soul Pleasure**.

In 1976, **Terry Moran** and **Phil Hughes** teamed up again in a Cabaret duo called **Tandem**, but apparently this did not last for too long, as in 1978, **Phil Hughes** became a member of **Lazy Grey.** Besides **Phil Hughes**, this group also included **Steve Roberts** (lg) and **Colin Roberts** (bg), both brothers of popular singer, **Cliff Roberts** who, in the Sixties, was very successful on the scene with his group – the **Cliff Roberts' Rockers**.

Terry Moran continued on with his acting career but later quit showbiz completely and went back to a normal day job.

So the **L.S.D.'s** legacy is certainly not a big name, but it includes an interesting acetate, worth looking out for . . .

Discography

Oh Carol / I washed my hands in muddy water　　　　　　　　UK – Unicord (?) acetate / 1964

RAY LEWIS & THE TREKKERS

This group was formed in Preston, Lancashire in late 1963 and soon became very popular with local audiences playing the normal circuit of youth clubs, coffee bars and some of the larger venues.

One night in 1964, **Ray Lewis & the Trekkers** were playing the Flamingo club and they were spotted by a certain **Robert Hartford-Davis**, who signed them immediately for a part in a music film which he was going to produce - 'Gonks Go Beat'.

A little later, they went down to London where they did the filming at Shepperton studios, in a line-up with:

Ray Lewis	(voc)
Dave Hall	(lg/voc)
Ken Simpson	(rg)
Paul Nichol	(bg/voc)
Barry Roberts	(dr)

Of **Paul Nichol**, it is known that he was a former member of the **Marksmen** and one or two of the others are thought to have previously played with the **Asteroids**, but there are no precise details available.

Ray Lewis & the Trekkers at the Top Rank Ballroom

The film itself was some nonsense about aliens in a sort of 'Westside Story' musical style, which was described by **Phil Eaves** in his book, *'Xtrabop'*, as "...a fantasy tale of battles between the inhabitants of Beatland (Rockers) and Balladisle (Mods)".

Even though the film featured **Lulu & the Luvvers**, the **Nashville Teens**, the **Graham Bond Organization** and the Lancashire groups the **Long & Short** (Liverpool/St. Helens), the **Vaqueros** (Whiston/St. Helens), the **Trolls** (Wigan) and of course, **Ray Lewis & the Trekkers**, it was quite embarrassing and, not surprisingly, it was unsuccessful.

However, the film obviously did not do any harm to the group and **Ray Lewis & the Trekkers** continued as professionals on the scene, playing throughout England until **Ray Lewis** decided to leave in 1966. He was followed shortly thereafter by **Ken Simpson**. Unfortunately, it is not known what happened to either of them after they had left.

The remaining three members continued on with **Mike Hurst** as their new singer under the name of **Mike Hurst & the Trekkers**.

To avoid confusion, it should be mentioned that this **Mike Hurst** was not the same person as the well-known producer of the same name, who had led the group **Mike Hurst & the Method**.

Probably, in late 1966 or early 1967, **Barry Roberts** had also left and was replaced by **Dave Hunt**.

Mike Hurst & the Trekkers kept on touring the national club circuit and became very popular in the northwest of England. In 1968, when the good times for the touring Beat groups were over, **Mike Hurst & the Trekkers** decided to continue on the cabaret scene as a sort of Rock and Comedy act and, therefore, changed their name to the **Trekkershow**.

Dave Hunt left at this time and his replacement was **Bill Hart**, who came from the **Shyms**, but this line-up only lasted for a little over a year as, in 1969, **Mike Hurst**, who was a Jehovah's Witness, left to concentrate on his religious studies.

At the same time, **Bill Hart** moved down to London and was replaced by the returning **Barry Roberts**. This trio successfully continued to play the social clubs until the early Eighties and then the **Trekkershow** called it a day.

Mike Hurst & the Trekkers - L to R: Dave Hall. Mike Hurst, Dave Hunt & Paul Nichol (1966)

The Trekkershow

Paul Nichol became a compere at a Preston club and **Barry Roberts** joined the **Old Peculiar Band** in 1984 as did **Dave Hall**, who followed him to this group in the early Nineties.

It is known that **Mike Hurst** later returned to the music scene as one-half of the **Mike Hurst Duo**, which at one time was also backed by drummer **Bill Hart** again.

After that **Mike Hurst** went solo, but he sadly died a few years ago.

Discography

Ray Lewis & the Trekkers (see note):

As young as we are / Drum battle (in "Gonks Go Beat")　　　　　　**UK-Decca　4673 / 1964**

There is absolutely no doubt that **Ray Lewis & the Trekkers** participated in the Titan Film Production **"Gonks Go Beat"** and they are also included in the cast list on the original poster for the film. However, the soundtrack album which includes 'As young as we are' credits this song to **Dougie Robinson with the Titan Studio Orchestra.** Therefore, we are unable to accurately confirm if this song was performed on the album by **Ray Lewis & the Trekkers** or if their drummer, **Barry Roberts** is included in the album's 'Drum battle' number.

THE LIVERPOOL RAIDERS

This story is about a group that was part of Liverpool's so-called 'Gospel-Beat-Scene' but, in the beginning, such a development was not that obvious. The story begins when the friends **Peter Lewis** (voc/g), **Peter Helsby** (g), **Billy Buxton** (t-bass) and **Colin Chestnutt** (wb) formed the **Union City Skiffle Group** in Childwall in the late Fifties.

Approximately one year later, **Billy Buxton** was replaced by **Keith Lord** and, in 1962, the group disbanded because **Peter Lewis** and **Keith Lord** decided to break into the Beat-scene and got together with **Steve Lister** (lg), **Derek Fulwood** (rg) and **Johnny Brown** (dr). This new line-up now appeared under the name of **Peter Lewis & the Raiders** and they were mostly playing **Cliff Richard & the Shadows** numbers. **Keith Lord**, who had switched from t-bass to a real bass-guitar, did not stay with them for too long and, in 1962, was replaced by **Dave Dover** (bg/harp), who came from **Deke Wade & the Ambassadors**. The group had grown tired of playing **Cliff Richard** and similar style music and wanted to expand their repertoire, this resulted in **Peter Lewis** leaving and the **Raiders** then changed their name into the **Cordes***.

L to R: Mike Espie, Bill Geeleher, Del Tubb

Peter Lewis, a member of the local church choir, somehow got together with the **Vaqueros** that were formed at the 'Trinity Methodist Youth Club' in Tuebrook. This group in a line-up with **Mike Espie** (lg), **Derek 'Del' Tubb** (rg), **Neil Ford** (bg) and **Ray Stringer** (dr) occasionally backed **Peter Lewis** using the name **Peter Lewis & the Raiders** but played the majority of their bookings without him under the **Vaqueros** name. This arrangement was going well until the **Vaqueros** split in 1963. **Mike Espie** and **'Del' Tubb** teamed up with **Ian Colyer** (bg), **Billy Geeleher** (dr) and a singer called **Ronnie** under the name **St. John's Precinct** – a very short-lived association. **Peter Lewis**, without a backing group again, disappeared from the scene for a while but was back in 1965 – with a group that was called the **Liverpool Raiders** and consisted of:

Peter Lewis	(voc/g/p)
Malcolm Sim	(bg/voc)
Mike Waiting	(dr/voc)

They did not take part in the normal club-scene but appeared in churches, youth-clubs, church-halls and related religious institutions. A complete 'Carol Concert' of the **Liverpool Raiders** was recorded at the Liverpool Anglican Cathedral in 1965 but never released. They apparently played throughout the UK as, in 1966, their story was featured in the 'Church Times' paper, where they were described as 'missionaries with a difference'. In that same year the trio can be seen in the opening of a documentary film called 'Liverpool Sounding', playing a good rocking version of the **Ray Charles** classic "Talking 'bout you" and this classified the **Liverpool Raiders** as still being a real Beat-group.

They were signed to the religious Tower label from London which, of course, had no connection to the big U.S. label of the same name and towards the end of 1966 an EP "Big Story" was released by the **Liverpool Raiders**. This record had some echoes of Beat in its rhythm, although not comparable to their above mentioned "Talking 'bout you" recording. Musically it was not very exciting but it did feature very good lead and backing vocals. As it seems, still in 1966, the group disbanded as the next EP "Sing About Christmas" was a solo record by **Peter Lewis** and there is no mention of the backing group on the label. It appears that **Malcolm Sim** emigrated to Canada at some later date but it is a known fact that the **Liverpool Raiders** in 1967 appeared in the following line-up:

Peter Lewis	(voc/g/org/p)
Rodney Brown	(bg/voc)
George Bewick	(dr/voc)

Due to the style of music they played, the group never made major headlines, but they obviously had no problems existing on the scene. By 1967, this new line-up had another EP released on the Tower label, simply called "The Rock". On the rear cover of this record, for the first time, **Peter Lewis & the Liverpool Raiders** are named as the artists.

What happened after that is somewhat confusing as it appears that, in 1969, **Peter Lewis** had two more solo-releases on the Tower label with the EP "Father Forgive Him" and an album "Give Yourselves To Me". He then switched to the Pilgrim label and released another solo-album "Sing Life, Sing Love". There was no indication on any of these three recordings that he was backed by the **Liverpool Raiders**. 1970 saw him back at Tower records with his final EP "A Chance To See" and this one was released as **Peter Lewis & the Liverpool Raiders** again. It was a very soft recording as drummer **George Bewick** played with brushes and not with sticks. It is not known how long **Peter Lewis & the Liverpool Raiders** continued to perform together but, **Peter Lewis** later formed the music-project **Family Folk,** which no longer had any connection with beat music and appeared in a number of ever changing line-ups.

Discography:

<u>as the **Liverpool Raiders**</u>:

EP **"Big Story"**

The big story / I wish I knew / Lord and giver of love / Rhythm in religion / There is God	UK-Tower CLM 224 / 1966

<u>as **Peter Lewis & the Liverpool Raiders:**</u>

EP **"The Rock"**

The Rock / Blest are the poor who know / Servants of God / There's a lot of good things on earth	UK-Tower CLM 229 / 1967

EP **"A Chance to See"**

When Jesus walked in Galilee / Cana town's in Galilee / What do I see / The son of God is with us	UK-Tower CLM 234 / 1970

Unreleased tracks:

A full 'Carol Concert' of the **Liverpool Raiders** was recorded at the Anglican Cathedral in Liverpool in 1965 but none of those songs was ever released on record. In addition, in 1966 the **Liverpool Raiders** recorded the **Ray Charles** classic **"I'm talking 'bout you"**, a good driving Beat-number that was used as the introduction to the documentary film "Liverpool Sounding" but sadly it never came out on record.

<u>**Peter Lewis** – solo:</u>

EP **"Sing About Christmas"**

The merry bells / Lucy's carol / Eighteen shopping days to Christmas / The lights on the Christmas tree / The farm-yard Christmas service	UK-Tower CLM 228 / 1966
EP **"Father Forgive Him"**	UK-Tower CLM 231 / 1969
LP **"Give Yourselves To Me"**	UK-Tower SCM 802 / 1969
LP **"Sing Life, Sing Love"**	UK-Pilgrim JLP 164 / 1969

*The story of this group can be followed in 'Beat Waves 'Cross The Mersey' (*VelocePress ISBN 978-1-58850-201-8*).

THE MAFIA GROUP

L to R: Johnny Burns, Arthur Owen & Ken Duggan (Circa 1962)

The development of this interesting group from the Wavertree area of Liverpool is somewhat typical for that time.

Arthur Owen and his school mate **Ken Duggan** started to play guitar together at a very young age in the late Fifties and, as their ability improved, **Arthur Owen** then got together with **Jimmy Moran** for a short time and played some **Shadows** instrumentals and similar numbers.

Arthur Owen and **Ken Duggan** then continued together and, in early 1960, briefly joined a band run by **Billy Roberts** and **Jimmy Moran** – the **Apaches**, though they never made a public appearance.

Glyn Wall

In 1961, **Arthur Owen** and **Ken Duggan** did some pub and club gigs together with a singer and a drummer, but they apparently did not have a name at this time. On one of these occasions, two of **Arthur Owen**'s work colleagues were in the audience, one of whom sang and played guitar and the other who had just begun learning to play the drums. In early 1962, the four got together for rehearsals but, prior to their first public appearance, **Ken Duggan** gave up playing to become a motor mechanic.

Arthur Owen

The remaining three recruited a new bass player and, from then on, continued as the **Mafia** in the following line-up:

Johnny Burns	(voc/rg)
Arthur Owen	(lg/voc)
Harry Williams	(bg/voc)
Glyn Wall	(dr)

The Mafia at the Sink Club - L to R: Harold Williams, Ian Bailey, Norby Del Rosa & Tony Priestly

Harry Williams had some prior musical experience, having previously played with the **Knights** and the **Abstrax**.

Johnny Burns, a former member of **Johnny Burns & the Renegades**, was an impressive front man with his good looks and great voice and so it was not really surprising that they were billed as **Johnny Burns & the Mafia** at a band contest held at the Tunnel Cinema, but that was a one-time use of that name. It was probably at this contest that they came to the attention of **Alan Williams**, who immediately booked them to appear regularly at the 'Blue Angel'.

```
KINGS R & B CLUB
    LITTLE SUTTON
  GRAND OPENING
  BARGAIN NIGHT
Saturday, 15th February at 7-30
The Mafia
   and
Joan and the Deamons
4/6 inc. 12 months membership
fee of 2/6. Members must be 17
and over
Sunday, 16th February at 7-30
Carol & the Corvettes
   plus
Kluke's Klan Rhythmic
    Group
Members 4/6. Non-members 5/6
Thursday, 20th February, 7-30
The Kosmenauts
   and
The Cave Dwellers
Members 3/6. Non-members 4/6
Friday, 21st February at 7-30
The Kresters
   and
Joan and the Deamons
Members 3/6. Non-members 4/6
Saturday, 22nd February, 7-30
The Concords
   (EMI Recording tests)
   and
The Cave Dwellers
Members 4/6. Non-members 5/6
Sunday, 23rd February at 7-30
Jonny Paul & the DJ's
  Runners-up in the Blackpool
  1963 R & B Contest
   plus
Joan and the Deamons
Members 4/6. Non-members 5/6
```

Although they were a real Rhythm & Blues group, playing numbers by **Slim Harpo**, **Jimmy Reed** or **Lightnin' Hopkins**, the **Mafia** were very well received at that famous club and, as a result, they were booked by other major venues including the 'Cavern' and the 'Iron Door'.

One day in 1963, **Harry Williams** introduced the group to the coloured vocalist, **Norby Del Rosa**, a great singer and showman. He and **Johnny Burns** now fronted the group as a really terrific double act, similar to **Derry Wilkie** and **Freddie Starr** with **Howie Casey & the Seniors**.

During their 'Blue Angel' period, they were spotted by **Neil English**, the owner of a snack bar called the 'Rumblin Tum' at the top of Hardman Street. He had created a Blues club called the 'Sink' in the basement of the snack bar and he booked the **Mafia** to become the resident group and also took over their management.

As well as being very busy with their residency, the **Mafia** kept on playing the local scene and also outside Liverpool, for example, the 'Kings R&B Club' in Little Sutton.

During that time, a live performance at the 'Sink' was recorded as a demo for **Neil English's** management group, which was most probably cut on acetate in parts but, unfortunately, nobody can remember any details or what happened to the recordings.

In late 1963, **Johnny Burns** left the group for work reasons and disappeared from the scene. His departure was soon followed by **Glyn Wall**, who was replaced by **Ian Bailey**, a great, powerful drummer who is said to have previously played with the **Cossacks.**

For unknown reasons, it seems **Arthur Owen** was not with the group for a period of time and, during his absence, he was replaced by **Tony Priestly**, a former member of **Mike & the Merseymen** and the **Beatcombers**, who went on to join **Earl Preston's Realms** when **Arthur Owen** returned.

Also, for unknown reasons, **Norby Del Rosa** left, and the **Mafia** continued on as a trio with **Ian Bailey** taking over the lead vocals. As such, they were going strong on the scene until **Ian Bailey** returned to his old group who, in the interim, had become the **Challengers**. His replacement in the **Mafia** was **Pete Wiggins.**

Around that same time, a rhythm guitarist, **Jimmy Ikonomides,** was added to their line-up. **Jimmy Ikonomides** is a cousin of **Harry Williams** with whom he had already played in the **Abstrax** and the **Knights.** Prior to joining the **Mafia**, **Jimmy Ikonomides** had been taking a break from the music scene.

Norby Del Rosa also returned to the group, but this final line-up only continued on the scene for a few months and the **Mafia** broke up totally when, in early 1964, **Arthur Owen** had to move to St. Helens for work related reasons.

Pete Wiggins joined the **Profiles**, who also performed as **Peter & the Profiles** for a time and, after that, he replaced **Danny Bell** in the **Kruzads.**

Jimmy Ikonomides joined the newly formed **Calderstones** and, in January 1965, **Norby Del Rosa**, who in the interim had sung with the **Challengers,** also joined them.

Jimmy Ikonomides

In April 1965, **Jimmy Ikonomides** followed **Pete Wiggins** to the **Kruzads**. He was later a member of the **Detours** who, in the meantime, had returned from London to Liverpool.

Harold Williams became a long-time member of the **Secrets** and went to Italy with them, where he lived for a couple of years. He sadly died at the very young age of 39 in 1985.

Arthur Owen initially kept playing on the St. Helens scene with groups that included the **G.T.O.s**, the **John Barry Trio** and **Candy's Crowd**. In 1969, he returned to Liverpool and joined **Peyton Place**, who also became quite popular in the Chester area and in North Wales. In the early Seventies, he moved to London where he was active as a solo performer until he moved again – this time to Wales, where he became a member of **Kelvin & the Absolute Zeros**. He then moved back to London and joined the **Steve Jones Backbeat Band**, where he played until 2010.

Discography

No details could be found about the live recordings by the **Mafia** which were made at the Sink club in 1963, but **Jimmy Ikomidis**, a later member of the group, remembers that there at least was one acetate out before he had joined.

> *"Certainly those Sink Club days were very good times, and in fact so good it's all like a dream now. I have very many great memories from my long lasting career, but I still treasure those days as the most, and always will . . . "*
>
> **(Arthur Owen / The Mafia)**

THE MAGGOTS

Here an explanation is required as to why it has taken such an incredible length of time before their story came to light: The main reason was due to the fact that this group spent almost all of its active time in Germany and, therefore, is mainly known there, predominantly in record-collector circles, as their only record was released in Germany on the cult-label 'Star-Club' Records. However, there was absolutely no information about them in the Star-Club archives as they obviously never appeared at the main Star-Club in Hamburg. That is why it was always assumed that the **Maggots** were either an unknown German group or one of the numerous short-lived English groups that toured Germany in the first half of the Sixties. It was not until their band-leader, **Jim Moran,** placed a short note about them in one of the internet-forums for record-collectors that I was able to confirm that the **Maggots** were a group of Liverpool origin.

As this mystery has now been solved, we can start at the beginning and follow the path of **Jim Moran** who, by the way, is not the Liverpool musician of the same name who had played in **Frank Knight & the Barons** and later, for many years, in the Country-group **Idle Hours**.

It was in 1957 when the **Alan Mack Skiffle Group** was formed in Liverpool by **Alan Mack** (voc/t-bass), **Jim Moran** (g/voc), **Cyril Evans** (g) and **Bernie Deevey** (wb). One year later, **Jim Moran** and **Bernie Deevey** teamed up with **Tony Jackson** (voc/rg) and **Eddie Silver** (lg) under the Name of the **Mavericks**. In 1959, this Toxteth group changed their name into the **Martinis** and soon after, they also changed their sound from Skiffle to more Rock'n'Roll. As they were in need of a real drummer, their washboard player, **Bernie Deevey,** was replaced by **Norman McGarry**.

Norman McGarry & Jim Moran

The Martinis L to R: Jim Moran, Bernie Deevey, Tony Jackson, Eddie Silver

This group did not last for very long and broke up when both **Tony Jackson**, who also went out as a solo-performer under the name of **Clint Reno**, and **Norman McGarry** became founding-members of the embryonic **Searchers*** that later had worldwide hits. It was not long before **Norman McGarry** left the **Searchers** and then later appeared as a member of the **Sassenachs** from London (another story in this book).

Tony Jackson remained with the **Searchers** and his lead-vocals can be heard on some of their early hit-records. In 1964, he left to form **Tony Jackson & the Vibrations*** that later became the **Tony Jackson Group**.

After the **Martinis** broke up, **Eddie Silver** disappeared from the scene but **Jim Moran** got together with two work-colleagues from the Joseph Lucas Engineering Factory. They were **Irene Grey** (voc) and **Edward Jones** (voc/g) who had already performed as a duo under the name '**Irene & Eddie**' and, when they were joined by **Jim Moran**, they changed their name into **Irene & the Santa Fe's.** As such, they had an appearance at the famous 'Cavern' on 4th November 1960 – playing a sort of Folk, Country and Pop in the style of the **Kingston Trio**. The three then changed their name into the **Irene Grey Trio** and they continued to play the social and working men's clubs on the local scene until one day they spotted an advert for an agency that was seeking groups that included a female vocalist to entertain the G.I.s on the American bases in France. They made contact, got the job, and, in December 1963, went to France for the first time. For ten days, they played at the USAF base in Toul Rosieres where they realized that they were in need of a drummer as one guitar, a bass-guitar and a girl-singer was simply not sufficient to play the rock music that the G.I.s wanted to hear. Their agency arranged for a drummer to be flown in and that was **Trevor Stott**, who came from **Eddie Prince & the Creoles** from Princes Risborough in Buckinghamshire UK. With this new member, the group changed the name slightly into the **Irene Grey Quartet**. Their next gig took them to Verdun and, after a few shows, it was again their agency that decided that a second guitarist should be added to the line-up and so **Dave Simmonds** joined them, who formerly had also played with **Eddie Prince & the Creoles**.

In addition to a few Folk and Country numbers, they now played the more current Rock 'n' Roll and songs of **Johnny Kidd & the Pirates**, the **Beatles** and the **Rolling Stones.** It was Easter 1964 when they played at the USAF bases in Chateauroux and that's when **Irene Grey** decided to leave the group and to return to England.

This meant that another name-change was necessary and so this quartet now called themselves the **Komos** but, as their agency insisted on a girl singer, they soon were joined by a certain **Val**, whose surname is sadly lost with time. She hailed from Melton Mowbray in the UK and the group now appeared as **Val & the Komos**. This new association did not work as well as with **Irene Grey** and, when the group was sent from France to the American 'Rhein-Main' base in the Frankfurt-area of Germany, **Val** left the group.

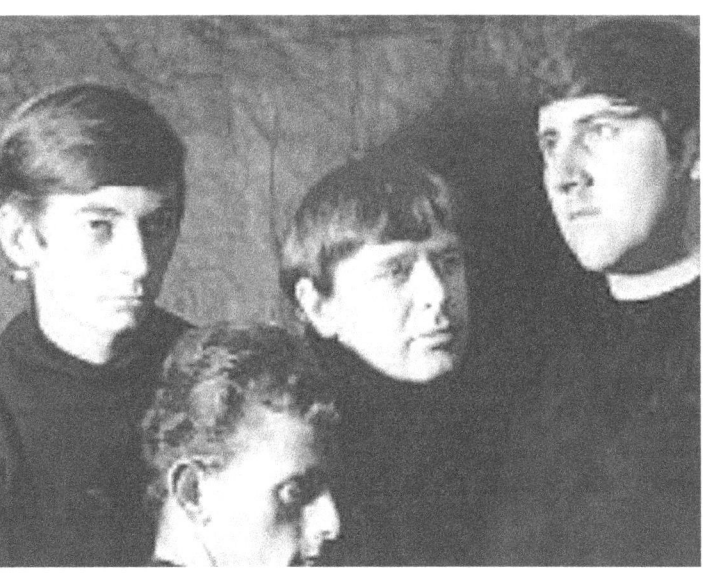

The Maggots L to R: Trevor Scott, Dave Simmonds, Jim Moran, Eddie Jones

While it's not absolutely sure, she could have been the **Val** of **Val & the V's**, that cut one single with "Do it again a little bit slower" for German CBS at a later date. Anyway, back to the **Komos** that at first continued under that name but then, for whatever reasons, changed the name into the **Maggots** – in a line-up with:

Jim Moran	(voc/bg)
Dave Simmonds	(lg/voc)
Eddie Jones	(rg/voc)
Trevor Stott	(dr)

They went down well in Germany and their agency over there also allowed the group to play gigs in private clubs outside the base. A certain **Klaus Stürmer** arranged for them to appear at a large theatre in Fulda where they had tremendous success and, from there, they were booked to appear regularly at the 'Club E' in Fulda. At one of those appearances, they were introduced to a D.J., who allegedly hosted a pop-programme on Radio Frankfurt and who had been contacted by several fans about the **Maggots**. He listened to their show, was impressed by their music and asked the musicians if they were interested in making a record. This really surprising offer was, of course, accepted by the group and, a few days later, they found themselves in the recording-studio of **Hans Podehl** in Frankfurt. Here they recorded the title, "Ha, Ha, Mister Froggie", an up-dated adaption of "Froggie went a' courtin'" – an old traditional that, years before, had been a hit for **Burl Ives**. The other recorded song was an original of **Eddie Jones** called "It's no Good".

After their recordings were finished, **Hans Podehl** introduced the group to the German singer **Kid Clausen**, who was about to record two numbers that evening and was in need of a backing-band. For that, the **Maggots** would receive the equivalent of fifty pounds as a one-off payment, which was a lot of money in those days, so the group promptly accepted. The A-side track was a song called "Ganz allein", which turned out to be the German version of the Brian Wilson/Gary Usher composition "In my room", which the **Beach Boys** had already recorded in German language – specifically for their German fan-club. The B-side, called "Nimm Dir endlich Zeit" was written by **Franz Rüger**, a local songwriter. Regardless, it worked out well for both the **Maggots** and **Kid Clausen,** but more about that later. At that time, the **Maggots** didn't know and, obviously didn't care, what happened to their recordings and left Frankfurt to fulfil an engagement at the 'Kakadu Club' in Karlsruhe.

Kid Clausen

During their stay in Karlsruhe, they received an offer to be cast in a low-budget film, 'Das Haus der Sünde' (The House of Sin), which was filmed, at that time, in nearby Baden-Baden. Needless to say, this little erotic film went nowhere. After that, the Maggots travelled North where they played in Duisburg and there they were contacted by a certain **Reg Owen**, who introduced himself as an A&R-man of Star-Club records, which is highly unlikely as his name was never confirmed by any of the insiders of that time as ever being associated with the Star-Club. Anyway, he obviously got them engagements at the 'Star-Club'-branches in Bochum and Hamm but they never played the main club in Hamburg. Therefore, it is really surprising that their record, "Ha, Ha, Mister Froggie", was eventually released on the Star-Club label.

According to the author's intensive research, **Hans Podehl** and his production company worked together with the 'Peter Schaeffers publishing-house' in Hamburg and he offered the two **Maggots** recordings and the two recordings backing **Kid Clausen** to them. They accepted and, in turn, they were able to make a deal with Fontana for the two **Maggots** recordings. Eventually, with the agreement of **Manfred Weißleder** (Owner of the Star-Club), "Ha Ha, Mister Froggie" was released on the Star-Club label. It should be noted that **Reg Owen** was not involved whatsoever in this process. Unfortunately, "Ha Ha, Mister Froggie" did not become the success it was hoped for and so the media did not show any interest in the group. That is why nothing was known about them for such a long time.

The **Kid Clausen/Maggots** recording of "Nimm Dir endlich Zeit" was given to Polydor and was released on the B-side of the next **Kid Clausen** Polydor single, "Ein Tag ohne Dich" (the German cover-version of **Paul Anka's** "My home-town"), backed by the popular **Orchestra Horst Wende**. However, the **Maggots** were not named on the B-side label, but the **Orchestra Reg Owen (?)** was credited as performing the backing. The whole matter is highly unfathomable – but probably all about royalties. Unfortunately, the **Maggots** did not have any copyright protection over the situation as they had accepted that one-off payment which falls under the 'work for hire' legal statute.

The **Maggots**, in the meantime, became a five-piece as **David Parker** had joined them as their piano-player. In 1965, they took up long residencies at the 'Club 99' in Cuxhaven and the 'Waterkant' in Norddeich. Here they ended up living in a run-down camper in a caravan-park and that was the only time that something was written about them in the 'Star-Club News' – but it only mentions their miserable living conditions, lack of bookings and money, but no other details about the group.

The **Maggots** then moved back down South, probably to the Frankfurt region again but, in 1966, gave up and returned to England, where they disbanded totally.

Trevor Scott, **Dave Simmonds** and **David Parker** went back to Buckinghamshire, **Eddie Jones** did not appear on the Liverpool-scene again and, only of **Jim Moran** it is known, that he became a member of the Liverpool Country-band **Country Five**, who made headlines when they became the backing-group for US-songstress **Tammy Wynette** on her 1966 Germany-tour and the few gigs she did on Merseyside. After that, he played in various groups and is still active on the scene, together with **Jimmy McGuirk** in a Country duo called the **Two Jims**.

Discography:

Ha, Ha, Mister Froggie / It's no good   G- Star-Club 148527 STF / 1965

backing **Kid Clausen** (not named on the label) :
Nimm Dir endlich Zeit (B-side of "Ein Tag ohne Dich") G- Polydor   52 512 / 1965

> "The producer said we could record anything we wanted but asked if we could include a few 'Ha-Ha-Ha's'. The reason was, a couple of English groups that were enjoying top positions in the charts had used this device. Casey Jones & his Engineers were one such Liverpool group and currently had a number one with "Don't ha ha".
>
> Most of our repertoire did not improve with the addition of 'Ha Ha's' and so I came up with the idea of using a traditional folk-song, of which I happened to know the words. It was "Froggie went a' courtin'".
>
> We turned it into a rockin' version and re-titled it "Ha Ha Mr. Froggie, which met everyone's approval in the studio."

*The stories of these groups can be followed in 'Beat Waves 'Cross The Mersey' (*VelocePress ISBN 978-1-58850-201-8*).

THE MAGIC LANTERNS

The foundation stone for this group was laid when a group called the **Sabres** was formed.

To prevent any confusion, this was definitely not the **Sabres** from Warrington or Manchester as is often stated, who at a certain point, also included **Kevin Godley** and **Lol Creme** of subsequent **10CC** fame.

The Sabres

The **Sabres** in this story that are connected with the **Magic Lanterns** were originally an instrumental group from St. Helens, close to Liverpool, where they were formed in 1961. In their original line-up, they consisted of **Peter Bond** (lg), **Ken Hobin** (rg), **Derek Jolley** (bg) and **Allan Wilson** (dr).

In 1962, **Maurice Tickle** from the **Blue Beats** Skiffle group got up on stage and sang with them and the other musicians liked him so much they asked him to join the **Sabres** there and then, an offer he accepted. The new singer adopted **Vince Reno** as his stage name and so the group became **Vince Reno & the Sabres**, probably to avoid confusion with the other **Sabres**, a fact which is often overlooked by some researchers.

Anyway, about one year later, **Derek Jolley** decided not to pursue a musical career and left. **Maurice Tickle** remembered his old friend from the **Blue Beats** and so **Ian Moncur** took over on bass guitar.

At that time, **Vince Reno & the Sabres** had become a real Merseybeat group, playing the typical venues in their hometown including the 'Plaza' or the 'Hellena' in the Co-op Hall and they also had gigs in many of the Liverpool clubs.

The next to leave was **Peter Bond** and his replacement was **Gerald Blackman**, who had formerly played with **Jimmy Martin & the Martinis** from Wigan.

1964 seems to have been a difficult year for the **Sabres**, as first **Ken Hobin** left and was not replaced and when **Maurice Tickle**, now known as **Vince Reno,** decided to go his own way, the **Sabres** continued in the following line-up:

Vince Reno & The Sabres

Jimmy Bilsbury	(voc/p)
Gerald Blackman	(lg/voc)
Ian Moncur	(bg/voc)
Allan Wilson	(dr/voc)

This development left **Allan Wilson** as the only remaining member of the original line-up.

Jimmy Bilsbury was a former member of the **Dominoes Skiffle Group** from Leigh, where he had replaced **Clive Powell**, who soon found international stardom as **Georgie Fame**. In the meantime, the **Dominoes Skiffle Group** had become the **Beat Boys** and recorded for Decca.

In 1965, **Gerald Blackman** left and was replaced by **Peter Shoesmith**, whose former group is not known, but he came from Nelson, Lancashire and was influenced by the local group **Ricky Shaw & the Dolphins**, whose guitarist, **Tony Hicks,** and bass player, **Bernie Calvert,** went on to play with the **Hollies**.

Jimmy Bilsbury was a very active and talented songwriter and so the **Sabres** now started to include more and more original songs in their live act. Because of this, not only did their sound change but also their name – to the **Hammers**.

The Hammers

The Hammers

When they had a gig at one of the biggest clubs in their area, the 'Garrick' in Leigh, they met up with the singer-compere, **Roy Hastings,** who liked their songs and convinced the **Hammers** to cut a demo that he could take to his publishers in London.

The group went into a studio and recorded the two **Jimmy Bilsbury** originals, "Long long time" and "Greedy girl". Both numbers were melodic Beat songs with a slight touch of Folk. The publishers Campbell/Connelly Music accepted the songs and **Mike Collier** of that company took over their management. He secured a record deal with CBS but insisted on a name change and so the **Hammers** became the **Magic Lanterns**.

1966 saw the first single by the **Magic Lanterns** with **Arthur Wayne's** "Excuse me Baby", coupled with "Greedy girl", the song from the above mentioned acetate. The record climbed to No. 44 in the charts, doubtless a big success, and so there was a follow-up with "Rumpelstilskin" still in the same year – but this record went nowhere.

The Magic Lanterns

After their version of "Knight in rusty armour" also flopped, CBS put out the LP "Lit up with the Magic Lanterns", an interesting and varied album with great vocal work but, unfortunately, it did not become a bestseller. The highlights of this LP, in addition to their version of **Curtis Mayfield**'s "You must believe me" and "Romeo & Juliet" (co-written by **Mike Collier**) are, without doubt, the **Jimmy Bilsbury** originals, "I'm only dreaming", "Long, long time" and "Too bad it hurts".

Their following single, "Auntie Grizelda", also sold quite well, but it did not get the **Magic Lanterns** back into the charts.

Alistair 'Les' Beveridge joined the group as an additional guitarist and singer and was featured on their next single, "We'll meet again", which had quite a few plays on Radio One and became a favourite with Radio Caroline. In spite of this, it was their last record for CBS.

The management of the **Magic Lanterns** was transferred to Double-R Productions but it took until 1969 before the next single was released – on the little known and apparently not very well organised, Camp label. While "Shame, shame", despite good promotion on radio shows and even being introduced on 'Top of the Pops', did not do anything in England, it was also released in the U.S.A. on Atlantic, climbed up to No. 17 in the American Billboard and became a top hit in Canada, as well as a really popular record throughout Europe.

Around that time, **Ian Moncur** left the group and returned to St. Helens, where he later joined the group, **Harmony Street** and, after that, continued on as a solo performer.

The new bass guitarist with the **Magic Lanterns** was **Mike 'Oz' Osborne** who, despite statements to the contrary, had nothing in common with **Ozzie Osborne**.

This change was followed by **Peter Shoesmith** leaving, as well as the only remaining original member, **Allan Wilson**. Neither of them appeared on the scene again. The new members in the **Magic Lanterns** were **Pete Garner** (lg) and **Harry Paul Ward** (dr).

In 1969, this line-up recorded a great Pop/Rock album on Atlantic, which was named after their big success "Shame Shame", though surprisingly it did not contain any **Jimmy Bilsbury** numbers. For some unknown reasons, this LP, produced by **Steve Rowland** of **Family Dogg** fame, was only released in the USA where it sold very well.

The following single, "Melt all your troubles away", was not as strong and, accordingly, not that successful while "One night stand" in 1970 clearly was an improvement and had much better sales.

In the interim, **Mike Osborne** had left, his replacement was **George Lynam**.

The **Magic Lanterns** toured Sweden quite successfully and, after that, had long engagements at both the 'K52' club in Frankfurt and the legendary 'Top Ten' club in Hamburg. When these engagements were over, the group disbanded. **Jimmy Bilsbury** remained in Hamburg, where he became a member of the very successful **Les Humphries Singers** in 1971.

The Magic Lanterns

Surprisingly, two more singles were released in England in 1972, with "Country woman" (written by Dutch **Piet Veerman** of the **Cats**) and "Stand for your rights", as well as an album "One night stand" – all on Polydor. If the songs featured on that album were not leftovers from previous recordings, they were most probably just studio issue that included **Steve Rowland** sessions that just used the name of the **Magic Lanterns** for their release.

Jimmy Bilsbury sadly died in Germany of heart failure in 2003.

Discography

as "The Hammers":

Long long time / Greedy girl	UK - acetate / 1965

The "Magic Lanterns":

Excuse me Baby / Greedy girl	UK - CBS 202094 / 1966
Rumpelstilskin / I stumbled	UK – CBS 202250 / 1966
Knight in rusty armor / Simple things	UK – CBS 202459 / 1967
Auntie Grizelda / Time will tell	UK – CBS 202637 / 1967
We'll meet again / What else can it be but love	UK – CBS 2750 / 1967
Shame Shame / Baby I gotta go now	UK – Camp 602207 / 1969
Melt all your troubles away / Bossa Nova 1940 – Hello you lovers	UK – Camp 602009 / 1969
One night stand / Frisco Annie	UK - Polydor 2001-013 / 1970
Country woman / You ring a bell	UK - Polydor 2058-202 / 1972
Stand for your rights / Pa Bradley	UK – Polydor 2058-322 / 1972

LPs:

LIT UP WITH THE MAGIC LANTERNS   UK – CBS 62935 / 1967

- You must believe me / What else can it be but love / No milk today / Greedy girl / I'm only dreaming / Long long time / Excuse me Baby / The In-crowd / Look at you / Romeo and Juliet / I stumbled / Too bad It hurts / Simple things / Knight in rusty armor

SHAME SHAME   US- Atlantic SD 8217 / 1969

- Impressions of Linda / Shame, shame / Brunette Lady / Never gonna trust my heart again / Sarah, wear a smile / Give me love / Highway of dreams / Feelings / Missing out on you / Out in the cold again / Pussy willow dragon / When the music stops

ONE NIGHT STAND   UK- Polydor 2460 113 / 1972

- Why can't people be people / One night stand / Pa Bradley / Carolina Brown / Mama sure could swing a deal / Sad thing / Another place, another time / Sara's coming home / Frico Annie / Let the sunshine in

RAY MALCOLM & THE SUNSETS

To relate the story about this early, very good and really interesting group, it might be the best to start with the **Zephyrs**, formed in St. Helens in January 1960 and originally consisting of **Ray Malcolm** (voc), **Frankie Wan** (lg), **Tony Waddington** (p/bg) and **Gordon Marsh** (dr).

In the mid 1960's, **Frankie Wan** and **Tony Waddington** teamed up with singer **George Spruce** (later **Earl Preston**) in **Gene Day & the Django-Beats**, who later became the **Comets**. When this group split, **Frankie Wan** joined **Sonny Webb & the Cascades**, while **Tony Waddington** became a member of **Lee Curtis & the All-Stars**, from which the **Pete Best Four** evolved.

The two remaining members, **Ray Malcolm** and **Gordon Marsh**, got together with three former members of **Bobby & the Cadillacs** and continued as the **Zephyrs** in a line-up with:

Ray Malcolm	(voc)
Geoff Taggart	(lg/voc)
Len Ryan	(rg/voc)
Mike Whitehead	(bg)
Gordon Marsh	(dr)

Prior to **Bobby & the Cadillacs**, **Geoff Taggart** and **Len Ryan** had already played together in **Johnny Kenton & the Nitehawks**.

Mike Whitehead did not stay for too long and became a member of the C&W outfit, the **Vigilantes**, who later continued as the **Aristocrats**. He was replaced by **Johnny Olive**.

The Zephyrs
L to R:
Geoff Taggart
Bert Morris (Manager)
Ray Malcolm
Len Ryan
&
John Olive

In this line-up, the **Zephyrs** became very popular on the Merseybeat scene and, amongst other clubs and venues, they also appeared at the 'Cavern'. They recorded their first acetate with a mobile unit in St. Helens. This was an EP at 78 rpm with **Billy Fury's** "That's love", the Rock 'n' Roll favourites, "Mean Woman Blues", "Twenty Flight Rock", "Whole lotta shakin' goin' on" and the **Johnny & the Hurricanes** instrumental, "Sandstorm".

Len Ryan left directly after the recording and was replaced by **Les Stocks**. Then **Gordon Marsh** left and joined the **Pontiacs**. The new drummer was **Mel Gallagher** who went by the stage name of **Mel Preston** and who came from the **Fireflites**.

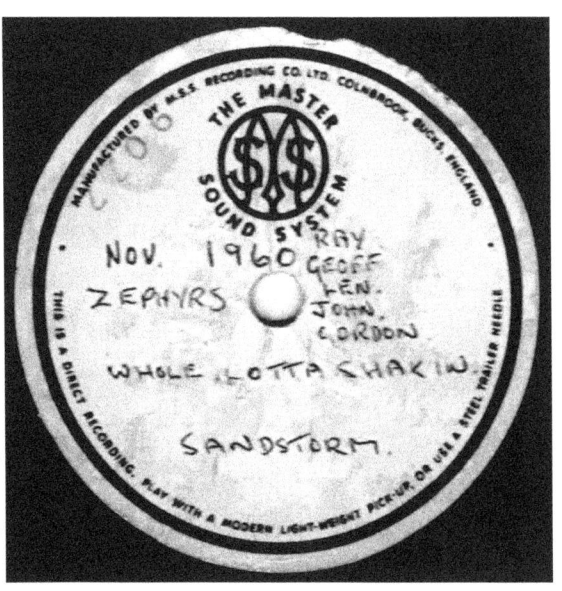

The Zephyrs - L to R: John Olive (bg), Ray Malcolm, Geoff Taggart, Gordon Marsh & Les Stocks

The Zephyrs continued until April 1962, in the interim, **Johnny Olive** was replaced by **Dave Jackson**, also a former member of the **Fireflites**, who were very popular locally.

The group disbanded when **Les Stocks**, **Mel Preston** and **Johnny Olive**, got together with **Stan Gibbons** (bg), and formed the **Classics**, another story in this book.

The remaining members of the **Zephyrs,** together with the returning **Len Ryan,** then formed **Ray Malcolm & the Sunsets**, with the following line-up:

Ray Malcolm	(voc)
Geoff Taggart	(lg)
Len Ryan	(rg)
Dave Jackson	(bg)
Dennis Casey	(dr)

Ray Malcolm & the Sunsets - L to R: Dave Jackson, Len Ryan, Geoff Taggart & Ray Malcolm

Their programme was a mixture of Rock & Roll, **Cliff Richard & the Shadows** and instrumentals in style of the **Ventures** and **Johnny & the Huricanes**.

This was a very good group, appearing at all the important venues in Liverpool including the 'Iron Door', the 'Cavern', 'Holyoake', 'Bradstones', the 'Aintree Institute', the 'Litherland Town Hall' and the 'Lowlands' in West Derby. **Ray Malcolm & the Sunsets** also had a residency at the Carlton club in Warrington and appeared regularly at the 'Casino' in Leigh and various clubs in Manchester, Blackburn and Bradford and, of course, in their hometown, St. Helens, with residencies at the 'Plaza' and the 'Co-Op Ballroom'. In addition, after organising and promoting their own dances at the 'Oddfellows' and the 'St. George' Assembly rooms, they opened a club in St. Helens called the 'Blue-Club'.

Towards the end of 1962, **Len Ryan** left again and was replaced by **Les Painter**, who came from **Dee Young & the Pontiacs**. The drummer carousel kept on turning and **Dennis Casey** was replaced by **Jimmy Lynch** who was then replaced by **Harry Horsley**.

This line-up of **Ray Malcolm & the Sunsets** continued until August 1963 and when **Ray Malcolm** decided to go solo this, of course, led to the group disbanding at that time.

Sometime later, **Harry Horsley** was a member of **Sonny Kaye & the Reds**.

Geoff Taggart, together with **Dave Jackson** and **Lionel Peel** as their new drummer, continued as a trio under the name of the **Sunsets** – but only for a few months and then they changed their name to the **Vogue**.

Geoff Taggart and **Lionel Peel** now shared the vocals and the group was doing really well on the scene. They went into the **Percy Phillips**' studio in Kensington and recorded the **Geoff Taggart** originals, "After the sun goes down" and "Do you think of me", on an acetate.

In March 1965, this trio was joined by **Rita Mather**, a great and, sadly, a much underrated female vocalist who had formerly sung with the **Riot Squad**.

The Vogue - L to R: Geoff Taggart, Lionel Peel, Dave Jackson

The group adopted the name of **Rita & the Vogue** and recorded the **Geoff Taggart** originals, "If I really knew" and "There he goes", on a **Percy Phillips** acetate. An interesting record from which "If I really knew" was re-recorded by **Shakin' Stevens** in 1989.

Shortly after this, **Lionel Peel** left and was replaced by **Ged Murphy**.

Rita Mather left in late 1965 to join **We Few**, who had evolved from **Sonny Kaye & the Reds** and **Reds Inc.**, respectively. They performed under the name **We Few & Rita** until the end of 1966. In early 1967, she sang with the **Crusaders** from Widnes before going solo under the name **Toni West** and, as such, she is still active on the scene.

Rita & the Vogue - L to R: Ged Murphy,

Alby Gornall, perhaps better known as **Alby Cook**, a former member of the **Blackwells**, replaced her for a short time. When he left, the **Vogue** added a new rhythm guitarist, **Morris Scott**, who came from the St. Helens group the **Whirlwinds**. After one more year, the **Vogue** finally disbanded in December 1966.

The Vogue (1966) - L to R: Morris Scott, Ged Murphy, Geoff Taggart & Dave Jackson

Geoff Taggart joined the **Kaytones**, a group that also included **Mel Preston** on drums for a period of time, and **Ray Malcolm** as their vocalist from 1968 until 1969. After that, **Ray Malcolm** formed a new group with his old comrades, **Len Ryan** and **Jimmy Lynch,** under the name, **First Reunion,** which existed until 1975.

The Kaytones - L to R: Ray Malcolm, Geoff Taggart & Mel Preston (1968)

Ray Malcolm then went solo again and sometimes worked in a duo with **Geoff Taggart**.

In 1973, **Geoff Taggart** left the **Kaytones** and teamed up again with **Morris Scott** in the **Ray Regan Attraction**, where they backed singer **Ray Regan** until 1975.

Then, the two former **Vogue** members, **Geoff Taggart** and **Morris Scott,** recruited **Len Ryan** on bass guitar and continued on as a trio under the name **Full Circle**. When **Len Ryan** left in late 1978, **Geoff Taggart** and **Morris Scott** continued as a duo under that name until they finally split in December 1999.

One month later, **Geoff Taggart** formed **In The Mood**, another trio where he reunited with his old comrades **Alby Gornall** (rg) and **Dave Jackson** (bg). They continued on the scene until **Dave Jackson** sadly died in 2005.

Alby Gornall then stopped playing, while **Geoff Taggart**, together with **Ian Picton** (bg) and **Jimmy Donaghue** (rg), still continue as **In The Mood**.

Every now and then there is a **Ray Malcolm & the Sunsets** revival in St. Helens where, besides the singer **Geoff Taggart** always playing lead guitar, the other places in the group are also taken by former members, although they do change from time to time.

Finally, it should be pointed out that **Geoff Taggart** always was a great songwriter who also wrote successfully for other artists. Besides the above mentioned **Shakin' Stevens** release, he wrote "Breakthru" for the **Shadows**, co-wrote "Still 19", recorded by **Charlie Gracie** and **Hayden Thompson**, as well as "Lover boy" for **Charlie Gracie**. Amongst the other artists who released his songs on record were **Carl Mann**, **Ben Hewitt** and **Ray Anthony**.

Discography

as The Zephyrs:

Mean woman Blues / Twenty Flight Rock / That's love /

Whole lotta shakin' goin' on / Sandstorm   UK – Master Sound System 78rpm acetate / 1960

The Vogue:

After the sun goes down /

Do you think of me   UK – Phillips acetate / 1965

Rita & the Vogue:

If I really knew / There he goes   UK – Phillips acetate / 1965

THE MEDALLIONS

As far as it could be ascertained, this Wirral based group with musicians from Birkenhead and Wallasey was formed sometime in 1963 by **Warren Gundry** and **Brian King** – at least, they are the ones that survived from the original four-piece line-up. Unfortunately, the names of the drummer and rhythm-guitarist have been lost with the passing of time. Their original drummer was replaced by **Alfie Youd** but, he also did not stay too long and left when he got engaged to get married. Accordingly, the **Medallions**, as they obviously were named from the beginning, in 1964 consisted of the following musicians:

John Wooley	(voc/harp)
Warren Gundry	(lg)
John Priestley	(rg)
Brian King	(bg)
Kenny Marshall	(dr)

It is not known if any of the new members had played in other groups previously and **Warren Gundry** is sometimes referred to by his nickname, 'Ben' after Benn Gunn, a character in 'Treasure Island'.

With this new line-up, the Medallions had transitioned itself from a pop-group to a Rock & Blues-band – mostly from pressure by **John Priestley** and **John Wooley**. After playing the usual local youth and social clubs, **Donald MacDonald**, manager of the **Prowlers** and father of **Prowlers'** drummer, **Ian MacDonald,** took the **Medallions** under his management.

They now had regular appearances at the 'Princess Ballroom', the 'Callister' and the 'Left Bank Club' in Birkenhead, the 'Victoria Hall' in Upton and they also travelled to venues in Greasby and Bromborough. The purchase of a second-hand van and the addition of a 'roadie' became necessary due to the fact that their bookings in Liverpool, Cheshire and North Wales were quite some distance apart. The **Medallions** had a small but very vocal fan-base that followed the group around and had become a regular audience.

Necessarily, the next step was to record and, for that, their manager arranged a session with a mobile recording-unit at the group's rehearsal-room in the basement of his home in Birkenhead. The **Medallions** went through some of their favourite numbers and it is believed that two **Chuck Berry** songs were recorded onto an acetate, but nobody remembers the titles of those songs. Their manager took this acetate to London in order to promote the group but, sadly, did not come back with any sort of a recording contract.

So the **Medallions** just kept on playing the scene until **Kenny Marshall** left to join the **Klubs***. He sadly died a little later in a boat-accident on the River Dee. This was also the end of the **Medallions** as **John Priestley** and **Warren Gundry** gave up Merseybeat and pursued other forms of music. **Brian King** became a member of the **Shake-Spears** and, after that, joined forces again with **John Wooley** but, it is not known in which group that was. It is known that **John Priestley** later was successful in the international Jazz-scene and, in the late Nineties, founded the Jazz-label 'Sirocco Music' and began producing albums in New York. None of the other members of the **Medallions** appeared on the scene again.

Discography:

In late 1964 the **Medallions**' management set up a recording session with a mobile recording unit and, of that session, two numbers were put on an acetate. It is assumed that both were **Chuck Berry** songs but nobody can remember the titles.

MIKE & THE THUNDERBIRDS

This group, formed in 1959 by two musicians from West Derby and two from the Roby, Huyton area, were sometimes billed as either the **Thunderbirds** or **Mike Byrne & the Thunderbirds**.

Mike Byrne had his first stage appearance on his last day of school at a party at St. Edwards College in West Derby when he, on piano, and his mates, **Pete Dunn** (guitar) and **Ronnie McLoughlin** (voc), performed some Rock 'n' Roll numbers.

A little later, **Pete Dunn** joined the **Pegasus Four**, a group which soon became **Ogi & the Flintstones** and, after that, he was a member of the **Clayton Squares**.

Mike Byrne, together with some friends, formed a new group which, at that time, did not have a name. One night, he went to see **Rory Storm & the Hurricanes** at the Grosvenor Ballroom in Wallasey and asked Rory what he thought of the **Thunderbirds** as a group name. Rory suggested that the name **Mike & the Thunderbirds** would be better.

A few days later, this new group had its first appearance under that name at the C.I. Coffee Bar in West Derby, with a five-piece line-up but the original bass guitarist, called **Paul**, did not stay for too long so **Mike & the Thunderbirds** continued as a four-piece, in a line up with:

Mike & the Thunderbirds - L to R: 'Paul', Dennis Apinall, Mike Byrne, Rod MacDonald & Clive Smith

Mike Byrne	(voc/bg)
Rod McDonald	(lg/voc)
Dennis Aspinall	(rg)
Clive Smith	(dr)

It was the first real group for all the members and, in the beginning, their programme was a mixture of Rock & Roll standards and instrumentals in style of the **Shadows** and **Ventures**.

Mike & the Thunderbirds now started to play the local clubs and dance halls with increasing success and it did not take too long until they also appeared at the popular Liverpool clubs including the 'Iron Door' and the 'Cavern', they also played quite regularly at the 'Klik Klik' club in Southport.

Mike & the Thunderbirds gradually changed their musical style and, from 1962 onwards, they even featured some early **Beatles** numbers in their repertoire.

In 1963, the group went into the Phillips recording studio in Kensington and recorded the **Mike Byrne/Rod McDonald** number, "Web of love" on acetate, coupled with an instrumental by the same writers called "Guitar Espaniola". This was an interesting record but, before **Mike & the Thunderbirds** could do anything with it, **Rod McDonald** decided to join a newly formed group called **Them Grimbles**.

The whole group split up and **Dennis Aspinall** quit the scene, while **Clive Smith** joined the **Cordes**.

Mike Byrne became a member of **Tiffany's Dimensions** but only for a very short time then **Rod McDonald** asked him to join **Them Grimbles**. However, **Rod McDonald** did not want to turn professional and soon quit the music business.

Them Grimbles - L to R: Rob (Burns) Little, Tony Crawley, Mike Byrne, Rod McDonald & Chris Hatfield

Them Grimbles then consisted of the following musicians:

Mike Byrne	(voc)
Ernie Hankin	(lg/voc)
Chris Hatfield	(org/voc)
Trevor Browne	(sax)
Robert Burns	(bg)
Tony Crawley	(dr)

Robert Burns adopted the stage name **Rob Little** and **Ernie Hankin** was a former member of the **Press Gang**.

Them Grimbles, by the way, took their name from the small cartoon-like monsters drawn by their organist, **Chris Hatfield**, which were also used for the group's advertisements. They were handled by the Arcade Variety Agency and **Jim Turner,** himself, became their personal manager. This very professional group, soon established a great name for themselves throughout the entire Lancashire area.

In 1964, they toured Germany and, amongst other venues, played at such well-known clubs as the 'Star Palast' in Kiel, the 'Storyville' in Frankfurt and the 'Savoy' in Hanover, where they went down quite well.

Because their music - a sort of Jazz-influenced Rhythm & Blues - was somewhat unusual for that time, **Them Grimbles** were never signed by a recording company and were never able to make the breakthrough they deserved.

In spite of this, **Them Grimbles** became a really popular group in the northwest and were able to exist very well from their numerous live bookings on the scene.

In late 1964 or early 1965, **Robert Burns**, alias **Rob Little,** and **Tony Crawley** left to join the **Denny Seyton Group** who, a little later, went to Italy as the **Motowns** where they became a very successful recording act.

The new drummer with **Them Grimbles** was **Pete Clarke**, a former member of **Vince & the Volcanoes, Groups Inc.**, the **Escorts** and the **Krew**.

Still in the same year, **Mike Byrne** joined the **Roadrunners** and, after that, played with the **Cordes**. His replacement in **Them Grimbles** was **Adrian Wilkinson**, better known as **Adrian Lord**, a former member of the **Missouri Drifters**, the **Nomads**, the **Mojos**, the **Mastersounds**, the **Bluesville Bats**, the **Faces** and Liverpool's **Easybeats**.

But the group did not exist for too long after that and it was probably in late 1965 that **Them Grimbles** disbanded totally.

Adrian Wilkinson went to Germany to join the **Mersey Five**, who had a long residency over there.

Pete Clarke, after a short stint with the **5 A.M. Event** (a Canadian group based in Liverpool, formerly known as the **Crescendos**), returned to the **Escorts**. After that, he played with the **Fruit Eating Bears,** he then became a founding member of the **Liverpool Scene**.

Chris Hatfield joined **Henry's Handful** and, in the late Seventies, appeared again as a member of **Karl Terry & the Cruisers**.

Of **Mike Byrne,** it is known that after taking a break he played with **Colonel Bagshot's Incredible Bucket Band**, a group that had evolved from the **Cordes** via **Fringe Benefit**. After that, he performed as a solo act at the Liverpool clubs, he was also the manager of the 'Beatles Museum' in the Albert Docks. He then got back on the group scene as a member of **Persuader** and **Rocket 88** before he joined the **Juke Box Eddies**. Today, he is the leader of **Mike Byrne & the Sun Rockers** - a very good Rock 'n' Roll group.

Discography

Mike & the Thunderbirds:

Web of love / Guitar Espaniola   UK- Phillips-acetate / 1963

THE MINITS

The originator of this group from Seacombe on the Wirral was the young and musically talented, **Ian Heath.** At 12 years of age, he already played the chromatic harmonica and, when he joined the 'Boys Brigade', he played bugle in their band. Then he started to play drums and became so good that he occasionally sat in with the **Astronauts**, the beat-group of the 'Boys Brigade', whose leader was the guitarist, **Doug McCleod**.

The members of the **Astronauts** were approaching 18 years of age which required that they had to leave the 'Boys Brigade' and so they decided that it would be good to train some of the younger members to be their replacements. The plan was that **Ian Heath** would be the drummer but, as there did not seem to be any progress with the guitarists, **Ian Heath** also practised this instrument at home and **Doug McCleod** eventually decided that **Ian Heath** would be the lead-guitarist of the new 'Boys Brigade' group but, in the end, nothing ever became of the project.

Ian Heath then decided to start a group of his own and began to rehearse with some friends. Their drummer, **Bobby Gray,** only had a snare-drum, which was okay for rehearsals but not for public performances and so he had to be replaced. Finally, on 17th June 1963, the group had their first booking at the 'Memorial Hall' in Wallasey, supporting the already established **Nightwalkers**. They called themselves the **Conspirators** and appeared in the following line-up:

Ian Heath	(lg/voc)
John Duggan	(rg)
Barry Henry	(bg)
Phil 'Dice' Dyer	(dr)

At this time, they mainly played instrumentals in the style of the **Shadows**, the **Ventures**, and the **Spotnicks**. In August 1963, they decided on another name for the group and so the **Conspirators** became the **Minits**, but things were progressing slowly and there were only two more gigs that year — one at the 'Wallasey Labour Club' and the other on New Year's eve at the 'Gandy Club' in Egremont.

In the meantime, **John Duggan** had decided to focus on his academic art studies at university and had left the group. The new rhythm-guitarist was **Ken Laidlaw**, who probably was also a newcomer. This line-up then played the 'Witch's Cauldron' for the first time, a venue where the **Minits** later appeared on a regular basis.

L to R: Phil Dyer, John Duggan, Ian Heath, Barry Henry

Other clubs they played at around that time were the 'Bronze Club' in Liscard, the 'Tavern' in Wallasey, the 'Boathouse' in Runcorn, the 'West Houghton Casino' and the opening-night at the 'Hole In The Floor' in Seacombe, where they also became regulars.

Occasionally, whenever he was available, the group also worked with **Trevor Thomas** as their guest-singer and, for those gigs, they appeared as **T.T. & the Minits.** When **Trevor Thomas** went on to join another group, **Roy Thomas** came in as their guest singer and the group did not have to change their 'guest' name as he was nicknamed **'Tommo' Thomas.** Whenever they performed without a guest singer, they were billed just as the **Minits** with **Ian Heath** doing the vocals.

T.T. & Minits L to R: Barry Henry, Roy 'Tommo' Thomas, Phil Dyer,
Ian Heath, Ken Laidlaw

On the 2nd March 1964, the **Minits** played the 'Cavern' for the first time when they took part in the *'Rael Brook Beat-Competition'* and placed third. They were approached by **Glady Morais**, probably the father of **Faron's Flamingos*** drummer **Trevor Morais**, who wanted to manage their bookings. He got them gigs at the 'Nigerian Social Club' and the 'Yarouba', both in Toxteth. He also arranged for the **Minits** to participate in another band-competition at the 'Rialto Ballroom', which they won. A little later, **Billy Crabtree** took over the management of the **Minits** and they now played the usual Liverpool clubs such as the 'Iron Door', 'Hope Hall', the 'Peppermint Lounge' and the 'Temple Bar' and also venues outside Merseyside including the 'Lido' in Prestatyn and the 'Carlton' in Rochdale.

In spite of their improving success, there were further changes in the line-up, firstly when **Ken Laidlaw** left towards the end of 1964, followed by **Barry Henry** in early 1965. The new members were **Steve Curtis** on rhythm-guitar and **Paul Sissons** as their new bass-guitarist, who also sung. This must have been the line-up of the **Minits** that, in mid-1965, went into the Unicord studio in Moorfields and recorded an acetate-single with the **Ian Heath** compositions, "This is the hour" and "Minits Stomp", that were both also sung by **Ian Heath**.

In the meantime, the group occasionally worked with a guest-singer, **Steve Dowd**, of whom it is remembered that he looked like **Freddie Garrity** of **Freddie & the Dreamers** and also sounded like him. But this co-operation did not last too long and, later on, **Steve Dowd** became a steady member of the **Vampires** (another story in this book). His place was taken by **Mike Pemberton** (voc/harp), who became a steady member of the **Minits** but he did not stay with them for too long. Then when **Steve Curtis** left and a little later was followed by **Phil Dyer**, the **Minits** continued as a trio with **Ian Heath** (lg/voc), **Paul Sissons** (bg/voc) and a new drummer, **Peter Fenlon**, who formerly had played with the **Breakdowns** and the **Globetrotters**.

This line up lasted until the end of 1965 and, then **Ian Heath,** who had married in the meantime, left the group. **Paul Sissons** disappeared from the scene and **Peter Fenlon** also became a member of the **Vampires**.

Local Beat Five

A young beat group that has become very popular since its formation eighteen months ago is 'The Minits' who have appeared at many well-known night spots including Liverpool's famous Cavern. All Wallasey boys, they are seen here with their new vocalist Mike Pemberton. Left to right: Phil Dyer (drummer), of Jubilee Grove; Ken Laidlaw (rhythm guitar), of Gorsey Lane; Barry Henry (bass guitar), of Wheatland Lane; Mike Pemberton, of Breck Road; and Ian Heath (lead guitar), of Shirley Street.
Photo: Bob Bird, Wallasey

But this was not the entirely end of the **Minits** as, in July 1970, **Ian Heath** and **Ken Laidlaw** got together as a duo again, using the old group-name. By September of that year, the **Minits** had become a quartet again – together with **John Barlow** (bg) and **Lawrence Hill** (dr). They were really busy playing the scene, getting their bookings from the Hal Hose agency. When **John Barlow** left, he was replaced by **Paul Clement** from the **Eclipse**, who was not only an outstanding bass-guitarist but also a great singer.

November 1965—Embassy Club

HOLE IN THE FLOOR
OPENS FRIDAY 26th JUNE
featuring
THE MINITS
7-0 till 11-45 p.m.
106 BRIGHTON ST., SEACOMBE, WALLASEY

His expertise in the use of harmonies and chord-structure led to the band wanting to expand their musical repertoire. Consequently, they also thought a different name was required and so, in July 1971, they became **Vocal Point**. They continued on the scene up to the mid-Seventies but, at some point, they changed their name into **Sweet Life**.

Discography :

This is the hour / Minits Stomp   UK-   Unicord acetate / 1965

> *. . . in those group-days there was a lot of improvisation. The craziest things could happen – and believe me, they did! There are many memories with the Minits but one is outstanding:*
>
> *We played the Attic Club in Bolton and Roy 'Tommo' Thomas was our singer. He loved shaking his maracas, really good ones and not cheap. On the night before we had played in Wallasey where Roy somehow had mislaid his maracas. So he was really upset when he found out they were missing. Somehow he managed to get hold of a pair from a family-member – so all well and good . . .well, maybe not quite. These maracas were cheap plastic ones, that kind you buy for kids . . .*
>
> *Roy was on stage in the middle of a Stones' number, singing his head off and enthusiastically shaking his maracas . . "I used to lover her, but it's all over now" . . when, unknown to him the seams began to split.*
>
> *Now these toy maracas were filled with something like lead shot and black dust began to steep out of it, sticking to Roy's heavily sweating face. Everybody watched as Roy's face got darker and darker but nobody had the heart to tell him. Someone in the audience then offered Roy a hankie to wipe his face and when it came away looking like a chimney-sweeps rag, he realised he was the butt of everyone's laughter. He took it in good part and didn't clean up till after we had finished the set.*
>
> *We had many a good laugh over Roy's maracas after that night.*
>
> Ian Heath / The Minits

*The story of this group can be followed in 'Beat Waves 'Cross The Mersey' (*VelocePress ISBN 978-1-58850-201-8*).

THE MOONRAKERS

To set things right at the very start, this is a sort of 'it could have been this way' story as the described development is highly probable but un-proven as no direct contact could be made with the musicians and no detailed information was available about this group that came from the Allerton area of Liverpool.

So let's start with an ascertained fact: In the second half of the Fifties there was a Skiffle group formed in the South of Liverpool called the **Moonrakers** that consisted of the following musicians:

Mike Cox	(voc)
Ian Pugh	
Mike Cove	(g/voc)
Dave Richards	
Alex Sinclair	(perc/wb)

Now, could it be that **Mike Cox** was identical with **Michael James Cox**, who as **Michael Cox** of 'Angela Jones'-fame in April 1959, appeared for the first time as a solo-singer in the highly popular TV-programme 'Oh Boy!' and, following this, had quite a few records released that were initially produced by **Jack Good** and then by **Joe Meek**. As this is only a possibility or an unproved assumption, it is not reasonable to go into deeper details about this.

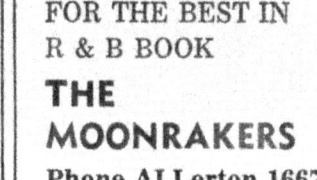

In the late Fifties to early Sixties, the majority of the Liverpool Skiffle-groups changed their music to Rock & Roll or Rhythm & Blues, essentially becoming Beat-groups. This most probably happened with the **Moonrakers** who, in spite of that change, kept their old name, which also was not that unusual. It is certain however, that, sometime in 1963, there was a Rhythm & Blues group from Allerton that was called the **Moonrakers** and that they were joined by a guitarist named **Tommy Caulfield**. It is also known that **Mike Cove** left the **Moonrakers,** around that same time, to join the re-formed **Asteroids** from Stoneycroft, that originally had been known as **Danny & the Asteroids**. These two facts do not prove anything but there is a probability that **Tommy Caulfield** replaced **Mike Cove** in the **Moonrakers**.

The **Moonrakers,** with **Tommy Caulfield,** played the usual Liverpool Beat-clubs and had at least three documented appearances at the Cavern – on 30th July and 15th October in 1963, as well as on 28th June 1964. Also in March 1964, they took second place in the 'Rael Brook Beat Competition' held at the 'Cavern'.

In 1964, they went into the Kensington studio of **Percy Phillips** and recorded an acetate with **Willie Dixon's** Blues classic, "Hoochie Coochie Man", that had been a hit-record for **Muddy Waters**.

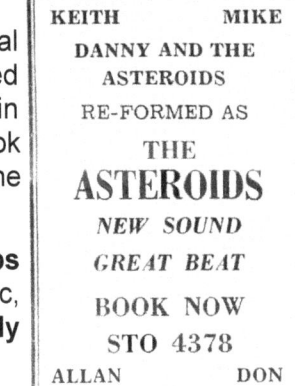

For the B-side of that single, they recorded the **Chuck Berry** song, "Beautiful Delilah". A really interesting record that showed the **Moonrakers** to be a pure R&B-group but, it sadly did not help them obtain a recording-contract or any kind of major breakthrough. They kept playing the Liverpool clubs for one or two more years and, after they disbanded, none of the (known) musicians appeared on the scene again.

Discography

Hoochie Coochie Man / Beautiful Delilah   UK- Phillips Kensington acetate / 1964

Author's note :
This is not a fictitious story but as it proved to be impossible to establish any direct contact, it was assembled from bits and pieces of information that came from various sources.

These facts mixed with assumptions of what was possible or probable does not give a guarantee of correctness. The possibility also exists that the Moonrakers Skiffle group and the R&B group of the same name were two completely different bands . . . .

THE MOROCKANS

This group was formed in Hoylake on the Wirral in 1958 and in its original line-up consisted of **Frank Burns** (voc), **Colin Rimmer** (lg), **Robin Cartwright** (rg), **Brian Woods** (bg) and **John Thomas** (dr).

L to R: John Thomas, Brian Woods, Robin Cartwright, Colin Rimmer & Frank Burns

Initially, they played exclusively at the local Y.M.C.A. dances and their set consisted of the popular tunes of that time. These routine performances continued for a period of almost two years until they decided to expand both the group and their musical repertoire, which led to the first personnel changes.

Brian Woods had left to become a member of **Gus Travis & the Midnighters** and, after that, he played with **Freddie Starr & the Midnighters.** He then went down to London and joined **Heinz & the Wild Boys**. It appears that, sometime in 1966, he returned to Liverpool and joined **Just Us.** He then became the singer and rhythm guitarist with **Art & Sound**, who, besides him, included **Paul Prince** (lg), **Derek Hatton** (dr) and **Cliff Williams** (bg), later of **AC/DC** fame. In the 70's, **Brian Woods** played in a group called **Country Style** and, after that, he was a member of the re-formed **Gus Travis & the Midnighters** throughout the 80's.

But let's go back to the story of the **Morockans**, where **Robin Cartwright** had switched to bass guitar.

A little later, **Colin Rimmer** had to quit the music business as he got a job as a sales representative which included extensive travel throughout the UK.

When **John Thomas** also split from the group, he was replaced (for a short time) by **Pete Williams**, who came from **Gus & the Thundercaps** and who had nothing in common with the musician of the same name, who played the bass-guitar with the **Koobas**.

After **Pete Williams** left, the **Morockans** continued in the following line-up:

Frank Burns	(voc/rg)
Pete Watson	(lg/voc)
Robin Cartwright	(bg/voc)
Derek Cooper	(dr)

They performed at venues all over the Wirral, initially playing a lot of **Cliff Richard & the Shadows** type of music but then they gradually changed their repertoire to include American Rock & Roll numbers. Over time, they eventually developed their own musical style.

The **Morockans** became very popular with the audiences on the west side of the river and, in the early Sixties, they crossed the Mersey to Liverpool where they appeared regularly at the 'Cavern' and the 'Kon Tiki' club.

They signed with the **Gordon Vickers** agency in Chester and often appeared there at 'Quantways' and the 'Flamingo Club', as well as throughout North Wales.

In 1963, the **Morockans** took part in a Beat contest in Bolton and reached the semi-finals and, a little later, they placed fourth in the 'Kings of Beat' contest at the Tower Ballroom in New Brighton. No doubt their biggest success was winning another contest at the Crane Theatre in Liverpool for the 'Best Group of the Northwest'. Obviously, it can be concluded that they were a really good group.

From 1964 on, the **Morockans** organised their own shows and dances on the Wirral as this brought in more money for the group. In addition, they also played the normal club circuit and appeared quite often at the 'Majestic' in Birkenhead, the 'Hoylake YMCA', the 'Grosvenor Ballroom' in Wallasey, as well as in New Brighton at the 'Witch's Cauldron', the 'Kraal' and of course the 'Tower Ballroom', where they shared the bill with such famous names as **Jerry Lee Lewis**, **Joe Brown & the Bruvvers** and **Emile Ford & the Checkmates**.

It was probably around that time that they went into a studio and cut an EP acetate with their original, "That's why I love you", the instrumentals, "Saturday night at the duck pond" and "Casatchok" and the song, "Steve Heighway", which was about a Liverpool footballer adapted to the melody of **Frank Sinatra**'s "My way". This recording got some plays on local radio but, of course, in the end, this did not help the groups popularity, let alone to get signed by a recording company.

The **Morockans** kept playing all the Merseyside venues and existed very well on the scene as they had made a really good name for themselves. They managed to adapt their music to the continuously changing 'tastes' of their audiences. Consequently, they continued to play in the same line-up for an extended period of time.

It was most probably in 1969 that **Pete Watson**, together with **Derek Cooper**, formed a group called the **Familiar Sounds** which, in addition to them, also included **Brian Wadsworth** (rg) and **Ian Baird** (bg). This group played the cabaret circuit extensively and lasted until 1983.

The remaining two founding members of the **Morockans, Frank Burns** and **Robin Cartwright**, were joined by **Kenny Harper** on lead guitar and **Jimmy O'Brien**, a former member of the **Soul Survivors**, as their new drummer. In this line-up, the **Morockans** continued well into the Seventies and were the resident group at the Parkgate Club in Neston.

It is not exactly known when the **Morockans** finally disbanded, but **Jimmy O'Brien** later had a short stint with the **Dark Ages** and then played with the **New Image** and with the second take of **Rockin' Horse**. Today he is a member of the **Undertakers**.

In the early Eighties, **Robin Cartwright** and **Derek Cooper** teamed up again with **Brian Woods** in the re-formed **Gus Travis & the Midnighters,** a group which also included **Pete Watson** who, after **Familiar Sounds**, formed a duo with his wife Tina and played in the local pubs and clubs until 1996.

Discography

Steve Heighway / That's why I love you /
Saturday night at the duck pond/ Casatchok   UK - acetate-ep   / 1964

THE MOTOWNS

In some way, this is the continuation of the **Denny Seyton Group** or the **Denny Seyton Showgroup**, as they were named (and recorded) in Germany. But that is another story that can be followed under **Denny Seyton & the Sabres.*** In late 1966, **Denny Seyton** left the group which then continued on with **Dougie Meakin** from the Liverpool recording group, the **Masterminds*,** under the new name of the **Lovin' Kind,** which they ultimately changed into the **Motowns** and, soon after, that went to Italy in the following line-up:

Dougie Meakin	(voc/rg)
Harold 'Lally' Stott	(voc/lg)
Mike Logan	(org/voc)
Rob Little	(bg)
Tony Crawley	(dr)

All of them were experienced musicians from the Merseybeat-scene and so **Dougie Meakin**, whose full name is **Albert Douglas Meakin**, was originally a member of the **Dingle Dices** and **Clay & the Classics** prior to becoming a founding member of the **Mindbenders** who, a little later, changed their name into the **Masterminds***. **Lally Stott** hailed from Prescot and formerly was a member of the **Black Jacks**, the **Vaqueros** and, for a short time, with the **Four Just Men***. **Rob Little,** whose real name is **Robert Burns**, and drummer, **Tony Crawley,** came from the disbanded **Them Grimbles**. **Mike Logan** was, at one time, the original organist of **Lee Eddie & the Chevrons***.

Originally, they only went to Italy for the 'Festival Delle Rose' for which **Albergio Crocetta** had produced the single, "Prendi la chitarra e vai" with them, which was the Italian version of the **David & Jonathan** success, "Lovers of the world unite". They arrived in Florence during the huge floods of 1966 and lost all their gear through water damage. **Albergio Crocetta** helped them with regular appearances at the legendary 'Piper Club' in Rome and also arranged for the **Motowns** to take part in the RAI television contest-show, 'Canta Giro', which they won in 1967 – with the result that they were contracted by RCA-Italiana and their above mentioned single was re-released with just a different B-side. It was a huge success and the **Motowns** became a big name in the Italian music-business. They were also featured in the music-movie, "L'immensita", together with the Italian stars, **Don Backy** and **Patti Pravo**.

Still in 1967, RCA released the album "Si, Propiro" by the **Motowns**, as well as one more single with "Sagamafina" and "Mister Jones", which were the Italian versions of the **Dixie Cups**' "Iko Iko" and the **Bee Gees**' "New York mining disaster 1941". After that, the **Motowns** were signed to the Durium label and, up to 1969, there were five more singles released, including the Italian versions of **Arthur Brown's** smash hit, "Fire", the **Lemon Pipers**' chart-success, "Blueberry Blue" and **Steam's** "Na, Na, Hey, Hey, kiss him Goodbye".

1970 saw them on the Carosello-label with one single called "Lassu'" after which, **Lally Stott** left and was replaced by **Dave Sumner** (lg), who came from the **Primitives**. This change was followed one year later by **Rob Little** leaving and he allegedly returned to Liverpool. The new bass-guitarist was **Mick Brill**, also an English musician, whose former group is not known. As such, the **Motowns** continued on the Italian scene and, in 1971, had another album released on the Cinevox-label of which the songs, "Wings of a bird" and "Back to my Baby", were coupled out for a single. Both numbers were co-written by **Mike Logan**.

It was in the mid Seventies that the **Motowns** disbanded totally and all of the members remained in Italy where they each started a solo-career and they were all involved in various recording-projects, mainly as studio-musicians or solo-artists for the RCA label. **Mike Logan** later released some solo-singles as did **Dougie Meakin** who, for his releases, used the name of **Sir Albert Douglas**.

By far, the most successful of the members was **Lally Stott** who, previously in 1968, had a solo-single released on Philips with his own composition, "Signora Jones". In 1970, he recorded another original on the same label called "Chirpy, Chirpy, Cheep, Cheep", which became a worldwide hit for the Scottish group, **Middle Of The Road**, for whom he also wrote "Tweedle Dee, Tweedle Dum", another chart-success. Of the releases in his own name against that overwhelming success, only "Jakaranda" (1971) and "Sweet "Meenie" (1972) sold quite well internationally. In 1971, he released the single, "Smiles lots of gentle smiles", using the pseudonym of **Larry Cochran** on the MiMo-label but, unfortunately, it was a flop. Throughout the early seventies, he wrote and produced records for other acts, amongst them the successful Liverpool outfit, **Candlewick Green**. In 1975, together with his wife **Cathy Stott**, they formed the **Lovebirds**, a quite successful disco-act until **Lally Stott** tragically died at age 32 in a bike-accident during a visit to his hometown in Whiston on 6th June 1977.

Discography:

Prendi la chitarra e vai / Per quanto io ci provi	IT - RCA-Italiana PM 45-3374 / 1966
Prendi la chitarra e vai / Una come lei	IT- RCA-Italiana PM 45-3414 / 1967
Sagamafina / Mister Jones	IT- RCA-Italiana PM 45-3420 / 1967
Dentro la fontana / In un villagio	IT- Durium LdA 7585 / 1968
Fuoco (Fire) / In the morning	IT- Durium LdA 7594 / 1968
Dai vieni giu/Los Marcellos Ferial	IT- Durium LdA 7616 / 1968
Sogno, sogno, sogno / Hello to Mary	IT- Durium LdA 7629 / 1969
Na, Na, Hey, Hey, kiss him Goodbye /	
In the morning	IT- Durium LdA 7667 / 1969
Lassu' / Sai forse t'ameró	IT- Carosello CI 20254 / 1970
Wings of a bird / Back tom my Baby	IT- Cinevox MDF JB 026 / 1971

Different foreign releases:

Hola Maria / Sueno, Sueno, Sueno	Peru - Durium DU 7-7038 / 1969
Miraggio d'Estate / Lassu'	Brazil - Fermata FB 33.398 / 1970

Lally Stott – solo:

Signora Jones / Io piego le ginocchia	IT- Phillips PF 363743 / 1968

LP's:

"SI, PROPIRO"   IT- RCA-Italiana S 14 / 1967

Se la va, la va / Si, Si, Silvana / L'uomo in cenere / Don't fight it / Everybody loves a lover / Per quanto io ci piovi / Prendi la chitarra e vai / Um, um, um, um, um, um / Cuore facile / Last train to Clarksville / Something you've got / Una verita

"THE MOTOWNS"   IT- Cinevox MDF 33/48 / 1971

I want to die / Move on out / Wings of a bird / Promise / My sleeping Lady / The eagle /

Back to my Baby / My kind of loving / Woman pig / A trip around the world

*The stories of these groups can be followed in 'Beat Waves 'Cross The Mersey' (*VelocePress ISBN 978-1-58850-201-8*).

THE MYSTERY FOUR

In the beginning, they were **Mark Anthony & the Alpha-Beats**, a group that was formed by the two friends, **Tony Burns** and **Terry Quinne,** in the Kirkdale area of Liverpool in 1962.

Terry Quinne played lead guitar and **Tony Burns** was the vocalist using the adopted stage name of **Mark Anthony.** The other original member was **Tony Baker** on rhythm guitar, while the bass-guitarists and drummers kept steadily changing. However, it is known that, at one point, **Vic Brunskill** was a member, he had recently started to play drums as, prior to that, he had been a guitarist with the **Statesmen** from West-Derby. Later on, he was a member of **T.L.'s Bluesicians*.**

Mark Anthony & the Alpha-Beats played the local youth-clubs, pubs, social clubs and church-halls, including 'St. Luke's Hall', better known as the 'Jive-Hive', and their music-style ranged from Rock'n'Roll and R&B to pure Pop. In 1963, **Tony Baker** decided to leave and disappeared from the scene. Consequently, **Tony Burns** took over on rhythm-guitar and dropped his stage name. As there was already a group from Litherland using the name of the **Alphabeats,** they also decided it was time for a new name, so they became the **Mystery Four** in the line-up with:

Tony Burns	(voc/rg)
Terry Quinne	(lg/voc)
Brian Scott	(bg)
Tommy Maguire	(dr)

The Mystery Four

It is not known, if **Brian Scott** and **Tommy Maguire** had played in other groups previously, but the **Mystery Four** now finally had a steady line-up and started to play the popular beat venues in Liverpool's city-centre such as the 'Iron Door', the 'Way Down', the 'Bear's Paw' and the 'Cavern'.

As they had built up quite a large following, the inevitable next step was a record. So, in 1964, the quartet went into **Charlie Weston's** Unicord-studio in Moorfields to record the **Tony Burns** composition, "Don't Say You're Sorry", as a demo-disc, that most probably was a one-sided acetate. An interesting record but, in the end, it did not help expand the popularity of the **Mystery Four.** This may have been due to the fact that, very soon after the recording, they had to change their name again. The reason was that they were joined by **Ray Renns** on saxophone, as an additional member, who came from the **Vibrators**. Being a five-piece, they became the **Mysteries** and, as such, they kept playing the scene until, for unknown reasons, they disbanded totally towards the end of 1964.

Brian Scott disappeared from the scene while it is stated that **Terry Quinne** became a member of the **Boys**. Sax-player, **Ray Renns,** joined the **Inmates** from West-Derby that, at times, also appeared as **Shades Of Purple**. From there, he went on to play with the **Terry Hines Sextet** that evolved into **Eddie Cave & the Fyx. Tony Burns,** a really great singer, became a member of the **Dominators,** that also backed girl-singer, **Jacki Martin**.

From there, he joined the **Kwans** and then was a member of the Decca recording-trio, **Signs**. **Tommy Maguire,** at first became the drummer of **Them Calderstones,** but then followed **Ray Renns** to the **Inmates** (aka **Shades Of Purple**). After that, he had a short spell with the **T-Squares** before he joined the **Cryin' Shames**, played with the **Fruit Eating Bears** and the **New Merseybeats** and, finally, he became a member of **Karl Terry & the Cruisers**.

In retrospect, it can be said that, despite the quality of the musicians, it's unfortunate the **Mystery Four** or **Mysteries** did not leave a greater impression behind them. However, it is obvious that the individual members left a lot of footprints in the scene.

Discography

Don't Say You're Sorry   **UK- Unicord acetate / 1964**

*The stories of these groups can be followed in 'Beat Waves 'Cross The Mersey' (*VelocePress* ISBN 978-1-58850-201-8).

OGI & THE FLINTSTONES

This is another early, important and highly admired pioneer group of the Liverpool scene. Formed under the name of the **Pegasus Four** in June 1959 by a lead guitarist from Anfield, a bass guitarist from Gateacre together with a rhythm guitarist and drummer from the Toxteth area.

The Pegasus Four

After intensive rehearsals, they played their first gig in December 1959 for the Merseyside Cycling Club at the 'State Ballroom' in Dale Street, which was followed by an appearance at the 'Black Cat' club.

It seems they very soon changed their name into the **Toglodytes** for a short time before they became known as the **Flintstones.**

A misprint in a newspaper advert, which should have read *'Ugh ! It's the Flintstones'* but instead was printed as **Ogi & the Flintstones,** gave the group the name that stayed with them. Although none of the members owned up to being 'Ogi', it was mainly associated with their lead singer.

Right from the beginning, the group, now called **Ogi & the Flintstones**, consisted of the following musicians:

        Ray Walker   (voc/rg)

        Pete Dunn   (lg/voc)

        Keith Crellin   (bg/voc)

        Len Holden   (dr)

Here it should be pointed out that this **Ray Walker** was not the singer of the same name who appeared with the **Del Renas** and the **Escorts** and **Pete Dunn** was not the musician of the same name who played with the **Fontanas** and the **Anzacs**.

From March 1961 onwards, **Ogi & the Flintstones** were the resident group at the 'Zodiac' club. However, in September 1961, they changed their residency to the 'Beat Route' coffee club in Smithdown Road where they were recorded on a reel-to-reel. These highly interesting recordings include "Peppermint Twist", "I love you more than I can say", "Twist in the hall of the Mountain King" (an instrumental corruption of Grieg's 'Peer Gynt Suite'), "Sweet little sixteen", "Let's twist again" and "Reelin' and rockin'", - the latter one being a real knockout, even if the vocals were not really captured on these tapes.

In addition, they played quite regularly at the 'Top Hat', the 'Holyoake', the 'Lowlands' in Haymans Green, 'Blair Hall', 'Hambleton Hall' and 'Knotty Ash Town Hall' and also at the 'Columbus Hall' in Widnes and the 'St. Helens Town Hall', as well as various places on the Wirral – until they became something of a favourite group at the famous 'Iron Door' in early 1962.

Ogi & the Flintstones, with their outstanding musical quality and powerful Rock & Roll sound, were probably the first *'group's group'* on the Merseybeat scene; they were especially admired by the other musicians, a qualification that was also attributed to the **Big Three**.

One major reason for their unusually powerful sound was their self-built bass amplifier, which **Pete Dunn** described as follows : ". . . that had an enormous loudspeaker, which looked like a ship's canon, 22 inch cone, a British Thompson-Houston from the cinema. The box was the size of a telephone-box . . . "

Ray Walker

From October 1962 onwards, they also played regularly at the 'Cavern' and, until May 1963, they had no fewer than 13 appearances at the club.

This was also around the time when **Keith Crellin** moved to Leeds and **Ogi & the Flintstones** broke up - too early to make any sort of a breakthrough, as the Merseysound was only just beginning to gather momentum on both the national and international scene.

Ray Walker later went down to London and became a famous mural painter. He received worldwide acknowledgment for his work. He sadly died much too young in 1984 in London, aged 39.

Peter Dunn

Pete Dunn stayed on the Liverpool scene and became a founding member of the fabulous **Clayton Squares**, where he played until 1967. After that, he continued on as a solo performer for many years. He also became a recording studio technician and worked at Hessy's music shop. In 1983, he emigrated to Australia, where he is still living in Perth and working as an electronics engineer in marine science for the Australian Government. As a hobby, he is still building guitars and amps.

Keith Crellin returned to Liverpool in mid 1964 and, together with **Len Holden,** formed a new group under the name of the **Pilgrims** who, to avoid any confusion with the already existing Wirral group of the same name, changed their name to the **Ferrymen**. Besides **Keith Crellin** and **Len Holden**, this group consisted of **Dave Richardson** (voc/lg) and **John Austin** (rg/voc). This line-up was sometimes joined by **George Georgeson** on vocals and harp, but he never became a steady member of the **Ferrymen**.

Len Holden

The Flintstones live

John Austin did not stay for too long and was replaced by **John Rekkas**. When **Dave Richardson** also emigrated to Australia in 1965, he was replaced by **Alan Millington**, whose former group is not known. The **Ferrymen** continued to play the Liverpool club circuit for quite some time and it is not known when they finally broke up. As far as it could be researched, none of them ever played in another group again.

On 14 March 1968, a group named the **Flintstones** played a one-off gig at the 'Cavern' but, unfortunately, it was not possible to find out if that was a revival gig of the original line-up or an appearance of the **Ferrymen** under the **Flintstones** name. It is also possible that it was a totally different group.

However, what was left of **Ogi & the Flinstones**, besides the interesting reel-to-reel recordings made at the 'Beat Route' coffee club in Smithdown Road in 1961, is a legendary name, never to be forgotten . . .

THE FLINTSTONES
Guaranteed Pure Beat Extract
GAT 2405.

THE PLAZA THEATRE · BIRKENHEAD
W.K. PROMOTION PRESENTS

LITTLE RICHARD

WITH

**THE FLINTSTONES · THE UNDERTAKERS
THE ROADRUNNERS
RORY STORM & THE HURRICANES**

Compere : MIKE COYNE

FRIDAY, 15th MAY · 6 p.m. & 8.30 p.m.

TICKETS
STALLS   3/-, 7/6, 10/6
CIRCLE   7/6, 10/6

S.A.E. with P.O. to Plaza Theatre,
Borough Road, Birkenhead
BOX OFFICE NOW OPEN

THE CAVERN

FRIDAY, 2nd NOV.— The Dennisons; The Spidermen; The Four Mosts; Johnny Martin and the Tremors.

SATURDAY, 3rd NOV.— Group One; The Mersey Beats.

SUNDAY, 4th NOV.— The Big Three; Johnny Sandon and the Remo Four; The Zenith Six Jazz Band.

TUESDAY, 6th NOV.— The Undertakers; Freddy and the Dreamers; Dee Young and the Pontiacs; Alby and the Sorrals.

WEDNESDAY, 7th NOV.— Pete MacLaine and the Dakotas; Lee Curtis with the All Stars; The Big Three.

FRIDAY, 9th NOV.— The Four Mosts; The Zodiacs; The Statesmen; The Flintstones.

Discography:

Ogi & the Flintstones never made a record but were taped on a reel-to-reel at a live performance at the 'Beat Route' coffee club' in Smithdown Road in September 1961 with the songs, **"Peppermint Twist"**, **"I love you more than I can say"**, **"Twist in the hall of the Mountain King"**, **"Sweet little sixteen"**, **"Let's twist again"** and **"Reelin' and rockin'"**.

> " . . . I think the 'Storyville' was the real scene, all the beatniks would go there and the most amazing band in the world at that time – Ogi & the Flintstones. They were better than the Beatles, by far . . .
>
> **(Paul Pilnick / Vince & the Volcanoes, Big Three, Stealer's Wheel, Deaf School and others)**

Author's note:

Pete Frame, in his book of Merseybeat Family trees, mentions a line-up of **Ogi & the Flintstones** that, besides **Ray Walker** and **Pete Dunn**, consisted of **Bob Gurney** (bg) and **Steve Barnes** (dr), but according to **Pete Dunn** such a line-up never existed.

THE PERFUMED GARDEN

As can be inferred from the name, this was one of the later groups on the Liverpool scene. They were formed by the great guitarist, **Jon Fitzgibbon**, in early 1967 after he had played with various Merseybeat groups – amongst them the **Profits**.

A few months after their formation, the original keyboard player **Jimmy Kaileth** left the group and emigrated to the U.S.A.

His replacement was **Barry Cohen**, who had originally played with the **Wild Things** and then the **Washington Soul Band** who, a little later, evolved into the recording group, **Selofane**.

Towards the end of 1967, the group was joined by a stand-alone singer as additional member. Being a five-piece now, **Perfumed Garden** appeared in a following line-up:

Charlie Berwick	(voc)
John Fitzgibbon	(lg/voc)
Barry Cohen	(key/voc)
Les Higgins	(bg)
Peter Pates	(dr)

After gigging around for a while, the musicians decided that they needed to market themselves and went into **Charlie Weston's** Cam studio in Moorfields and recorded a private single with the two originals, "Cover girl" and "A girl like you". The a-side, "Cover girl", was a melodic Rock number with a certain psychedelic element in its arrangement – a very interesting and attractive mixture for the musical tastes of that time. However, the musicians were very critical and unhappy with the final mix. Accordingly, they did not promote it so it did not result in a contract with a major recording company.

After playing the usual club circuit for some time, including the 'Cavern', the 'Vicoriana' (the former 'Downbeat'), the 'Mardi Gras', 'Dino's' and the 'Lowlands in Hayman's Green, **Perfumed Garden** started to play gigs throughout England. Amongst others, they also appeared at the legendary 'Marquee' in London.

On the 7th of December 1968, they were booked to play BBC Radio Merseyside's 'Kaleidoscope' Concert at the Liverpool stadium, where they shared the bill with popular names including **Pink Floyd**, the **Move** and **Cliff Bennett**, another highlight in the career of this talented group.

This line-up of **Perfumed Garden** continued playing on the national scene until late 1969 but, despite some success, they were never able to make a major breakthrough.

Barry Cohen left the group and the music scene to concentrate on his business as a hairdresser and discount shop owner before becoming a hotelier. Recently, he got involved in the music scene again when he took over the management of the female Blues-Rock singer/guitarist, **Kim Karma.** He has also written a book about his time spent in various groups called, 'Cavern After Hours'. Anyone interested should look out for this or have a look at his website, which has the same name as his book.

His replacement, in **Perfumed Garden,** was **Dave Goldberg**, a former member of the **Incident** and **Action Line**. The group kept on touring for a few more years but then called it a day, leaving behind a very good name on the scene.

John Fitzgibbon continued to play in various groups, of which the names are not known, while all the others disappeared from the scene – with the exception of **Dave Goldberg**, who later played with **Lex Lupin, Bobby Sox & the Prize Guys**, before becoming a member of well-known groups including **Liverpool Express**, the newly formed **Merseybeats** and the **Pete Best Band**.

Discography

Cover girl / A girl like you   UK – CAM - acetate / 1968

MARDI GRAS CLUB
ROY 2401

MEMBERS NOTICE

TONIGHT 7.45—2 a.m.
(BAR UNTIL 2 a.m.)
Hit Recorders 'Baby Come Back'
THE EQUALS
On Stage 11.30 p.m.
TOMORROW
CURIOSITY SHOPPE
SUNDAY
PERFUMED GARDEN
ALSO
Familiarity Breeds

MARDI GRAS CLUB
ROY 2401

MEMBERS NOTICE

TOMORROW NIGHT
7.45 — Midnight
Members' Christmas Bonus
Atlantic Recording Star
SHARON TANDY
with FLEUR-DE-LIS
also THE PERFUMED GARDEN
plus MICHAEL HENRY GROUP
Members Normal Prices of
Admission.

LICENSED BAR
HOT MEALS
+ DANCING
CABARET +
GAMING

MEMBER'S NOTICE
dino's
1A, FRAZER STREET, LIVERPOOL 3

TO-NIGHT (THURSDAY)
DANCING 7.30 to 2 a.m.
PERFUMED GARDEN
MICHAEL HENRY
TOMORROW (FRIDAY)
The Fantastic
RUMBLE FAT BAND
with STUART CHARLES
THE PERFUMED GARDEN
Come and enjoy yourselves at
Dino's the in club for the 20's

JOIN THE WILD
SCENE &
THE SOUND

Saturday:
THE BUSINESS
Sunday:
The Perfumed Garden

Members' Notice
OPEN NIGHTLY
8.0—Midnight
Mon. & Wednesday
excepted.
40 SEEL STREET,
LIVERPOOL 1.
ROYAL 0788.

MEMBERS NOTICE
ALL FOURS CLUB
3 EBERLE STREET

SATURDAY:
PERFUMED GARDEN
SUNDAY:
CURIOSITY SHOPPE
MONDAY:
REASON WHY

"The 60s truly were something special and it was great being there to play at so many fantastic venues and meet so many big names at such a young age . . . . "

Barry Cohen / Perfumed Garden

THE PIKKINS

It was sometime in 1962 that two neighbourhood-friends from Orrell Park, a singer and a guitarist, had the idea of forming a group. They found a drummer who lived in the same street and, with two other friends, who could play rhythm and bass-guitar, they were complete. All were newcomers to the scene – the classic way to start a group in those days. Right from the start, they called themselves the **Pikkins** and, in the beginning, their music consisted of Rock & Roll and Beat standards before they discovered Rhythm & Blues and Motown Soul, which later made up the major part of their programme. The **Pikkins** started to play the local dock workers and miners social clubs in the line-up with:

Tony Brown	(voc)
Walter Walmsley	(lg/voc)
Jim Dempsey	(rg)
Philip Donaldson	(bg/voc)
Ged Walsh	(dr)

L to R: Walter Walmsley, Tony Brown, Ged Walsh,
Philip Donaldson, Jim Dempsey

In 1963, the **Pikkins** also started to play the clubs in Liverpool's city-centre such as the 'Mardi Gras' and the 'Iron Door' and they also became regulars at the 'Blue Angel' and the 'Beachcomber'. Although being a very good group, it took them until November 1965 before they played the 'Cavern' for the first time. By then, **Jim Dempsey** had left the group and disappeared from the scene.

The **Pikkins** continued as a four-piece and went into **Charlie Weston's** studio in Moorfields to record an acetate-demo with versions of **Fats Domino's** "Hello Josephine", the **Every Brothers'** "So How Come No One Loves You", the **Johnny Cash** song, "Give My Love To Rose" and **Ben E. King's** "Amor". Quite a musical mixture but an excellent way to demonstrate their musical ability. Soon after that recording, **Ged Walsh** left the group and disappeared from the scene.

The new drummer was **Brian Dodson**, who came from the **Nightguys**, but he did not stay for too long and then went on to play with the **Earthlings** and later became a member of **Liverpool Scene**.

Towards the end of 1965 or possibly early in 1966, the **Pikkins** were joined by **John Gee**, a very experienced drummer, who had started with the **Tokens** and then had played with **Danny Havoc & the Secrets**, the **St. Louis Checks*** and **Freddie Starr & the Delmonts**. At that time, they became professionals and, at the end of 1966, this line-up toured Europe for three months playing the American bases in France (Tours, Nancy, Orleans and Verdun) and Germany (Fulda, Bad Hersfeld, Worms and Babenhausen). Here, it is an interesting fact that their former rhythm-guitarist, **Jim Dempsey,** went with them as a 'roadie'.

Pikkins in Germany

Pikkins in France

On that tour, they had to vary their repertoire to meet the expectations of the servicemen and so they added some Country songs. When they returned to Liverpool in 1966, they kept this mixture and mainly played the cabaret-scene, where they became very busy.

It was in the early Seventies that **Philip Donaldson** left to join Liverpool's Country-scene and became a member of the **Country Gentlemen** and, after that, played with the **San Antones**. He was replaced in the **Pikkins** by **Terry Kennaugh** (aka **Terry Kenna**) who formerly had played together with **John Gee** in the **Tokens** and in the **St. Louis Checks**. After that, he was a member of the **Terry Hines Sextet*** and the **Fyx** (formerly **Eddie Cave & the Fix***). After almost one year with the **Pikkins,** he left and the new bass-guitarist was **Charlie Dunn**, whose former group is, sadly, not known. In that line-up, the **Pikkins** continued until the mid-seventies and then **Tony Brown** left as he moved with his family down to Falmouth in Cornwall. He was replaced by **Philip Donaldson** who returned to the group as their lead-vocalist and rhythm-guitarist.

For another five years, the **Pikkins** kept playing the scene until, after almost seventeen years, they finally disbanded in 1979. This alone shows that it must have been a very good group. As far as it is known, all the members quit the music-business after that.

Discography

**Hello Josephine / So How Come No one Loves You /
Give My Love To Rose / Amor**   UK- Unicord acetate / 1965

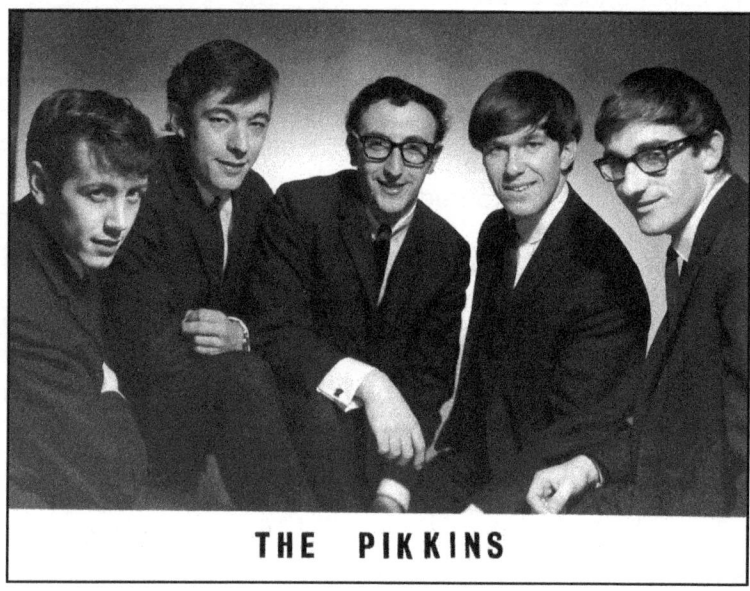

L to R: Ged Walsh, Jim Dempsey, Philip Donaldson,
Tony Brown, Walter Walmsley

*The stories of these groups can be followed in 'Beat Waves 'Cross The Mersey' (*VelocePress ISBN 978-1-58850-201-8*).

THE PILGRIMS

This interesting group was formed on the Wirral in the second half of 1963. The members were apparently all newcomers to the scene and came from different locations, including Birkenhead, Upton and West Kirby, one of the members was even from the Liverpool side of the River Mersey.

A few months after their formation, their original lead guitarist, whose name no one can recall, left the group and, from October 1963 onwards, the **Pilgrims** appeared in the following line-up:

            Keith Ellis   (voc/bg)

            Dave Keighley   (lg/voc)

            Peter Corcoran   (rg/voc)

            Tony O'Reilly   (dr)

Tony O'Reilly was a former member of the **Counts**, who became **Adam & the Sinners** after his departure. **Keith Ellis** formerly had played with the **Thunderbeats** from Moreton, that had changed their name to the **Talismen**.

Dave Keighley was the replacement for the original lead-guitarist and he had previously played with the **Four Sounds**, who, at one time, were also the backing group for **Gus Travis** and, as such, appeared as **Gus Travis & the Midnighters.** During the association with **Gus Travis,** the **Four Sounds** also appeared without him under their own name. **Dave Keighley** also had short stints with the **Rainchecks** and the **Exiles**, formerly known as **Pharoh & the Exiles**.

After playing the usual clubs on the Wirral, including the 'Hoylake YMCA', the 'Majestic' and the 'Cubik' in Birkenhead, the **Pilgrims** very soon became a popular group on the entire Merseybeat scene, playing an attractive mixture of Rock 'n' Roll, Rhythm & Blues and real Blues numbers.

By now, they were appearing at the major clubs in Liverpool's city centre including the 'Cavern', the 'Locarno', the 'Iron Door' and 'Hope Hall'. They were also playing the 'Orrell Park Ballroom', 'St. Luke's Hall' in Crosby (then known as the 'Jive Hive'), the 'Plaza' in St. Helens, the 'Floral Hall' Southport and 'La Scala' in Runcorn. They even made a weekend trip to Edinburgh where they played at three different clubs.

In September 1964, the **Pilgrims** went down to London and recorded the **Keith Ellis** originals, "Save your love for me" and "All night long", on acetate at the Regent Sounds Studio. This acetate caught the interest of the people in charge at the PYE recording company and they invited the **Pilgrims** for test recordings in their studios in London.

Their return trip to London in October 1964 was coupled with an appearance in the 'Beat City' club in Oxford Street, mainly to cover the money for petrol. The **Pilgrims** recorded the above-named songs again; the only problem was that **Keith Ellis** had a bad throat that day and was unable to sing and so he had to go back a few days later to record the vocals.

This led to an argument in the group as **Pete Corcoran** and **Dave Keighley** were not prepared to take any more time off work and so the **Pilgrims** disbanded shortly after the October 1964 recordings. As far as it is known, **Keith Ellis** went back to PYE and recorded the vocals but, of course, the record was never released.

Keith Ellis and **Tony O'Reilly**, the two members that wanted to turn professional, accepted an offer to join the **Koobas**, where they played until this great recording group broke up in 1968.

Regent Sounds Studio - London

Keith Ellis became a member of **Van der Graaf Generator** and, after that, played with the **Misunderstood** and **Juicy Lucy**. He then went to America for some time and, from 1975 until 1978, was a member of **Boxer**, a group that also included **Mike Patto** and **Ollie Halsall** from **Timebox**. Still in 1978, he joined **Iron Butterfly** but sadly died a little later in Darmstadt during their tour of Germany.

The Pilgrims - L to R: Keith Ellis, Tony O'Reilley, Dave Keighley & Pete Corcoran

After the **Koobas**, **Tony O'Reilly** was associated with **Yes** and **Bakerloo** but then he apparently returned to Liverpool where he continued as the resident drummer at a club in Walton Village.

When the **Pilgrims** broke up in 1964, **Pete Corcoran** became a member of the **Coins**, who had evolved from two different groups, **Alby & the Sorrals** and the **Young Ones**.

After the original group had disbanded, there were still some gigs outstanding and so **Dave Keighley** formed another line-up under the **Pilgrims** name. Besides him, it consisted of **Graham Nugent** (rg/voc), **Ray Adams** (bg/voc) and **Alan Denton** (dr).

Graham Nugent was a former member of Liverpool's **Scorpions** and the **Rainchecks**.

Ray Adams came from the **Concords**, while **Alan Denton** was the original drummer of the **Four Sounds** and had played with them under the name of **Gus Travis & the Midnighters** before he joined the **Exiles**.

This line-up of the **Pilgrims** continued to play the Liverpool clubs well into 1965 but then disbanded without having recorded again, as **Dave Keighley** had to move away from Merseyside due to his job as a newspaper journalist.

In 1970, **Dave Keighley** was back with a newly formed line-up of **Gus Travis & the Midnighters** but left the group and the area again in late 1971. He moved to the northeast where he was a member of a group called **Government** for three years but then moved down to London. During the 80s, he did not play at all but, from the early to the mid-Nineties, he was back on the scene as a member of **Roadhouse Blues** from Kent.

After that, he played sporadically with **Gus Travis & the Midnighters** again and formed a trio with his old drummer, **Alan Denton** and former **Avengers** bass guitarist, **Mike Rudzinsky**. In the very late Nineties, they were joined by the former **Dennisons**' singer and guitarist, **Ray Scragge** and continued under the name of the **New Dennisons** but that came to an end when **Ray Scragge** sadly died in 2000 after a long illness.

Today, **Dave Keighley** lives in Kent but he no longer performs.

Discography

Save your love for me / All night long   UK – Regent Sound acetate / 1964

(These songs were also re-recorded by the **Pilgrims** for PYE in October 1964, but unfortunately they were never released)

THE PROWLERS

The history of this highly-interesting Birkenhead group leads back to the formation of the **Confederates** in the early Sixties though, it should be pointed out that this was not the group of the same name that included the future **Searchers** vocalist/guitarist, **Mike Pender**.

The **Confederates**, a group of pupils from Birkenhead, originally consisted of **Johnny Hankin** (voc/g), **Ray Brown** (lg), **Ian MacDonald** (bg) and **Malcolm Coram** (dr). As all the members were still very young, they did not play the usual club circuit, they only performed at local youth clubs.

Malcolm Coram left when his family moved to Liverpool, where he became a member of the **Inbeats**, while his place in the **Confederates** was taken over by **Alex McLachlan**.

When, for unknown reasons, **Ray Brown** also left in late 1962, the remaining members continued as the **Blackjacks**, sometimes presented as the **Original Blackjacks** together with **Phil Norman**, a newcomer to the scene, on lead guitar.

In early 1964, after they had done a few promising gigs together, **Johnny Hankin** left the group to get married.

Obviously, this was a major setback, but they recruited two new members and continued as the **Prowlers** with the following line-up:

Alan Davies	(voc/harp)
Phil Norman	(lg)
Dave Stanton	(rg/voc)
Ian MacDonald	(bg/voc)
Alex McLachlan	(dr/voc)

Dave Stanton was a school mate of **Alex McLachlan** and had formerly played with the local Blues-orientated **Abstracts**, who later became the **Michael Allen Group**.

Alan Davies, another school mate who had a great Blues/Rock voice, was also available because his former group had just disbanded.

As a result of those changes, it was not surprising that the musical direction of the **Prowlers** developed into a sort of Rhythm & Blues where they took obscure American Blues songs and arranged them in a more modern Rock style.

Although they still played the youth clubs, including the 'Methodist Y.C.', Charing Cross, the 'Woodchurch Y.C.' and the 'Callister Y.C.' in Birkenhead, the **Prowlers** now also started to play the usual live clubs such as the 'Majestic' in Birkenhead, the 'Kraal' and the 'Tower Ballroom' in New Brighton and they appeared regularly at the 'Cubik' in Birkenhead. Their first steps towards conquering Liverpool were made with appearances at the 'Temple Bar', the 'Bears Paw' and the 'Rumblin' Tum', which later became the 'Sink'.

BRITISH LEGION HALL
PARK ROAD EAST

THE PROWLERS
THE SHAKESPEARS
Monday, 7th December
7.30 — 11 p.m.

ADMISSION 3/6.

No Pass-outs

No admission after 9 p.m.
In aid of O.A.P's and Dacre House (s)

The **Prowlers**' bid to build their local popularity was given a boost one night in mid-1964 at the Callister Youth Club in Birkenhead. A few young female fans who followed the group were in front of the stage, clapping along to the music, when suddenly they started screaming. Many others joined in not knowing what was going on. The club manager ran from his office, stopped the show and sent everyone home. Of course, the group was thrilled with the audience reaction and were surprised to find a much bigger crowd than expected at their next local gig. Clearly, word had spread and, as soon as the band opened up, the screaming started and continued throughout the show. From this point on, the group's following grew rapidly and screaming audiences became the norm at Wirral venues and later also at out-of-town gigs.

The Prowlers - L to R: Mally Coram, Ian MacDonald, Phil Norman, Dave Stanton & Alan Davies

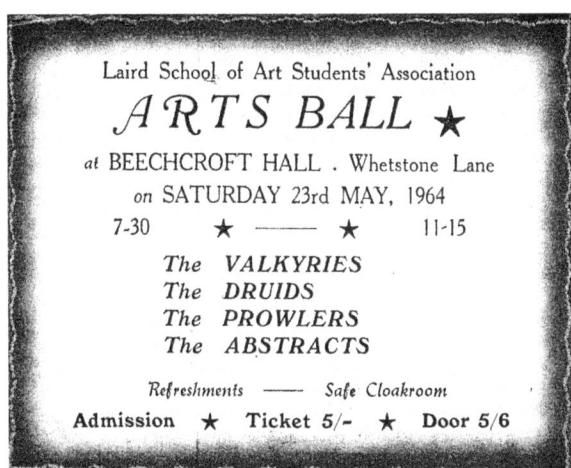

With their popularity rising fast, the **Prowlers** came to the conclusion that they needed a demo disc to continue building up their career. Recognising that they probably had to do something original and more pop in style, they wrote the ballad "Lost and alone". Their fans loved it and shouted for the song at every show.

It was in mid 1964 that they recorded it with a mobile unit at the 'Callister Youth Club' and, for the flipside, they chose the **Slim Harpo** song, "I'm a kingbee". Copies of this interesting demo were sent to the big recording companies, but the **Prowlers** only got polite letters of rejection from them.

Alex McLachlan left the group and was replaced by the returning **Mally Coram**, who in the interim, had played with **Vince Earl & the Talismen**.

The **Prowlers**, with their ever increasing success, spread their activities over Lancashire and Cheshire and into the North Midlands, playing regularly at venues including the 'Teen Beat' in Crosby, the 'Cubik' in Rochdale, the 'Klic Klic' in Southport, the 'Catacombs' in Preston, the 'Sportsman' in Wigan, Hope Hall in Warrington, the 'Fareways' in Wrexham and the 'Majestic' in Crewe.

In September 1964, the **Prowlers** took part in an audition at the Grosvenor Ballroom in Wallasey for the 'Star Palast' in Kiel/ Germany. The Star Palast manager, **Bob Xavier**, from the London group **Bob Xavier & the Jury**, selected the **Prowlers** and, at the same time, **Ken Darville-Smith,** who ran the 'Darville Entertainment' agency, became their new manager.

When the time came to go to Germany, in January 1965, the group members found out that you had to be at least 18 years old to work in Germany but their drummer, **Mally Coram,** was only 17. He threatened to leave the group if he did not go with them and so the **Prowlers** engaged a stand-in drummer in **Tony McGuigan** from the **Saracens**, and, also (at their own expense), took **Mally Coram** along. Of course, **Mally Coram** actually played at most of their gigs in Germany.

In January 1965, they went to Kiel for a month-long engagement, taking over from **Freddie 'Fingers' Lee** and his group, which also included a young **Ian Hunter**, later of **Mott The Hoople** fame.

The **Prowlers** went down very well and soon established a following of fans at the 'Star Palast', where, at one time, they shared the bill with the all American female group **Goldie & the Gingerbreads**. However, the drummer for **Goldie & the Gingerbreads** was not feeling well so the **Prowlers** 'stand-in drummer', **Tony McGuigan**, 'stood-in' for him at some of their gigs. On another occasion, the **Prowlers** backed coloured American singer, **Davy Jones**, whose group had not arrived in time for his performance.

German work permit (1965)

Prior to the **Prowlers** returning to England, they also played a few days at the 'Star Palast' in Eckernförde but then they were recalled to Kiel by public demand. All in all, this was not only a great experience for the group but also a very successful trip, as they were re-booked for April and July 1965.

Arriving home, they received a very warm welcome from their fans, who hardly had time to see their favourite group as they were soon off again to tour Scotland.

Following that tour they got repeated engagements at the well-known Liverpool clubs, including the 'Iron Door', the 'Peppermint Lounge', the 'Orrell Park Ballroom' and, of course, the 'Cavern', where they became regulars with four to five appearances per month. They also played the major venues throughout England where they became very popular, especially in the Birmingham area.

On their second trip to Germany, they moved around the 'Star Palast' chain in Eckernförde, Rendsburg and Lüneburg, but mainly played in Kiel again.

They were offered recording contracts by both Philips and Polydor but, in the end, turned both down, as a prerequisite for these contracts were long residences in Germany to promote the records, which the group did not want to do.

1965 really looked like it would become a big year for the **Prowlers** and, acknowledging this, the group cut a new demo with "I believe to my soul" and "You don't own me" at the Northampton Sound studios. PYE seemed to be interested in signing the group, but, again, in the end there was no contract.

Star Palast Club - Germany

A few months after their third, very successful German trip, **Dave Stanton** left to form a new group called the **A-Go-Go-Set**, which, in the end, never made a public appearance. The **Prowlers** continued as a four-piece until **Alan Davies** also decided to leave in early 1966. That was the beginning of the end for this promising group.

The Prowlers - L to R: Alan Davies, Dave Stanton, Ian MacDonald, Phil Norman & Mally Coram

Alan Davies and **Dave Stanton** later ran a disco together and, after that, disappeared from the music scene.

After a short break, the **Prowlers** were back on the scene with two new members, **Mick Thackery** (voc) and **Pete Wharton** (rg), though their previous groups are not known. This only lasted for a few weeks and then **Mick Thackery** was replaced by **Phil Munro,** who came from the just disbanded **Detroits.**

Max Wilson became the new manager for the group, who still played regularly at the 'Cavern' and who were also very popular in the Ellesmere Port and Chester clubs, where they often appeared a 'Quantways' and the 'Warren'.

Suddenly, just when things appeared to be turning around again for the **Prowlers**, another change occurred when **Pete Wharton** left and was replaced by **Dougie Hughes**.

With this line-up a third acetate was recorded at Lynsound in Wallasey with "Cadillac", which had been a huge European success for the **Renegades** from Birmingham. Coupled with the **Max Wilson** original, "Motor car", this demo caught the interest of Decca but, for some unexplainable reason, once again, no recording contract was signed. Although "Cadillac" was not released commercially, it was heard hundreds of times on the pirate station Radio Caroline as an introduction for the 'Cavern' advertisements.

In April 1967, **Phil Munro** and **Dougie Hughes** left and effectively this was the end of the **Prowlers.** They decided to change their material, add a keyboard and a sax player and start afresh with a new name, the **Hartford Sound** having already been chosen.

Unfortunately, this planned group did not become reality . . . so the **Prowlers**, who had shown such promise in 1964/65, were no more.

The members went their separate ways on the scene but, in 1988, **Phil Norman**, **Ian MacDonald** and **Mally Coram** teamed up together again in the six-piece Blues band, **Out Of The Blues**. The line-up also included **John Peacock** on keyboards, a former member of the **Roadrunners**, as well as the sax player **Jack Curtis**, who had played in many groups in the 60's including the **Renegades**, the **Night Walkers**, the **Secrets** and the **Dresdens**. The singer of that sextet was Jack's son, **Paul Curtis**.

```
PEPPERMINT LOUNGE
Fraser Street, Liverpool
To-night — Friday — To-night
Currently riding high in the hit parade
    the fantastic sound of the
   RICHARD KENT STYLE
Saturday — Saturday — Saturday
       THE PROWLERS
       THE REACTION
Sunday — Sunday — Sunday
    THE CONNOISSEURS
        THE COLTS
Have you seen our startling
      DISC-AFRIQUE
Made a date this week-end and go
to the club which always sets the trends
     THE PEPPERMINT
         LOUNGE
   STRICTLY OVER 18 ONLY
    LICENSED RESTAURANT
```

This group lasted for around four years and, after that, **Ian MacDonald** played in groups including **Overdrive** and **Smiley**, while **Phil Norman** was part of a studio band called **Upturned Collar**.

Mally Coram, who ran a small recording studio, kept playing on the scene until he emigrated to Australia, where he played with the **Duke Wilde Band** but, sadly, died unexpectedly in Brisbane in February 2008.

None of the other members of the **Prowlers** appeared on the scene again.

Discography

Lost and alone / I'm a kingbee	UK – (?) acetate / 1964
I believe to my soul / You don't own me	UK- Northampton Sound acetate / 1965
Cadillac / Motor car	UK – Lynsound acetate / 1966

"The Prowlers proved their success by attracting over 500 teenagers to see them again. To that popular beat group, The Prowlers, the enthusiasm shown by Ellesmere Port's teenagers has been something like the sparkling cascade of champagne on a ship's bows"

Ian Craig / Ellesmere Port Pioneer – June 1965

TOMMY QUICKLY

Thomas Quigley was born on 7 July 1943 in Liverpool and he is often documented as one of **Brian Epstein's** failures, although that does not do justice to his talent and the significant role he played on the Merseybeat scene.

He was a fragile character and highly immature for his age. Consequently, it can be a difficult task to trace a serious photo of him, as he would normally be making silly faces. In addition, due to his immaturity, he was easily influenced and he probably did not object when he was lead the wrong way musically, as also happened to some other artists from the NEMS stable.

However, he started his career, together with his sister, **Patricia Quigley,** in the **Challengers** in 1961 or 1962. Besides these two as a singing act, the group consisted of **Bob Gilmore** (lg), **Pete Wilson** (rg), **Ray Pawson** (bg) and **John Bedson** (dr). Their manager, at that time, was **David Bramwell**. It was a good group, playing a sort of Rhythm & Blues-influenced Beat and all three guitarists could read and write music, which was not normal for the groups at that time.

The Challengers with Patricia and Tommy Quigley

Tommy Quickly & the Challengers became regulars at the famous 'Iron Door' in Liverpool and, in 1963, when they appeared on the same bill as the **Beatles** at the 'Majestic' Ballroom in Birkenhead, **Brian Epstein** became interested as, in his opinion, the singer had the same sort of impish personality as **Gerry Marsden**. He suggested a name change to **Tommy Quickly & the Stops**, but this simple-minded idea was declined right away by the musicians.

When **Dave Bramwell** had to give up managing the **Challengers** in 1963, **Brian Epstein** took his chance and signed up the singer but not the group, whom he considered to be "too ugly" – a short-sighted decision as the group was an integrated entity. The **Challengers** continued on the scene, backing R&B singer **Steve Aldo**.

As with others artists he managed, **Brian Epstein** gave **Tommy Quickly** a Lennon/McCartney composition for his first record release but, "Tip of my tongue" was a poor song and, accordingly, it went nowhere.

Still in 1963, **Tommy Quickly** was put together with the **Remo Four** who, until then, had been backing singer, **Johnny Sandon,** who had just started a solo career. Doubtlessly, one of the best Liverpool groups ever, at that time, the **Remo Four** consisted of **Colin Manley** (lg), **Phil Rodgers** (rg), **Don Andrews** (bg) and **Roy Dyke** (dr). **Tommy Quickly & the Remo Four** made quite an impact on the live scene but, unfortunately, not with their records.

Tommy Quickly

"Kiss me now" was written by **George Martin** and, despite having a better musical arrangement, it was somewhat harmless and boring, and so, it was as unsuccessful as Tommy's debut. The next one was written by **Gerry Marsden** and he probably knew exactly why he did not record it himself – "Prove it" was another flop.

The **Tommy Roe** song, "You might as well forget him", was the first acceptable material that had been given to **Tommy Quickly & the Remo Four** for a recording and it turned out well but, unfortunately, it did not make the charts.

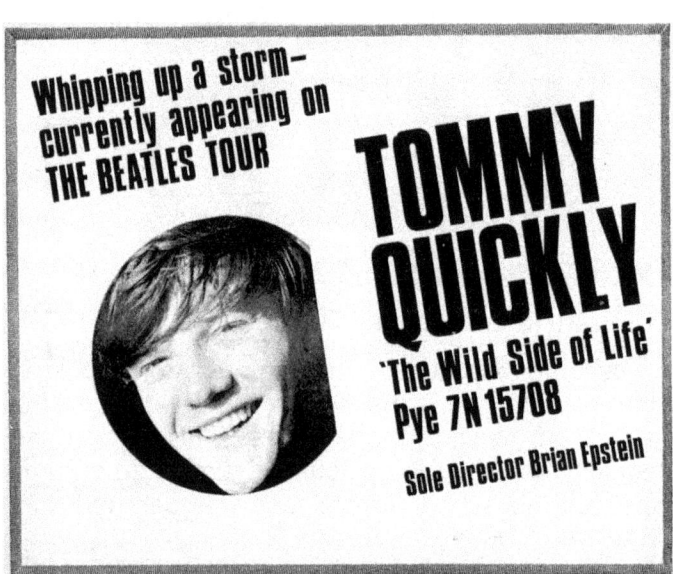

An international breakthrough seemed to be within reach when the follow-up, **Hank Thompson**'s Fifties success, "Wild side of life", climbed up to No. 33 in the British charts, despite being a Country-based number. It was also released on the European continent, including the Netherlands, Germany, France and parts of Scandinavia where it became quite popular. This song was successfully covered in the Seventies by **Freddie Fender** (1976) and **Status Quo** (1977), where the latter version was clearly taken from the arrangement on the **Tommy Quickly & the Remo Four** recording.

A good singer with a great group and an ambitious record meant it was clearly on the well-deserved way up. Even the Americans showed interest and invited **Tommy Quickly** to tour the U.S.A. Apparently, the management did not understand the signs of the times when it allowed, influenced or even decided on the live version of the childish drivel "Humpty Dumpty" for their next record. It is not really surprising that it became the next flop. However, it was clear that the musical style of the flipside, "I'll go crazy", suited the singer much better. This was the type of music that **Tommy Quickly** had previously sung with the **Challengers**.

In 1965, he was backed by the **Take Five** from Southport on another nationwide tour but his management was unable to push him any further. Disappointed with the lack of success of his recordings, **Tommy Quickly** retired from the music business never to return.

In retrospect, it can be said that had he continued with the **Challengers** and their R&B influenced Beat and without **Brian Epstein**, **Tommy Quickly** most probably would have made a much bigger impact in showbiz.

For more information on **Tommy Quickly** please see the **Challengers** & the **Remo Four** stories in the book *"Mersey Beat Waves"* – *ISBN 1588502015 or 9781588502018.*

Discography

Tommy Quickly – solo:

Tip of my tongue / Heaven only knows	UK – Piccadilly 7N 35137 / 1963

as **"Tommy Quickly & the Remo Four"**:

Kiss me now / No other love	UK – Piccadilly 7N 35151 / 1964
Prove it / Haven't you noticed	UK – Piccadilly 7N 35167 / 1964
You might as well forget him / It's as simple as that	UK – Piccadilly 7N 35183 / 1964
Wild side of life / Forget the other guy	UK – PYE 7N 15708 / 1964
Humpty Dumpty / I'll go crazy	UK – PYE 7N 15748 / 1964

EP: THE WILD SIDE OF LIFE   F - PYE Vogue PNV 24124 / 1964

- Wild side of life / It's as simple as that / Tip of my tongue / Heaven only knows

THE QUINTONES

It was in the Spring of 1960 that this group was formed in Prescot, a small town on the outskirts of Liverpool. Fortunately, they had the availability of a room in the local 'Crown Hotel' where they could rehearse every Thursday night. Their music-repertoire in the beginning consisted of Rock & Roll, the popular hits of the day, some standards and a little Rhythm & Blues. That mixed bag of music had the advantage that the **Quintones**, as they were named from the beginning, were able to play all different types of bookings.

Their original vocalist, **Michael Gillgannon,** was older than the other musicians who were unhappy with his singing style, as they considered it to be a little 'old-fashioned'. One night during their rehearsal session, there was a private party going on in an upstairs function-room and there was a group playing with a singer who met their expectations. They asked him to join, he agreed and, from late 1960 onwards, the **Quintones** appeared in the following line-up:

Tony Lewis-Gilbert	(voc)
Robert Cane	(lg/voc)
John Naylor	(rg/harp/voc)
Ray Naylor	(bg)
Bill Holden	(dr)

John Naylor was the younger brother of bass-guitarist, **Ray Naylor,** and, with exception of the new vocalist, none of the musicians had been in another group previously.

The Quintones 1962—L to R: John Naylor, Bill Holden, Ray Naylor, Tony Lewis, Robert Cane

The **Quintones** played the local pubs and clubs in Prescot but had also appearances at some of the major venues, such as the 'Plaza' in St. Helens and the 'Casino-Ballroom' in Bolton, both not too far away from their hometown. In 1962, they decided to participate in the 'Battle of the Bands' competition which was held at the 'Neptune Theatre' in Liverpool. For that they needed a demo and therefore they booked into the **Percy Phillips** studio in Kensington where they recorded the vocal-number, "With you", a group-original. For the B-side they chose a **Shadows** number of which it is assumed that it was 'Nivram', but no one could recall for certain.

The **Quintones** did not become the winners of the band-competition but, probably through their participation, they now also started to play the Liverpool venues. Among others, they had regular bookings at the 'Gorsey Cop' in Gateacre, a 'posh' private club that was extremely popular at that time. In addition, on the 25th September 1963, the **Quintones** appeared at the 'Cavern' for the first time.

Shortly after the 'Cavern' appearance, the brothers, **Joseph & Stanley Kelly**, who ran a small booking agency, took over their management and they suggested a name change and so the **Quintones** became the **Kobras** in early 1964. As such, they kept playing the local and Liverpool-scene but also had bookings further afield such as the 'Palace Cinema' in Pentre Broughton, near Wrexham, where they appeared quite frequently.

It was in mid-1965 that **Bob Cane**, **Billy Holden** and **Ray Naylor** got married, one after the other, and obviously did not have enough time for the **Kobras** anymore so, towards the end of that year, the group disbanded. As far as it is known, all members quit the music business.

Only of **Ray Naylor** it is known that he later played in a Country & Western group. In 1970, **John Naylor** moved to Johannesburg in South Africa for job related reasons and there he started to play again in a Boere-musiek group (a type of South African instrumental folk music). When he returned to Merseyside in 1983, he took up the bass-guitar and currently performs as part of the resident trio at the 'Wellington Pub' in Prescot.

Discography

as the **Quintones**:

With You / Nivram (?) UK- Phillips Kensington acetate / 1962

Kobras 1964—L to R: Bob Caine, Billy Holden, Tony Lewis, John Naylor, Ray Naylor

THE RENICKS

Formed in the north end of Liverpool in 1961, this group was inspired by the **Ravens**, later to become **Faron's Flamingos**, who lived in the neighbourhood and who used to rehearse in the garden during the summer. **Ted Wallace**, his brother **Len Wallace** and their school mate, **Trevor Blackham,** used to sit on the fence and listen to the rehearsals when, one day, they decided to form their own group. They convinced another friend from school to join in and started to rehearse in the basement of the Wallace's house.

They originally called themselves **Eddie & the Escorts** and soon found out that they were in need of a real lead guitarist. Through **Ted Wallace**'s girlfriend, they got in touch with a guy from her neighbourhood who could play all the **Shadows** numbers and he agreed to join.

As they were now a 'complete' group, they changed their name to the **Renicks** and soon got their first booking at the 'Blue Ball' in Liverpool – with the following line-up:

Ted Wallace	(voc)
Billy Lunt	(lg/voc)
Len Wallace	(rg/voc)
Trevor Blackham	(bg)
Jimmy Simpson	(dr/voc)

The **Renicks,** at that time, were playing a lot of **Arthur Alexander** songs, as well as Blues numbers by **John Lee Hooker**, **Sonny Boy Williamson**, **Howlin' Wolf** and others, all re-arranged in the Merseybeat style.

The group did an audition for manager/promoter, **Dave Forshaw**, who signed them on the spot. Almost immediately, the **Renicks** were booked six nights a week, playing at venues that included 'St. Johns Hall' in Bootle, the 'Litherland Town Hall', the 'Jive Hive' in Crosby and the 'Orrell Park Ballroom'. They also appeared quite often at the 'Kingsway Casino' in Southport, where they supported headliners such as **Johnny Kidd & the Pirates**, **Screaming Lord Sutch** and **Dusty Springfield**, just to name a few.

It was probably in 1963 that **Dave Forshaw** sent the **Renicks** to the CAM recording studio in Moorfields to record an acetate with the **John Lee Hooker** number, "Dimples" and **John Mayall**'s "Crocodile Walk" on the flipside. In addition, they were recorded live at the 'Craftsman' in Birkenhead, together with two other groups from the **Dave Forshaw** stable, one of which was most probably the **Mersey Gonks**.

The songs that were recorded live by the **Renicks** were "Dimples", which doubtlessly was one of their favourite numbers, "Little Queenie" plus two originals, the titles of which cannot be recalled. Unfortunately, neither the live recordings, nor the previously recorded acetate lead to a recording contract, so they were never released.

A little later, the **Renicks** did another live recording and a photo shoot at the 'Klic Klic' in Southport for an American magazine but, unfortunately, nobody knows what happened to that or which songs were recorded. Maybe there was some special edition released in the USA . . . . . ?

When **Dave Forshaw** wanted to send them to play the American military bases in France and Germany, only **Ted Wallace** and **Billy Lunt** were prepared to go, as the others had good jobs that they did not want to leave. This was the beginning of the end for the **Renicks**, the cohesion started to crumble.

The Renicks

Len Wallace left and formed a folk duo with the group's roadie, **Billy Driver**. He was followed by **Trevor Blackham**, who put the bass guitar aside and took a job as the resident drummer in a cabaret club. The next to leave was **Ted Wallace**, who became a member of the **Impact**.

The remaining **Billy Lunt** and **Jimmy Simpson** recruited **Vinnie Thomas** (bg) from the **Croupiers** and **Nick Cleary** (rg) and they teamed up with **Ricky Gleason**, who had just left the **Rebels**. He had previously been the leader of the well-known **Ricky Gleason & the Topspots**.

This new line-up of the **Renicks** only made a few appearances under their old name and then went on as **Ricky Gleason & the New Topspots** for a couple of years.

Ricky Gleason then became a member of the **St. Ive's Trio** and later teamed up in a cabaret duo with **David May**, formerly with **Mark Peters & the Silhouettes** and **Rory Storm & the Hurricanes**. After that, he quit the music business for many years and only recently reappeared again with a re-formed Sixties line-up of **Ricky Gleason & the Topspots**.

Billy Lunt and **Jimmy Simpson** formed a cabaret group under the name the **Twigg** with Jimmy's brother **Brian Simpson** as lead vocalist and **Colin Oates** on bass guitar.

Nick Cleary and **Vinnie Thomas** moved on to other groups whose names are not known.

Ted Wallace formed a new group together with his brothers, **Len Wallace** (rg), **Steven Wallace** (lg) and **Peter Wallace** (bg) - calling themselves the **Family Affair**. This four-piece harmony group became very successful on the cabaret circuit, working throughout the country.

In later years, **Ted Wallace** and **Billy Lunt** got back together and formed the **Squares**, a comedy show band, doing a lot of Motown and other Soul stuff. They were on the scene for quite a few years before they disbanded in 1999.

All the former members of the **Renicks** went back to normal day jobs and only **Billy Lunt** is known to still play the guitar – but just for fun.

Ted Wallace works for a film production company these days and his brother, **Len Wallace** sadly died far too young a few years ago, aged just 44.

Discography

Dimples / Crocodile Walk   UK - CAM acetate / 1963

The **Renicks** were also recorded by the Admiralty recording unit at the 'Craftsman' Club in Birkenhead in 1963, although this was not followed by a release. In addition to two originals, the songs **"Dimples"** and **"Little Queenie"** were recorded.

In 1964, another live recording was made at the 'Klic Klic' in Southport, which was for an American magazine, but nobody knows what happened to that and it is not known which numbers were recorded.

> *"The Beatles and other Liverpool bands had broken onto the world stage, this was an exciting time in pop music – something extraordinary and vibrant was happening and I wanted to be part of it."*
>
> *(Ted Wallace, The Renicks)*

THE RIGG

When the **Climaks** disbanded in 1964, two of their members, **Stuart Lynch** (bg) and **Pete Beckett** (rg) got together with **Derek Anfield** on lead-guitar and **William 'Billy' Geeleher** on drums, who came from the **Fab Five**, and formed a new group named the **Modes.**

Pete Beckett did not stay for too long and went on to join the **Thoughts*** and he was replaced in the **Modes** by **Kenny Parry**, a great singer and guitarist, who came from a Garston group, the **Scribes**, that were formerly known as the **Banshees**. The **Modes** obviously were a good Beat band and became very busy on the scene but that did not stop **Billy Geeleher** from leaving them to join the **Calderstones***. His replacement was **Ken Folksman**, who had formerly played with **Stuart Lynch** in the **Climaks** and, in the meantime, had been a member of the **Bo-Weevils**. In this line-up, the **Modes** existed until mid-1965 at which time they disbanded due to disagreements between the members over their musical direction.

The Modes—Billy Geeleher

Derek Anfield disappeared from the scene and **Ken Folksman** at first became a member of the **Verbs**. After that, he joined the **Admins** and then kept on playing in various other groups, mainly in the cabaret-circuit, until 2004. **Kenny Parry** and **Stuart Lynch** together with the drummer, **Mick Pappas,** formed a trio under the name of the **Rigg**. Their music was a sort of heavy R & B in the style of the **Yardbirds**, **John Mayall** or the **Paul Butterfield Bluesband**. They were enthused by the sounds of **Graham Bond** and even more so by **Zoot Money** but, for that they urgently needed a keyboard-player. It was not easy in those days to find the right individual but, in 1966, they were successful and the **Rigg** finally became a four-piece in a line-up with:

Kenny Parry	(voc/lg)
Geoff Russell	(key/voc)
Stuart Lynch	(bg/voc)
Mick Pappas	(dr)

Mick Pappas came from the **Lawrence James Federation** and, before that, had played with the **Blue Sounds** (another story in this book). **Geoff Russell** had started as a short-time member of the **Nashpool Four*** and, after that, had played with the **Bo-Weevils** from Speke, also featured in this book. The **Rigg** obviously hit the right music-nerve of that time and quickly became very busy on the scene, playing clubs such as the 'Iron Door', the 'C.I.-Club' in Sunfield Park, the 'Four Winds', the 'Waydown', the 'Mardi Gras' and they also became regulars at the 'Cavern'.

On April 5th, 1966, they played at a benefit-concert, 'A Night For Mike', at the Grafton Ballroom which was held in remembrance of the very popular **'Big Mike' Millward** of the **Fourmost*** who had recently died at a very young age. After their spot, the former **Searchers*** drummer and now record-producer, **Chris Curtis,** came up to them and offered the **Rigg** the opportunity of a recording test at PYE in London. Accordingly, a few weeks later they went to London for that audition and both **Chris Curtis** and the PYE label-director, **Tito Burns,** were present during the recording session. The **Rigg** recorded three numbers, namely "Good, Good Lovin'" by **Ike & Tina Turner**, the **John Mayall** title, "Heartache" and **Arthur Alexander's** classic, "You'd Better Move On". After the session, the musicians returned to Liverpool and waited for a decision from PYE.

When they almost had given up hope, they received a telephone call and were informed that they had passed the audition and would be contracted to PYE. **Gerry Jackson**, the brother of ex-Searcher, **Tony Jackson,** got in touch with them to arrange for press releases, photos and all of the publicity material that was needed to promote the **Rigg's** recording career. **Chris Curtis** asked the group to come to his house as he had a demo-record of a song that he wanted the **Rigg** to record for their first single. This demo turned out to be an advance recording of the **Doors** hit "Light My Fire", done by a singer called **José Feliciano**. The **Doors'** original record release of that great song had still not seen the light of day at that time and, accordingly, was not known anywhere. In addition, **José Feliciano** was also not very well-known in Europe and his version was not

The Rigg (1966)

Stuart Lynch (vocals/bass)   Kenny Parry (vocals/lead guitar)   Geoff Russell (vocals/keyboards)   Mick Pappas (drums)

The Rigg with Chris Curtis at PYE
L to R: Stuart Lynch, Mick Pappas, Chris Curtis, Kenny Parry, Geoff Russell

released until 1968. However, both versions became worldwide hits in 1967 and 1968, respectively, and developed into all-time classics! Looking back, this would have been a great and unique opportunity for an international breakthrough by the **Rigg,** as their 1966 release would have pre-dated both of the other recordings. In spite of this, the musicians were not too happy as the song was in too low a key and too folky for them. Regardless, they took the advice of **Chris Curtis** and half-heartedly started to arrange and to rehearse the song.

Then out of the blue, **Geoff Russell** got a telephone-call from **Kenny Parry** who told him that the **Rigg** was no more! **Mick Pappas** had made the decision to take up his studies at university, **Stuart Lynch** did not want to pursue the musical direction that **Chris Curtis** tried to steer the group in and **Kenny Parry** was also not too keen on it. Considering the fact that the group was given a song that obviously had the quality for a huge international hit, having a major record-company behind it and **Chris Curtis** as a top-notch qualified producer, this can only be seen as a fatal decision . . .

Stuart Lynch, a little later, joined the **Runaways*** and, in 1968, he teamed up again with **Kenny Parry** and together with drummer, **Tommy Maguire,** as the **Fruit Eating Bears.** They were the backing band for the **Merseys.** From there, **Stuart Lynch** and **Kenny Parry** both joined the **New Mojo Band** and, after that, became members of the group, **Birthday,** and **Stuart Lynch** stayed with that group until it disbanded. Still in 1969, **Kenny Parry** left to join **Colonel Bagshot's Incredible Bucket Band** (see story of the **Cordes***) and, after that, he was a member of the new **Merseybeats** and, finally in the late Seventies, he found international success as a member of **Liverpool Express**. A great singer and guitarist, **Kenny Parry,** is still active as part of the residential duo at the 'West Derby Social Club'. **Stuart Lynch** later appeared again as a member of the re-formed **Shooter**, where he is still playing today. **Mick Pappas** later returned to the scene with a group called the **Pappas** that only played local gigs. After that, he was a member of the **Good Earth Bluesband** where he played well into the

Birthday
L to R: Stuart Lynch, Paul Comerford, Ritchie Routledge, Kenny Parry

Seventies before he finally quit the music-business. **Geoff Russell** did not join another group and, in the mid-seventies, emigrated to South Africa where he lived for 25 years. He then returned to England and, as **Cowboy Geoff,** got into the Country scene. Additionally, as a DJ and presenter he hosts a Country-programme on Hailsham Radio these days.

Discography:

<u>Unreleased tracks</u>

Heartache / Good, Good Lovin' / You'd Better Move On   UK-PYE (unreleased) / 1966

*The stories of these groups can be followed in 'Beat Waves 'Cross The Mersey' (*VelocePress ISBN 978-1-58850-201-8*).

THE RIOT SQUAD

In the beginning there were five teenagers from Huyton who formed a group with the name **Lee Diamond & the Gems** in 1961. The line-up at that time was **Norman Reader**, alias **Lee Diamond** (voc), **John Taylor** (lg), **Bob Reece** (rg), **Pete Ritson** (bg) and **Paul Williams** (dr). They initially played the local youth clubs.

Towards the end of 1962, **John Taylor** and **Paul Williams** left to join the **Katz**. Their replacements were **Bill Ennis**, who apparently was a newcomer to the scene, and **Alan Noone** on drums, who came from the Prescott area and had formerly played with the **Vampires** from St. Helens. **Lee Diamond & the Gems** kept on playing the same youth clubs, but their manager, **Ted James,** also organised an appearance at the Locarno Ballroom, where they went down quite well.

Shortly after the changes in the line-up, the musicians decided to stop playing **Cliff Richard/Buddy Holly** numbers, which resulted in **Lee Diamond** leaving the band, he never re-appeared on the scene again.

The group then changed their name to the **Riot Squad** and continued as a quartet in a line-up with:

The Riot Squad - L to R: Alan Noone, Bob Reece, Bill Ennis & Peter Ritson

Bill Ennis	(voc/lg)
Bob Reece	(rg/voc)
Peter Ritson	(bg/voc)
Alan Noone	(dr)

Pete Ritson was a former member of the **Sundowners**, one of Liverpool's very early Country groups. **Bob Reece** had not previously played in a group. **Alan Noone** was sometimes known as **Alan Newman** as he once gave that surname to a journalist because he thought sounded more interesting.

Bill Ennis came from a Jazz background, being the brother of **Ray Ennis** from the **Swinging Blue Jeans**, who had previously been a Trad-Jazz group called the **Bluegenes**. Consequently, a mixture of Country and Jazz characterized the music of the **Riot Squad**, best described as varied commercial Beat with a Trad-Jazz influence. They played songs such as the **Ricky Nelson** version of "Fools rush in", the **Unit 4 plus Two** chart success "Concrete and clay", traditional numbers like "Red sails in the sunset" and some **Duane Eddy** numbers.

The **Riot Squad** were soon playing the major club circuit in Liverpool, probably not at least due to **Bill Ennis'** connections through his brother.

Johnny Hamp called the group into the Granada television studios where they recorded a few songs from their live programme under the wing of **Lally Stott** from the **Vaqueros**, who was later a member of the **Denny Seyton Group**. Unfortunately, nobody can remember which songs these were and what happened to the recordings.

Sometime in early 1964, **Bob Reece** left the group and quit show business completely. The others continued as a three-piece and a little later shortened their name to the **Squad**, probably because of an up and coming recording group from London that was also using the **Riot Squad** name.

When this trio was joined by the teenage songstress **Rita Mather** in 1964, they performed under the name of the **Squad & Rita** and their repertoire became even more varied with **Rita Mather** singing songs that included **Francoise Hardy's** "All over the world", **Dusty Springfield** songs and similar numbers.

The Squad & Rita - L to R: Bill Ennis, Pete Ritson, Rita Mather & Alan Noone

Towards the end of 1964, the **Squad** were approached by popular singer **Mark Peters**, who had just parted company with the **Silhouettes** and was now looking for a new group. The three musicians accepted the 'merger' and were joined by the singer's brother **Steve 'Tiger' Fleming** on the organ. They initially appeared as **Mark Peters & the Squad**, but very soon changed the name to **Mark Peters & the Method**.

Rita Mather was not included in this association with **Mark Peters** and in spring 1965, she joined the **Vogue** from St. Helens, who then went on to record as **Rita & the Vogue**. In late 1965 she was with the Widnes group **We Few**, which consisted of former members of **Sonny Kaye & the Reds** and in 1967 she sang with the **Crusaders** from Widnes, before she went solo under the name **Toni West**. She is still singing in the clubs under this name.

But back to **Mark Peters & the Method**, who in March 1966 went on tour to France and were apparently quite successful. On their return to Liverpool, **Roger Stanton** from the Epstein stable took the group into the CAM studios where they recorded the songs "I wanna walk with you" and "Come back to me" for a private single release. The record was handed to **Princess Margaret** as a gift on her visit to Liverpool, but apart from an article in the newspapers the recording did not do much for the group.

When a new offer for a tour of France came in May 1966, **Bill Ennis** did not want to go and he joined the **Corsairs**, while **Tony Coates** from that group became the new lead guitarist with **Mark Peters & the Method**. It was this line-up that recorded the **Four Seasons** number "Save it for me" and the **Jacki De Shannon** song "Don't turn your back on me Babe" for CBS. For unknown reasons neither of these songs were ever released.

Alan Noone left and went on to play with a group called **Sky**. He was replaced on drums by **Tony Sounders**, a former member of **Chick Graham & the Coasters**, who prior to joining **Mark Peters & the Method** had played with the **Silhouettes**. **Mark Peters & the Method** did not exist for too long after that and broke up in early 1967, when **Mark Peters** teamed up with the **Rats** from Wigan - of course as **Mark Peters & the Rats**.

Mark Peters & the Method - L to R: Bill Ennis, Pete Ritson, Alan Noone, Mark Peters & Steve Flemming

Tony Coates became a member of **Ian & the Zodiacs**, who had a long residency in Hamburg at that time. From there, he joined the **Hi-Fis** with whom he returned to England.

Steve Fleming teamed up again with **Alan Noone** and together with **Steve Darling** (bg) from the **Sky**, they formed a trio under the name of the **Steve Alan Set**, which in some way became a continuation of the **Riot Squad** and **Mark Peters & the Method**, respectively.

A little later, the **Steve Alan Set** was joined by **Mark Peters** and when **Steve Darling** left and quit the music business, his replacement was **Pete Bowden**, who came from the **Corsairs**, before that he had played with the **Katz**.

Then **Alan Noone** left and once again his place was taken over by **Tony Sounders**. Later, in the Seventies, **Alan Noone** appeared again as a member of the re-formed **Dimensions**.

Bill Ennis and **Tony Coates** also joined the **Steve Alan Set**, but then **Steve Fleming** and **Mark Peters** both left!

Pete Bowden left and was replaced by **Peter Ritson**, who in the meantime had been running a promotion business. He did not stay for too long as he emigrated to France. In 1974 he moved to Spain, where he is still living today and playing in a Jazz-Blues-Pop sextet called **Five Life**.

Pete Bowden then returned to the **Steve Alan Set** and when **Tony Sounders** was replaced by **Derek Cashin** in 1969, the group's name was changed to **Paper Chase**. In the mid Sixties **Derek Cashin** had been a member of the **New Avengers**.

This group continued successfully on the scene until, in late 1969, when **Tony Coates** and **Derek Cashin** became members of the **New Merseybeats**, who also recorded under the name **Crane** for the Buk Label. After that, they both teamed up with **Billy Kinsley** in the international hit group **Liverpool Express**. **Tony Coates** is currently a member of the **Vince Earl Attraction**.

When **Paper Chase** split up, **Bill Ennis** and **Pete Bowden** continued together with a new drummer as the **Steve Alan Set** again. This trio was active on the scene for a few years, until **Bill Ennis** left and apparently quit showbiz. **Pete Bowden** then teamed up with **Alan Noone** in a duo, which did not have a name.

Of the earlier members, it is known that **Steve Fleming** later played with the **Fourmost** and its successor **Clouds**. After that he was also a member of the **Vince Earl Attraction** for some time. **Mark Peters** emigrated to Sri Lanka, where he sadly died a few years ago.

Discography

as **"The Riot Squad"**:

In late 1963 or early 1964, **Johnny Hamp** took the **Riot Squad** into the Granada Television studios in Manchester where, under the wings of **Lally Stott**, they recorded some songs from their live repertoire. Unfortunately, it is not known which songs were recorded or what happened to these recordings.

as **"Mark Peters & the Method"**:

I wanna walk with you / Come back to me	UK- Cam acetate / 1966
Save it for me / Don't turn your back on me, Babe	UK- CBS unreleased / 1966

THE ROCKING VICKERS

It was sometime in 1962 that **Rev. Black & the Rockin' Vicars** were formed in Blackpool, Lancashire.

In the beginning it was a notorious Rock 'n' Roll band that originally consisted of vocalist **Harry Feeney**, known as Reverend Black, lead guitarist **Alex Hamilton**, bass guitarist **Peter Moorhouse** and drummer **Cyril 'Ciggy' Shaw**. In 1963, this quartet was joined by **Ken Hardacre** on rhythm guitar.

Besides the clubs in and around Blackpool, **Rev. Black & the Rockin' Vicars** very often played the famous 'Iron Door' club in Liverpool, where they became firm favourites with the audience.

In 1964, for unknown reasons, all three guitarists left the group, the remaining two members recruited new musicians and continued as **Rev. Black & the Rockin' Vicars** with the following line-up:

Harry Feeney	(voc)
Nicholas Gribbon	(lg/voc)
Ian Holbrook	(rg/harp)
Stephen Morris	(bg/voc)
Ciggy Shaw	(dr/voc)

Nick Gribbon, **Ian Holbrook** and **Steve 'Mogsey' Morris** were all former members of **Lee Wade & the Wild Ones**, who had apparently just disbanded.

Now Merseybeat and Rhythm & Blues also characterised their sound and they became very popular for their wild stage act, appropriately dressed as members of the clergy! Still in 1964, they were signed to Decca but the record company insisted on a name change as they feared problems may arise with the religious organisations.

Rev. Black & the Rockin' Vicars

So **Rev. Black & the Rockin' Vicars** became the **Rocking Vickers** and under that name, they released an exciting version of **Neil Sedaka**'s "I go ape" as their first single in October 1964, which sold quite well but unfortunately, it did not get into the charts.

The **Rocking Vickers**, sometimes still billed as **Rockin' Vicars**, were one of the first British acts to play behind the 'Iron Curtain' when they toured Yugoslavia as a part of a cultural exchange with the Red Army Youth Orchestra in July 1965. Amongst other places, they appeared in front of thousands of enthusiastic teenagers at the Olympic stadium in Zagreb.

In October of the same year, the group toured the northern parts of Finland as **Rev. Black & the Rockin' Vicars** and with this name they signed a contract with Decca! (in Finland).

They recorded eight songs, of which their great version of "Zing went the strings of my heart" and the original "Stella" were chosen to be on their first single released in Finland, in November 1965. This record sold really well – so well that the group was invited back again to tour the south of Finland in December 1965, but surprisingly, there were no further records released.

After their second tour of Finland, where the group brought Lapp national costumes for their stage act, the **Rocking Vickers** were signed to CBS in England and with "It's alright", they recorded an alternative version of the **Who** success "The kids are alright". It was a great record but, once again, it did not have any major success.

When this single was released in March 1966, **Ian Holbrook** and **Nick Gribbon** had already left the group. **Ian Holbrook** disappeared from the scene and of **Nick Gribbon** it is known that he later became the leader of the local group **Nick Unlimited**. They were replaced by a single guitarist and the group continued as a quartet.

The new guitarist with the **Rocking Vickers** was **Ian Willis**, a highly-interesting musician, who was born as **Ian Frazer** in Stoke-on-Trent but then adopted his stepfather's surname, a real priest by the way, with whom he moved to Wales. It was there that he also joined his first group – the **Sundowners** from Anglesey. He then moved to Manchester, where he became a member of the **Rainmakers** and after that he played with the **Motown Sect**, before joining the **Rocking Vickers**.

It was this line-up of the group that cut their final single, a version of the **Ray Davies** number "Dandy". Unfortunately, this was not a good choice and it was also not as interesting as their earlier records. It did not become a hit as the **Kinks** and **Herman's Hermits** versions were far better sellers.

In spite of having such bad luck with their records, the **Rocking Vickers** made a good living as a professional group, playing throughout England, where they were especially popular in the northwest, mainly in the areas of Liverpool, Manchester and of course their hometown Blackpool.

Towards the end of 1967, the lead guitarist, **Ian Frazer** (alias **Ian Willis**) who in the meantime called himself **Ian Kilminster** but was better known under his nickname **'Lemmy'**, went down to London. He initially joined **P.P. Arnold's** band, before he became a member of **Sam Gopal's Dream** and **Opal Butterfly**, which evolved from **Sam Gopal's Dream**. After that, he joined the internationally successful Rock band **Hawkwind**, where he sang their biggest hit "Silver Machine".

The new guitarist with the **Rocking Vickers** was **Jeff Carter** and for a short time the former **Bruce & the Spiders** guitarist **Dave Rossall** was also said to have been involved with the group.

The **Rocking Vickers** toured Finland for one last time in December 1967 and after that they practically broke up. **Ciggy Shaw** was replaced by **Steve Wilks** on drums and **Harry Feeney** quit the music scene and became a very successful car dealer,

The remaining members continued for a while as a trio, but then **Jeff Carter** and **Steve Wilks** left, later playing together again in the group **Manitou**. However, the original drummer **Ciggy Shaw** returned to work with **Steve Morris** and they recruited two new guitarists, **Stuart McGarry** and **Phil Coggan**. At one time they both had been members of **Lee Wade & the Wild Ones**, and prior to that **Phil Coggan** had played with the **Five Commandments**.

Phil Coggan was only with the group for a short time but **Stuart McGarry** (g/voc), **Steve Morris** (bg/voc) and **Ciggy Shaw** (dr) continued on the cabaret scene as the **Rocking Vickers** until 1972 though it is more than probable that during this period there were some personnel changes in the line-up.

It is said that the trio were joined again by **'Lemmy' Kilminster**, but he did not stay for too long and went back to London to reform **Hawkwind**. After that he became a real legend as a guitarist with **Motörhead**. As well as playing with this heavy Rock group, **'Lemmy'** also played in a Rockabilly outfit called **Head Cat**.

It is known that **Ciggy Shaw** was later a member of **Solomon King's** band.

An interesting obscurity is the fact that one short-term band member, **Dave Rossall**, emigrated to Australia in 1967, where he joined the Wollongong band the **Finks** as vocalist and re-styled that group as **Rev. Black & the Rockin' Vicars**, modelled after the Blackpool original. They kept going until 1969 and during this time they toured throughout Australia and recorded five singles for the Z.O.T., Leedon and Sunshine labels.

The Rocking Vickers

Discography

as **"The Rocking Vickers"**:

I go ape / Someone like you	UK- Decca F. 11993 / 1964
It's alright / Stay by me	UK - CBS 202051 / 1966
Dandy / I don't need your kind of love	UK – CBS 202241 / 1966

(Please note that the final single was also released on US Columbia 4-43818)

as **"Rev. Black & the Rockin' Vicars"**:

Zing went the strings of my heart / Stella   SF – Decca SD 5662 / 1965

(Please note that this record was also released on Decca in Ireland in 1966)

Previously unreleased tracks

Baby never say Goodbye / I just stand there / Say Mama / Shake, rattle and roll / What's the matter Jane / Little Rosy.

These could be the six remaining numbers from their Finnish recording session in 1965. Besides all their released tracks, these numbers, plus some rehearsal extracts were released on the RPM CD 196 in 1995 and re-released in 2000.

PAUL ROGERS

Paul Murphy was born in Liverpool and grew up in Broadgreen, an area where many of the early Merseybeat musicians hailed from, including **Bob Hardy** from **T.L.s Bluesicians**, **Eddie Cave & the Fix** and some other well know groups. The guitarist **Dave Gore** of **Johnny Tempest & the Tornadoes** that evolved into **Earl Preston & the TTs** was also from Broadgreen, as was **Alan Caldwell** better known as **Rory Storm**. **Paul Murphy** started his career as a guitarist with the **Alan Caldwell Skiffle Group**, that later became the legendary **Rory Storm & the Hurricanes**, via the **Raving Texans** and **Al Storm & the Wild Ones**.

By 1957, **Paul Murphy** and the other guitarist in that group, **Johnny 'Guitar' Byrne**, had already gone into the Phillips studio in Kensington and as a duo recorded a metal single with **Little Richard's** "She's got it" and the **Charlie Gracie** success "Butterfly".

Paul Murphy then changed his musical style and, under the stage name **Paul Rogers**, became the singer with the **Wilf Rigby Orchestra** from Warrington. From there he was signed to the Geoff Patterson Agency in London and joined the **Cyril Stapleton Orchestra** as a singer. Around that time he somehow obtained a recording contract with HMV and in 1961 he cut his first record with the "Twenty four thousand kisses", which was the English version of the Italian success "24 Mila Baci" by **Adriano Celentano**. This was not a big success so **Paul Rogers** continued on as a vocalist with the **Cyril Stapleton Orchestra**.

Paul Rogers (Paul Murphy)

1963 saw his second single on HMV with "Always", a nice, gentle rocking number which, like its predecessor, was not too successful. The session line-up which was featured on both records is interesting. It included **Clem Cattini** (dr), **Jimmy Page** (g), **Big Jim Sullivan** (g), **Herbie Flowers** (bg), **Andy White** (dr) and **Ian Frazer** (org).

In between these two records **Paul Rogers** appeared again as **Paul Murphy** with some of the other Merseybeat groups, including the **Galvanisers** and **Eddie Dean & the Onlookers**, where he played the bass guitar.

After his second single, his agency offered him the chance to go to Germany to sing at the American bases for six months, which was an extremely well paid opportunity for him. However, as he was still employed by **Cyril Stapleton** he was only granted four weeks 'leave'. He decided to go to Frankfurt, only to find out that he had been 'set up' by his London agent who, during his absence, had told **Cyril Stapleton** that he was not coming back to England so the orchestra recruited a full-time singer to replace him!

Just as it appeared that things could not get any worse, he was unable to get his pay from the agent in Germany. So he stopped performing for the American servicemen and went to live with his parents-in-law in Würzburg, where he got a job in a radio/TV shop.

 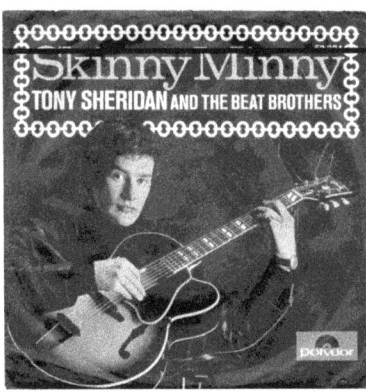 

However, as he wanted to get back to singing, he travelled to Hamburg to contact **Bert Kaempfert** in an attempt to get a job with his orchestra. This did not work out, but he was able to get a job as a record producer with the German Polydor label.

For his first assignment, he produced the **Audrey Arno** single "Mir geht es wieder besser". This also happened to be the first recording by **King Size Taylor & the Dominoes**, who backed the songstress on that release under the name of the **Tony Taylor Band**.

Following this, **Paul Murphy**, who was sometimes named **Paul Mersey** on the scene, produced records with **Tony Sheridan**, the **Alex Harvey Soul Band, King Size Taylor & the Dominoes** (as the **Shakers**), the Hamburg groups the **Bats** and the **Giants**, as well as the Scottish **Tremors**. (He also occasionally performed with the **Tremors**).

The Tremors (1963)

1964, he self-produced his next single for Polydor with "Meine Liebe wird niemals enden", the German version of "All my sorrows", which sold well but did not become a hit. He was backed by the **James Last Orchestra** on this.

From Polydor he then switched to Telefunken, where he successfully produced German singing stars including **Catharina Valente, Abi Ofarim** and **Drafi Deutscher & his Magics**, as well as the great and legendary first album by the **Boots** from Berlin, one of the best, if not the best German Rhythm & Blues group of the Sixties.

In 1967, he self-produced another single on the Telefunken label. For the song "This is the time", he used the pseudonym **Benny** and he was backed by session musicians – one of whom was **Byron Grant**, the great lead guitarist of the above-mentioned **Tremors** and who **Paul Murphy** also booked for some of his **Catharina Valente** productions.

Later he got involved with the newly founded BASF label and then founded the English Buk label, which became a subsidiary of the English Polydor.

He continued successfully as record producer for well-known artists such as **P.J. Proby**, **Billy J. Kramer**, **Malcolm Roberts**, **Donna Hightower** and **Magna Carta**, to name just a few. In addition, he was associated with **Engelbert Humperdinck** and **Jigsaw**.

In conclusion, it can be said that if his career as a singer was not too successful, he made it really big as a producer…..

Discography

as **Paul Rogers**:

Four and twenty thousand kisses / Free to love	UK – HMV POP 872 / 1961
Always / Joanie, don't be angry	UK – HMV POP 1121 / 1963

different German release:

Meine Liebe wird niemals enden / Angela	G – Polydor NH 52 349 / 1964

as **Benny**:

This is the time / Michael, Marc & Christian	G – Decca D 19826 / 1967

JOHNNY SANDON

The singer/guitarist, **William Beck,** was born in Liverpool in 1941 and, in the late Fifties, he started to sing Country & Western songs under the name of **Billy Beck** in the local pubs and clubs.

John McNally had just formed his first group, which soon became known as the **Searchers**. When their vocalist, **'Big Ron' Woodbridge** left, **John McNally's** mother, who worked in a bakery together with **Billy Beck's** mother, suggested their sons co-operate. And so, in 1960, **Billy Beck** became the new lead singer with the embryonic **Searchers**, where he adopted the stage name **Johnny Sandon**. The name Sandon was taken from a pub close to Liverpool's football ground.

L to R: Joe Kennedy (?), Tony West, John McNally, Mike Pender, Johnny Sandon

The original line-up of **Johnny Sandon & the Searchers** consisted of **Johnny Sandon** (voc), **John McNally** (lg), **Mike Pendergast** (rg/voc), **Tony West** (bg) and **Joe Kennedy** (dr). **Mike Pendergast**, who shortened his name to **Mike Pender**, was a former member of the **Wreckers** and the **Confederates** and had just replaced the original guitarist **Brian Dolan**. **Tony West** and **Joe Kennedy** left successively and were replaced by **Tony Jackson** (bg/voc) and **Norman McGarry** (dr), who both came from the **Martinis**.

The new drummer did not stay for too long, he later appeared as a member of the **Sassenachs**. His replacement was **Chris Crummey**, then known as **Chris Curtis**.

Within a short time, **Johnny Sandon & the Searchers** became very popular on the scene and they were always one of the top placed groups in the 'Mersey Beat' newspaper popularity polls. Despite this popularity, **Johnny Sandon**, who was more of a C&W singer, left them in February 1962. This was just prior to the **Searchers** going to Germany to play the 'Star Club' in Hamburg, the starting point of their worldwide success.

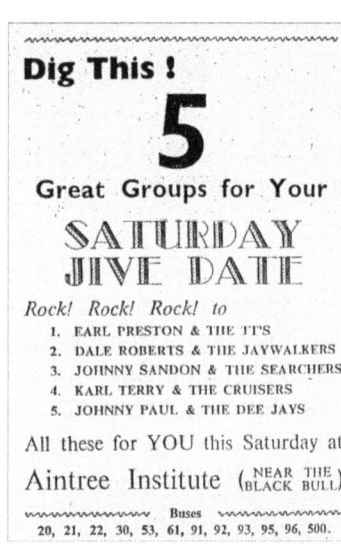

Johnny Sandon & the Searchers

Johnny Sandon then teamed up with Liverpool's top instrumental group – the **Remo Four**. They were signed to PYE and in 1963 they had their first single with the **Colin Manley** original "Lies". This was an interesting and very good Merseybeat record, unfortunately, it was not a major chart success. In spite of this disappointment, **Johnny Sandon & the Remo Four** stayed together with the following line-up:

Johnny Sandon (voc), **Colin Manley** (lg), **Phil Rodgers** (rg), **Don Andrews** (bg) and **Roy Dyke** (dr).

Their next record "Yes" was also good 'Merseybeat' and maybe would have done better if PYE had switched the Bacharach/David song "Magic potion" to the A-side. The record did not make the charts and soon after this **Johnny Sandon** and the **Remo Four** parted. The **Remo Four**, besides backing 'other' singers including **Tommy Quickly** and **Gregory Phillips** on their records, also recorded in their own right and later became a cult group on the so-called 'Star Club'-circle.

Johnny Sandon continued recording for PYE as a solo act. His next release, a version of **Merle Travis**' standard "Sixteen tons" was still interesting, but as expected, it was a step towards Country & Western, and it did not get anywhere in the charts. The follow-up was **Gene Pitney**'s "Donna means heartbreak" - a nice, well-sung ballad but his great version of the **Drifters**' success "Some kinda wonderful" on the B-side would probably have done better at that time.

JOHNNY SANDON & THE REMO FOUR
(PHIL, ROY, JOHNNY, DON & COLIN)
TEL ROYAL 7749

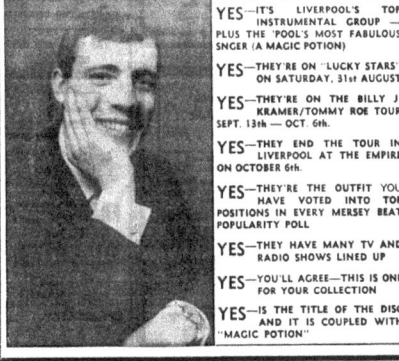

The end of 1964 saw **Johnny Sandon**'s final release with the re-recorded version of his first solo single's flip-side, called "The Blizzard". This song, as well as "I'd be a legend in my time" on the B-side, was pure Country. With that record **Johnny Sandon** had turned his back on Merseybeat and instead he became active in Liverpool's lively C&W scene as a solo act for some time. Around that time there was a C&W group by the name of the **Sandons** which may have been connected to him, but this is just an assumption.

Later, **Johnny Sandon** tried his luck as a comedian on the cabaret circuit, but by then he was **Billy Beck** again. He then quit showbiz completely, became a taxi-driver and did not try a comeback – until 1992, when all of a sudden he appeared at the 'Merseycats' shows in the Hotel Victoria in New Brighton. Initially, he sang with scratch bands, but a steady group using the name **Johnny Sandon & the Specials** soon evolved from these sessions. In addition to him it consisted of **Dave Myers** (lg), **Colin Roberts** (bg) and **Alan Schroeder** (dr). This was a really good group, mainly consisting of experienced musicians from the Sixties.

Dave Myers had been a member of **Cliff Roberts' Rockers**, the **Climbers**, the **Renegades** and the **Pawns**. **Alan Schroeder** had played with **Cliff Roberts' Rockers** and the **Black Knights**. **Colin Roberts** was a newcomer to the scene but his connection was his older brother, Liverpool's successful 60's singer **Cliff Roberts**.

For the next year or so, **Johnny Sandon & the Specials** made various appearances on the local scene, but they mainly played for the 'Merseycats' organisation, where **Johnny Sandon** proved that he was still a great singer. Unfortunately, he suffered from depression, which in the end caused him to leave the group. After **Johnny Sandon** left, the group continued for two more years on the scene as the **Mersey Specials**, **Mick Swift** having joined them as a singer/guitarist. On occasions, they would also be joined by **Mike Byrne** (voc/key), who in the Sixties had been a member of **Mike Byrne & the Thunderbirds**, **Them Grimbles** and the **Roadrunners**, amongst others.

Johnny Sandon occasionally sang with the **Mersey Specials** until the group finally broke up in 1995.

On 25 December 1996 **Johnny Sandon** committed suicide in his flat in Rock Ferry – what a sad end for a great singer . . .

Discography

as "**Johnny Sandon & the Remo Four**":

Lies / On the horizon	UK - PYE 7N 15542 / 1963
Yes / Magic potion	UK - PYE 7N 15559 / 1963

Johnny Sandon – solo:

Sixteen tons / The blizzard	UK - PYE 7N 15602 / 1964
Donna means heartbreak / Some kinda wonderful	UK - PYE 7N 15665 / 1964
The blizzard / I'd be a legend in my time	UK - PYE 7N 15717 / 1964

> *"Johnny had a brilliant deep Country & Western-voice – a bit like Jack Scott"*
>
> **(John McNally / The Searchers)**

For more information on **Johnny Sandon** please see the **Searchers** & the **Remo Four** stories in the book *"Mersey Beat Waves"* – *ISBN 1588502015 or 9781588502018*.

THE SANTONES
(THE ANZAKS)

Very little information could be found about the early days of this group but it was ascertained that they came from a small locale called Ford, which is north of the Litherland area of Liverpool, where they were formed in or around 1962.

The **Santones**, as they were named right from the beginning, never made the headlines but they played the usual club circuit in Liverpool, including the 'Litherland Town hall', the 'Jive Hive' in Crosby, the 'Iron Door', the 'Downbeat' and once at the 'Cavern'. According to people who saw them live, they were one of the better Merseybeat groups.

In 1963, the line-up of the **Santones** consisted of the following musicians:

Eddie Lane	(voc/rg)
Johnny Wild	(lg)
Chris Ellis	(bg)
Kenny Mundye	(dr)

Johnny Wild's real name was **John Winder** and, although the drummer's name is often reported differently, the correct spelling is **Kenny Mundye.** Also, from the fact that none of the members had appeared in other groups previously, it can be concluded that they were all newcomers to the scene.

It was in the summer of 1964 that **Eddie Lane** accepted an offer to play in Alicante in Spain for two weeks, though it is not known if he went on his own or as a singer for another group. Regardless, while he was there he was spotted by a talent scout who offered him additional work and the possibility of a recording contract.

On his return to Liverpool, **Eddie Lane** rejoined the **Santones** and recorded a demo disc, though it is not known if it was with or without this group. Unfortunately, there is also no information about which studio it was or what songs were recorded.

Eddie Lane likely returned to Spain, but even this could not be confirmed.

```
OLD ANSELMIANS' R.U.F.C.
       present a
  GREAT BEAT NITE
       TONIGHT
          at
Birkenhead Technical College
         with
  THE FLINTS (Tributes)
   THE PROWLERS
      THE ANZACS
     ADMISSION 6/-
Licensed Bar.   Pay at Door.
No admission after 9.30 p.m.  (s)
```

What is certain is that the group's cohesion was not the same after the singer's Spanish adventure and so, in 1965, the **Santones** parted from **Eddie Lane**.

They recruited other musicians, changed the name to the **Anzaks** and to have something unique about their name, they spelled it with 'k' instead of a 'c', but that was not honoured by promoters who kept advertising them as **Anzacs** (see advertisement above).

Anyway, regardless if it was written with a 'k' or a 'c', the **Anzaks** appeared in the following line-up:

Pete Dunn	(voc)
John Winder	(lg)
Ken Duckers	(sax)
Chris Ellis	(bg)
Kenny Mundye	(dr)

Pete Dunn was a former member of the **Fontanas**, but he was not the same person as the guitarist who played with the **Flintstones**, sometimes known as **Ogi & the Flintstones**, who also played with the **Clayton Squares**.

The Anzaks
(Note the spelling on the drum)

The group recorded some songs for a demo acetate in **Charlie Weston's** Unicord studio in Moorfields, but the titles of these recordings are sadly not known.

By now the **Anzaks** had evolved into a real Blues group and their management tried to get them bookings in Germany. For unknown reasons this did not happen, so the **Anzaks** decided to move to London, as there was a greater demand for their style of music down there.

In London they played all the major clubs, including the 'Greyhound' in Croydon and the 'Crawdaddy', they appeared regularly at the 'Cellar Club' in Kingston and even had a short residency at the world famous 'Marquee', before they became the resident group at the 'Café Des Artists' in Chelsea.

It was none other than **Who** manager **Kit Lambert** who saw them there and was so impressed by their drummer that he signed him for session and studio work for his Tracks records. This meant additional money for **Kenny Mundye**, who, besides his session work, continued to play with the **Anzaks.**

When the **Merseybeats**, who at that time were also being promoted by **Kit Lambert**, played in London and their drummer **John Banks** went missing for a week, **Kenny Mundye** sat in for him at various gigs.

These sorts of substitutions were not uncommon in those days and normally there was no concern about it, but unfortunately, this situation was the beginning of the end for the **Anzaks**.

It was not too long after this that the **Merseybeats** disbanded. **Billy Kinsley** and **Tony Crane** continued as a duo under the name of the **Merseys** and they were in need of a backing group. That was when the **Fruit Eating Bears** were formed, which in their original line-up consisted of the former **Masterminds** members **Joey Molland** (lg), **George Cassidy** (rg), **Chris Finley** (bg) and ex **Escorts** drummer **Kenny Goodlass**. However, **Kenny Mundye** was also included as a second drummer in the group.

Initially, the **Anzaks** used a replacement drummer but they soon disbanded and the musicians returned to Liverpool where they all vanished from the scene.

It was sometime in 1967 that **Kenny Mundye** parted from the **Fruit Eating Bears** and joined the final line-up of the **Roadrunners** with **Bruce McCaskill** (voc/rg), **Mike Kontzle** (lg), **Stuart McPherson** (bg) to play the American military bases in France and Germany. They toured in Europe for almost two years and ended up in Gstaad in Switzerland, playing for the Swiss high society for a long time.

Back in Liverpool in 1969, **Kenny Mundye** teamed up once again with **Billy Kinsley** and **Tony Crane** in a three-man line-up of the **Merseybeats**, who continued to perform on the cabaret scene until 1974. **Kenny Mundye** then took a long break from the music scene but came back as a member of **Liverpool Express** in the mid-Seventies.

He then returned to London and joined a Punk Rock group called **Tricycle Turds** who, a little later, changed their name to the **Fruit Eating Bears** of which, he was the only original member. From there, he went on to play with the **Mice** and finally settled down somewhere in Kent where he has a music shop and also teaches percussion.

Discography

As far as it is known, there was never an official record released by the **Santones** but, according to a newspaper article in 1964, the group recorded an acetate at **Charly Weston's** Unicord studio in Moorfields. This could well have been the demo for their singer, **Eddie Lane,** as mentioned in the story. No further details are known about this.

In mid-1965, prior to going to London, the **Anzaks** again went to the same studio and recorded another demo—the songs, sadly, are not known.

While they were in London, under the guidance of **Kit Lambert**, the **Anzaks** should have recorded for the Immediate label but, again, no further details were available.

THE SARACENS

It was in 1963 that the Irish drummer, **Tony McGuigan,** from Newry in Northern Ireland had to leave his group, the **Heartbeats**, due to the fact that his family moved to his Mother's native city of Liverpool. They settled down in the Kirkdale area of Liverpool. Things were going well and **Tony McGuigan** had no initial plans to take up drumming again. However, his older sister soon became good friends with the girl who lived next door, **Jaqueline (Jackie) Lewis**, who told her that she was playing the guitar in a Beat-group that she had formed with some friends but that they could not perform because they were missing a suitable drummer. Tony's sister had the solution and **Jackie Lewis** invited **Tony McGuigan** to join the group that did not have a name at that time. They rehearsed together a few times and **Tony McGuigan** joined them. After watching a horse-race on TV in which one of the horses was named 'Saracen', **Tony McGuigan** had an idea. He got in touch with the other group-members and they all agreed to call their group the **Saracens**. Now it was time for the first public appearance in the following line-up:

L to R: Phil Simpson, Jackie Lewis, Derek Relly, Tony McGuigan, George Gibson

Derek Reilly	(voc/perc)
Phil Simpson	(lg)
Jackie Lewis	(rg/voc)
George Gibson	(bg)
Tony McGuigan	(dr)

After getting some experience in local youth-clubs, the **Saracens** played the smaller clubs on Merseyside such as the so-called 'Blue House' in Everton or 'Up The Creek' in Egremont, where they appeared quite regularly. On 10th June 1964, they went into the **Percy Phillips** studio in Kensington and recorded an acetate with the **Rolling Stones** hit rave-up of **Buddy Holly**'s "Not fade away" and **Chuck Berry's** all-time classic, "Maybelline". This acetate showed that they had a real good driving Rhythm & Blues sound but, unfortunately, it was not of any great help in advancing their career.

In September 1964, the **Saracens** auditioned at the 'Grosvenor Ballroom' in Wallasey for **Bob Xavier**, who had been instructed by **Manfred Woitalla** to find a Merseybeat-group to play at his 'Star-Palast' club in Kiel, Germany for an extended booking. It was the **Prowlers** from Birkenhead who finally passed this audition and were contracted to go to Germany. This would ultimately prove to have a significant effect on the future of the **Saracens**.

THE SARACENS

Very soon after that audition, **Derek Reilly** left the **Saracens** and was replaced by **Frank Larkin** as lead-vocalist, who had adopted the stage-name of **Franklin Day**. The **Saracens** now proceeded to play the major venues, including a date at the 'Cavern' in December 1964. It was during that 'Cavern' gig or immediately after that the **Prowlers** contacted **Tony McGuigan** as they had found out that you had to be at least 18 years of age in order to obtain a work permit to play in Germany – and their drummer was too young. So they asked **Tony McGuigan** if he was prepared to go with them to Germany. He was, but the **Saracens** were not too enthusiastic about this development as it was not just for a few days but for a number of weeks.

Tony McGuigan (dr) with Goldie & the Gingerbreads at Star Palast, Kiel

Anyway, that did not change **Tony McGuigan's** decision and, in January 1965, he went to Germany with the **Prowlers**. The **Prowlers** members obviously had a close relationship as they also took their regular drummer, **Mally Coram,** to Germany who, of course, ended up playing at most of their gigs. Consequently, **Tony McGuigan** jammed with other groups and played quite a few gigs with the American all-girl group, **Goldie & the Gingerbreads**, that were on a German tour at that same time and whose drummer had become ill and was unable to play. After the **Prowlers** returned to England, **Tony McGuigan** discovered that in the meantime the **Saracens** had recruited **Keith Workman** as their drummer and so, there was no way back for him.

Tony McGuigan

Accordingly, he joined **Lee Eddie & the Chevrons*** where he played until that group disbanded. He then went to London to do some session-work but returned to Liverpool and joined **Karl Terry & the TTs** with whom he obviously went to Germany for their first tour as the **T-Squares**. After that, he was a long-time-member of **Derek Joy's Showband** from Waterford in Southern Ireland. When he returned to Liverpool, he became a member of the **Lettermen** recording-group. Later, he played with the **Paddy Kelly Band** (Country), with **Time & Place** and the **Signs** (which has no connection with the sixties Liverpool group of the same name) and, after that, he was a member of **Karl Terry & the Cruisers***.

But now back to the **Saracens** that at a later stage were also joined by their lead vocalist's sister, **Moreen Larkin,** as an additional vocalist and they became more of a Country-group, which obviously resulted in further changes in the line-up. **Jackie Lewis** left and was replaced by **Dave Rogerson** on rhythm-guitar, who brought **Margaret Hill** (his future wife) as a vocalist with him. This development resulted in **Frank** and **Moreen Larkin** leaving and **Tommy Griffiths** was added as a lead vocalist, who could have been the former singer of **Tommy & the Satellites,** but there is no real evidence for this. With only two remaining members of the original **Saracens,** the group, in 1965, changed its name into the **San Antones** and became a busy part of Liverpool's very successful Country & Western scene.

In late 1967, they toured Germany backing US Country singer, **Charlie Walker,** and it is said that they may have recorded with him after their return to England but no further details are known. However, it is confirmed that in 1965 the **San Antones** recorded the title "Roll In My Sweet Baby's Arms" at the **Percy Phillips** studio in Kensington and then, in 1968/1969, recorded **Joe Dolan's** "Love Of The Common People" and "Dated Yesterday" for Mercury, but none of these recordings were followed by an official release.

THE SAN-ANTONES

Discography:

as the **Saracens**

Not Fade Away / Maybelline   UK- Phillips Kensington acetate / 1964

as the **San Antones**

Roll In My Sweet Baby's Arms   UK- Phillips Kensington acetate / 1965

**Love Of The Common People /
Dated Yesterday**   UK- Mercury (unreleased) /1968

THE SASSENACHS

Researching this story was no easy task. Most of the data that could be found continually revealed the same information on the drummer only. Otherwise, the **Sassenachs** were normally referred to as a *'lesser known Merseybeat group'* or an *'obscure Liverpool outfit'* – a judgement most likely based solely on their one recording.

To call this group 'Merseybeat' or 'Liverpool' is incorrect, as the only Liverpool connection here is the drummer. The group hailed from the southeast of London, where it was formed and run by two brothers, **Dennis Shiret**, singer and rhythm guitarist, and **Ron Shiret**, the groups' roadie. They were originally named **Danny & the Torinos** and, after a change in the line-up, in 1963 they consisted of:

        Dennis 'Danny' Shiret   (voc/rg)
        Eddie Eager   (lg/voc)
        Chris Maskell   (bg/voc)
        Norman McGarry   (voc/dr)

The group leader, **Dennis 'Danny' Shiret,** and the drummer, **Norman McGarry,** shared the lead vocals. **Eddie Eager** and **Chris Maskell** were former members of the **Crusaders**, a **Shadows** type group from London.

The Crusaders

Norman McGarry hailed from Liverpool and, prior to joining **Danny & the Torinos,** he initially played with the **Martinis** before becoming the original **Searchers** drummer. It is often said that he was also a member of **Rory Storm & the Hurricanes** for a short time, but there is no real evidence for this.

Danny & the Torinos, who included a female organist for a short time (whose name is not known), signed with the Norman Jackson Agency who arranged an audition with the Bron Music Company in London.

In 1964, they went to the Lansdowne Studios and recorded the two **Eddie Eager/ Chris Maskell** originals "That don't worry me" and "All over you". These songs were passed on to the production and songwriting duo **Les Reed** and **Barry Mason**, who organized the songs to be released as a single on the Fontana label in 1964. However, the producers insisted the group change their name to the **Sassenachs** for the release.

This record showed the **Sassenachs** to be a really good group with a typical Merseybeat sound. The up-tempo A-side featured powerful drums and **Norman McGarry's** lead vocals, the lower registers were sung by **Chris Maskell** while the others sang harmony, **Barry Mason** also dubbing on the higher notes. The B-side, a lovely melodic ballad, featured **Dennis 'Danny' Shiret** as the lead singer with close harmony work by all the other members. It is an interesting record which apparently sold quite well but did not make the charts.

The **Sassenachs** were called into the studio again and recorded the great original "You're gonna be mine" and the Reed/ Mason song "Bittersweet" for their next single. However, due to petty jealousies about royalties it was not released and subsequently **Gerry Bron,** the owner of Bron Music, dropped the group.

In 1965, **Chris Maskell** left to join **Marc Adams Inc**. and the **Sassenachs** continued with a new bass player and later added a brass section. As far as it is known, they did not record again and none of the musicians other than **Chris Maskell** ever re-appeared on the scene.

Chris Maskell got married and quit showbiz for 15 years. He moved to Plymouth and started playing again with local groups including **Cement Bag O'Brien & the Humming Melons**, who played a sort of Bluegrass Folk music. He then joined **Bus Stop**, a successful pop group with whom he also toured in Germany. Today he performs as a solo artist, playing 60's music in the pubs and clubs, in addition, he is also a member of a group called **Dixie Grass**.

Discography

That don't worry me / All over you   UK- Fontana   TF 518 / 1964

Unreleased tracks:

The **Sassenachs** recorded the **Eddie Eager/Chris Maskell** original **"You're gonna be mine"** and the **Les Reed/Dave Mason** song **"Bittersweet"** in 1964 for their follow-up single, which unfortunately, was never released.

Author's note:

Of course, featuring this group in a book on the Merseybeat scene can be debated, as the group clearly came from London and only had a minor connection to Liverpool through their drummer. What made me make this decision is the fact that they were and still are always referred to as a Liverpool or Merseybeat group and if someone wanted to find out about them, this book is probably the first place one would look. Therefore, I could not think of a better place to put things right, as the Sassenachs will continue to be included in the Merseybeat scene as long as people do not know the truth about their origins.

SAVVA & THE DEMOCRATS

It is best that we begin the story of this Bebington group with **Peter Goodall** who, at a very young age, was already an accomplished guitar-player and played in a school-band called the **One Trojan's Form Band** that won an inter-school competition. His family was member of the Lower Bebington Methodist Church and he often went to the parish youth-club. With other teenage members, he formed his first group in 1959 that was named the **Black Diamonds**. As the members were too young to play in pubs or clubs, they concentrated on other youth-clubs in addition to church and school events. In a room of the above named Bebington youth-club there was also an established Rock 'n' Roll group that rehearsed there and sometimes this group invited **Peter Goodall** to play a few numbers with them. It was in 1960 that this group was in need of a new lead-guitarist and asked the 15 year old teenager to join them. Peter's father approved and so **Peter Goodall** became a member of his first real band – and this was none other than **Lee Crombie & the Sundowners**, who hailed from Rock Ferry. He remained with them until 1962 at which time he formed his own group, which he named the **Democrats**.

After the **Democrats** played the local clubs for a few months, one of his friends told him that he had a cousin who would be coming over from Cyprus to live on the Wirral – a good singer, who had already sung in a number of Cyprus nightclubs. This cousin was of Greek origin and his name was **Savva Eracleus**. After some rehearsals with the group, he joined, changed his name to **Savva Hercules,** and the group, from that moment on, appeared as **Savva & the Democrats** in a line-up with:

Savva Hercules	(voc)
Peter Goodall	(lg/voc)
Jimmy Mearns	(rg)
Malcolm Shelbourne	(bg)
Billy Robinson	(dr)

Malcolm Shelbourne came from **Clay Ellis & the Raiders***, while the former groups of the other members, if there were any, are not known. **Savva Hercules** was an excellent singer but there was a problem in that he did not have a Merseybeat background and he had sung mostly Jazz, Swing and Sinatra style vocals in Cyprus and could not get the right 'feeling' for the rocking numbers. So the group took these melodic Jazz and Swing standards and rocked them up – a real musical challenge for the members but it was successful in the end.

Accordingly, the repertoire of **Savva & the Democrats** was different from that of other Merseybeat groups but the audiences obviously liked it – especially the promoter **Walter 'Wally' Hill**, the owner of 'Peak Promotions'. He took over their management and, in 1963, sent the group into the **Percy Phillips** studio in Kensington where they recorded an EP with the titles, "Too Much", "Shaking All Over", "Mean Woman Blues" and "Please Don't Tease". This acetate was just for promotion and, within a very short time, **Savva & the Democrats** became popular all over the scene and appeared regularly at the 'Cavern', the 'Iron Door', the 'Mardi Gras', the 'Peppermint Lounge' and the other Beat clubs in Liverpool and on the Wirral. They also performed at the 'Plaza' in St. Helens, the 'Majestic' in Birkenhead, the 'Empress' in Wigan, the 'Carlton' in Rochdale, 'La Scala' in Runcorn, 'Kings R&B Club' in Little Sutton, 'River Park' in Chester. In addition, there were the larger halls, where **Wally Hill** organised shows such as – 'Holyoake' in Wavertree, 'Blair Hall' in Walton, the 'Civic Hall' in Ellesmere Port, 'Queens Hall' in Widnes and 'Hambleton Hall' in Huyton. This obviously was too much gigging for **Jimmy Mearns**, so he left the group and did not appear on the scene again. His replacement was not another guitarist but a distinctive piano-player with the name of **Roger Parrot**, who had not previously played in a group.

Wally Hill

In 1965, **Savva & the Democrats** played a gig at the 'Empress Ballroom' in Wigan together with the London based group, the **Graham Bond Organisation,** that played a sort of early Jazz-Rock and **Peter Goodall** was fascinated with their sound. He talked to the musicians and they told him to come to London as there would always be work for such an excellent guitarist and that they would be willing to help him. **Peter Goodall** wanted to give it a try but, before he could leave Liverpool, he needed to obtain a certain academic qualification in order to continue his studies at a London University. Consequently, he had to cut back the number of gigs he was playing so he quit **Savva & the Democrats** and was replaced by **Ted Thompson**. **Peter Goodall** joined the **Keystone Combo**, a Blues group from Wallasey that had a less exacting gig schedule and, besides this, he played 'folky' style solo gigs for the promoter **Brian Kelly** under the name of **Timothy**. Finally in 1966, he went to London and had a great career there, but more about that later in this story.

Wally Hill kept **Savva & the Democrats** very busy on the scene and they established an excellent name for themselves throughout the Northwest of England. Still, during 1965, there was an announcement made that the group would do a private recording for which they had chosen a group original with the title, "You Know". This song was written in 1964 by **Roger Parrot** for the **Gerry & the Pacemakers*** film 'Ferry Cross' The Mersey' and **Savva & the Democrats** were in the running for a part in the film. Unfortunately, they did not get to appear in the film and it could not be confirmed if this recording was ever released. If so, it was most probably on the Unicord label as, during that time period, they were doing vinyl records in addition to acetates.

It was sometime in 1967 that **Savva & the Democrats** called it a day. **Malcolm Shelbourne** joined **Gerry DeVille & the City Kings*** and played with them until 1972. After that, he became a member of **Purple Grass**, that later changed their name into **Rainbow**. When this group disbanded in 1982, **Malcolm Shelbourne** quit the music-business. **Ted Thompson** also continued playing in the scene and, in the late Seventies, he teamed up with **Les Williams** and **Mike Easthope** from the **Dimensions*** in a trio called **Pendulum** that was active for some years on Liverpool's cabaret-circuit – sometimes also appearing as the **Dimensions** again. After that, nothing was heard of **Ted Thompson** but it is very likely that he kept on playing. It is also likely that **Roger Parrot** continued in the music-business, as he was very talented and, besides keyboards, he could play guitar and drums. Unfortunately, there was no information available about his further activities. It is highly probable that **Savva Hercules** continued as a singer on the cabaret-scene after the **Democrats**

SAVVA WITH THE DEMOCRATS
PETE GOODALL
ROC 6279

had disbanded but, once again, there are no further details known.

Now back to **Peter Goodall** who, at first, started busking in London, then became resident at a club called 'Bunjie's' and was a member of a multimedia-group (this is a type of group that would include other types of entertainers, dancers, magicians, ventriloquists etc. as part of their performances) called the **Pentameters.** However, through the 1965 gig at the 'Empress Ballroom' with the **Graham Bond Organisation,** he was able to renew connections with **Dick Heckstall-Smith** and **Gerry Temple** and, while he was still appearing with the **Pentameters,** he co-operated with them on various special projects which helped him achieve the recognition he deserved. This ultimately resulted in him leaving the **Pentameters** and he played with **Zoot Money, Chris Farlowe** and a group called **Annapurna** and, from there, he joined the **Alan Bown Set**. In the mid-Seventies, he was a member of the **Troggs** and, after that, toured with **Percy Sledge** in Germany and Africa. He then joined the backing-group of **Carl Douglas** who, at that time, had big hit with "Kung-Fu Fighting". As a studio-musician, he also worked with **George Martin** and **Dick James** and his guitar can be heard on numerous recordings. It was through **Dick James** that he also got into producing and was responsible for quite a few of the **Foundations** hit-records. He kept on producing and playing and today he lives in Herefordshire, where he has his own studio, record-label and publishing company – all very successful. Obviously, his 1960's journey to London was the right move . . . .

Discography:

Too Much / Shaking All Over /

Mean Woman Blues / Please Don't Tease   UK- Phillips Kensington acetate / 1963

Furthermore, in 1965 it was announced that **Savva & the Democrats** would make a private recording with the original **"You know"** that **Roger Parrot** had written previously in 1964 for the musical film 'Ferry Cross' The Mersey'. Sadly no further details are known.

*The stories of these groups can be followed in 'Beat Waves 'Cross The Mersey' (*VelocePress ISBN 978-1-58850-201-8*).

THE SHAKE-SPEARS

Dave & Chris Pownall

It was probably sometime in 1962 that **Chris Pownall** started to guest as a singer with the resident groups that played the various pubs and social clubs in the Birkenhead area. Then he and his brother, **Dave Pownall,** who had learned to play the guitar, teamed up in an **Everly Brothers** style duo. This duo did not have a name but, when they were joined by **Harry Miller** as a second guitarist, they called themselves the **Shake-Spears** (original spelling in two separate words). This line-up was expanded with the addition of **Brian King** on bass-guitar but only for a short time as he went on to become a member of the **Medallions**. His replacement was **Desmond (Des) Fenning** and, by the end of 1964, the **Shake-Spears** had expanded into a quintet with the addition of **Billy Maybury** on drums and had become a real Beat-band in the following line-up:

Chris Pownall	(voc/harp)
Dave Pownall	(lg/voc)
Harry Miller	(rg)
Desmond (Des) Fenning	(bg)
Billy Maybury	(dr)

If **Des Fenning** had played in a group before, it is not known but **Billy Maybury** was a former member of the **Strollers**, the **Page-Boys** and the **Globetrotters**, the last two being one and the same group. In 1964, **Harry Miller** was temporarily replaced by **Stan Ferguson** who was also a former member of the **Page Boys** and the **Globetrotters** but, in the interim, had played with a short-lived group called the **Set-Up**. However, **Harry Miller** returned to the group when **Stan Ferguson** got married and quit showbiz for about ten years.

The **Shake-Spears**, who appeared regularly at the 'Callister' youth-club in Birkenhead also played the major venues such as the 'Tower-Ballroom' in New Brighton and the 'Grafton' and the 'Blue Angel' in Liverpool. They also had regular appearances at the 'Silver Blades' ice-rink on Prescot Road and a single booking at the 'Cavern' on the 14th March 1965.

It was probably in early 1965 that the group decided to make a record for promotional purposes and so they went into the Kensington-studio of **Percy Phillips** to record an EP on acetate. For that recording they chose the R&B-classic, "Little Egypt", the **Doris Troy** success, "What'cha gonna do about it", **Bob Dylan's** "She belongs to me" and an original called "Satisfy", that they had composed an hour or so before going into the studio. While this was an interesting record it did very little to help boost the popularity of the **Shake-Spears**. It was also sometime in 1965 that they were joined by **Steve Robinson** on organ.

The group was kept busy with plenty of bookings but their cohesion was starting to crumble. The first to leave was **Billy Maybury**, who was replaced by **Mike Nolan**. Then **Steve Robinson** left and he was soon followed by **Harry Miller** and **Des Fenning**, none of them appeared on the scene again. This left **Chris** and **Dave Pownall** who, along with the new drummer, **Mike Nolan**, formed another group in 1966, which was more Soul orientated and appeared under the name of **Chances Are** with the following musicians:

Chris Pownall	(voc/harp)
Phil Morgan	(lg)
Dave Pownall	(rg/voc)
'Big Louie' Lewis	(bg)
Mike Nolan	(dr)

To make one thing clear right now, this Liverpool group had nothing in common with the Columbia recording-group of the same name.

Unfortunately, by that time, there were not too many places that were booking groups with the style of music that **Chances Are** played and they only had one 'Cavern' appearance on the 1st March '67. They occasionally played the 'Mardi Gras' but mostly played the cabaret clubs and social-clubs. They did not use that group-name for too long, very likely because of the above mentioned recording group, so the **Chances Are** from Birkenhead became the **Handful**. In early 1968, they were booked to play the 'Kings Hall' in Stoke-on-Trent together with the **Rockin' Berries** hit-group from Birmingham. Much to the astonishment of the Liverpool musicians, the **Rockin' Berries** started to do comedy on stage. **Chris** and **Dave Pownall** considered that to be a great idea and from that night on wanted to incorporate comedy into their repertoire. This plan did not meet the consent of the other members and resulted in a series of replacement musicians starting with **Phil Morgan** who was replaced by **Peter Cooke** from **Earl Royce & the Olympics***, who was then replaced by **Vinnie Thomas** from the **Croupiers,** who eventually was replaced by **Sid Edwards** from the **Nashpool Four***. On bass guitar, **'Big Louie' Lewis's** place was taken over by **Ronnie Woods**, who came from the **Delmonts** who was then replaced by **Kenneth Webb**. Then, **Mike Nolan** was replaced by **Jimmy Whelan** on drums, who at one time had played with **Jerry & the Juveniles**. Most probably there were more changes in the line-up over time but the **Handful** kept going into the Seventies and, at one stage, it is known, that they won a national talent-contest organised by the 'Top Rank' ballroom-chain, but no more recordings were made.

Discography:

as **The Shake-Spears** :

Little Egypt / What'cha gonna do about it /
She belongs to me / Satisfy   UK- Phillips Kensington acetate / **1965**

*The stories of these groups can be followed in 'Beat Waves 'Cross The Mersey' (*VelocePress ISBN 978-1-58850-201-8*).

SOLOMON'S MINES

Allan Devon hailed from the area of Norris Green and, just like many of the other Liverpool musicians, he was first infected with the Skiffle virus which prompted him to start playing the guitar. His big influence was **Lonnie Donegan** (of course) and he soon became a member of a local Skiffle group who played regularly at the 'Regal Cinema' in Norris Green. They also played at some of the local youth clubs - just for fun and without having any particular name.

It was in 1962 that he formed a Rock 'n' Roll group together with some classmates from the Florence Melly Senior School in Walton. Heavily influenced by **Buddy Holly** and **Chuck Berry,** they started to rehearse with instruments borrowed from family members and friends.

This group, still without a name, made its first public appearance at St. Aidans Hall in Walton in 1962 and their equipment for that night consisted of one microphone, acoustic guitars and two drums. The older brother of their rhythm guitarist was **Norman Dunn**, a guitarist with the established **Spidermen**, who also managed to get them a few other gigs. In 1963, they all left school and they were able to get new equipment on hire purchase from Hessy's music shop.

Now what they needed was a name and one night after a rehearsal they decided on **Solomon's Mines**, after the famous book. In its original line-up the group consisted of:

Allan Devon	(voc/bg)
David Livingstone	(lg/voc)
Allan Dunn	(rg/voc)
Tony Owen	(dr)

The group now had equipment and a repertoire of standards such as "Roll over Beethoven", "Nadine", "Roadrunner" and "Walking the dog" and started to play the club scene. After a few local gigs, **Peter Rowlands**, manager of the **Maraccas**, became aware of them and took **Solomon's Mines** under his wing.

They rented a PA system on long-term finance from 'Alpha Sound' in Litherland, owned by **Brian Kelly**, who also promoted shows at Litherland Town Hall. Through him, **Solomon's Mines** got their first booking at that very popular venue and, from there, things started to take off.

In 1964, they got an offer to go to Germany but had to turn it down because **David Livingstone**'s parents wouldn't allow him to go as he was serving an apprenticeship as a toolmaker.

Solomon's Mines - L to R: Tony Owen, David Livingstone, Allan Dunn & Allan Devon

So **Solomons's Mines** kept on playing the local venues with ever increasing success and, in 1965, they went into the Phillips studio in Kensington and recorded an acetate with the **Everly Brothers** success, "All I have to do is dream", coupled with **Buddy Holly**'s classic, "Well alright". Not too long after this, **Tony Owen** left for personal reasons and he was replaced on drums by **John Sorsky**, apparently a newcomer to the scene.

It was in early 1966 that **Allan Devon** put his instrument aside and stepped in front as lead singer, while **Jimmy Humphreys,** from the recently disbanded **Deans,** joined as their new bass guitarist.

Allan Devon and **Jimmy Humphreys** became very close friends and this distanced them somewhat from the rest of the group. This meant that the cohesion started to crumble and so the two of them decided to disband the old group and to team up with **Jimmy Humphrey's** old band mates from the **Deans**. This new group also appeared as **Solomon's Mines** in a line-up with:

Allan Devon	(voc/bg)
Eddie Williams	(lg/voc)
Tommy Flude	(org/p/voc)
Jimmy Humphreys	(rg/voc)
Derek 'Dell' Robinson	(dr)

Prior to joining **Solomon's Mines, Dell Robinson** had been a member of the **Abstracts** from Crosby. However, he did not stay for too long, as he left to get married and **John Sorsky** returned to the group to replace him, meanwhile having played with the **Liverpool Scene**.

L to R: Eddie Williams, John Sorsky, Tommy Flude, Allan Devon & Jimmy Humphreys

It was this line-up of **Solomon's Mines** that now started to play regularly at all the established Beat clubs, for example the 'Cavern', 'Grafton', 'Iron Door' and 'Blue Angel', the 'Orrell Park Ballroom', the 'Floral Pavilion' in New Brighton, 'Parr Hall' in Warrington, as well as some venues in Manchester. They were also regulars at the 'Silver Blades Ice Rink' in Kensington, and it was there that a national group competition called 'Search For Sound' originated.

Solomon's Mines got through all the qualifying contests and made it to the finals in London, where they placed second. Although this really was a remarkable success, **Allan Devon** lost heart in the music scene and, in 1967, he became a merchant seaman and **Solomon's Mines** disbanded.

Tommy Flude joined a group called **Grand Prix** and, after that, played with the **Rockets** and the **Sensations**, while **Eddie Williams** became a member of the nationally successful cabaret group called **Charlie Boy**. He later emigrated to the United States, where he is still living. **Jimmy Humphreys** emigrated to Canada, where he played the clubs as a solo-performer.

In the early Seventies, **Allan Devon** left the Merchant Navy, returned to Liverpool and formed a new group, once again performing under the **Solomon's Mines** name.

This new Rock & Blues group included **John Sorsky** and **David Livingstone** again, as well as **Tony Owen's** brother **Steven Owen** on bass guitar and **Frank Baker**, a great guitarist and former member of the **Maraccas**' on lead guitar.

L to R: Jimmy Humphreys, John Sorsky, Allan Devon, Tommy Flude & Eddie Williams

For almost a year, **Solomon's Mines** had a strong presence once again on the scene, but the line-up was not very stable and they finally split in or around 1972. **Allan Devon** and **Frank Baker** retired from the music business, while **John Sorsky** became a successful comedian on the cabaret scene.

It is worth mentioning in connection with **Solomon's Mines** that **Tony** and **Steven Owen's** sister, **Jean Owen,** was a member of the **Vernon's Girls** and lived together with **Larry Parnes** in London for a few years and later found international fame as **Samantha Jones**.

Discography

All I have to do is dream / Well alright   UK – Phillips acetate / 1965

SOME OTHER GUYS

The Young Britians (1960) - L to R: Jimmy Cross, Gerry Norton, Ray Lee, Colin Prescott & Colin Lee

This group came from the west side of the River Mersey, where it was formed in Wallasey as the **Young Britains** in late 1959. Its original line-up consisted of **Colin Prescot** (voc), **Jimmy Cross** (lg), the brothers **Ray Lee** (rg) and **Colin Lee** (bg), as well as the drummer, **Gerry Norton**.

It was the first group for all the musicians, but **Colin Prescot** did not stay for too long and, in 1960, he was replaced by vocalist, **Eric Vernon**, also a newcomer to the scene. The **Young Britains**, playing a sort of Rock & Roll and mixed pop, appeared at the usual youth clubs in the Birkenhead and Wallasey area for a little over a year and then the group disbanded.

While the other members quit the music scene, **Jimmy Cross**, **Ray Lee** and **Gerry Norton** recruited two new members and, from 1961 onwards, they appeared under the name **Some Other Guys** with the following line-up:

Mike Morrisey	(voc/cornet)
Mick Lamb	(lg/voc)
Ray Lee	(rg/voc)
Jimmy Cross	(bg/voc)
Gerry Norton	(dr/voc)

Micky Lamb was a former member of the **Woodchoppers**, but it is not known whether **Mike Morrisey** had played in a group previously or if this was his first group.

Some Other Guys, now more of a typical Beat group, very soon accepted a residency at 'Rock Point', which was in the grounds of the New Brighton Tower. For three summer seasons they played there every Friday, Saturday and Sunday, afternoons and evenings.

In addition, they also appeared at other venues on the Wirral, including the 'Witch's Cauldron' in Wallasey, the 'Old Wirralians' in Ellesmere Port, as well as the 'Rakers', the 'Lakeside Bar' (later 'Sadies'), the 'Tavern' and 'Fort Perch Rock' in New Brighton.

In addition to playing with the group, **Gerry Norton** became a DJ and compere at the Tower Ballroom, he continued with both of these jobs throughout the Sixties.

It was in spring 1963 that **Some Other Guys** went into the Johnny Rodehouse Studios in Manchester to record the **Jimmy Cross** original, "I don't do me no good", and the **Shadows** instrumental, "Nivram". This acetate was sent to 'Radio Caroline' and got some plays but, ultimately, it didn't help the group obtain a recording contract or to make any sort of significant breakthrough.

Some Other Guys continued to play the club circuit on the Wirral on a semi-professional basis and established quite a following but, unfortunately, they never made the headlines.

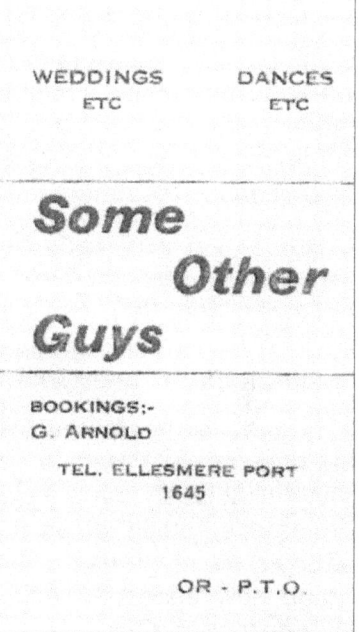

Sometime in 1964, the group disbanded when **Jimmy Cross** quit to get married and **Mike Morrisey** and **Mick Lamb** also decided to leave the music business.

Ray Lee went on to play with various groups, including the **Pioneers**, the **Abileens**, **Katie Jones & the Rivermen**, **Kenray Country** and **Tennessee Twist,** he is still an active performer on the scene.

Of **Gerry Norton** it is known that, after his time as a DJ, he became the resident drummer at the St. Josephs Club until the 80's.

In 1996, **Jimmy Cross** returned to the scene and started a band called **Buckshot**, which lasted for five years. He then played with **Del Rio** until 2007 and, since then, he has been a member of **Blueridge**, who are still playing the clubs today.

None of the other members of **Some Other Guys** ever appeared on the music scene again.

Discography

I don't do me no good / Nivram   UK- Rodehouse acetate / 1963

GEOFF STACEY & THE WANDERERS

The history of this group from Widnes goes back to the year 1957 when the three friends **Denny O'Neill** (g/voc), **John Halliburton** (g/voc) and **Ernie Hayes** formed the **Deltics** Skiffle group. In the beginning, **Ernie Hayes** played a tea-chest bass but a little later he switched to guitar, while **Denny O'Neill** took over on bass. Denny's father, who was a very good banjo player, sometimes joined the **Deltics** at gigs and he also coached the group.

It was in the very early Sixties that they were joined by the drummer, **Dennis Keeley**. Following that, their music direction changed to Rock 'n' Roll and the group's name first changed to the **Electrons** and then to the **Wanderers**.

In 1962, **John Halliburton** left to become a member of the **Paladins** from Runcorn. A new rhythm guitarist and a new lead vocalist - the drummer's cousin joined the group. The singer adopted the stage name, **Geoff Stacey,** and the group now appeared as **Geoff Stacey & the Wanderers** with the following line-up:

The Wanderers - L to R: Ernie Hayes, John Haliburton, Dennis Keeley & Denny O'Neil

Geoff Stacey	(voc)
Ernie Hayes	(lg)
Graham Garner	(rg/voc)
Denny O'Neill	(bg/voc)
Dennis Keeley	(dr)

Geoff Stacey's real name was **Geoff Keeley** and, although he was the front man and lead singer, **Denny O'Neill** and **Graham Garner** would sometimes team up and sing in **Everly Brothers**' style harmony.

Geoff Stacey & the Wanderers
L to R: Graham Garner, Dennis Keeley, Geoff Stacey & Denny O'Neil

John George Jr. took over their management and the group very soon became popular on the local scene and also gigged around the Liverpool area. They became the resident group at the 'Jokers' in Edge Lane, where they played every Thursday, Friday, Saturday and Sunday night from 1 a.m. until 4 a.m., which meant that they were working on a professional basis. This, of course, led to an improvement in their musical quality and also gave them the chance to play other gigs before their 'set' at the 'Jokers'.

```
NEMS ENTERPRISES
    PRESENT:—
MONDAY, SEPTEMBER 10th
QUEENS HALL, WIDNES
   THE BEATLES
Rory Storm and the Hurricanes
Geoff Stacey and the Wanderers
```

In August 1962, **Geoff Stacey & the Wanderers** reached second place in the Widnes/Runcorn Popularity Poll held at the Deacon Road Labour Club. As a result, the following month they were booked to play at a Nems concert at the Queens Hall in Widnes, on the same bill with the **Beatles** and **Rory Storm & the Hurricanes.**

This helped their popularity but, in spite of that success, **Geoff Keeley** and **Dennis Keeley** teamed up with two musicians from the **Cadillacs** and formed the **Addicts**, who later recorded for Decca.

Ronnie Ince, a former member of the **Cheetahs** and the **Dominant Four,** joined the **Wanderers** as their new vocalist. **Ronnie Ince** was better known on the scene as **Paul Francis**. Their new drummer, **Chris James,** had also played with the **Dominant Four**. In spite of these changes, the group was still occasionally presented as **Geoff Stacey & the Wanderers**.

The Wanderers - L to R: Ronnie Ince, Chris James, Ernie Hayes, Denny O'Neil & (Front) Graham Garner

When **Howie Casey & the Seniors** split in 1963, the **Wanderers** backed singer, **Derry Wilkie,** for some months while also continuing to play in their own right. **Derry Wilkie** then teamed up with the **Pressmen**, with whom he was featured on the Oriole album, "This Is Merseybeat" Vol.1. This co-operation did not last and, when **Derry Wilkie** was looking for a new group, he contacted **Ernie Hayes** again and they formed **Derry Wilkie & the Others.** Sometime later, this line-up, also backed **Screaming Lord Sutch** and, in the mid-Sixties, evolved into a 10-piece Soul band called **This 'N' That**, a name that was often shortened to **TNT**.

The **Wanderers** were joined by another lead guitarist and continued on the scene. Still in 1963, they cut a demo disc for Decca with the song, "It ain't necessarily so", which, unfortunately, was not followed by an official record release.

**The Wanderers - L to R: Ernie Hayes, Denny O'Neil,
Paul Francis (aka Ronnie Ince) Dennis Keeley & Geoff Stacey**

When **Denny O'Neill** also left to join the **Addicts**, the **Wanderers** disbanded totally in 1964. It is known that **Denny O'Neill** and **Graham Garner** later teamed up again and, together with Denny's wife, they are still active on the cabaret scene.

For the complete story of the **Addicts** please see the book *"Mersey Beat Waves" ISBN 1588502015 or 9781588502018*.

Discography

It ain't necessarily so / ???   UK- Decca-demo (acetate) / 1963

THE TEENAGE REBELS
(Vince Earl & various)

Let's start with a comment that was made about this group, by the great **Bob Wooler** with his immense knowledge about the Merseybeat-scene - taken from his biography, 'The Best of Fellas', written by **Spencer Leigh** in 2002.

"In 1958 at the 'Winter Gardens', Garston, Vince Earl was in a group called the Teenage Rebels. They were 16 year olds from Birkenhead and he was the Elvis of the group. I am convinced that if any group could have challenged the Beatles, it would have been the Teenage Rebels . . ."

This, of course, is a strong statement for someone known to pick his words very carefully and this fact definitely underlines the quality and significance of this group, that was formed as a real Skiffle-group under the name of the **Rebels** in Birkenhead in 1957. After changing over to mainly Rock & Roll and other popular music of that time, they had a huge success in the 'Boys' Clubs Federation' show, 'Ace Of Spades', in Manchester. Their original guitarist, **Jerry Dempsey,** left and, a little later, the group's management was taken over by **Ron Tucker**, who was the secretary of the Northwest Boys' Clubs. Following his advice, the group changed their name into the **Teenage Rebels** that, at that time, consisted of the following musicians:

Vince Earl	(voc/bg)
Pete Wright	(lg/voc)
Joey Aptor	(rg)
Dave Pears	(g/voc)
John Cruice	(voc/dr)

Dave Pears was the new guitarist and **Pete Wright** was the bandleader and the oldest member of this very young-aged group. The exceptional thing about the **Teenage Rebels** was that all the members were great singers and shared the lead-vocals. So, for example, **Vince Earl** sang **Buddy Holly** and **Elvis Presley** hits, **John Cruice** all the **Pat Boone** songs, **Pete Wright** the **Lonnie Donnegan** songs and **Dave Pears** was the specialist for **Tommy Steele** vocals.

Ron Tucker arranged regular appearances for **Wally Hill's** 'Peak Promotions' at the 'Winter Gardens' in Garston and the promoter was so enthusiastic about them that he also booked the **Teenage Rebels** for his premiere events at the 'Holyoake', where they were billed as a 'Special Attraction'. The group now played at many places all over North Wales, Cheshire and Lancashire.

When **Pete Wright** had to join the Army in 1960, this promising group broke up totally, much too early to make any real impact on the Merseybeat scene. What is most surprising is that, with only one exception, none of the

members of this really good group appeared on the scene again. That exception was **Vince Earl**, who became the lead vocalist of the already established **Zeros** from Birkenhead who then changed their name into **Vince Earl & the Zeros** and appeared in a line-up with:

Vince Earl	(voc)
Barry Ezzra	(lg/voc)
Brian Hilton	(rg/voc)
Ray Whitehead	(bg)
Mike Oldham	(dr)

Only of **Barry Ezzra** it is known that he was a former member of the **Firecrests** (another story in this book). **Vince Earl & the Zeros** was an excellent Beat group that appeared regularly at all the popular venues on the Wirral, as well as in and around Liverpool. In

Vince Earl & the Zeros

spite of their success, they did not exist for too long and, for unknown reasons, **Vince Earl & the Zeros** broke up towards the end of 1962. **Barry Ezzra** joined **Steve Day & the Drifters**, that then became **Gus Travis & the Rainchecks*** and finally continued just as the **Rainchecks*** and recorded for the Solar label. **Brian Hilton** became a member of **Group One*** but then changed over to Liverpool's Country-scene and joined **Sonny Web & the Cascades***, that very soon changed their name into the **Hillsiders,** where he played until they split off in the Nineties. What happened to **Mike Oldham** is not known but **Ray Whitehead**, for sure, continued to play the scene – but more of that later in this story.

Vince Earl then became the vocalist of the **Talismen** from Moreton, formerly known as the **Thunderbeats**. Due to the popularity of their new singer, they changed their name into **Vince Earl & the Talismen***. **Vince Earl** stayed with the **Talismen** until early 1965 and then became the bass-guitarist with **Rory Storm & the Hurricanes***. After that, he was a member of the **Connoisseurs***, who were also very popular group on the Merseybeat scene. When the **Connoisseurs** disbanded, **Vince Earl** joined a cabaret-group, called the **Trend** that, besides **Peter Cooke** (lg) and **Jimmy Jordan** (dr), both former members of **Earl Royce & the Olympics*** and **Bobby Wild** (rg) also included **Ray Whitehead** (bg) of the **Zeros**.

VINCE EARL & THE TALISMEN

When, at the end of the Sixties, the two guitarists, **Peter Cooke** and **Bobby Wild** left, the remaining three teamed up with **Barry Triggs** (org/p/voc) and **Barry 'Baz' Davis**, the former lead-guitarist of the **Connoisseurs, King Size Taylor*** and the German group **Mike Warner & the New Stars** from Bielefeld. This new group was called the **Vince Earl**

Attraction and after **'Baz' Davis** was replaced by **Graham Jones**, they recorded an album on the Liverpool Sound label, simply called, 'First'. **Jimmy Jordan** then was replaced by **Billy Dunlop** and when **Ray Whitehead** also left, **Vince Earl** took over the bass-guitar. That was the line-up on the second album, 'Can't Get Enough', on the Amazon label. In the mid Seventies, this group disbanded but **Vince Earl** kept the name for various line-ups. The next record, a privately recorded EP was released on the Realm label (this was a 'fantasy' label created by him and there were no further releases on that label) featured **Billy Hughes** (bg), **Tony Jennings** (dr) and **Alan Greer** (lg), the former leader of **Wayne Calvert & the Cimarrons**.

As the good times for groups were declining, also in the cabaret-scene, the **Vince Earl Attraction** only had sporadic live-engagements, which led **Vince Earl** to the decision to go out as a solo-act – as singer and comedian. In the early Eighties, he successfully concentrated on a career as actor, was featured in various films but, is probably best known for his portrayal of the character, Ron Dixon, in the soap-opera, 'Brookside', that was on British TV from 1990 until 2003. Besides all this, **Vince Earl** kept active on the music-scene and the **Vince Earl Attraction** is still going to this day, even if only sporadically and in steadily changing line-ups, which always feature well-known Merseybeat veterans. At times, it has included guitarist, **Charlie Flynn** (ex-**Ian & the Zodiacs*** and the **Connoisseurs**), keyboarder, **Steve 'Tiger' Fleming** (ex-**Mark Peters & the Silhouettes***), drummer, **Dave Lovelady** (ex-**Fourmost***) and guitarist, **Tony Coates** (ex-**Ian & the Zodiacs**) and guitarist, **Ian Hunter** (lg) and bassist, **Allan Burton** (bg) both formerly of the **Valkyries***.

Discography

There are no recordings of **Vince Earl** from the Sixties - neither with the **Teenage Rebels**, the **Zeros** or the **Talismen**, nor with any of the other groups he played in. It was only in the Seventies that he made records with the **Vince Earl Attraction** but of course they were not Beat anymore.

as <u>**The Vince Earl Attraction**</u>:

Album **'First'**	UK-Liverpool Sound LS 1778 / 1973
Album **'Can't Get Enough'**	UK- Amazon (unnumbered) / 1974

<u>**Vince Earl** – solo-EP</u>:

Love Hurts / I Believe /

You'll Never Find Another Love Like Mine /

God Only Knows   UK- Realm (private)   VE 006 / 1976

*The stories of these groups can be followed in 'Beat Waves 'Cross The Mersey' (*VelocePress* ISBN 978-1-58850-201-8).

THE THUNDERBEATS

In addition to the **Dominators**, the **Vendors**, the **Asteroids** and **Bob Johnson & the Bobcats**, the **Z-Men** were one of the early groups from Preston, Lancashire, where they were formed as a four-piece by drummer, **Keith Hartley,** in or around 1959.

In 1960, the group was joined by a singer who called himself **Johnny Thunder**, whose real name is not known. The group then changed their name to **Johnny Thunder & the Thunderbeats** and, around the same time, their rhythm guitarist, **Johnny Clegg,** left and probably quit the music business completely. His replacement, on guitar, was **John Brierley**.

It was still in 1960, that **Johnny Thunder** left and disappeared from the scene. The group then shortened their name to the **Thunderbeats** and continued as a four-piece, with all members sharing the vocals.

After having played the local youth clubs, such as the 'Blessed Sacrament' in Ribbleton for some time, they began to get bookings at the real Beat clubs, including the 'Flamingo', the 'Derby Arms' and the 'Catacombs' coffee bar. Liverpool's **Big Three** also played the 'Catacombs' on a regular basis and they had a strong influence on the musical style of the **Thunderbeats**, who at that time consisted of:

Peter Atkinson	(lg/voc)
John Brierley	(rg/voc)
Jimmy Whittle	(bg/voc)
Keith Hartley	(dr)

The **Thunderbeats** were one of the best hard-driving Rock 'n' Roll groups in the Preston area and they had become a significant group on the local scene. Consequently, they were now playing at some of the larger venues including the 'Odeon' and the 'Top Rank'.

Their management was taken over by two wrestlers who knew a lot of promoters in the north of England and so the group frequently appeared at the major dance halls in Lancaster, Kendal, Southport and Blackpool. They even became the regular band at the 'Leyland Public Hall' for some time and also played at the 'Cubik Club' in Birkenhead quite often, where they became very popular.

A certain **David John Smith** had been hanging around with the group for some time and he would occasionally help out with backing vocals. The group members eventually allowed him to take on some lead vocals and he ultimately became member by default!

In June 1963, **Keith Hartley** left the group. He went to Liverpool and joined **Rory Storm & the Hurricanes** for a few months before moving on to play with **Freddie Starr & the Midnighters**.

Shortly after, **Jimmy Whittle** left to join a re-formed trio line-up of the **Bobcats** who soon changed their name to the **Puppets** and recorded for **Joe Meek**. In the 70's, he appeared with the **Four Just Men** for a short time before he retired from the music business.

The Thunderbeats

The remaining **Thunderbeats** members, **David John Smith**, **Peter Atkinson** and **John Brierley** were joined by **Gene Carberry** from the **Crusaders** as their new drummer and the former **Rebels** lead guitarist, **Reg Welch**. They continued as the **Questions** on the scene, but only played four gigs under that name. Their final gig was at the 'Daily Herald Beat Festival' in Liverpool and, as well as doing their own spot, they backed **Ricky Valance** at that show.

After that, **John Brierley** and **Reg Welch** teamed up with **Keith Hartley** again in **Freddie Starr & the Midnighters**.

Gene Carberry toured Poland with the **Atoms** but then, as **Gene Richie,** he became a member of the **Prestons**. After that, he played with the **Executives** from Blackpool and then joined the Belfast recording group, the **Wheels**.

David John (Smith) joined the **Falcons** from Preston, who became the legendary **David John & the Mood**. A little later, this group also included **Peter Atkinson** once again.

When the **Midnighters** disbanded in April 1964, **John Brierley** also joined **David John & the Mood**, while **Reg Welch** initially became a member of the **Nashpool Four** but then joined the **Suspects**. He sadly died in March 2006.

David John & the Mood split up in 1966 and **David John** became a member of the **Sound Five** and later sang with the groups, **Barbed Wire Soup** and **Thundermother**.

John Brierley joined the **Police Force** (the group, not the constabulary), while **Peter Atkinson** disappeared from the scene.

Now back to **Keith Hartley** who, in the meantime, changed his name to **Keef Hartley** and, after playing with **Midnighters**, was a founding member of the **Ice Blues** together with **Bob Garner** (bg), **Roger James** (p/org) and **Dave McShane** (sax). This was an interesting group, who settled down in Blackpool and also toured Germany at one time. At the end of 1964, **Keef Hartley** was a member of the **Artwoods** from London, where he played until he joined **John Mayall's Bluesbreakers** in 1967. After that, he formed his own successful group called the **Keef Hartley Band** and, in the mid 70's, he played with the **Michael Chapman Group** before he became a member of **Chicken Shack**.

Completely unexpectedly, the **Thunderbeats**, who at one time formed the backbone of **Freddie Starr & the Midnighters** and **David John & the Mood**, re-united in 1998 in a line-up with **Keef Hartley**, **David John**, **Peter Atkinson** and **John Brierley**, and were sometimes joined by other Preston musicians they were friendly with. As far as it is known, they have not made a public appearance (yet), but have recorded a private CD with six songs in a local studio.

Sadly, **Keef Hartley** died on November 27th. 2011

For the complete story of the **David John & the Mood** please see the book *"Mersey Beat Waves" ISBN 1588502015 or 9781588502018.*

Discography

The **Thunderbeats** did not make any recordings in the Sixties but when they re-united in 1998, they recorded a highly interesting private CD with **"Three steps to heaven"**, **"Shake, rattle & roll"**, **"Memphis Tennessee"**, **"Bony Moronie"**, "**Slow down"** and an unedited version of **"Bony Moronie"**.

THE TIMEBEATS

The driving force behind this interesting group, and the other two that evolved from it, and basically always consisted of the same musicians, most probably was the multi-instrumentalist and singer, **Jose McLaughlin.** In his younger years, he was known as **Joe McLaughlin** and he originally hailed from Norris Green but, at a very young age, had moved with his parents to the Orrell Park area of Liverpool.

In 1961, he joined the teenage-group, the **Vulcans,** as drummer, with whom he played the local venues for about two years. But this was only the starting point and, in 1963, he became a member of the much more established, **Timebeats**, where, besides being the lead-singer, he also played guitar and piano. In 1963 their line up consisted of:

Jose McLaughlin	(voc/p/g)
Leslie Morris	(lg/voc)
Eddie Jones	(rg/voc)
Ray Madden	(bg)
Colin Hewitt	(dr)

The **Timebeats** were a typical Merseybeat group, playing Rock 'n' Roll and a bit of early Motown. All the members came from the Orrell Park area, with the exception of **Eddie Jones**, who lived in the south end of Liverpool. That fact was also the reason for him leaving the group sometime in 1964. It was just too difficult for him to travel from the other end of the city by public transport, carrying his guitar and heavy amplifier to rehearsals and gigs. There is nothing further known about him ever joining another group.

The Timebeats - L to R:
Eddie Jones, Les Morris,
Ray Madden, Colin Hewitt
& Jose McLaughlin

The **Timebeats** carried on as a four-piece and continued to play all the clubs in the north end of Liverpool, as well as the larger local venues including the 'Orrell Park Ballroon', the 'Aintree Institute' and the 'Litherland Town Hall', where they often supported the big names but also established a large following of their own.

Still in 1964, **Jose McLaughlin** had also formed a group with some of his school-mates under the name of the **Fortune Tellers**. However, he continued to play with the **Timebeats** besides playing with the **Fortune Tellers.** The **Fortune Tellers** only existed for a few months but, during that time, amongst other clubs, they also managed to appear at the 'Cavern'.

Towards the end of 1964, **Leslie Morris** decided not to pursue a career as a musician, quit the **Timebeats** and went back to school to become an electrical engineer. He still has his bright red Fender Stratocaster although, as far as it is known, he never played in another group.

Jose McLaughlin, together with **Ray Madden** and **Colin Hewitt,** then continued on as a trio but, co-incident with the leaving of the two guitarists, they decided to change their name from the **Timebeats** to **Joe, Ray & Me**, which was a play on the musical solfège "Do-Re-Mi".

This trio continued successfully on the scene until **Jose McLaughlin** joined the **Dials** in early 1966 and, after that, he became a member of the **Dee Jays** for a short time. It was in early 1967 that he teamed up with his old comrades again and formed the **Modern Blues Quartet** in a line-up with:

Jose McLaughlin	(voc/org/g)
Chris Toffa	(voc/sax/harp)
Ray Madden	(bg)
Colin Hewitt	(dr)

Chris Toffa was of Greek descent and also hailed from the Orrell Park area, he was also an excellent singer and musician. This group, in spite of it's 'bar-music' sounding name, actually was a rocking combo that, in it's style, concentrated on American Rhythm & Blues, Soul, Motown and classic Rock 'n' Roll. All performed with their own interpretation and presented in a well rehearsed programme.

The Modern Blues Quartet

The **Modern Blues Quartet** turned professional and they were immediately booked by the major venues on the Liverpool scene, including the 'Cavern', the 'Iron Door', the 'Victoriana' and the 'Mardi Gras'. They were also featured regularly on BBC local and national radio and that fact might have led to the decision for them to make a record.

Still in 1967, the group went into **Charlie Weston**'s studios in Moorfields and recorded the very soulful "Summertime" and an exciting version of "La Bamba", which always was a favourite at their live-gigs. This single on the CAM label received significant airplay but did not help the group to get signed by a major recording-company.

Shortly after this recording, for unknown reasons, **Chis Toffa** left and disappeared from the scene. His replacement in the **Modern Blues Quartet** was the guitarist and singer, **Paul Booth**, who had already played together with **Jose McLaughlin** in the **Dials**. They both now shared the vocals and the group continued in that line-up until the end of 1968, when the **Modern Blues Quartet** finally broke up.

Paul Booth continued to play with various groups on the scene, while **Colin Hewitt** joined a Hawaiian group and **Ray Madden** quit the music-business. Of **Colin Hewitt,** it is known that he later emigrated to New Zealand, where, today, he owns a printing business in Invercargill.

During his time with the **Modern Blues Quartet, Jose McLaughlin** also played with, and became a member of, **Amos Bonny & Friends**, an exceptional group that consisted of many well known Merseybeat-musicians (see the **5 A.M. Event** story).

After that, **Jose McLaughlin** joined the group, **Highly Inflammable**, that, besides him on keyboards, consisted of **Mike Evans** (tenor-sax) – ex **Clayton Squares** and **Liverpool Scene**, **Graham 'Bobby' Robertson** (alto-sax) – ex **Almost Blues**, **Percy Jones** (bg) from **Liverpool Scene** and **John Sorsky** (dr) – ex **Solomon's Mines** and **Liverpool Scene**.

That group played on a national level, touring throughout England. They had appearances at the famous 'Marquee' in London and recorded an interesting album on the CAM label ("Highly Inflammable" CLP 010).

In late 1970, **Jose McLaughlin** was a member of the **Mike Byrne Band**, a group that had evolved from **Amos Bonny & Friends**. In 1972, he was part of the newly formed **Gerry & the Pacemakers** and, in 1974, he emigrated to Australia, where he has been an integral part of the national music-scene ever since.

Discography

as **The Modern Blues Quartet** :

Summertime / La Bamba	**UK- CAM Records CAM 027 / 1967**

THE TIMEBOX

In many ways, this legendary group had its origins in two Southport outfits that were, of course, part of the Merseybeat scene, even if they were more into Rhythm & Blues.

The first group is the **Music Students**, formed at the Southport Technical College in 1962 by **Chris Holmes** (org) and **Bill Lovelady** (lg/voc), together with **'Bugsy' Mullen** (rg/voc), **Max Hornby** (bg) and a drummer, whose name unfortunately is not known. Also, In the very beginning, they were said to have had a lead vocalist, but unfortunately, nothing is known about him either.

In 1963, the original drummer was replaced by **Peter 'Ollie' Halsall**, who had played with the **Gunslingers** (formerly known as the **Rebels**), **Pete & the Pawnees**, as well as with **Rhythm & Blues Incorporated** for a short time.

A little later, **Max Hornby** also left and his replacement was **Chris Parr**, who was a member of **Gerry De Ville & the City-Kings** in later years.

This real Blues group became more and more popular and played all the local clubs, such as the 'Klic Klic', the 'Beachcomber', the 'West End Club', the 'High Park Club' and the 'Floral Hall'. They also appeared quite regularly at the 'Jive Hive' in Crosby, and they played all the popular Liverpool venues including the 'Iron Door' and the 'Cavern'.

The second group was **Take Five**, formed in 1963 by **Clive Griffiths** (bg) together with **Peter Liggett** (voc), **Geoff Deane** (dr) from the **Sandgrounders**, **Stella James** (voc/perc) and her brother **Peter James** (g/voc), who both came from the **Rondels**. Prior to joining **Take Five**, **Peter James** had played with **Little Gene & the Outlaws** and the **Toledo Four**, who were also known as the **Toledos with Dee James**.

It is not known how it came to happen but, in early 1965, **Take Five** obtained a two-month engagement in Koblenz in Germany, which apparently was a very stressful time for the group as, immediately following this booking, they started to 'come apart at the seams'.

When the group returned to the UK, **Stella James** remained in Germany for some months and joined the **Dogs** from Koblenz, a forerunner of the **Rebbels**, a great German group who had a national hit in 1966 with "Monkey, Monkey". When she eventually returned to Southport, she quit the music business forever.

Peter James also left **Take Five** immediately after their return. In the late Sixties, he fronted the **Peter James Bluesband**, before he adopted the stage name, **Eddie Vincent**. Today he lives in North Wales, where he is still active in showbiz.

Around that same time, the **Music Students** had also disbanded. **Bill Lovelady** joined **Rhythm & Blues Inc**. and then he started a successful solo career. He later had a massive international hit with "Reggae for it now".

Now a three-piece, **Take Five** recruited a new lead guitarist and two members of the recently disbanded **Music Students** - and so **Take Five** continued as a six-piece in a line-up with:

Peter Liggett	(voc)
Kevin Fogerty	(lg)
Chris Holmes	(org)
'Ollie' Halsall	(vib)
Clive Griffiths	(bg)
Geoff Deane	(dr)

Kevin Fogerty was a former member of the **Teenbeats**, who were very popular locally and also played a lot in Liverpool.

As they were a sort of local super group now, **Take Five** decided to go fully professional. They backed Liverpool singer, **Tommy Quickly,** on a nationwide tour and, after that, they backed US singer, **Lou Christie**, whose "Lightnin' strikes" had just climbed up the British charts. In 1966, they settled down in London where they met **Laurie Jay**, leader and drummer of the **Laurie Jay Combo**, who took over their management.

An engagement for a summer season at a Butlin's Holiday Camp secured their position as professionals. However, for unknown reasons, at some point during that booking, **Peter Liggett** left and returned to Southport. His replacement was **Frank Dixon** as lead singer and front man.

Timebox

In November 1966, the group changed its name to **Time Box** (initially written with two words), but unfortunately, that did not seem to be a good omen. Shortly after the name change, **Frank Dixon** became ill with tuberculosis and left in early 1967. A little later, **Geoff Deane** was diagnosed with the same illness, he also left the group and returned to Southport. As far as it is known, **Geoff Deane** never joined another group but became the resident drummer at a number of various Merseyside clubs over the years.

At about the same time, **Laurie Jay** had secured a recording contract for the group with Piccadilly. However, they needed to quickly re-build their line-up, so they were joined by the black American singer, **Richard Henry**, who came from the **Zig Zag Band** and the drums were temporarily taken over by **Laurie Jay** himself. **John Schroeder** was the producer for **Time Box's** first single, "I'll always love you", which was coupled with the instrumental, "Save your love". As their debut, this Soul-influenced record sold quite well, but wasn't a huge success.

Richard Henry was an American soldier and the musicians were not aware of the fact that their new singer had gone 'absent without leave' from the US Army. Accordingly, it took them by surprise when the Military Police turned up to arrest him after a gig in a London club in March 1967. He never returned to the group and all that was heard from him later was a solo single on Regal Zonophone with "Oh girl/Lay your head on my shoulder" (ZG 3014) in 1968.

Thus, the next single by **Time Box** was a pure instrumental called "Soul sauce" which was coupled with the group's original "I wish I could jerk like my uncle Cyril", which was a sort of Latin Rock number. The session drummer, **Ronnie Verrel**, had been engaged for that recording but very soon the group was joined by **Andy Peters** as their new drummer, having come from the **Band Of Angels**.

However, it took until July 1967 before they found a new singer in **Michael Patrick McCarthy**. He had adopted the stage name **Mike Patto** and was very experienced as a former vocalist with the **Fretmen** and the **Breakaways** (who had evolved from the **Fretmen**), the **Bluesbottles**, the **Continentals**, the **Bo Street Runners**, as well with **Patto's People** and the **Chicago Line Blues Band** who, amongst others, also included drummer, **Viv Prince** of the **Pretty Things**. In addition, prior to joining **Time Box**, **Mike Patto** had a solo single released in December 1966 with "Can't stop talking 'bout my Baby" (Columbia DB 8091).

This was not the end of the personnel changes, as **Andy Peters** left and was replaced by **John Halsey** from Finchley, who had formerly played with **Barry Reed & the Avengers**, the **VIPs** and **Felder's Orioles**.

Then **Kevin Fogerty** left to join the **Dave Davani Four**. He later played in a group called **One** and then in **Tommy Hunt's** band. He was active on the music scene in America until he sadly died in December 2010. He was not replaced in **Timebox** and from then on **Ollie Halsall** concentrated on playing the guitar, an instrument he excelled on. This was the line-up of **Timebox** that was signed to Deram in 1967 and it is considered by many to be their ultimate line-up.

In October of that year, the single, "Don't make promises", was released on the Deram label, which was coupled with "Walking through the streets of my mind" which, for the first time ever, featured the lead vocals of **Ollie Halsall**.

It was a great record and showed **Timebox** to be a Soul-influenced, vocal harmony group, although, at live appearances, they played a more aggressive mixture of Soul and Jazzrock. They became something of a 'band's band' on the scene, meaning they were admired by other musicians – especially the outstanding guitar work of **Ollie Halsall**.

After that release, **Timebox** toured France and the tour was extremely successful. They were recorded at a show in Paris for a planned live album, unfortunately, it was never released.

Their next record was a version of the former **Four Seasons** hit, "Beggin", which was zapped up with a full orchestral backing arranged by **Mike Vickers** of **Manfred Mann** fame. The female backing vocals came from none other than **Kiki Dee** and **Madeleine Bell**. It was an interesting record which became the first (and only) chart success for **Timebox,** when it climbed up to No. 38. This was followed by extensive and successful tours in Europe and the United States.

Back in London, a complete album was recorded, which is said to have included the two **Young Rascals** songs, "Come on up" and "How can I be sure", as well as the original numbers, "Love the girl", "Leave me to cry", "Black dog", "Treehouse", "Barnabas Swain", "Gone is the sad man", "Country Dan & Lil" and "A woman that's waiting", for the most part written by **Mike Patto** and **Ollie Halsall**.

For some reason, the LP was not released at that time but "Come on up" and "A woman that's waiting", recorded at that session, were issued as a single - in France only. (*The complete recordings can be found on the 1998 CD "The Deram Anthology" which sold very well, especially in America.*)

In November 1968, the follow-up release to their chart success in England finally came with the **Leon Huff** song, "Girl don't make me wait", a typical Tamla Soul sound, while the B-side, "Gone is the sad man" (from the album session), had more of a Beat touch. They were not able to repeat the success of "Beggin" with this record, although it sold fairly well.

Maybe as a result of this recording, Liverpudlian **Wayne Bickerton** became their new producer. He had played in various Merseybeat groups, amongst others with **Lee Curtis & the All Stars** and the **Pete Best Four**. Their first record under his wings was "Baked Jam-Roll in your eye", which had moderate success. It is hard to understand why the really great rocking number, "Poor little heartbreaker", with **Mike Patto's** fantastic singing and the excellent guitar play of **Ollie Halsall** was relegated to the B-side. If it had been marketed as the A-side, it most probably would have become a second chart success for **Timebox**. The Deram divisions in Belgium and Denmark obviously saw its potential and swapped the sides but, apparently, it was not the right market for it.

The next single, "Yellow van", did not get any attention at all and this lack of success with their records may have led to **Chris Holmes** deciding to leave in November 1969. He joined **Funky Fever** and, after that, he backed the black US singer **Tommy Hunt** for a number of years. In 1978, he was a member of **Babe Ruth** but then returned to the **Tommy Hunt Band**, before he joined the **Showstoppers** in 1980. He was an exceptional keyboarder, who is still active today as a member of **No Spring Chicken**.

He was not replaced in the group, which continued as a four-piece and, a little later, changed their name to **Patto**, following a suggestion by their new manager and producer, **Muff Winwood**. They were signed to Vertigo and, judging by their two LPs, "Patto" (1970) and "Hold your fire" (1971), they had developed into a really Progressive Jazz-Rock group.

Patto was firmly established among the leading groups on the British scene but their record sales were apparently not satisfactory enough for Vertigo. This led **Patto** to change to Island Records in 1972, where they cut another album with "Roll 'em, smoke 'em, put another line out".

In 1973, **Ollie Halsall** left the group and, a little later, they disbanded totally. He joined **Jon Hiseman's Tempest**. After that, he played with **Kevin Ayers** and then became a member of **Boxer**, where he met up again with **Mike Patto**, who died in 1979. **Ollie Halsall** became a part of the **Rutles** but then returned to work with **Kevin Ayers**. Over the years, he had developed into a phenomenal guitarist and was deemed to be in the same league as **Eric Clapton**, **Jeff Beck** and **Jimmy Page**.

John Halsey, who later became a very successful session drummer, once said of him: *"Ollie may not have been the best guitarist in the world, but he was certainly among the top two!"* **Ollie Halsall** died of a heroin overdose in Spain in June 1992.

Discography

I'll always love you / Save your love	UK-Piccadilly	7N 35363 / 1967
Soul sauce / I wish I could jerk like my Uncle Cyril	UK-Piccadilly	7N 35379 / 1967
Don't make promises / Walking through the streets of my mind	UK- Deram	DM 153 / 1967
Beggin' / A woman that's waiting	UK- Deram	DM 194 / 1968
Girl, don't make me wait / Gone is the sad man	UK- Deram	DM 219 / 1968
Baked Jam Roll in your eyes / Poor little heartbreaker	UK- Deram	DM 246 / 1969
Yellow van / You've got the chance	UK- Deram	DM 271 / 1969

Diferent French release:

Come on up / A woman that's waiting	F - Deram	17.010 / 1968

*(For collectors it is interesting to note that in 1976 an album was released in the USA with the title **"The original moose on the loose"** (Peters International 9016) with all songs from the released Deram singles)*

THE TOKENS

John Gee

This group cannot be placed to a particular district of Liverpool as their founders **Terry McAdam** (voc/rg) came from the Anfield area and **Terence Kenaugh** (lg/voc) from Aigburth. Apparently, they began as a four-piece group sometime in 1961/1962 and, in the beginning, had some personnel changes until they came to a steady line-up when they were joined by **John Gee** on drums, who also hailed from the Aigburth area. Sadly, as the bass-guitarist position kept changing, the name(s) could not be established. Regardless, all of the members were newcomers to the scene but, by 1963, the **Tokens** had built up an excellent name for themselves on the Liverpool Beat-scene – not at least thanks to their manager **Mike Chamberlain**, who was very active in promoting them.

Then the line-up problems started again. **Johnny Gee** left and joined **Danny Havoc & the Secrets,** and, after that, he went on to play with the **St. Louis Checks*** where he met up with **Terence Kenaugh,** again, who, in the meantime, had also parted ways with the **Tokens**. Then, **Johnny Gee** left the **St. Louis Checks** and became a member of **Freddie Starr & the Delmonts** until sometime in 1966 when he joined the **Pikkins** (another story in this book), with whom he played until they disbanded in 1979 (!). After that, **Johnny Gee** quit showbiz. Then, **Terence Kenaugh** or **Terry Kenna,** as he was sometimes reported in the press, left and joined the **Terry Hines Sextet*** that developed into the **Fyx** and then he became a member of the Scottish group, **Blues System,** that, for a long time, were the resident group at the 'Blue Angel' in Liverpool. Following that, he was a member of the **Pikkins** for a short time. But now back to the **Tokens** as **Terry McAdam** kept the band going with new members and, in early 1964, the group consisted of the following musicians:

Terry McAdam	(voc)
Richard Quilliam	(lg)
Stan Davis	(rg)
Charlie 'Chez' King	(bg)
Derek Averton	(dr)

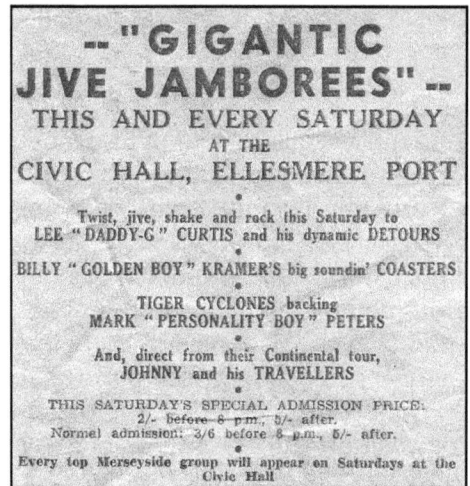

Charlie King's real name is Charles Robinson and both he and Richard Quilliam came from the Detours* that, for a time, had also backed Lee Curtis. Derek Averton, who is sometimes reported as Derek Atherton, was formerly a member of Lee Shondell & the Boys, while the former group of Stan Davis is sadly not known. It is also possible, that for a short time, the Tokens were joined by an additional female vocalist from North Wales, as documented in an article that appeared in the Mersey Beat Newspaper, but no further details are known.

However, it is a fact that the Tokens in the above line-up recorded a demo-disc (acetate) for well-known producer, Norrie Paramor (Columbia Records), in May 1964 but this sadly was not followed by a release. The recorded numbers were most probably originals by the group but as it proved to be impossible to establish any direct contacts, it could not be determined, which songs were recorded or in which studio.

On 10th August 1964, the Tokens made it into the finals of the 'Rael Brook Beat Contest' at the 'Tower Ballroom' in New Brighton but, sadly, did not win. They kept on playing in the scene for one more year and then both Charlie King and Richard Quilliam left the group. Nothing was heard of Charlie King again but Richard Quilliam, together with Billy Churchill, re-formed the Detours. After that, Richard Quilliam also quit the music-business. It is not known if the Tokens continued with new members or disbanded totally in 1965. There is also the possibility that they changed their name because of the American hit-group of the same name. Fact is, that after 1965, nothing more was heard of the Tokens in the Liverpool scene and neither Terry McAdam, Stan Davis or Derek Averton appeared again in other groups.

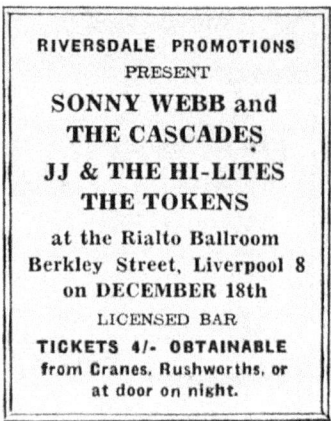

Discography :

The Tokens never had an official record out but in 1964 they recorded a demo-disc, probably with originals by the group, for the well-known producer Norrie Paramor. As this was not followed by a release it is sadly not known which songs were on it.

*The stories of these groups can be followed in 'Beat Waves 'Cross The Mersey' (VelocePress ISBN 978-1-58850-201-8).

TOMMY & THE METRONOMES

The **Metronomes** were formed in 1957 as a Skiffle-group in the Vauxhall district of Liverpool, better known in Liverpool slang as 'Scottie Road'. The founding members were the childhood friends **Tommy Lowe** (voc/rg) and **Frank Fullerton** (dr) together with **Bobby Dean** (lg/voc) and **Jimmy Ennis** (t-bass).

In 1958 the group changed their music into Rock & Roll and, accordingly, were one of Liverpool's pioneering groups in that music-style. This change resulted in **Bobby Dean** leaving the group and he was replaced by **Bert Byrne**, who hailed from Croxteth. **Jimmy Ennis** also left and was replaced by **Phil Clancy**, who played rhythm-guitar. As it is difficult to play Rock & Roll without bass, it was likely that **Tommy Lowe** substituted as their bass guitarist by playing just the bass-strings of his six-string guitar.

Metronomes 1959 - L to R: Bert Byrne, Frank Fullerton, Phil Clancy, Tommy Lowe

It was obviously this line-up of the **Metronomes** that first played the Cavern in May 1959, still advertised as a Skiffle-group - *(see **Frank Fullerton**'s comment at the end of the story)*. However, it is also known that on special occasions they still played Skiffle. For example; the Cavern's weekly '**Lonnie Donegan** Appreciation Society' sessions.

Still in 1959, the **Metronomes** went to Manchester where they successfully auditioned for a summer season at Middleton Towers, a holiday-camp near Morecambe and, as this was a professional engagement, they became what is most probably the first professional group of the Merseybeat-scene.

Phil Clancy did not want to turn professional and decided to concentrate on his studies. It is said that **Tony Webster** stood in as a guitarist on a few occasions but without becoming a permanent member of the group. He eventually joined **Mark Peters & the Cyclones** which, after the departure of **Mark Peters,** continued on as the **Cyclones**, recorded a single for Oriole and then changed their name to the **Few**.

Shortly before their engagement at Middleton Towers, **Frank Fullerton** was called up for the National Service and also had to leave. With the arrival of a new drummer, the group adopted the name of **Tommy & the Metronomes** in the following line-up:

Tommy Lowe	(voc/g/bg)
Bert Byrne	(lg)
Johnny Winder	(rg)
Donald Singleton	(dr)

Johnny Winder was the steady substitute guitarist for the band and, of **Donald Singleton**, a fantastic drummer, it is known that he hailed from Toxteth. Unfortunately, there is no further information available about his former musical activities.

In addition to their Cavern appearances, **Tommy & the Metronomes** were regulars at many of the major Liverpool venues such as the 'Civil Service Club' on Lower Castle Street, the 'Peppermint Lounge', 'Holyoake Hall' on Smithdown Road, the 'Orrell Park Ballroom', the 'Mardi Gras', 'Wilson Hall' in Garston and the 'Mersey View' in Frodsham – just to name a few. As professional musicians, they also played seasonal engagements at various holiday-camps such as Butlins and the Golden Sands in Rhyl.

Early 1960

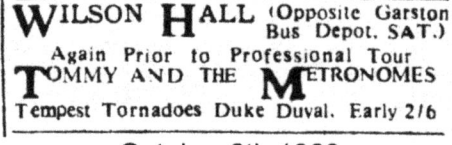
October 8th 1960

Don Alcyd

In the Spring of 1961, the drummer, **Donald Singleton**, who in the interim, had changed his name to **Don Alcyd**, accepted an offer to join **Faron & the Tempest Tornadoes,** formerly known as **Johnny Tempest & the Tornadoes** that ultimately shortened their name to the **T.T.s**. It is known that **Tommy & the Metronomes** continued for a short time with another drummer but totally disbanded mid 1961.

Tommy Lowe continued on as a singer on the scene and guested with various groups, including **Derry & the Seniors** and **Gerry & the Pacemakers**. It is also rumoured that he was one and the same individual as the singer, **Tommy Jordan.** He then gave up music completely and both he and **Bert Byrne** disappeared from the scene. **Johnny Winder** changed his stage name into **Johnny Wild** and became the lead guitarist for the **Santones**, who soon changed their name into the **Anzaks.** They recorded at the Unicord studio and had a long and very successful residency in London.

Don Alcyd, after the **Tempest Tornadoes,** became a member of the **Renegades** from Liverpool that eventually became the new **All Stars** for **Lee Curtis** and went to Germany.

For quite some time, they mainly played the Star-Club circuit until they returned to Liverpool. However, **Don Alcyd** remained in Germany and became a member of the **Mersey Five** who, at that time, were also backing **King Size Taylor** in Germany.

When **Don Alcyd** finally returned to Liverpool, he joined the **Delmonts,** who later also backed the well-known singer, **Freddie Starr.** After that, he moved to London, where he disappeared from the scene.

Finally, it can be said that although **Tommy & the Metronomes** obviously never made a recording, they are fondly remembered as being one of the really great Liverpool groups and, because of their early professional status, a really important part of the embryonic days of 'Merseybeat'.

> "At the Cavern we were listed as Skiffle despite being a Rock & Roll group, probably played Skiffle due to the Cavern's strict 'no Rock & Roll'-policy."
>
> Frank Fullerton (The Metronomes)

THE TRIBUTES
(Robbie Gray Soul Band)

This highly interesting group was formed in the early Sixties in Bebington on the Wirral under the name of the **Flints**. They began much like many of the groups, at that time, playing the usual Beat standards. However, after a year or so, they changed their name to the **Tributes** and their musical style into Soul and Rhythm & Blues, playing a lot of **Chuck Berry**, **Ray Charles** and, especially **Coasters** numbers because, with **Paul Glynn**, they had the ideal singer for that kind of music. The **Tributes** became very busy appearing regularly at all major venues on the Wirral and the Liverpool circuit – in a line-up with:

Paul Glynn	(voc/bg)
Perry Kurylo	(lg/voc)
Richard Mumford	(rg/voc)
Peter Cooke	(dr)

The Tributes (1962) - L to R: Perry Kurylo, Paul Glynn, Peter Cooke, Charlie Cooke (Manager) & Richard Mumford

WIRRAL BEAT FANS
OLD WIRRALIANS
MARQUEE BEAT DANCE
7.30 SAT., JUNE 20
5/- PATHFINDERS 5/-
TRIBUTES
Crosville Buses C1, C3, C4 to Hooton War Memorial.

OLD ANSELMIANS' R.U.F.C.
present a
GREAT BEAT NITE
TONIGHT
at
Birkenhead Technical College
with
THE FLINTS (Tributes)
THE PROWLERS
THE ANZACS
ADMISSION 6/-
Licensed Bar.   Pay at Door.
No admission after 9.30 p.m.   (s)

Perry Kurylo was a former member of the **Rebels** from Port Sunlight and **Peter Cooke** had previously played in another group whose name is sadly, not known. Also unknown is the reason why, in a 1964 advertisement for the 'Great Beat Nite' at the Birkenhead Technical College, the **Tributes** were billed as the **Flints** with the **Tributes** name shown in parenthesis, whatever the reason, this was an absolute exception.

Around that time, the **Tributes** went into **Charlie Weston's** Unicord studio in Moorfields and cut an EP on acetate. In spite of intensive enquiries, it sadly could not be established which songs were recorded — only that one of the numbers was a group's original written by **Richard Mumford** and another one was the cover-version of a **Timi Yuro** song — probably "What's The Matter Baby". Only a very small number of these acetates were cut and it is not known if any survived.

The **Tributes** established a good name for themselves and kept playing the Merseybeat circuit until **Richard Mumford** left sometime in late 1964. He became a member of the **Executioners** and, after that, he was possibly associated with a later line-up of the **Pathfinders**.

It was at that time, that the remaining three members decided to expand the line-up and to become more of a real Soul band. **Paul Glynn** stepped in front as singer and the group was joined by **Robbie Strand** as new bass-guitarist, a former member of the **Routers**, who also was a good singer. Besides this, a brass-section was added, with **Kenny Newton** (sax) and **Graham Lamb** (tr), and the groups name was changed into the **Robbie Gray Soul Band**.

Sometime in late 1965 or early 1966, the group was approached by manager, **Geoff Leack**, who was looking for a new group for female vocalist **Irene Green**, then better known as 'Tiffany'. She had formerly sung with the **Liverbirds**, was a member of **Tiffany's Dimensions**, had recorded solo and, after that, was backed by the **Thoughts**, with whom she had also recorded.

The **Robbie Gray Soul Band** played some gigs with '**Tiffany**' in the south of England. Following those bookings, they were called into the Decca studios in London, where they backed her on a recording of "Hallelujah, I Love Her So". At the same time, the **Robbie Gray Soul Band** did a recording in their own right with **Paul Glynn** singing "All Night Worker". Neither one of the recordings were ever released. Shortly after, due to problems with their management, the **Robbie Gray Soul Band** parted from **Irene Green.**

Allen 'Gaz' Gaskell, who came from the **Nightwalkers** joined them as an additional saxophonist. He had formerly played with the **Young Ones**, the **Tiyms**, the **K-Ds** and **Combo Six.** However, he did not stay for too long and went to Italy with the **Valkyries**. He then left the **Valkyries** and joined the **Secrets**, who at that time, also had a long residency in Italy. **Allen 'Gaz' Gaskell** was replaced in the **Robbie Gray Soul Band** by **Tony Harper**.

Sometime in 1967, **Kenny Newton** also went to Italy, where he joined the

The Robbibe Gray Soul Band at the 'Old Wirralians' 1967

Valkyries after **Allen Gaskell** had left them. When **Ken Newton** returned to Liverpool in late 1967, **Paul Glynn** had just left the **Robbie Gray Soul Band**. The remaining members and **Ken Newton** now formed **Kasper's Engine** in a line-up with:

Norman Yardley	(voc)
Perry Kurylo	(lg)
Robbie Strand	(bg/voc)
Keith Taylor	(key)
Graham Lamb	(tr)
Ken Newton	(sax)
Keith Wilson	(sax)
Peter Cooke	(dr)

It is not known, from which groups **Norman Yardley** and **Keith Taylor** came, but **Keith Wilson** had been together with **Ken Newton** in the **Valkyries** in Italy and, before that, he had played with the **Doug Barry Sound** and **Beckett's Kin**.

The brass-section was constantly changing and, at one time, **Terry Guyle** (tr) was also a member. However, the other musicians in the group remained unchanged and **Kasper's Engine** became one of the most distinctive groups on Merseyside and throughout the northwest. They had a huge following on Merseyside and appeared on a regular basis at the 'Victoriana' and the 'Mardi Gras'.

Their popularity did not go unnoticed, a large London agency even offered them the opportunity to support major US Blues musicians on their British tours. Ultimately, the offer was declined as the musicians considered the pay to be inadequate and they really just wanted to do their own thing.

In the middle of 1970, **Robbie Strand** left and was replaced by **John Megginson** on bass. However, **Kasper's Engine** only continued until the end of that year and then disbanded. After that, **Perry Kurylo**, **Peter Cooke** and **Ken Newton** teamed up again with **Robbie Strand** in the **Screw**, a group that only existed for a few months.

Discography

The Tributes:

It is known that in late 1964, the Tributes recorded an acetate on the Unicord label. Of this four-track EP, the titles are not known, only that one was an original of **Richard Mumford** and another one was a cover-version of the **Timi Yuro** song—probably **"What's The Matter, Baby"**.

The Robbie Gray Soul Band :

"All Night Worker"   UK- Decca unreleased / 1966

Tiffany & the Robbie Gray Soul Band :

"Hallelujah, I Love Her So"   UK- Decca unreleased / 1966

(Please note, that both above mentioned songs were recorded during the same session at Decca studios)

THE TROPICS

Here, everything started in the Anfield area of Liverpool when members of the 'Queens Road Youth Club' formed two Rock & Roll groups in the late Fifties.

The **Kingfishers** were **Stan Collier** (voc), **Don Black** (lg), **Alan Lowry** (rg), **Billy Cox** (bg/voc) and **Bert Thornhill** (dr), while the **Valiants** consisted of **Larry Clarke** (voc/rg), **Frank Williams** (lg), **Syd Allen** (bg) and a drummer named **Reg**.

Frank Williams had previously played with the **Reece Alan Five** and had, on various occasions, stood in with **Hobo Rick & the Cityslickers**. It is interesting to note that **Hobo Rick** was later the very successful actor, **Ricky Tomlinson**.

When the 'Queens Road Youth Club' went on holiday to Belfast in the summer of 1960, **Frank Williams** and **Syd Allen** from the **Valiants** and **Billy Cox** from the **Kingfishers** decided to form a new group under the name of the **Tropics**, with the following line-up:

Billy Cox	(voc)
Frank Williams	(lg)
George Taylor	(rg)
Syd Allen	(bg/voc)
Albert Gibb	(dr)

However, this was not the end of either the **Valiants** or the **Kingfishers**. The **Kingfishers** continued with a new bass player and a new line-up. The **Valiants** continued as **Jet & the Valiants**. 'Jet' was none other than **Larry Clarke**, who later played with **Karl Terry & the Cruisers** and then led the group, **Jet & the Centerbeats**.

Now back to the **Tropics**. As far as it is known, **George Taylor** and **Albert Gibb** had not played in any other groups prior to the **Tropics**.

The music of the **Tropics** was a mixture of Rock & Roll, Country and instrumentals and they soon gained popularity on the scene. They became something of a resident group at the 'Paladin Club' on Norton Street and appeared quite regularly at 'Ogden's Social Club' on West Derby Road, 'Connolly's Social Club' in Kirkby and the 'Victor Silvester Dance Studio' in Anfield. They also played at venues such as the 'Liverpool Red Triangle', the 'Aintree Institute', the 'Orrell Park Ballroom' and 'Fazakerley Hall'.

In 1961, the **Tropics** went into the Percy Phillips recording studio in Kensington and cut an acetate EP with the **Johnny Cash** song, "Five feet high and rising", **Buddy Holly's** "It's so easy", the **Shadows** number, "F.B.I." and the **Santo & Johnny** movie hit, "Come September". This was a very interesting record, the same size as a 78 but playing at 45 rpm.

The Tropics at St. George's Hall (1961)

In October 1961, they even had a gig at the big 'St. George's Hall' in Liverpool, but they did not appear very often on the Liverpool club scene. In fact, they played the Cavern only once.

In late 1963, **George Taylor** left the group, he was replaced by **John Grace** who, apparently, was a newcomer on the scene. Shortly after **George Taylor** left, **Billy Cox** got married and quit the music business. **Stan Collier** from the **Kingfishers** replaced him as the new lead singer for the **Tropics**

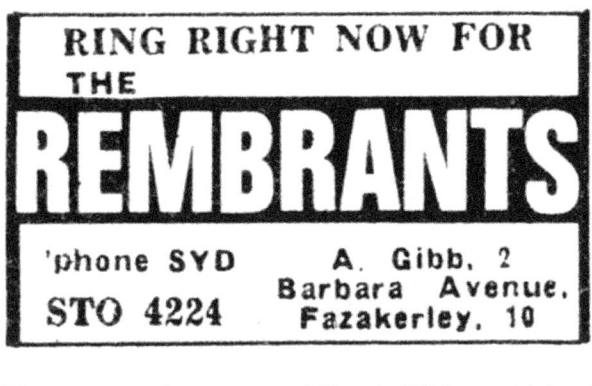

In 1964, **Frank Williams** left the group as he was not prepared to turn professional. As far as it is known, he never joined another group. After **Frank Williams** left, **John Grace** took over on lead guitar while **Dave Relph** joined as their new rhythm guitarist. Then, with the addition of female vocalist, **Lynn Stiles**, the group changed their name to the **Rembrants** (it should be noted that the letter 'd' was intentionally omitted from their name).

The next to leave was **Albert Gibb** and his place on drums was taken by **Alan Menzies**, who came from Southport's **Rhythm & Blues Inc.** Prior to joining the **Rembrants,** he had played with the school band, the **Kestrels**, **Jan & the Vendettas** and the **Gems**, who were formerly known as **Chris & the Quiet Ones**.

All of these changes, within a quite short time, meant **Syd Allen** was the only remaining original member. The **Rembrants** continued successfully on the scene but it seems the cohesion of the group was not the same as it had been and they disbanded totally in 1965, without having recorded again.

All the band members quit the music business at that time – with the exception of **Alan Menzies**, who first joined the **Tabs** and then played with the **Expressions**, **Wall Street Diversion** and **Jasmin-T**, before he formed the **Bootles**, a group he still leads.

It is known that **Syd Allen** soon emigrated to Australia, where he is still living today.

The original singer **Billy Cox** returned to the scene in 1977 when he became a member of **Dandelion Wine**, who later evolved into the **Plazzy Bags**, who also included **Alan Crowley** (who played with **Billy Butler & the Tuxedos** in the 60's) and **Les Williams** of the **Four Dimensions**.

Albert Gibb sadly died much too young in the Nineties.

Discography

as **The Tropics**:

Five feet high and rising / It's so easy / FBI / Come September

UK-Kensington-acetate EP / 1961

THE VAMPIRES

This group was formed in Wallasey in the early Sixties and started off under the name of **Eddie Falcon & the Vampires** in a line-up with **Eddie Falcon** (voc), **Kris Williams** (lg), **Terry Hughes** (rg), **Ron Marshall** (bg) and **Mike Cooper** (dr).

Eddie Falcon's real name is not known but the group very soon changed their name to the **Vampires**, which may mean that **Eddie Falcon** had left them as the new singer's name was **Mark Clifton**. Of course, the other possibility is that **Eddie Falcon** and **Mark Clifton** were one and the same person and that he had decided to drop his stage name.

Whatever the case, **Ron Marshall** had also left and he was replaced on bass by **Tony Kenny**. It is interesting to note that the new bass guitarist's brother **Nigel Kenny** stood in on drums for **Mike Cooper** a couple of times without ever becoming a member of the group. It is even possible that both of them played together at some gigs, which would explain the group's advertisements referring to a 'double drum-beat'.

The 'Double Drum Beat' advertisement

It was sometime in 1962 that the group almost disbanded after **Tony Kenny, Mark Clifton** and **Terry Hughes** left one after the other. **Tony Kenny** was replaced by **Mike White**, who came from the **Strollers.**

Barry Roberts, who called himself **Bob Barrie**, took over their management. The **Vampires** musical style was orientated towards American Rock 'n' Roll, with that typical Merseybeat touch. They soon became very popular on the Wirral scene and after playing the church halls, coffee bars and social clubs; they started to appear at venues including the 'Majestic' in Birkenhead and the 'Kraal' in New Brighton. They often played five nights a week, which included a residency at the 'Witch's Cauldron' in New Brighton.

In late 1963 the **Vampires** were signed to the Fosters Agency in London, who wanted the group to relocate to London. Manager **Bob Barrie** did not agree and neither did **Mike White**, who did not want to turn professional. **Bob Barrie** quit as their manager and **Mike White** joined a group called **Brook Bond & the T- Men**, whose singer was **Pete Clarke**, this band eventually evolved into the **Tiyms.**

Sometime later, **Mike White** was a member of the great Merseyside Soul group **Y-Kickamoocow** and played with both **Otis & the Elevators** and **Gaz & the Groovers**. He is still active on the scene and today plays Latin Melodic-Jazz in the **Bossa Nova Trio**, together recording career for the **Vampires** never materialised.

After a few months in London they returned to Merseyside, took up a residency at the 'Grosvenor Ballroom' in Wallasey and resumed playing all the usual clubs on Merseyside.

On the way to or from a gig in August 1964, the group was involved in a bad accident and their van was written-off. As they could not afford a new van, the **Vampires** initially decided to play at local gigs only.

A few weeks later **Ray Clegg** left and joined the Liverpool group the **Defenders**. **Ray Clegg** was later a member of **Mungo Jerry**, with whom he went to America. His replacement was **Ted Hayes** but it seems this line-up did not exist for too long, and the **Vampires** ultimately disbanded in 1964.

The Vampires (1963)

Mike Cooper joined the **Tiyms** where he met up again with **Mike White**. When that group split, both became members of the **Colin Brent Trio**. **Mike Cooper** then disappeared from the scene and sadly died a few years ago.

Dave Hughes, who always was very much involved with charity work in Romania, died there in 2006 after being struck by a car.

Kris Williams later re-formed the Vampires in a line-up with Ted Hayes (bg) and Steve Dowd (rg/voc) and Kris Williams Took on the task of lead vocalist. The group had various drummers, amongst them Stewart Jones from the Blue Diamonds and Mike Smith, before they were joined by Peter Fenlon, who formerly played with the Breakdowns, the Globetrotters and the Minits. It was probably this line-up of the Vampires that became the resident group at the 'Corona Ballroom' in Crosby, where they played every Friday night.

In February 1968, they made one more appearance at the Cavern – their only one after 1964. The press did not take much notice of the group after their Cavern appearance and so it is not known when Kris Williams, Ted Hayes and Peter Fenlon joined up with John Hawkes (voc). Jowith Alan 'Gaz' Gaskell.

```
TRANMERE ROVERS SUPPORTERS'
          ASSOCIATION

        BEAT - NITE
    BIRKENHEAD TECHNICAL
          COLLEGE
             on
        SATURDAY
    5th SEPTEMBER, 1964

   THE PETE BEST FOUR
      THE VAMPIRES
      THE PROWLERS
     7.30 TO 11.45 P.M.,
        LICENSED BAR
   (No admission after 9.30

      TICKETS 6/- EACH

Tickets from Rushworth Grange Road,
or Club Offices, Committee Members
```

Following all these personnel changes, at the end of 1963 the Vampires appeared with the following line-up:

Dave Hughes (voc/g)
Kris Williams (lg/voc)
Ray Clegg (bg/voc)
Mike Cooper (dr/voc)

This line-up, with Kris Williams and Mike Cooper as the only remaining original members, sometimes also appeared as **Dave & the Vampires**.

They went down to London where the Fosters Agency had arranged for them to play at the famous '2 i's Coffee Bar' and also arranged a recording session with Columbia. The **Vampires** recorded the two Kris Williams originals "I'll do what I like" and "My life", which almost certainly were cut on an acetate.

The Vampires (1967)

Unfortunately, this was not followed by an official release so the opportunity of a hn Hawkes was the former singer with the Blue Diamonds and this new line-up continued as the Blue Diamonds. When John Hawkes left they were joined by Tony Hines (rg) and apparently continued as Argus. It is not known for how long that group lasted . . .

Discography

I'll do what I like / My life   UK- Columbia (?) acetate / 1964

VIC TAKES FOUR

The great Liverpool vocalist **Vic Wright** started his singing career in the early Sixties and it is said that initially, he was **Pete Picasso** of the Merseybeat group **Pete Picasso & the Rock-Sculptors**.

This group apparently did not exist for too long and after they split the singer joined the **Spidermen** in 1962, a band which became very popular as **Vic & the Spidermen**. They played all the major clubs on Merseyside and also made some demo recordings.

However, when **Earl Preston** left the **T.T.s** (short for **Tempest Tornadoes**) to work with the **Realms** and shortly thereafter their other lead singer **Cy Tucker** also left to form **Cy Tucker & the Friars**, the remaining members of the **T.T.s** asked **Vic Wright** to join them. As the **T.T.s** were considered to be one of Liverpool's top groups he accepted the offer, and the **T.T.s** now became **Vic & the T.T.s**.

For some unknown reasons this partnership ended in mid 1964 and **Vic Wright** joined up with some musicians from Widnes under the name of **Vic Takes Four** in a line-up with:

Vic Wright	(voc)
Ray Faulkner	(lg/voc)
Bill Faulkner	(rg/voc)
John Ashton	(bg)
Frank Houghton	(dr/voc)

Ray Faulkner and his cousin **Bill Faulkner** had formerly both played together in the **Syndicate** from Widnes, a group that had already appeared at the 'Cavern' and other well-known venues.

Vic Takes Four

John Ashton came from the **Cheetahs**, which were a local attraction in Widnes, while **Frank Houghton** had formerly played with the **Senators**, who became **Ricky & the Dominant Four** a little later.

They signed a management contract with **Andrew Harris** of Anchor Promotions and from August 1964 onwards they appeared at all the important venues in Liverpool, Widnes and Runcorn. They also played the clubs in Manchester, Warrington, Altrincham, Wigan, Leigh, Bolton and Llandudno in North Wales.

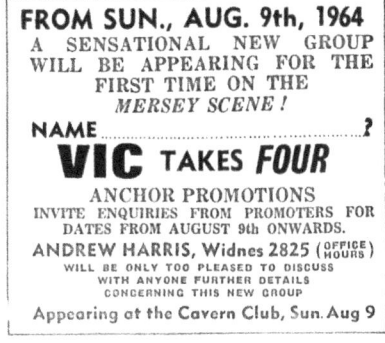

As Anchor Promotions were a very professional agency, **Vic Takes Four** were sent into a studio and recorded a demo acetate with **Betty Everett's** "It's in his kiss" along with three other numbers. That demo recording proved that they were one of the really good Merseybeat groups but, unfortunately, while is quite hard to understand, it did not lead to a contract with a record company.

In spite of the lack of a recording contract, it seems that **Vic Takes Four** turned professional in 1964 and apparently made a good living as they had numerous bookings throughout the north of England. However, for unknown reasons, sometime in 1965 the group broke up.

Vic Wright was possibly associated with the **Script** from Liverpool, prior to emigrating to Australia, where he is still living.

Bill Faulkner joined the **Almost Blues** from Liverpool and after that quit show business.

John Ashton later played with various groups, while **Frank Houghton** disappeared from the scene.

Ray Faulkner joined the **Exotics** from Chester. A little later, the **Exotics** amalgamated with **Allan Parkinson** from the recently disbanded **Rats** from Wigan and under the name of **Dave Allen & the Exotics**, they went on a tour of Spain, where they also released a record. After that the group had a long residency in Italy, where they changed their name to the **Bigs**.

Ray Faulkner later went back to Spain, where at one time he was a member of a group called **East Coast Jazz**. He is still living there and apparently still playing.

Discography

It's in his kiss /   UK- acetate / 1964

VINCE & THE VOLCANOES

This was one of the interesting, early Liverpool groups. They were formed in the Toxteth area by musicians who would soon go on to become both successful and famous on the Merseybeat scene.

At the beginning of the Sixties, **Paul Pilnick**, a young and very talented guitarist was playing with two fabulous musicians who had a great influence on him – **Ritchie Atkinson** and **Tommy Lamb**. They kept busy doing gigs in the local clubs and pubs playing **Hank Williams** numbers when one day, **Paul Pilnick** was approached by **Vinnie Ismail**, who was looking for a guitarist to form a Rock 'n' Roll group. **Paul Pilnick** agreed to join and this was the birth of **Vince & the Volcanoes** who hit the scene a few weeks later in a line-up with:

Vinnie Ismail	(voc/rg)
Paul Pilnick	(lg/voc)
Rob Eccles	(bg/voc)
Pete Clarke	(dr)

Vinnie Ismail's real name was **Vincent Tow** and **Pete Clarke** was also known as **Peter Gaskell**.

The group had worked out a pure Rock 'n' Roll programme with **Vinnie Ismail** doing **Jerry Lee Lewis** songs and **Paul Pilnick** doing **Carl Perkins** numbers. They also included some Rhythm & Blues numbers in their repertoire. After playing their first big gig with **Faron's Flamingos** at the 'Aintree Institute', **Vince & the Volcanoes** started to make a name for themselves on the club circuit.

They became the resident group at the 'Bamboo Club' on Parliament Street but they also played the usual venues including 'St. Johns Hall', the 'Civil Service Club', 'Blair Hall', 'Lathom Hall' and 'Holyoake Hall'.

Vince & the Volcanoes at the 'Iron Door'

Things became really interesting when **Vince & the Volcanoes** started to play at the 'Iron Door' (formerly known as the 'Storyville' or the Liverpool Jazz Society). It was here that they met **Freddie Starr** and **Beryl Marsden** and also **Bruce McCaskill**, founding member of the **Bluegenes** and after that he formed the **Kansas City Five**. **Bruce McCaskill** became a very close friend and supporter of the group and sometimes even appeared with them on stage though he never was a member. The 'Iron Door' became something of a new home for **Vince & the Volcanoes**.

The 'Iron Door' club itself was in the basement of a former warehouse and there was a coffee bar on ground floor and lots of floors above. The group members got some sleeping bags and moved into one of the empty floors. They slept there and played afternoon gigs or rehearsed during the day. Some of these sessions were recorded but no one knows what happened to the recordings.

The other club where they appeared on a regular basis was the 'Beat Route' in Smithdown Road, where they also had a large following.

Vince & the Volcanoes were very popular at this time – because they had the musical 'thunder' plus really good and very powerful equipment including an ex-military quad bass amp and two Vox AC30's for the guitarists.

Vince & the Volcanoes

It was in early 1963 that **Pete Clarke** left to join a group formed by **Bruce McGaskill** to back **Freddie Starr** on a tour of France. This group was called **Groups Incorporated**, occasionally shortened to the **G.I.s**. After **Groups Inc.**, **Pete Clarke** became a member of the **Escorts** and then he played with the **Krew** and **Them Grimbles**. He then had a short stint with the Canadian group **5 A.M. Event** (formerly the **Crescendos**) during their two-year residency in Liverpool before he rejoined the **Escorts**. Later he was a member of the **Fruit Eating Bears** and he was also the founding member of **Liverpool Scene**. After that, he emigrated to the USA, where he is still lives today. His replacement in **Vince & the Volcanoes** was **Dave Preston.**

Paul Pilnick also joined **Groups Inc.** and when they disbanded, he played with the **Renegades**, who became the **All Stars** for **Lee Curtis**. He spent a considerable period of time in Germany with the **All Stars** and he also recorded with this group.

Back in Liverpool, **Paul Pilnick** played with the **Big Three** but then went back to the Star-Club to join **Tony Sheridan & the Big Six**. He then returned to Liverpool, became a member of **Steve Aldo & the Fix** and after that met up with **Pete Clarke** again in the short-lived group **Blockhouse**. Both of them were also members of the **Apple-Band**, formed by **George Harrison** as an in-house group for the Apple studios, which also included **Jackie Lomax** of the **Undertakers** and **Billy Kinsley** of the **Merseybeats**. **Paul Pilnick** later played with such well-known groups as **Stealers Wheel** and **Badger**, before he joined **Deaf School**.

But back to **Vince & the Volcanoes**, who after **Paul Pilnick** left continued on as a trio. They then changed their name to the **Harlems** and became the backing group for the successful Liverpool vocal-quintet the **Chants**.

Dave Preston, left the **Harlems** sometime in 1964 to join the **Secrets**. After that, he played with the **Kinsleys** and then he joined **Mark Four** from Cheshunt. **Mark Four** later changed their name to the **Creation** and had some international hits in the second half of the Sixties.

When the **Harlems** finally split up in Hamburg in 1965, **Rob Eccles** returned to Liverpool and joined **Henry's Handful**, while **Vinnie Ismail** remained in Hamburg for some time and played with the **Top Ten All Stars** before also becoming a member of **Henry's Handful**. After that he played with the **Detours** and then with the **Valentinos**, who later changed their name to the **Harlems**, but this is another story in this book. In the Eighties, **Vinnie Ismail** was a member of **Karl Terry & the Cruisers** but sadly died much too young at the end of that decade.

Of **Rob Eccles** it is known that he later emigrated to France, got married and is still living there.

Discography

There were never any official records or acetates released by **Vince & the Volcanoes**, who really were one of the very interesting groups on the early Merseybeat scene. However, some of their afternoon sessions at the 'Iron Door' were recorded, but no one knows what happened to them.

CARL VINCENT & THE COUNTS

For sure this was one of the very early groups on the Liverpool-scene, originally formed as a Skiffle group in the Bootle and Litherland region of Liverpool. Their name most probably, from the beginning, was **Carl Vincent & the Counts** and, after the original lead-guitarist, **Pat 'Curly' D'Arcy,** left followed by their bass-player, **Don** and **Dave** (p/bj), whose surnames could not be recalled, **Carl Vincent & the Counts** appeared in the following line-up:

CARL VINCENT and the FABULOUS COUNTS
★ Rock and Roll Entertainment ★
Booking Manager: Harold Hill.   Phone Bootle 3815

Carl Vincent	voc)
Dave Williams	(lg)
John Kennedy	(rg)
John Cardownie	(bg)
Les Mason	(dr)

Carl Vincent

Besides **Carl Vincent**, whose real name was **John Olson**, **John Cardownie** and **Les Mason** were the remaining original members. **Les Mason,** whose real name was **Les Fillis,** had formerly used the stage-name, **Count Baron. John Kennedy** came from the embryonic **King Size Taylor & the Dominoes*** while the former group of **Dave Williams** is not known. **John Kennedy** did not stay too long and went on to join the **Rayburn Five. Dave Williams** switched to rhythm guitar and **Dave Fillis,** the drummer's brother, came in as their new lead-guitarist but he also changed his name to **Dave Kent**.

Although **Carl Vincent & the Counts** at first only played the usual clubs and halls in the North of Liverpool, such as 'St. John's Hall' in Bootle, the 'Jive Hive' in Crosby, 'Lathom Hall' in Seaforth and the 'Litherland Town Hall', they soon became popular all over the scene. An individual that showed a great deal of interest in the group was the well-known promoter, **Walter 'Wally' Hill** of 'Peak Promotions' who, not only engaged them for his premiere shows in the Southern part of Liverpool but, as it seems, took the group under his wings as their booking-manager. Around that time, the group likely made some demo-recordings for **Wally Hill** to use as a promotional tool but it could not be established if the recordings were on tape or acetate or which songs were possibly recorded.

When the Beat-sound started to become more and more popular among the Liverpool groups and audience, the group changed its name into the **Kingpins**. Although Rock & Roll was still their dominating sound, they began to include beat oriented music within their repertoire. Unfortunately, this change was obviously not liked very much by **Carl Vincent** and, in late 1961, he turned his back on the group and he was replaced by **George Baker** as their new singer. **Carl Vincent** did not join another group as a steady member but had guest-appearances with various other groups prior to joining up with his old band members a little later on. **Les Mason** also left the group and his place on drums was taken over by **Colin Moir**. However, the **Kingpins** did not stay together for long and totally disbanded. **Dave Williams** became a member of the **Profiles*** and **Dave Kent** joined the **Galaxies**, who had evolved from the **Banshees**. Although it looked like it was all over, this was not the end of the story.

The Kingpins

The **Galaxies**, did not exist for too long and, after that, **Dave Kent** for a short time continued as a cabaret duo with **Doreen Savage**, the girl vocalist from the **Galaxies.** However, he soon discovered that was not what he wanted to do, so he got together with his old comrades from the **Kingpins** and they formed a new group under the name of the **Corvettes**. After a few bookings, they were joined by **Carl Vincent** again and, of course, they now continued as **Carl Vincent & the Corvettes** in the line-up with:

Carl Vincent	(voc)
Dave Kent	(lg)
Hank Johnson	(rg/voc)
John Cardownie	(bg)
Colin Moir	(dr)

The former group of **Hank Johnson** is sadly not known. **Carl Vincent & the Corvettes** became a popular live-act again and continued successfully on the scene until they finally disbanded in 1964. **Carl Vincent**, a really great singer and stage-personality, most likely continued to play the cabaret-circuit, while the other musicians disappeared

Carl Vincent
and
The Corvettes

from the scene with the exception of **Dave Kent**, who teamed up with his brother **Les Mason** again and, who in the interim, had played with the **Soul Seekers** and, together with **Colin Fabb** on bass-guitar, formed a trio under the name of the **Mersey Gamblers**. In 1964, this trio completed the line-up of the **Connoisseurs*.**

Discography

Of this group in its various line-ups no recordings are known, other than the demos that were recorded for **Wally Hill** – still as **Carl Vincent & the Counts** but no details are known.

*The stories of these groups can be followed in 'Beat Waves 'Cross The Mersey' (*VelocePress ISBN 978-1-58850-201-8*).

THE VOCALS

Due to lack of information, it proved almost impossible to document a story about this group. The **Vocals** are remembered by other Merseybeat veterans but no one could provide any details and there was no information to be found in the music-press of the day. It is believed that they hailed somewhere from the Old Swan, Broadgreen or Knotty Ash areas of Liverpool, where they were formed in the early Sixties. However, it is a known fact that, in 1963, the **Vocals** were a trio, consisting of the following musicians:

Jimmy Swinnerton   (g/voc)
Les Herdman   (bg/voc)
Kevin O'Connor   (dr/voc)

It is not known, if they were a trio from the very beginning and, it seems that none of the members had played in another group previously, so they were probably all newcomers to the scene. There are indications that a harp-player named **Joe Barrow**, known on the scene as 'Joe The Blow', occasionally guested with them, but it could not be ascertained if that was in the Sixties or during a later reunion of the members.

They played the local pubs and clubs and a few times at the 'Peppermint Lounge' but never appeared in the advertisements for any of the other prominent Liverpool venues. From that, it could be concluded that they were obviously not interested in any kind of a musical career but there is one point that is contrary to this theory: In 1963, the **Vocals** went into the Kensington studio of **Percy Phillips** and recorded an EP on acetate with the songs, "Little latin lupe-lu", "She said yes", "Love potion No.9" and "Shakin' all over". This EP proved the **Vocals** to be a really good Merseybeat-group but, needless to say, nothing more came from it.

They kept gigging in the local pubs and clubs for a few more years and then disappeared as quietly as they had come. The only one that later appeared on the scene again was **Les Herdman** when he was a member of the **New Undertakers**, formed by **Geoff Nugent** in the mid-eighties, that also recorded a private EP in 1987.

In the Nineties, the **Vocals** had a revival for the Merseycats Charity Organisation and, on behalf of that organisation, they appeared quite often at the 'Hotel Victoria' in New Brighton - in their original trio line-up with repeated guest appearances by **Joe Barrow**. Of **Kevin O'Connor,** it is known that he became the chairman of the Merseycats Charity Organisation in the late Nineties and quite often was the stand-in drummer with a group called **Strawberry Fields**. The **Vocals** were just one of the groups that helped to create the 'Mersey Sound' and who left behind an interesting recording, which hopefully will be picked up by a re-issue label someday.

Discography :

**Little latin lupe-lu / She said yes /
Love potion No.9 / Shakin' all over**   UK- Phillips Kensington acetate / 1963

THE WARRIORS

David Foster was born in Liverpool but, in the late Fifties, moved with his family to Accrington, Lancashire where, as a teenager, he was the founding member of the highly interesting Beat group, **The Warriors**.

In 1961, In addition to himself on bass, their line up included brothers, **Tony Alveston** (voc) and **Ian Alveston** (rg), **John Hill** (lg) and **Derek Thornhill** (dr). The group played the local youth and social clubs and soon obtained a level of popularity in their hometown.

Because of disagreements between the members, the group disbanded in early 1963. **Tony Alveston**, **Ian Alveston** and **John Hill,** along with some other musicians, went on to form **Tony & the Tea-Leaves**. However, **David Foster** and **Derek Thornhill** formed a new group under the old name and so the **Warriors** continued in a line-up with:

Anthony Anderson	(voc/harp)
Mike Brereton	(lg)
Rodney Hill	(rg)
David Foster	(bg/voc)
Derek Thornhill	(dr)

A little later, the **Warriors** were joined by the singer's brother, **John Anderson** (later he dropped the 'h' and became **Jon Anderson**), as an additional singer. They now played the working men's clubs, sport's clubs and small halls throughout Lancashire with ever-increasing success.

Very soon they found their way to Liverpool where they were signed by **Jim Turner** to his 'Arcade Variety Agency' and played clubs such as the 'Cavern', the 'Majestic' and the 'Iron Door'. Besides this, they often appeared on the Manchester scene, especially at the 'Oasis' as well as the Mecca Ballroom circuit.

It was probably around this time that **Derek Thornhill** left and returned to Accrington, his place on drums was taken by **Ian Wallace** who came from Bury, where he had previously played with the **Jaguars**.

In 1964, the **Warriors** reached the finals of a NME (New Musical Express newspaper) sponsored Beat competition in London and, following that, they did a test for Decca where four or five of their own numbers were recorded – among them, "I found you" and the **David Foster** song "Don't make me blue".

The Jaguars

This test resulted in a contract with Decca and, in early 1964, they had their first single released with the catchy Merseybeat number, "You came along". The B-side of this record, which was produced by **Ivor Raymonde**, was "Don't make me blue" from the initial recording session.

"You came along" was heavily plugged on BBC's 'Juke Box Jury' and ATV's 'Thank your lucky stars' and the group was also featured in the film 'Just for you' with the song "Don't make me blue". Unfortunately, neither song had any major success in the charts, so there were no further releases by the **Warriors**.

Their management was taken over by the owners of the 'Beachcomber' nightclub chain and, as a result, the group toured the UK extensively. However, they kept their residences in Liverpool and, between March and November 1965, they also made 17 appearances at the 'Cavern'.

In addition, the **Warriors** toured Europe where, amongst other venues, they played the 'Carousel' in Copenhagen, the legendary 'Top Ten' in Hamburg as well as the various 'Storyville' clubs in Germany.

Tony Anderson and **Mike Brereton** left the group during their stay in Germany and returned to England in late 1965.

While **Mike Brereton** disappeared from the scene, **Tony Anderson** initially joined **David Walmsley** in the **Wami**. In 1968, he stepped back into the limelight when he became the lead singer with the Spanish group, **Los Bravos**, who had a previous international hit with "Black is black", as well as some other, minor, chart successes. **Tony Anderson** kept recording with this group and charted again with "People talking around" in 1970. After that he had a short stint with a Mallorca group called **Zebra** before he quit show business, returned to England and became a priest.

The **Warriors** were joined by **Brian Chatton** on keyboards, while **Rod Hill** switched to lead guitar and **Jon Anderson** and **David Foster** shared the lead vocals. They continued to play throughout Europe until, in 1967, after an appearance at the 'Storyville' in Frankfurt, they spit up.

The Warriors

The reason for the split may have been the fact that **Jon Anderson** had signed a solo recording contract with Parlophone. In 1968, he released two singles under the name **Hans Christian**. The first was a nice version of the **Association** hit "Never my love", which sold quite well in England and other European countries, while the follow-up "(The autobiography of) Mississippi Hobo" did not go anywhere.

Disillusioned, **Jon Anderson** joined **Gun** for a short time but then became a member of **Mabel Greer's Toyshop**, that a little later evolved into the legendary Rock group, **Yes,** who found international stardom under his leadership. In the mid-Seventies, **Jon Anderson** recorded solo again for Atlantic.

After the Warriors, **Brian Chatton** went on to play with **Phil Collins**, **Boys Don't Cry** and **Meatloaf** and also worked with many other well-known artists.

Rod Hill apparently returned to his hometown Accrington, while **David Foster** and **Ian Wallace** joined the **Big Sound**, who became very successful in Scandinavia and ,for a time, also backed Danish rock star, **Nalle**.

Ian Wallace then went to London as a session drummer and amongst others played with **Sandy Shaw**, **David Garrick** and the American Soul star, **Marv Johnson**. He then joined the **Bonzo Dog Doo Dah Band**, who became the **World**, and after that, he was the drummer with the legendary Rock group, **King Crimson**. Following that, he played with **Alexis Korner**, **Bob Dylan** and the **Teabags**. After a really successful career, **Ian Wallace** died in February 2007 in Los Angeles, aged 60.

In 1968, **David Foster** and his old comrade **Rod Hill** formed the group **Sleepy** and, following that, they both played with **Accrington Stanley**. In the interim, **David Foster** had also teamed up again with **Jon Anderson** as a song writing duo. Amongst others, they wrote the **Yes** songs, "Sweet dreams" and "Yours is no disgrace".

Together with **Tony Kaye** from **Yes** and the Liverpool drummer **Roy Dyke** (ex **Karl Terry & the Cruisers** and **Remo Four**), **David Foster** formed the group, **Badger,** in the early Seventies. Later line-ups of **Badger** also included Liverpudlians **Paul Pilnick** (ex **Vince & the Volcanoes** and **Lee Curtis & the All Stars**) and **Jacki Lomax** (ex **Undertakers**). **David Foster** later went solo and also became a producer of modern Celtic music.

Discography

The Warriors:

You came along / Don't make me blue	UK- Decca F. 11926 / 1964

Jon Anderson (solo) as **Hans Christian**:

Never my love / All of the time	UK- Parlophone R 5676 / 1968
(The autobiography of) **Mississippi Hobo / Sonata of Love**	UK- Parlophone R 5698 / 1968

It is known that the **Warriors,** prior to their single release, recorded the title, **"I Found You"** for Decca, as well as three other unknown songs. **"I Found You"** stayed unreleased until this day, while the three unknown titles from that session could well be the songs on the A-side of the below mini-album (7-inch, 33 rpm).

Furthermore, the **Warriors** made some test recordings for EMI in 1965 / 1966, which most probably are the ones on the B-side of that record:

Jon Anderson & the Warriors—The Lost Demos   UK-Plane Groovy OLIAS 90127 / 2020

Too Much (Please don't feel too bad) / Can't live it down / Summer girl (Poor little lonely) / The Doll house is empty / Run to me / She's gone (instrumental) **/ She's gone** (vocals)

CLIFF WARWICK & THE DOLLYBEATS

To immediately set matters straight, this is a very obscure story, possibly totally fictitious, with a big question-mark hanging above it from beginning to end. There was only one source for the information and there was no possibility to cross-check it elsewhere.

The story of this group, whose name is guaranteed to be fictitious, tells that it was formed in or around 1965 by **Cliff Warwick** at the Liverpool School of Art and, at least under the name of **Cliff Warwick & the Dollybeats,** never had a public appearance in **any** of the usual Liverpool venues.

So there is the possibility that they had a different name or that it was just a 'casual' school-group, consisting of:

Cliff Warwick	(voc/org)
Terry Coombes	(lg)
Paul May	(bg)
Richard B. Graham	(dr)

All members were students at the Liverpool School of Art and with the exception of drummer, **Richard B. Graham**, who came from Weston-Super-Mare, they all hailed from Liverpool. However, none of their names had appeared in any other groups previously.

Cliff Warwick & The Dolly-Beats

At the end of a school-term, **Cliff Warwick** was charged with organising a student dance but, as he could not find a suitable band for the event, he decided to book his own group. Of course, this should have resulted in bookings to appear at the Liverpool Beat-clubs. However, (by a stroke of luck!) a talent-scout from London apparently just happened to be at the dance and was so impressed that he signed them right away.

What happened after that is somewhat unclear but, in 1966, there was a publicity-record released by the London Pedigree Dolls Ltd. for their bestselling doll 'Sindy'. This doll was based on the American 'Tammy' doll, which became much more popular in the UK at that time than 'Barbie'.

This promotional record featured a spoken fairytale "Sindy Meets The Dollybeats" on the A-side and was coupled with a Beat-number, simply called 'Sindy' on the B-side, that was played by **Cliff Warwick & the Dollybeats**. This single was sent to all the retail stores as part of a sales promotion for 'Sindy' dolls. Needless to say, the record went nowhere, neither did the group, as nothing more was ever heard of them again after this recording – at least not under the name of **Cliff Warwick & the Dollybeats**.

If this story is fictitious, it poses the question, who was that group that played the Beat-number on the record? Also, by 1966, Liverpool had already lost its leading role on the UK music scene so why was a London group not used? Finally, why was such detailed information given about the origin of the musicians, "three from Liverpool and one from Weston-Super-Mare"?

Whatever the answers, as pointed out at the beginning, this story (as such) is probably totally fictitious, very likely a marketing 'con' – but what, if it is not?

Discography

Sindy / Spoken fairytale : **"Sindy Meets the Dollybeats"**   **UK – Sindy SD 3 / 4 / 1966**

DERRY WILKIE

This story is not about a group. Instead it concentrates on and is dedicated to a very talented and likeable person, a great dancer and one of the most brilliant performers that evolved from the Merseybeat-movement.

In September 1941, **Richard Derry Wilkie** was born in the Liverpool district of Toxteth, which was something of a melting pot for various nationalities, many of them African, Caribbean and Asian, including the oldest Chinese community in Europe. His father was a Nigerian seaman and his mother was born in Liverpool but also had African roots. There was always a lot of music and singing in the large Wilkie family and Derry soon became infected by the music-virus.

As a young teenager, he regularly went to the 'Whitehouse' pub in Duke Street on Sunday afternoons when it was closed. At that time, it had become a meeting-point for many local musicians who put on jam-sessions and young **Derry Wilkie** would often get up and sing with them. When he was eighteen years old, he joined his first group, the **Hy-Tones**, as their vocalist and frontman and, soon after he joined, they changed their name into **Derry & the Seniors**.

Initially, this group played mainly in the Toxteth area, appearing regularly at the 'Beacon Club' and the 'Rialto Ballroom'. They won a talent-competition held at the 'Holyoake' and that is where **Allan Williams** became aware of them. They became regulars at his club, the 'Jacaranda', and **Allan Williams** also booked them to be on his **Gene Vincent** show at the Liverpool stadium in 1960. The club-owner and promoter became their manager and, as such, he booked them to play the legendary '2 I's' coffee-bar in Soho, London. Here they were spotted by **Bruno Koschmieder**, a native of Germany who owned the

Derry & the Seniors

'Kaiserkeller' in Hamburg. He was so enthusiastic, especially about their frontman **Derry Wilkie**, who was constantly moving and dancing on stage and who could easily win over the audience and have them join in waving their arms and clapping their hands. He immediately booked them for his club and so, from July until September 1960, **Derry & the Seniors** played the 'Kaiserkeller' on the 'Grosse Freiheit' in Hamburg. They were a huge hit and pioneers of the very successful and long lasting Liverpool-Hamburg connection. It is important to note that, at that time, the famous 'Star-Club' did not exist, it was still a cinema, called 'Stern Kino'.

After their return to Liverpool, **Derry & the Seniors** became the house-band at **Allan Williams**' new club, the 'Top Ten', that, very soon after, burned down and destroyed the group's equipment. This disaster led to personnel changes in the group – **Freddie Fowell** joined as a second singer and the group's name was changed into **Howie Casey & the Seniors***, after the sax-player's name. This new line-up was signed to Fontana and became the first Merseybeat-group to have a record released – with the album "Twist at the Top" and, from that album, three singles were coupled out.

A little later in 1962, **Little Richard** appeared at the 'Tower Ballroom' in New Brighton. **Derry Wilkie** was in the audience and became so enthralled with the performance that he jumped onto the stage and sang along with the great US Rock'n'Roll-star. **Little Richard** liked it and asked **Derry Wilkie** to join his band but Derry declined because of loyalty to his band. If he had known that **Howie Casey & the Seniors** would break up soon after, he probably would have accepted the offer.

Derry Wilkie, now without a band, guested with various groups and was often backed by **Geoff Stacey & the Wanderers** from Widnes (another story in this book) until he teamed up with the **Pressmen**. Due to the popularity of their new singer, this Wirral-based group changed its name to **Derry Wilkie & the Pressmen***. In 1963, they were featured on the legendary Oriole sampler, "This Is Merseybeat" Volume 1, with the **Ray Charles** classic "Hallelujah, I Love Her So". Probably through that recording, Decca became interested in the group and **Derry Wilkie & the Pressmen,** among others, recorded a version of "Twist and Shout" which was intended for release as a single but, unfortunately, did not happen.

Derry Wilkie & the Pressmen

In early 1964, the **Pressmen** went to Hamburg as the **Flamingos** and so **Derry Wilkie** went to London and joined **Alexis Korner's Blues Incorporated** as a vocalist. On his return to Liverpool, he and his former **Pressmen** saxophonist, **Phil Kenzie,** formed **Derry Wilkie & the Others***, whose embryonic line-up also included the drummer, **Norman Chapman**, who formerly had played with the **Silver Beatles**. They became regulars at the 'Kraal' in New Brighton but also appeared at many of the major venues in the Northeast, such as the 'Mojo Club' in Sheffield and repeatedly at the 'Club A-Go-Go' in Newcastle, which was owned by the **Animals** manager **Mike Jeffries**.

It was **Mike Jeffries** who signed **Derry Wilkie & the Others** to his agency and got them a contract with Fontana, where they recorded the numbers "Sweet Tasting Wine" and "Can You Think Of Another" which was intended for release as a single but, unfortunately once again, did not happen.

In 1964, **Mike Jeffries** sent them to Germany to play the 'Star Club'-circuit, where they went down very well and **Derry Wilkie**, their tall, slender and handsome looking frontman was always the star of the show. After they returned to the UK, most of their gigs were in the London area playing the major clubs such as the 'Marquee' and the 'Crawdaddy'. They were then approached by **Screaming Lord Sutch** who asked them to become his support and backing-band for a European tour and they accepted. Under the name **Screaming Lord Sutch & the Savages,** they went to Europe and even had a single released in Sweden with "Purple People Eater" on the Hep House label. When **David Sutch** was on stage performing his horror-act, **Derry Wilkie** often played the victim.

Derry Wilkie & the Others

Back in London they were recruited by former US-boxer, **Freddie Mack,** for his 'This 'N' That' music-experiment. The group then parted from **Freddie Mack** but kept the name **This 'N' That** and, in 1966, they had two singles released – "Someday" on Mercury and "Get Down With It" on Strike. They then shortened the name into **TNT** and added the singer **Sonny Childe** as an additional vocalist to their line-up. Unfortunately, **Derry Wilkie** felt somewhat pushed aside and so he left the group. In late 1966, he re-joined the **Freddie Mack Show** and became the vocalist for the resident band at the 'Upper Cut Club' in London. As their vocalist, he appeared on the bill alongside many of the top stars of the day, including the **Who**, **Eric Burdon & the Animals**, **Jimi Hendrix**, the **Small Faces**, the **Spencer Davis Group** and many more.

In the summer of 1967, **Derry Wilkie** returned to Liverpool and sang on the local scene with various groups and musicians. He then moved to Paris where he formed a new group with a number of American musicians and, with them, he went to Italy in 1968 where they appeared in many of the major clubs and also on television. It was there that the great talent and ability of **Derry Wilkie** was soon discovered and he was cast to appear in

'Orfeo 9', probably the very first rock-opera that had its première in Rome in January 1970. In 1973, he returned to Liverpool and guested with various groups through the Eighties. In 1980, he appeared in the opening show of the new 'Star-Club' in Hamburg and can be found on the corresponding live-sampler with the song "I'm Going Home" mysteriously named as **Deryl Wilkie**.

He moved to London again and became a member of the **Full Moon Boogie Band** and, after that, kept performing through the Nineties with different groups, with some of them he appeared under the name of **Derry Wilkie & the Pressmen** once again. In the late Nineties, **Derry Wilkie** became terminally ill and in 2000 he finally returned to join his family in Liverpool. When his illness progressed, he moved into sheltered accommodation and sadly died in December 2001 – aged 60.

Discography:

* For the known **Derry Wilkie** recordings of the Sixties, see in the stories of:

    Howie Casey & the Seniors

    Derry Wilkie & the Pressmen

    Derry Wilkie & the Others

In 'Beat Waves 'Cross The Mersey' (*VelocePress ISBN 978-1-58850-201-8*).

as **Deryl Wilkie**:

"I'm Going Home"   G- Palm Records 7002 / 1980

On the sampler-album **"Live In Hamburg 80"**

THE WITNESSES

This was another of the religious – or so-called 'Gospel-Beat'-groups, very similar to the **Crossbeats** *(their story can be found in 'Beat Waves 'Cross The Mersey' ISBN 9781588502018).*

The **Witnesses**, as they were named from the beginning, also came from Merseyside (from the Wirral?), where they were formed sometime in 1964. Their religious songs were clearly in the Merseybeat style, even if played in a 'softer' manner. They mainly performed in church halls, youth clubs and related religious venues.

Accordingly, the **Witnesses** appeared in a typical line-up with:

Chris Keenan (voc/rg)
Phillip Jones (lg/voc)
James Nunnen (bg/voc)
Norman Smith (dr)

It is not known if any of the members had played in other groups previously.

A very important influence on the **Witnesses** was **David Eastwood**, an automobile mechanic from Prenton who, as a member of the Palm Grove Methodist Church, was the leader of the Merseyside 'Youth For Christ' movement. He was also very interested in pop music and sometimes appeared as a Christian DJ under the name of 'Dave the Rave' at various venues, among them the famous 'Peppermint Lounge' in Liverpool.

**'Dave the Rave' Eastwood
At the Peppermint Lounge**

He was a supporter of the group and got them to play at a number of church events. When he became involved with the popular 'Catacombs' Coffee-Bar in Manchester, the **Witnesses** became the resident group at this unusual club, which was very likely the first full-time operating Christian coffee-club in England.

There is nothing known about gigs at the usual beat-clubs or any TV-appearances by the group but, in spite of that, the **Witnesses** obviously established a good following.

In 1966, probably through the connections of **David Eastwood**, an EP was released by the **Witnesses** on the British Herald-label, which was part of Livingston Recording Ltd. from Watford.

This EP, which was untitled, included the **Chris Keenan** and **James Nunnen** originals, "Why", which was a nice melodic Merseybeat ballad; "The Winning Side", which had a little more drive in its rhythm; "Another Day", which had subtle overtones of the American Westcoast sound and the not so spectacular, "Everything Will Be", which was still real Merseybeat. All in all, it can be confirmed that it was both a pleasant and interesting record.

Dave Eastwood wrote the liner-notes on the sleeve in which he said: *"I was able to work closely with the **Witnesses** and watch them build a tremendous programme of songs, so that now they need use only material they have written themselves. I believe that they are unequalled in their ability to write contemporary Gospel-Beat songs"*. A strong statement by somebody who obviously knew what he was writing about.

Of course, this was not a record to climb up the charts but it obviously sold quite well and helped the group's popularity at that time.

There is nothing known about additional recordings by the **Witnesses.** Unfortunately, it could not be ascertained if there were any personnel changes in the line-up, or when the group finally broke up, or what happened to the individual musicians after that.

However, it is known, that **Dave Eastwood** later became more of a secular DJ and, as such, had his own shows on various Liverpool and Manchester radio stations, as well as on Essex Radio until he sadly died, much too young, in March 1989.

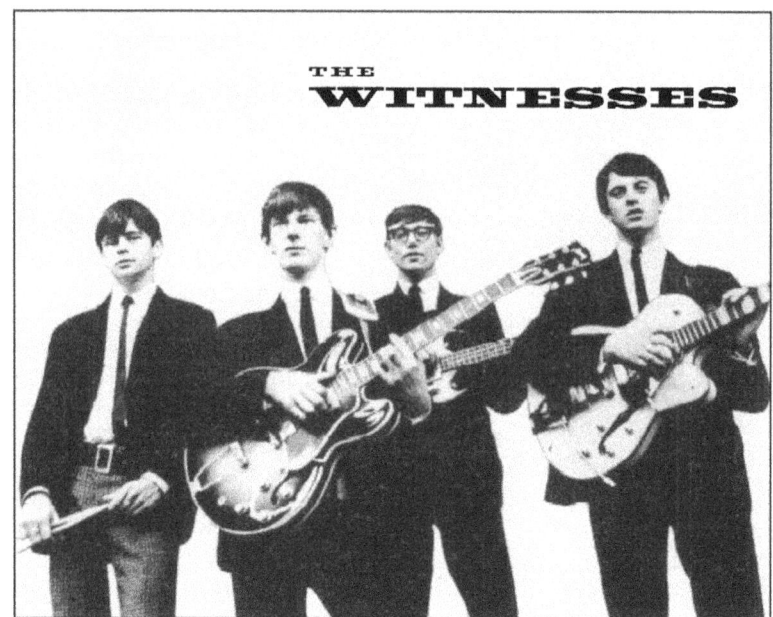

Discography

EP "The Witnesses"

Why / Everything Will Be / Another Day / The Winning Side   UK- Herald   ELR 1076 / 1966

DEE YOUNG & THE PONTIACS

This group was formed in Ormskirk in 1959 by three guitarists, **Michael Tromp**, **Derek Berkley** and **Rick Caldwell** under the name **Mark Flame & the Fireflies**.

They soon found that they were in need of a drummer and recruited **Jeff Hunter**, who hailed from Rufford. A little later, this line-up was expanded with the addition of singer, **Pete Molyneux** and the group's name was changed to the **Memphis Pontiacs**, which was soon shortened to the **Pontiacs.**

When **Derek Berkley** left, they recruited **Tommy Ashton**, who came from the **Jokers**, as their new lead guitarist. At that time, **Michael Tromp** switched to bass guitar.

The group played **Shadows** style instrumentals and Rock 'n' Roll numbers. They performed at the local venues in their area and became quite popular with audiences.

The Pontiacs at the 'Ivamar' club Skelmersdale

Pete Molyneux left and they were joined by a new singer, **Eddie Walsh** from Skelmersdale. It was probably him who organized their 1961 gig at the 'Ivamar Club' in Skelmersdale, which of course was run by Ivamar Promotions, owned by **Jim McIver** and **Doug Martin**. This resulted in an engagement at St. Luke's Hall in Crosby, at that time known as the 'Jive Hive', which was also managed by **Jim McIver** and **Doug Martin**.

From there, things started to take off and the group was ready to conquer the Liverpool clubs. However, before that happened, **Tommy Ashton** left and was replaced by **Sam Andrews** from St. Helens, while **Eddie Walsh** adopted the stage name **Dee Young**.

Following all of these changes, the group was called **Dee Young & the Pontiacs** now and consisted of:

Dee Young	(voc)
Sam Andrews	(lg/voc)
Rick Caldwell	(rg/voc)
Michael Tromp	(bg)
Jeff Hunter	(dr)

Michael Tromp is sometimes reported as **Michael Young** and this is because one of the group members jokingly told an interviewer for a newspaper article that Michael was the brother of **Dee Young**.

Dee Young & the Pontiacs

Rick Caldwell left the group to get married and the new guitarist was **Les Painter**, who had previously played with a St. Helens group whose name is not known.

It was **Bob Wooler** who initially recognised the group's talent and, after an audition at a 'Blue Genes guest night', immediately booked them for ten appearances on the 'Cavern'.

Dee Young & the Pontiacs became very popular at the downtown Merseybeat clubs, playing all the important venues including the 'Iron Door', the 'Odd Spot', the 'Locarno' and the 'Grafton', as well as the 'Majestic' in Birkenhead, where they appeared on the same bill with the **Beatles**, the 'Aintree Institute', the 'Litherland Town Hall', the 'Orrell Park Ballroom' and the 'Plaza' in St. Helens.

It must have been around that time that the **Pontiacs** recorded the two **Fentones** instrumentals, "The Mexican" and "The breeze and I", as well as the traditional "Hava Nagila", but surprisingly no recordings with **Dee Young** singing. Nevertheless, while these recordings remain as interesting documentation of the group, they did not result in any additional success for them at that time.

Dee Young & the Pontiacs at the Jive Hive, Crosby

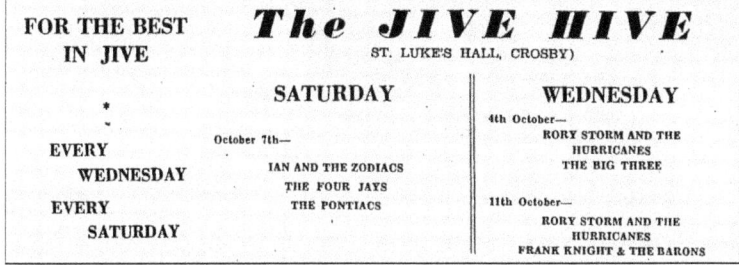

However, they continued to play the Merseyside scene and established a really good name for themselves. In spite of their popularity, **Dee Young & the Pontiacs** never became a professional group and disbanded in late 1962 after founding member, **Michael Tromp**, accepted a job offer in Denmark, where he stayed for more than a year. It seems the group did not even try to find a new bass guitarist and all the members went their separate ways.

Les Painter became a member of **Ray Malcolm & the Sunsets** and **Eddie Walsh**, now known as **Dee Young**, is said to have continued as a solo act on the cabaret scene. What happened to **Jeff Hunter** is not known.

However, **Sam Andrews** did not want to loose the excellent reputation that the group had worked to establish and so he formed a new group who continued as the **Pontiacs**. This group consisted of **Gary Heyes** (voc/rg), **Sam Andrews** (lg/voc), **Cliff Preston** (bg) and **Reginald Jackson** (dr).

Reg Jackson was soon replaced by **Gordon Marsh** of the **Zephyrs** from St. Helens. It was probably this line-up of the **Pontiacs** that the singer, **Gerry May,** booked to back him recording a song he had written called "You're just a dream". They went into the Kensington studio of **Percy Phillips** and recorded the **Gerry May** song on the A-side of an acetate and the **Pontiacs** played an instrumental on the B-side, the title of which nobody can recall. To promote this acetate, the group made an appearance at the 'Cavern' as **Gerry May & the Pontiacs,** they also did a few other gigs under that name.

Gerry May wanted to join the group as a fulltime member but the others decided against it. They continued to play the club circuit on Merseyside as a four-piece for another two years. However, during that time, there were some more personnel changes.

Cliff Preston left and was replaced by a certain **Danny** and then by **Leon Collins**, who was in turn replaced by **George Lynan**. When **Gordon Marsh** left, the new drummer was a certain **Bernard**, whose surname cannot be recalled. Consequently, **Sam Andrews** and **Gary Heyes** were the only stable members of the re-formed **Pontiacs**, who disbanded sometime in 1964.

The Pontiacs at the 'Paradise Club' (Wigan - 1963)

L to R: Bernard ?, Sam Andrews, Gary Heyes & George Lynan

It is of some interest that **Michael Tromp** from the original line-up re-appeared on the scene again on his return from Scandinavia. He occasionally jammed with the resident group at the 'Queens Head folk club' in Ormskirk, which by the way, also included drummer **Brian Anderton** of the **Blue Chips**. In 1965, **Michael Tromp** became a steady member of the folk group, **Mandella**, but a year later, he also quit the music business.

Discography

Dee Yong & the Pontiacs

The Mexican / Hava Nagila / The breeze and I   UK – acetate (?) / 1962

Gerry May & the Pontiacs

You're just a dream / Instrumental   UK – Phillips-acetate / 1963

THE ZEROS

It is always said that this group came from the Kirkdale area of Liverpool and that is correct, although their first business card shows two telephone-numbers – one for Aintree and one for Aughton. The fact is that this group was a result of a failed attempt by the Boys-Brigade of Kirkdale to form a band in 1962. Only guitarist **John Kitson** stuck to the plan and, together with two schoolmates and another friend, they formed the **Zeros**, as they were named from the very beginning.

To prevent any confusion, it should be pointed out that the **Zeros** of this story are not in any way whatsoever connected to the **Zeros** from Birkenhead that backed singer **Vince Earl** for a time. The **Zeros** from Kirkdale, in their four piece line-up, were a real Beat-group and, after their original lead-guitarist **David Brown** left, the group in 1963 consisted of:

John Parry	(voc/bg)
Steve Gibbons	(lg)
John Kitson	(rg/voc)
David Skinner	(dr/voc)

After playing the youth-clubs and the other usual venues in Liverpool's Northern locales, they conquered downtown Liverpool with their driving Beat-sounds and played all the major clubs, among them the 'Iron Door', the 'Locarno', the 'Peppermint Lounge' and the 'Cavern', as well as the 'Borgia' in Tranmere and the 'La Scala' in Runcorn. The **Zeros** obviously wanted to further their career and so, in March 1964, they entered the 'Rael Brook Beat Contest' but as is seems did not make it through to the finals.

So still during 1964, and looking for promotional opportunities, they booked into the Kensington studio of **Percy Phillips**, where they recorded an acetate with the **Little Richard** classic, "Lucille", and a rather outstanding version of the **Marcels'** success, "Blue Moon".

The selection of these two songs shows that, besides playing with a hard and somewhat aggressive Beat, the **Zeros** also put a great deal of importance into vocal harmony and, on this recording, **John Parry** was supported by the voices of **David Skinner** and **John Kitson**. This really interesting acetate sadly did not help in promoting the **Zeros** career, neither did it result in a recording-contract.

Maybe that was the reason why **Steve Gibbons** left - his replacement was **Ian Reynolds**, who came from the **Downbeats** that was not connected with the recording group of the same name. Around that same time, **John Kitson** took over on bass-guitar so that **John Parry** could concentrate on singing. A new rhythm-guitarist **Pete Fegan** was added and it was probably at that time that the **Zeros** became the **Munchkins** – a really weird choice of a name . . .

In late 1964 or early 1965, the group recorded the two originals, "Milkman" and "Soon", this time at the Cymbal Studios in Mount Pleasant. Demos were sent out to a number of record-companies but that effort failed to land a recording-contract. In 1965, **David Skinner** left and he was replaced, for a short time, by **Tony Peart** and then by **Eddie Bowers,** also a former member of the **Downbeats** but, in the interim, had played with the **Rift** and the **Mersey Gonks**. The group continued successfully on the local club-circuit and after **Pete Fegan** left, the **Munchkins** appeared in the following line-up:

John Parry	(voc)
Ian Reynolds	(lg/voc)
Norman Smeddles	(rg/voc)
John Kitson	(bg/voc)
Eddie Bowers	(dr)

Norman Smeddles came from Anfield and had formerly played with the **Madhatters** and the **Fabz** that later developed into the **Vandunes.** **John Parry** was still very keen on vocal harmony and he steered the other group members in that direction. So the **Munchkins** became something like a commercial Beat group. Therefore, it seems a bit surprising that, one day in 1966, they were booked to back the **Excelles*** at the Cavern, who had a lot of Soul numbers in their programme. Regardless, it worked out well, so well in fact that the **Munchkins** got a re-booking at the Cavern. But after that gig, according to **Norman Smeddles**, the group was not the same anymore.

The musicians were now infected by the Soul-virus and began to rehearse the songs of **Sam & Dave**, the **Temptations**, the **Four Tops** and **Smokey Robinson**. This development was not liked by **John Parry** and that was the reason he left the group in 1966 and formed a new group under the name of the **Country Folk,** together with former band-mate, **Pete Fegan**. The lead-vocals of the **Munchkins** were now split between **Norman Smeddles** and **Ian Reynolds**, which also worked very well.

The **Munchkins** got an offer to back the great Liverpool Soul singer, **Steve Aldo,** and after intensive rehearsals, they played quite a few successful gigs together. But the musicians did not want to end up as a backing-band and so they ended this association. Being a real Soul group now, they added two girl-singers to their line-up to extend their repertoire of Tamla Motown sounds. Their booking-management was taken over by the well-known Southport agent **Ron Ellis**.

When, for unknown reasons, **Ian Reynolds** left the group, the others made a decision not to replace him but to add an organist to their line-up. Not long after this, it was time for another name-change and so the **Munchkins** became the **Pattern People** with the following members:

Val Coughlin	(voc)
Margaret Garragan	(voc)
John Kitson	(g/voc)
Norman Smeddles	(voc/bg)
Mal Perry	(org/voc)
Eddie Bowers	(dr)

The former group of **Mal Perry** is not known, while **Val Coughlin** and **Margaret Garragan** were for sure newcomers to the scene. **Margaret Garragan** left quite soon for family reasons and was replaced by **Pat Davies**. **Norman Smeddles**, who had become somewhat of their bandleader by now, had always liked the American Folk-rock of the **Byrds** and **Bob Dylan**. One day, while listening to the radio, he heard the **Mamas & Papas** with their up-coming worldwide chart-success, "California Dreamin'" and he was absolutely stunned by their vocal-harmony sound. This sound was what he also wanted for his group so he convinced the other members and the music of the **Pattern People** was drastically changed into that so-called 'Folk with a psychedelic influence 'Westcoast' sound'. Their manager, **Ron Ellis,** saw an opportunity and, in 1967, promoted them as 'The North's Top Westcoast Group'. Between December 1967 and February 1968 they had five bookings alone at the 'Cavern'.

The Pattern People L to R: John Kitson, Norman Smeddles, Valerie Coughlin, Margaret Garragan, Eddie Bowers, Malcolm Perry

The **Pattern People,** with their new sound, were on the right groove with the Hippie-movement of that time. They became popular all over the UK but, in spite of this success, they disbanded totally in 1969. Here, it should be pointed out that the MGM-single, "Love is a Lover Loving to be Loved", by a group called the **Pattern People** from 1968, is definitely not by this Liverpool group.

Norman Smeddles and **Val Coughlin**, one year later, formed the group, **Petticoat & Vine**, which continued very successfully for quite some time on the Pop scene. Here it is interesting that this group included another girl-singer and the Liverpool guitarist, **Colin 'Sid' Maddocks**, who, in 1965, had been the successor of **Norman Smeddles** in the **Vandunes** and, in the meantime, had been a member of the **Buffalo Band**. **Petticoat & Vine** released three singles in the early Seventies and then evolved into the group **Champagne**, which became even more successful in the international arenas of Pop-music. All the other musicians of the **Zeros**, the **Munchkins** and **Pattern People** respectively did not appear on the scene again.

Discography

as The Zeros:

Lucille / Blue Moon   UK– Phillips Kensington acetate / 1964

As The Munchkins:

Milkman / Soon   UK– Cymbal (Studio) acetate / 1965

Line-Ups

The previous edition of this book included a listing of 104 line-ups. However, based on newly discovered information some of those line-ups have been deleted as they now have their stories included in this revision. Furthermore, my research unearthed an additional 35 line-ups which, as far as it could be ascertained, did not record during the 1960's and updates this list to a total of 133 groups. Please understand that for space reasons only one line-up of each group could be included.

Aarons (1963) L to R: Tom Cooney, Jimmy Thompson, John Smith, Carl Roper

The Aarons From Bootle (1962)

John Smith	(voc/rg)
Carl Roper	(lg)
Thomas Cooney	(bg)
Jimmy Thompson	(dr)

Adam & the Sinners

Adam & the Sinners
From Huyton / Kirkby (1963)

Paul 'Adam' Staunton	(voc/g)
Bill Cookson	(lg/voc)
John Abrahams	(bg/voc)
Roy Hesketh	(dr)

(Later evolved into the **Chimes**)

The Adds From Wallasey (1963)

Dennis Barton	(voc/rg)
Stanley Barr	(lg)
Alan Halliday	(bg)
Dennis Garner	(dr)

The Admins From Kirkby (1966)
Mike Dolan	(voc/lg)
John Allen	(rg/voc)
David Hives	(bg/voc)
Ken Folksman	(dr)

The Alamos From Sefton Park (1962)
Morris Knoakes	(voc/rg)
David May	(lg/voc)
Alan Bailey	(bg)
Walter Ellison	(dr)

The Alibis From Southport (1963)
John Surguy	(voc/rg)
Ian Grainger	(lg/harp)
Graham Powell	(org)
Chris Monk	(sax)
Keith Jenkins	(bg/sax/voc)
John Marshall	(dr)

The Alphabeats From Litherland (1963)
John Jenkins	(voc)
Alan Mather	(lg)
Ken Mills	(rg)
Robert Millett	(bg)
Ron Ingrams	(dr)

The Argonauts at the Riverside Club

The Argonauts From Southport (1962)
Ian Smith-Crellin	(voc)
Mike Rankin	(lg)
Brian Gilder	(rg/voc)
Gerard Todd	(bg)
Dave Taylor	(dr)

The Beatwoods From Liverpool (1964)
John Moorcroft	(voc)
Mike Kontzle	(lg)
Jan Coyler	(bg)
Len Smith	(dr)

Becket's Kin From Liverpool (1966)
John Gobin	(voc)
Alan Martin	(lg)
Alan Hanson	(rg)
Billy Hargreaves	(bg)
Ted Hesketh	(dr)

The Black Diamonds
From Southport (1962)
Rick Lawrence	(voc/harp)
Stuart James	(lg/voc)
Phil Brooks	(rg)
Andy Smith	(bg/voc)
Billy Franks	(dr)

The Blue Boys

The Blue Boys From Widnes (1962)
Dave Tomlinson	(lg)
John Price	(rg/voc)
Tony Gilhouley	(bg)
Ian Robinson	(voc/dr)

The Blue Diamonds
From Wallasey (1964)
Johnny Hawkes	(voc)
Kenny Edwards	(lg)
Malcolm Linnell	(bg)
Terry ???	(p)
Stewart Jones	(dr)

The Blue Prints From Garston (1965)
Alfie Pendleton	(voc)
Gary Crawford	(lg)
Billy Burgess	(rg)
John Roberts	(bg)
John Wheatley	(dr)

(Became the **Section Four**)

The Blues Angels

The Blues Angels
From Wavertree (1963)
John Clucas	(voc/lg)
Derek Armstrong	(rg)
Keith Turner	(bg)
Peter Watkins	(dr)

(Formerly known as the **Hangmen**)

Bobby & the Cadillacs
From Huyton (1960)

Bobby Dempter	(voc)
Geoff Taggart	(lg)
Len Ryan	(rg)
Mike Whitehead	(bg)
Billy ?	(dr)

The Bones Of Men

The Bones Of Men From Liverpool (1966)

Sid Edwards	(voc/lg)
Barry Hyam	(org/voc)
Paul Eker	(bg)
Eddie Edwards	(dr)

The Bonnevilles From Liverpool (1962)

Dennis Hulme	(lg)
Geoff Hulme	(rg)
Chris ???	(bg)
Kenny Guy	(dr)

The Breakdowns From the Wirral (1964)

Mike Lavelle	(lg)
Graham Carewell	(rg)
Rodney Lightfoot	(bg)
Peter Fenlon	(dr)

The Brokers From Warrington (1963)

Ian Walker	(voc/rg)
Ian Priest	(lg)
Robert Garner	(bg)
Derek Hough	(dr)

The Buffaloes From Garston (1963)

Kenny Brown	(lg/voc)
Stan Green	(rg/voc)
Peter Hulme	(bg)
Graham Ashcroft	(dr)

The Casuals L to R: Dudley Knowles, Simon Hind, Mike Bankes

<u>**The Casuals**</u> From Southport (1963)

Dudley Knowles	(lg/voc)
Simon Hind	(rg/voc)
Mike Bankes	(bg/voc)
Joe Walsh	(dr)

(Became the **All-Stars** for **Lee Curtis**)

<u>**The Cavemen**</u> From Liverpool (1965)

Barry Woods	(lg/voc)
Doug Eaton	(rg/voc)
Charles Woods	(bg/voc)
Ernie McIntosh	(dr)

(Later became **Abbey Road**)

The Centaurs

<u>**The Centaurs**</u> From Bootle ? (1963)

Peter Mercer	(lg/voc)
John Parry	(rg/harp/voc)
John Harrison	(sax)
Max Lunt	(bg/voc)
Ken Hollihead	(dr)

Occasionally with
Carla Diane Powsey	(voc)

<u>**The Cheetahs**</u> From Widnes (1963)

John Turner	(voc)
Ray Jones	(lg)
Derek Price	(rg)
John Ashton	(bg/voc)
David Preece	(dr)

Chris & the Quiet Ones

Chris & the Quiet Ones
From Litherland (1963)

Chris Rimmer	(voc)
George Eccles	(lg)
Ray O'Connor	(rg)
John White	(bg)
Barry Madden	(dr)

(Continued as the **Gems**)

The Climaks L to R: Stu Lynch, Ken Folksman, Peter Beckett, Eric Brown

The Climaks From Stoneycroft (1963)

Eric Brown	(lg)
Pete Beckett	(rg)
Stuart Lynch	(bg)
Ken Folksman	(dr)

The Columbians From Widnes (1964)

Les Bolger	(lg/voc)
Stan Skelhorne	(bg/voc)
Barry Severn	(dr)

The Cordelles From Liverpool (1964)

Jim Taylor	(voc)
Ken Blackburn	(lg)
Norman Finn	(rg)
Terry Marsh	(bg)
Ian Grey	(dr)

The Crosbys From Crosby (1963)

Ralph Williams	(voc)
Pete Jones	(lg)
Alan Myles	(rg)
Nick Scarborough	(bg)
Kenny Bayliss	(dr)

THE CONTRAST CLUB
85 LINACRE ROAD, LITHERLAND

PRESENTS FOR YOU
THURSDAY, 20th AUGUST
THE DELTAS
FRIDAY, 21st AUGUST
THE JAYBIRDS
SATURDAY, 22nd AUGUST
THE VAMPIRES
MONDAY, 24th AUGUST
THE DYNAMIC DAWNBREAKERS

EVERY TUESDAY
"TOP 20 SHOW"
JUKE BOX SESSIONS
EVERY LUNCH TIME

FOR A CHANGE GO TO THE CONTRAST

Membership only 5/-

The Dawnbreakers From Wallasey (1964)

Brian Dee	(voc/bg)
Robby Nolan	(lg/voc)
Willie Pitts	(rg)
Bob Evans	(dr)

Gene Day

Gene Day & the Django-Beats
From Liverpool (1961)

George Spruce (aka Gene Day)	(voc)
Frankie Wan	(lg)
Tony Waddington	(rg)
Tommy McGuirk	(bg)
Frank Worthington	(dr)

(Continued as the **Comets**)

The Deacons

The Deacons From Chester (1963)

Keith Watkinson	(voc)
Barry Hollinshead	(lg)
John Hughes	(rg)
Brian Partington	(bg)
John Walsh	(dr)

Buddy Dean & the Teachers
From Liverpool (1963)

Buddy Dean (aka **Richard Aspinall**)	(voc/dr)
Tony Cockayne	(lg)
Chris	(rg)
Mal Jefferson	(bg)
Peter Brooker	(dr)

(**Peter Brooker** would substitute on drums whenever **Buddy Dean** fronted the group as their lead vocalist)

Pete Demos & the Demons
From Wirral (1962)

Pete Sweeney	(voc/lg)
Les Lomax	(rg)
Paul Sweeney	(bg)
Terry McCusker	(dr)

The Denims

The Denims From Kirkby (1964)

Ray Kelly	(g/voc)
Ray Madden	(bg/voc)
Ray Thornton	(dr)

The Diablos From Southport (?) (1964)

Eddie O'Neill	(voc)
Tex Kelly	(lg)
Harry Cooper	(bg)
Peter Wade	(dr)

D.J. & the Four Jets
From Southport (1963)

Derek Ollerton	(voc)
Steve Kelly	(lg)
John Surguy	(rg)
Dave Ross	(bg)
???	(dr)

The Dresdens

The Dresdens From Liverpool (1965)

Ray Kelly	(lg)
Gerald Keegan	(rg/voc)
Mick Cunningham	(voc /bg)
Keith Butler	(dr)

The Drifting Sands From Southport (1964)

Harry Cooper	(voc)
Ellis Tomlinson	(lg)
Graham Dutton	(rg)
Ian McCloud	(bg)
Geoff Lee	(dr)

(Formerly **Sandy Shore & the Beach boys**)

The Drumbeats From Norris Green? (1963)

Ritchie Rutledge	(voc/lg)
Alan Walker	(rg)
Tommy Hanson	(bg)
Bobby Connor	(dr)

The Du-Fay From Seaforth (1962)
Peter Hinton	(voc)
John Quinton	(lg)
David Schroeder	(key)
Colin McCourt	(bg)
Colin Green	(dr)

The Elektones From Liverpool (1964)
Reggie Parr	(voc)
Jean Irving	(voc)
Dave Mullan	(lg)
Dave Hick	(rg)
Billy Lynch	(bg)
Harold Brown	(dr)

The Exit From Bootle (1965)
Tommy Gordon	(voc/rg)
John Jones	(lg)
Alan Jones	(bg)
Peter Whalen	(dr)

The Expressions From Liverpool (1965)
Peter Edge	(voc)
Bob Galvin	(lg)
Alex Galvin	(org/voc)
Les Martin	(bg/voc)
Brian Johnson	(dr)

The Fabz L to R: Phil Rogers, George Dean, Norman Smeddles

The Fabz From Aintree (1965)
Norman Smeddles	(voc/rg)
Phil Rogers	(lg)
Ian Tulloch	(bg)
George Dean	(dr)

(Evolved from the **Madhatters**)

The Fireflys From Southport (1961)
Keith Bottomley	(lg)
Mike McKay	(bg)
John Dixon	(dr)

The Flames

The Flames From Grassendale (1962)
Jeff Caddock	(voc)
Garth Henny	(lg)
Sid Edwards	(rg/voc)
Ray Barber	(bg)
Eddie Edwards	(dr)

The Futurists From Maghull (1963)
Jim Wylie	(lg)
Les Pelt	(rg)
Tommy Weston	(bg)
Pat McCall	(dr)

The Gerry Owen Four
From Liverpool (1958)
Gerry Whiteside	(voc/g)
Freddie Bradshaw	(rg)
Owen Clayton	(bass)
Roger Wilcox	(dr)

The Good Times From Speke (1964)
Maurice Banks	(lg/voc)
Geoff Langley	(rg)
Tommy Carter	(bg/org/voc)
Colin Moss	(dr)

The Graduates From Wirral (1964)
Fred Girven	(lg)
George Jones	(rg)
Pete Davies	(bg)
Derek Cashin	(dr)

Hank & the Drifters From Liverpool (1963)
Jimmy Jones	(voc)
George Davies	(lg)
Tony Fairley	(rg)
Billy Marsh	(bg)
Roy Jeffrey	(dr)

BRUCE and the CAVALIERS
BOOKING—
Phone: NORTHWICH 2794

Bruce Harris & the Cavaliers
From Warrington (1963)
Bruce Harris	(voc)
Ralph Hornby	(lg)
Brian Booth	(rg)
Ken Taylor	(bg)
Alan Fletcher	(dr)

The Hungry I's From Walton ? (1963)
Tony Coates	(voc/lg)
John Dunne	(rg/voc)
Peter Kilfoyle	(bg/voc)
Mike Short	(dr)

The Ice Blues From Liverpool (1964)
Roger James	(p/org/voc)
Robert Garner	(voc/bg)
Dave McShane	(sax)
Keef Hartley	(dr)

The Impact From Aintree (1963)
Colin Oates	(lg/voc)
Derek Box	(rg/voc)
John Farrell	(bg)
Arthur Maguire	(dr)

The Inbeats From Knowsley (1963)
Doug Hatfield	(lg/voc)
Tom Evans	(rg)
Norman Bellis	(bg/voc)
Malcolm Coram	(dr)

The Inmates From Norris Green ? (1964)
Peter Byrne	(voc/p/org)
Mike Espie	(lg/voc)
Brian Norris	(bg/voc)
Paul Comerford	(dr)

For Rhythm and Blues ...

The Inmates

P. Craig,
70 Orleans Road,
Old Swan, L'pool 13   Ring STO 7267

Inmates (West Derby)

The Inmates From West Derby (1964)
Derek Royl	(voc)
Peter Maxwell	(lg/voc)
Ken Smith	(rg)
Alan Chalkley	(bg)
Ray Renns	(sax)
Tommy Maguire	(dr)

(Also known as the **Shades of Purple**)

The Interns

The Interns From Southport (1963)
John Duncan	(voc/rg)
Steve Kelly	(lg/voc)
Roger Carter	(bg/voc)
Mike Astardjian	(dr)

The Jay-Els
From Birkenhead (1964)

Ray Lewis	(lg/voc)
Dennis Richards	(rg/voc)
Sid Colvin	(org/voc)
John Brooks	(bg)
Malcolm Jacobs	(dr)

Jerry & the Juveniles

Jerry & the Juveniles
From Birkenhead (1964)

Jerry Atherton	(voc/g)
James Nolan	(lg)
John Smith	(bg)
James Whelan	(dr)

The Jokers - at the Palace Ballroom Isle Of Man (1965)

The Jokers From Southport (1964)

Tony Emery	(lg/voc)
Mick Mullen	(rg/voc)
Kevin Short	(bg)
Ian Magee	(dr)

The Kegmen From West Derby (1966)

John Dunne	(lg)
Chris Monk	(rg)
Mark Clarke	(bg)
Mike Ball	(dr)

Keith's Kind From Huyton (1966)

Keith Billows	(voc)
Phil ?	(voc/g)
Peter Conway	(lg)
Joe O'Connor	(bg)
Alan Anderson	(dr)

The Kingpins

The Keystone Combo
From Wallasey (1965)

Pete Goodall	(g/voc)
Peter Mathews	(sax)
Mike Daley	(bg/voc)
Mike Jones	(dr)

The Kingpins From Litherland (1960)

George Baker	(voc)
Dave Kent	(lg/voc)
Dave Williams	(rg)
John Cardownie	(bg)
Colin Moir	(dr)

The Knights From Wavertree (1964)

Stan Blackmore	(voc)
Norman Revill	(lg)
Jimmy Ikonomides	(rg)
Harold Williams	(bg)
'Taffy' Evans	(dr)

The Kingfishers with Steve Day

The Kingfishers From Birkenhead (1962)

Kingsley Foster	(voc/bg)
John Williams	(lg)
Alan Swindles	(rg)
Steve Skelly	(dr)

The Kordas From Wallasy (1962)

Eddie Garner	(voc)
Derek Higginson	(lg/voc)
Peter Robbins	(rg)
Harry Thomas	(bg/voc)
Norman Smith	(dr)

The Kwans From Kirkdale (1965)

Tony Burns	(voc)
Mike Espie	(lg)
Derek Marl	(rg/sax)
Dave Davies	(bg)
Colin Quinn	(dr)

Lawrence James Federation
From Garston (1965)

Lawrence Swerdlow	(key/voc)
Gordon Humphries	(lg/voc)
Ray Gandy	(voc/rg)
Mike Wallis	(bg/voc)
Mick Pappas	(dr)

The Lay-bys From Huyton (1965)

Harry Shaw	(voc/rg)
Mick Rowley	(lg/voc)
Joe O'Connor	(bg)
Alan Anderson	(dr)

The Legends From Birkenhead (1965)

Norris Easterbrock	(voc/harp)
Roy ???	(lg)
Chris Brown	(rg)
Tony Hesketh	(bg)
Jimmy Gillison	(dr)

(Formerly known as **Cats Eyes**)

The Legends (Chester)

The Legends From Chester (1962)

Barry Tushingham	(lg)
Peter Massey	(rg)
Gordon Morris	(bg)
Graham Leigh	(dr)

The Marescas From Liverpool (1963)

Don Jackson	(voc)
Stan Broster	(lg)
Ian White	(rg)
Derek Griffith	(bg)
Pete Brooker	(dr)

The Mariners From Garston (1965)

Vinny Connelly	(voc)
Harry Martin	(lg)
Malcolm Drewitt	(rg)
Jimmy Harvey	(bg)
Philip Robinson	(dr)

THE NEW FACES OF 1963
THE MATADORS
Tel. WALlasey 3432
(AFTER 6 p.m.)

The Matadors From Wallasey (1963)

Pete Smith	(voc)
Tom Proctor	(lg)
Paul Wise	(rg/voc)
Dennis Jeffcoate	(bg)
Dave Matthews	(dr)

The Memphis R&B Combo
From Liverpool (1963)

Eddie Forte	(lg/voc)
Tommy Murray	(rg/voc)
Alan Collins	(bg)
Malcolm Browne	(sax)
Pete Orr	(dr)

A New Beat by Merseyside's Fab New Group
MERSEY BLUE-BEATS
You listen - you wonder - but you just gotta dance

The Mersey Bluebeats
From Anfield (1964)

Joe Halley	(voc)
Bill Cookson	(lg)
Joe Harrison	(rg)
Jimmy Bannon	(bg)
John Hart	(sax)
John Carney	(dr)

The M.I. 5

The M.I. 5 From Cressington (1962)

Sid Edwards	(voc)
Sid Jones	(lg)
Gordon Daly	(rg)
Gordon Mills	(bg)
Eddie Edwards	(dr)

The Moonstones From Frodsham (1962)

Barry Whittall	(lg/voc)
Chris Birtles	(bg/voc)
Brian Pugh	(sax)
Roger Burkhill	(dr)

(Later became the **Gonks**)

The Movement

The Movement From Crosby (1964)

Frank Glascott	(voc/lg)
Tony Doherty	(rg/voc)
Kevin Murphy	(bg/voc)
John Spence	(dr)

The Mustangs From Dingle (1962)

Dave Fowler	(voc)
Eddie Granite	(lg)
Terry Barrat	(rg)
Kenny Purdy	(bg)
Billy Conroy	(dr)

The Mustangs L to R: Dave Howard, Geoff Boow, Ian Clewes, Roy Barker, Chris Howard

The Mustangs From Runcorn (1962)

Ian Clewes	(voc)
Chris Howard	(lg)
Dave Howard	(rg)
Geoff Boow	(bg)
Roy Barker	(dr)

The Nutrockers

The Nutrockers From Grassendale (1963)

Sid Edwards	(voc)
Jan Ferguson	(lg)
Derek Watling	(rg)
Harry Scully	(bg)
Eddie Edwards	(dr)

The Otters

The Otters From Allerton (1965)

Trevor Jones	(voc/harp)
Mike Dickinson	(lg/voc)
Stuart Gilvey	(org/voc)
Geoff Jones	(bg/voc)
Nigel Forster	(dr)

The Paladins From Runcorn (1963)

John Halliburton	(voc)
John Davies	(lg)
Derek Gilbert	(bg)
Doug Hastings	(dr)

Johnny Paul & the Dee Jays
From Liverpool (1963)

Johnny Paul	(voc)
David James	(lg)
Bernie Galloway	(bg)
George Horton	(p)
Tommy Husky	(sax)
Alan Leyland	(dr)

Pharoh & the Exiles
From Bebington (1964)

Tony 'Pharoh' Silcock	(voc)
Phil Williams	(lg)
Paul Lowry	(rg)
Colin Humphreys	(bg)
Mike Charlton	(dr)

(Formerly as **Tony & the Quandros**)

Phase Four

The Phase Four From Liverpool (1963)

Frank Mangan	(voc/rg)
Jimmy Peak	(lg)
Jimmy Cowell	(bg)
Kenny ???	(dr)

(Formerly known as **The Decibels**)

Johnny President & the Senators

Johnny President & the Senators
From Mossley Hill (1962)

John Walker	(voc)
Kenny Green	(lg)
Brian Corfield	(rg)
Steve Lucas	(bg)
Mike Rice	(dr)

Pressure Points L to R: Geoff Langley, Arty Davies, Mike Hurley Graham Rice, Paul Lewis (1965)

The Pressure Points From Garston (1965)

Mike Hurley	(voc)
Geoff Langley	(lg)
Graham Rice	(rg/voc)
Paul Lewis	(bg)
Arthur Davies	(dr)

The Principals L to R: Peter Holgate, Glen Kelly, John Butcher, Keith Dodd & Ronnie Kelly

The Principals From Netherton (1964)

Glen Kelly	(voc)
Keith Dodd	(lg)
Peter Holgate	(rg)
Ronnie Kelly	(bg)
John Butcher	(dr)

The Pulsators From Aintree (1964)

Martin Sharp	(lg/voc)
Jimmy Chadwick	(rg)
Brian McWilliam	(bg)
Paul Comerford	(dr/voc)

The Pyramids From Bebington (1963)

Paul Scott	(voc/lg)
Steve Percy	(rg/voc)
Anthony Mayer	(p/voc)
Peter Silcock	(bg/harp/voc)
Christopher Charsley	(dr)

(From 1964 as the **T-Bone Blues Band**)

The Rebel Rousers
From Southport (1960)

Antony Travis	(voc/lg)
Dave Thompson	(p/voc)
John Carey	(bg)
Peter Rodwell	(dr)

The Rhythm Amalgamated
From Wallasey (1963)

Ray Hilton	(voc/rg)
John McNee	(lg)
Willie van Geffen	(bg/voc)
Rick Foulkes	(dr)

(Also known as the **Alleycats**)

The Rhythmics
From Birkenhead (1964)

Barry Gaskell	(voc)
Keith Huxley	(lg)
George Webster	(rg)
Alan Jones	(bg)
Robin Jackson	(dr)

Ricky & the Restless Four
From Litherland (1960)

John Jenkins	(voc)
Ricky O'Neal	(lg)
Neil Cowell	(rg)
John Bancroft	(bg)
Geoff Bamford	(dr)

(formerly the **Tuxedos**)

The Sandgrounders at the Riverside Club
L to R: Gordon Halsall, Tony Green (Sands), Geoff Deane, Norman Hardy, & Tommy Gregory 1962

The Sandgrounders From Southport (1962)

Tony Green	(voc)
Gordon Halsall	(lg)
Norman Hardy	(rg)
Tommy Gregory	(bg)
Geoff Deane	(dr)

The Scorpions From Wallasey (1963)

Mike Davies	(voc/rg)
Graham Nugent	(lg/voc)
Colin Briscoe	(bg/voc)
Robin Jackson	(dr)

The Rondels From Southport (1964)

Peter D. James	(voc/lg)
Stella James	(voc/perc)
Ian Robinson	(bg/voc)
Roger Biffin	(dr)

The Scribes From Garston (1964)

Kenny Parry	(voc/lg)
Terry Carney	(rg/voc)
Colin Daley	(bg/voc)
Ian 'Jock' Wright	(dr)

(Formerly known as the **Banshees**)

The Sinclairs From Liverpool (1964)

Stan Blackmore	(voc)
Garth Hennie	(lg)
Norman Revill	(rg)
Dave Robinson	(bg)
Dave Houghton	(dr)

The Smokestacks From Liverpool (1963)

Phil Robertshaw	(voc/rg)
Phil Cross	(lg/voc)
Graham Bell	(bg/voc)
John Matthews	(dr)

(Formerly known as the **Bentics**)

The Soul Searchers
From Litherland (1966)

Mike Aspinall	(voc/rg)
Howard Griffith	(lg)
Phil Mullarkey	(rg)
Tony Maher	(bg)
Jimmy O'Brien	(dr)

The Soul Seekers

The Soul Seekers From Crosby (1963)

Gary Barker	(voc/rg)
Dougie Appleton	(lg)
Duncan McCray	(rg/voc)
Alan Walton	(bg/voc)
Les Fillis	(dr)

The Sounds Plus One
From Liverpool (1963)

Vic Evans	(lg)
Dave Barber	(rg)
Ray Cooke	(bg)
Johnny Cook	(dr)

(No relation to the Tuebrook recording-group)

The Spekeasys From Speke (1964)

Mike Hurley	(voc)
John Harrison	(lg)
Ken Turnstall	(rg)
Derek Ainscow	(bg)
Jimmy Reynolds	(dr)

St. James Infirmary From Liverpool (1967)

Mark Clarke	(voc/bg)
Dave Martin	(lg/voc)
Pete Rooney	(dr)

(Formerly the **Locomotive**)

NOTE: Mark Clarke, a former member of the Kegmen, went down to London with this group. From there he joined Colosseum and then played with Uriah Heep, Tempest, Ritchie Blackmore's Rainbow and Mountain. He emigrated to USA and became a member of the Monkees, worked with Davy Jones and then re-joined Colosseum.

The Strollers (Broadgreen)

The Strollers
From Broadgreen/Knotty Ash (1962)

Brian Holden	(voc)
Trevor Aindow	(lg/voc)
Dave Williams	(rg)
Ian Taylor	(bg)
Jeff Skinner	(dr)

The Strollers From Wallasey (1960)

Pete Clarke	(voc)
Ivor Moore	(lg)
Mike White	(rg)
Neil McHugh	(bg)
Mike Harvey	(dr)

The Tagg From Wirral (1965)

Al Stone	(voc/bg)
George Furrie	(lg)
Geoff Lawlan	(rg)
Tony Williams	(dr)

The Teenbeats - L to R: John Wilkinson, John Bullock, Doug Edmondson & Kevin Fogerty

The Teenbeats From Southport (1961)

Robert Ashton	(voc)
Doug Edmondson	(lg)
Kevin Fogerty	(rg/voc)
John Bullock	(bg)
John Wilkinson	(dr/voc)

Richie Perkins Lead Guitar   Arnie Neale Bass Guitar   Geoff Smith Drums   Tony Berry Vocals

The Tempos From Birkenhead (1963)

Tony Berry	(voc)
Richard Perkins	(lg)
Arnie Neale	(bg)
Dave Jackson	(dr)

The Tenabeats From the Wirral (1961)

Mike Hart	(voc/g/sax)
Paul Williams	(lg)
Alan Jones	(rg)
Peter Mackay	(bg/voc)
Mike Hayes	(dr)

The T.Js

The T.J's From Southport (1962)
Tony Jones	(lg)
Eric Howie	(rg)
Tony Kennedy	(bg)
Joe Walsh	(dr)

Tommy & the Satellites
From Bootle (1961)
Tommy ?	(voc)
Martin Sharp	(lg)
Colin Burrows	(rg)
Kelvin Harrison	(bg)
Geoff Lloyd	(dr)

The Tombstones From Liverpool (1963)
Billy Wareing	(voc)
George Johnson	(lg)
Tony Johnson	(rg)
Brandon Brownbill	(bg)
Alfie Hoyles	(dr)

The Toreadors From Speke (1962)
Dave Kerrigan	(voc/rg)
Eddie Smith	(lg)
Fred Suarez	(bg)
Kenny Hogg	(dr)

The Trek From the Wirral (1966)
Mike Davies	(voc)
Brian Milsom	(lg)
Ray Costello	(rg/voc)
Ian Chadderton	(bg/voc)
Tony Davies	(dr)

The Tridents From Widnes (1965)

Barry Corker	(voc)
Ian Edwards	(lg)
Dennis Nolan	(rg)
John Shaw	(bg)
Barrie 'Baz' Lyons	(dr)

The Triffids From Liverpool (1963)

Matt Burke	(voc)
Steve Gibbons	(lg)
Peter Rowen	(rg)
Ray David	(bg)
Roy David	(dr)

The Tudors (Original?) L to R: Les Pinch, Terry Tasker, Keith Dutton, Graham Dutton

The Tudors From Southport (1963)

Stuart Gaukroger	(lg/voc)
Terry Tasker	(rg/voc)
Les Pinch	(bg/voc)
Keith Dutton	(dr/voc)

The Vandunes From Aintree (1965)

Colin Maddocks	(voc/lg)
John Sherry	(rg/voc)
John Rimmer	(bg/voc)
George Dean	(dr)

(Evolved from the **Fabz**)

The Vaqueros From Whiston (1964)
Harold 'Lally' Stott	(voc/g)
Gary Roberts	(lg)
Johnny Watkinson	(rg)
Alan Liptrot	(bg)
John Kearns	(dr)

The Varasounds

The Varasounds From Neston (1963)
Billy Keen	(voc)
Dave Jones	(lg)
Bruce Tebble	(bg)
Alan Jones	(dr)

(Until March 1963 as the **Vampires**)

The Vibrators From Wallasey (1963)
Dave Wells	(lg/voc)
Dave Christian	(rg/voc)
Ray Renns	(sax)
Frank Leech	(bg/voc)
Willy Tierney	(dr)

The Vulcans From Orrell Park (1961)
Joe McLaughlin	(voc/p)
Gordon Richardson	(voc/lg)
Kevin Gerrard	(dr)

The Wishbones From West Derby (1965)
Ken Hawksworth	(voc/rg)
Frank Williams	(lg)
Pete Duke	(bg/voc)
Pete Clements	(dr)

Zeniths at Formby Ice Rink
L to R: Tony Mullen, Greg Lathom,
Ray Bell, Keith Livingstone
& Ian Mason

The Zeniths From Southport (1962)
Ray Bell	(voc)
Ian Mason	(lg/voc)
Greg Lathom	(rg/voc)
Tony Mullen	(bg)
Keith Livingstone	(dr)

(Later became **Triology**)

APPENDIX

THIS IS MERSEYBEAT – Volume 3
(The Truth About the Lost ORIOLE Cavern-Recordings)

I know that with this note and comment, I will 'grasp the nettle' but, as it is important for my Merseybeat documentation, I'm convinced it is necessary. It is about the Oriole recording session for the third album that was meant to be a follow-up to their legendary albums, 'This Is Merseybeat' volumes 1 and 2, both recorded at the 'Rialto Ballroom' in Liverpool in July 1963. This recording session was scheduled to take place at the Cavern on February 1964. Unfortunately, there seemed to be no real evidence available and all the documentation about it was surrounded with a sort of vagueness. However, it is known for a fact that a third volume of 'This Is Merseybeat' was never released, but that's not the point, the important question was: Did the corresponding recording session for that third volume ever occur?

In the diary-section for the evening of Monday the 17th February 1964, **Phil Thompson's** book, 'The Best Of Cellars', mentions an Oriole recording session (no further details) and an appearance of **Wayne Fontana & the Mindbenders** from Manchester who, for sure, were not part of that session as they were already contracted to the Fontana label. It is also important to note that for Friday the 21st February, there is only mention of the lunchtime-session with the **Kinks** – nothing for the evening. In **Spencer Leigh's** book, 'The Cavern', the only mention of the Oriole recording session is the Sunday, February 23rd **Alexis Korner** session.

The only person who took up the challenge to shed some light on this matter was my publisher, **Dave McClure**, in his book, 'The Notions – The Cavern's Choice For 1964' (*VelocePress ISBN 9781588501752*). In the **Notions'** gig-list kept by their manager **Frank Delaney,** he found the following entry for the 21st February 1964:

```
FEB. 21. THE CAVERN. ORIOLE RECORDING "LIVE" AT THE CAVERN
             Present - CANADIAN BROADCASTING CORPORATION FILM UNIT
                      "Herman & the Hermits"."The Markfour"
                      "Chris & the Autocrats"."Bobby & the Bachelors".
```

(This clipping is reproduced from Frank Delaney's original 1964 gig-list for the Notions)

As that information was never meant to be published, the only reason and motivation for the purpose of such detailed notes could have been to keep a record of the truth!

Dave McClure, contrary to other Merseybeat historians, recognized the importance of that notation and took his researching from there. In the above mentioned **Notions** book, he refers to various newspaper reports, including *'Mersey Beat', 'Combo', 'Crosby Herald'* and others, but he was faced with vagueness and even contradiction. This confusion prompted a 2014 personal telephone-call between Dave and **John Schroeder** which, unfortunately, did not bring the enlightenment that was hoped for, as the Oriole A&R man could only confirm that volume three was never released and he could not recall any details regarding the recording sessions for that third volume.

Now I can add some information from my early interviews with musicians for my first book. However, in order to prevent getting lost in all this, let's start with the groups that, in various newspaper articles, were named as having recorded at the Cavern Oriole sessions. In alphabetical order they were:

Bobby & the Bachelors	**The Mastersounds**
Chris & the Autocrats	**The Notions**
Ricky Gleason & the Topspots	**The Panthers***
Herman & the Hermits	**The Roadrunners**
Sonny Kaye & the Reds	**The Secrets**
The Markfour	**Rory Storm & the Hurricanes**

*The **Panthers** changed their name to the **Kirkbys** in March 1964.

Here, it should be pointed out that in both the interviews and the various newspaper reports, the recording sessions were sometimes described as being for "This Is Merseybeat Vol. 3" and sometimes as being for Oriole's "Cavern Alive" album but it can be taken for sure that it was one and the same session. **Ricky Gleason** of the **Topspots** was the first who ever mentioned "Volume 3" to me. He insisted that his recordings of "I'm A hog for you" and "Johnny B. Goode" were chosen to be on it. At that time, he firmly believed that the album was released in the USA.

Bill Mullen of **Sonny Kaye & the Reds** stated that, the group as **Reds Inc.** (**Sonny Kaye** was ill at that time), recorded the songs, "Shake, Rattle and Roll" and "Lawdy Miss Clawdy" for Oriole's "Cavern Alive" album.

Vic Grace of the **Secrets** once said that **John Schroeder** had confirmed to him that, in his opinion, their "Mojo" (I've Got My Mojo Working?) was the best recording of that session.

Gordon Harrison of the **Markfour** confirmed that they were recorded by CBC (Canadian Broadcast Corp.) at the 'Cavern' for a TV documentary. No mention of Oriole but there is the confirmation that a Canadian film-team was at the 'Cavern' on the 21st February 1964 – at the same time as the Oriole recording-unit.

All these statements were given totally independent from each other and all at different times, but I was too inexperienced and too naive to see the real value in them and so failed to put them all together.

Now one may also wonder why **Herman & the Hermits** were included as they are considered to be a Manchester-based group. This connection probably comes from the fact that at least two members of their original line-up came from Prescot and/or Huyton (**Peter Noone**) and, at that time, they were handled as a local group with no outstanding success, let alone any kind of stardom. Only after substantial changes in the line-up did they become **Herman's Hermits** and were handled by the McKiernan agency from Manchester and, as a Manchester-based group, signed a contract with Columbia. It was only in August 1964 that they had their first chart success with "I'm Into Something Good".

However, after the discovery made by **Dave McClure**, I had to go over the old ground again – in a steady interchange with Dave. Sadly, new interviews did not bring us any additional details but, from a number of articles from various newspapers of that time, we came to the conclusion that the recording-sessions took place at the 'Cavern' from Monday, 17th February through Sunday, 23rd February 1964 and that Oriole's priority was most probably focused on recording **Alexis Korner's Blues Incorporated** when they performed at the Cavern on the 23rd February. It is also possible that Oriole's thought behind all this was that it was considered uneconomic to transport all the equipment from London to Liverpool for just the Alexis Korner recording and, as their volumes 1 and 2 of "This Is Merseybeat" had been quite successful, they could record some more Liverpool groups for a 3rd volume on the same trip.

However, a self-written article by **John Schroeder** for the *Mersey Beat* newspaper finally gave us the confirmation that the recordings really happened. In his write-up, he mentions that he recorded approximately 20 groups but we only knew about the above mentioned twelve groups. Further possibilities of Merseybeat groups that could have been recorded were many of the unadvertised groups that played at the Cavern's lunchtime sessions including the **Spidermen**, the **Ivan D Juniors**, the **Vibrators**, the **Corvettes**, the **Kubas**, the **Concords**, the **Georgians**, the **Astrals**, the **Remo Four** and the **Dominant Four** who were all billed to appear at the Cavern during the time of the recording sessions. However, that is just an assumption and we could not get any reliable confirmation. In this same article, he also wrote that it was estimated that two albums would be released from the Cavern sessions. This vague statement could have meant that one of those albums was "This Is Merseybeat Vol.3" and the other the "Cavern Alive", as some recordings were possibly made without an audience either during the daytime or on Thursday, 20th February 1964 when the Cavern was closed to the public, while others were obviously made during the group's live-performances. For sure, he had recorded enough tracks for two albums . . . . However, there is also the possibility that he meant the second album was the one of **Alexis Korner**, that was released as **"Alexis Korner's Blues Incorporated At The Cavern"** (Oriole PS 40058). This is another question that cannot be clarified as, sadly, **John Schroeder** died in 2017.

Finally, there is still the question why nothing ever became of the Merseybeat-recordings and, of course, what happened to the tapes? The reason could have been that **John Schroeder**, who obviously was the driving force behind the project, changed jobs and became the A&R-man for PYE in June 1964. In addition, the British branch of Oriole was absorbed by CBS in September 1964, just six months after the recordings took place.

The timeline that follows indicates that, up to September 1964, the album(s) were still a possibility but, after that, there was absolute silence and this might have been because CBS did not have the same interest in the Merseybeat-scene as Oriole, especially through **John Schroeder**. So it can only be assumed that the tapes ultimately became the property of CBS, as did the complete Oriole archive and, it can only be hoped that they survived and . . . maybe . . . some day will be released by CBS or one of the interested reissue-labels – once they have discovered the true meaning of Merseybeat as it relates to the birth of the European Rock-scene.

Timeline of newspaper reports regarding the
February 1964 Oriole Recording at the Cavern

January 02 – January 16, 1964 issue No.064 of the *Mersey Beat* newspaper under the heading **"MOBILE UNIT RETURNS"** includes the following quote: "Oriole A&R man John Schroeder will be returning to Liverpool this month......to make another Merseyside L.P.".

January 16 – January 30, 1964 issue No.065 of the *Mersey Beat* newspaper includes the following quote: "John Schroeder......is negotiating to record a 'live' L.P. at the Cavern and proprietor Ray McFall was in London this week to discuss plans".

January 30 – February 13, 1964 issue No.066 of the *Mersey Beat* newspaper, under the heading **"ORIOLE DISC"** includes the following quote: "John Schroeder......confirmed that he will be recording an L.P. at the Cavern Club. He will be arriving in Liverpool on Sunday, February 9th. Among the groups he will be recording will be the **Secrets**, the **Roadrunners**, the **Mastersounds** and the **Panthers**".

February 13 – February 27, 1964 issue No.067 of the *Mersey Beat* newspaper carries an advert for the Cavern that lists the groups that are scheduled for evening appearances between Wednesday, February 12th and Sunday February 23rd. This advert includes the **Notions** on Friday evening February 21st which supports (Notions Manager) Frank Delaney's note in their gig list. It's important to note that the advert is only for evening sessions and does not include any lunchtime appearances.

February 19, 1964 (The date is from Frank Delaney's notes which also included a clipping from the *Combo* newspaper - very possibly the February 7th through 20th issue). Under the heading **"CAVERN'S CHOICE NOTIONS ON RECORD"** the *Combo* clipping states that: "The **Notions** will also be featured on Oriole's third Mersey Sound L.P."

February 21 – March 5, 1964 issue of the *Combo* newspaper carries the following headline: **"CAVERN LP RECORDING UPSET BY HITCH"** and goes on to report: "Oriole's recording of Merseyside groups on an L.P. cut at the Cavern was disrupted......On Monday lunchtime **Ricky Gleason and the Topspots** were due to record but because of a technical hitch they were unable to do so. They were invited back for Tuesday's lunchtime session" (All of the Cavern's lunchtime sessions were open to the public so these would have been 'live' recordings).

February 21, 1964 issue of the *Crosby Herald* newspaper, under the heading **"CAVERN L.P. TO-NIGHT"** includes the following quote: "The **Notions** have been chosen......to play on a new L.P. which is to be recorded to-night" Once again, 'to-night' would be Friday, February 21st, which supports manager Frank Delaney's gig list note.

February 27 – March 12, 1964 issue No.068 of the *Mersey Beat* newspaper, under the heading **"LIVE RECORDING AT THE CAVERN"** includes the following quote: "Oriole has recorded several groups, including the **Secrets** and also **Rory Storm and the Hurricanes**".

February 28, 1964 issue of the *Crosby Herald* newspaper, under the heading **"SNAP CAVERN"** includes the following quote: "John Schroeder (Oriole) is making an L.P. Possible groups to be featured include the **Notions**, the **Secrets**, the **Roadrunners**, and **Ricky Gleason and the Topspots**".

March 12 – March 26, 1964 issue No. 069 of the *Mersey Beat* newspaper under the heading **"ALIVE AT THE CAVERN"** includes a photo of the **Secrets** at the Cavern. In that photograph Denny Alexander of the **Secrets** is shown singing into a very expensive Neumann microphone. These high-end recording microphones would have been used by Oriole in place of the inexpensive Reslo microphones that were normally used as part of the Cavern's PA system. An accompanying article written by John Schroeder himself includes the following statements: "Having literally been a Cave Dweller for the last 10 days......The success of the 'Mersey Beat' albums from this visit will be received with much acclaim......Approximately 20 groups were recorded......It is estimated that two L.Ps. will be released......of which further details regarding titles and composition will be announced in (the) Mersey Beat newspaper".

May 08, 1964 issue No. 074 of the *Mersey Beat* newspaper under the heading **"KORNER LP TO BE RELEASED SOON"** includes a statement that the Sunday, February 23rd (Oriole) recording of **Alexis Korner** at the Cavern is scheduled to be released shortly. It also includes the following quote "No release date has yet been set for another Oriole album recorded live in Liverpool and tentatively titled 'The Cavern Alive'".

June 04, 1964 issue No. 078 of the *Mersey Beat* newspaper under the heading **"NO RELEASE DATE FOR FARON"** includes a statement that the release date for the **Alexis Corner** Cavern album (recorded by Oriole on Sunday, February 23rd) and the **Faron's Flamingos'** E.P. are still not finalized.

July 02, 1964 this issue of the *Mersey Beat* newspaper includes a statement that: John Schroeder is no longer working for Oriole and has accepted a new position at Pye Records.

July 23, 1964 this issue of the *Mersey Beat* newspaper under the heading **"MERSEY ALBUM"** includes the following quote: "Oriole's (executive) Ron Bell tells us that the L.P......"The Cavern Alive" is to be released in the near future".

August 27, 1964 this issue of the *Mersey Beat* newspaper under the heading **"ORIOLE L.P."** includes the following quote: "First news we have regarding the forthcoming Oriole album recorded 'live' at the Cavern several months ago is (that)......the track on the album 'Peepin 'N Hidin' is sung by (**Rory Storm's**) guitarist **Lu Walters**".

September 03, 1964 this issue of the *Mersey Beat* newspaper under the heading **"REDS INCORPORATED"** includes the following quote: "They (Reds Incorporated) have two tracks on the Oriole L.P. 'Cavern Alive' which is due out in the near future".

Finally: In their *'Beat Wave 'Cross the Mersey'* stories, the following groups also mention as being chosen to participate in this **Oriole** recording session: The **Executioners** the **Four Clefs** and the **Renegades.** This brings the total up to 15 groups that were (supposedly) recorded, which at 4-5 songs each would be 60-75 songs in total....so where are those tapes?

Manfred Kuhlmann – January 2020

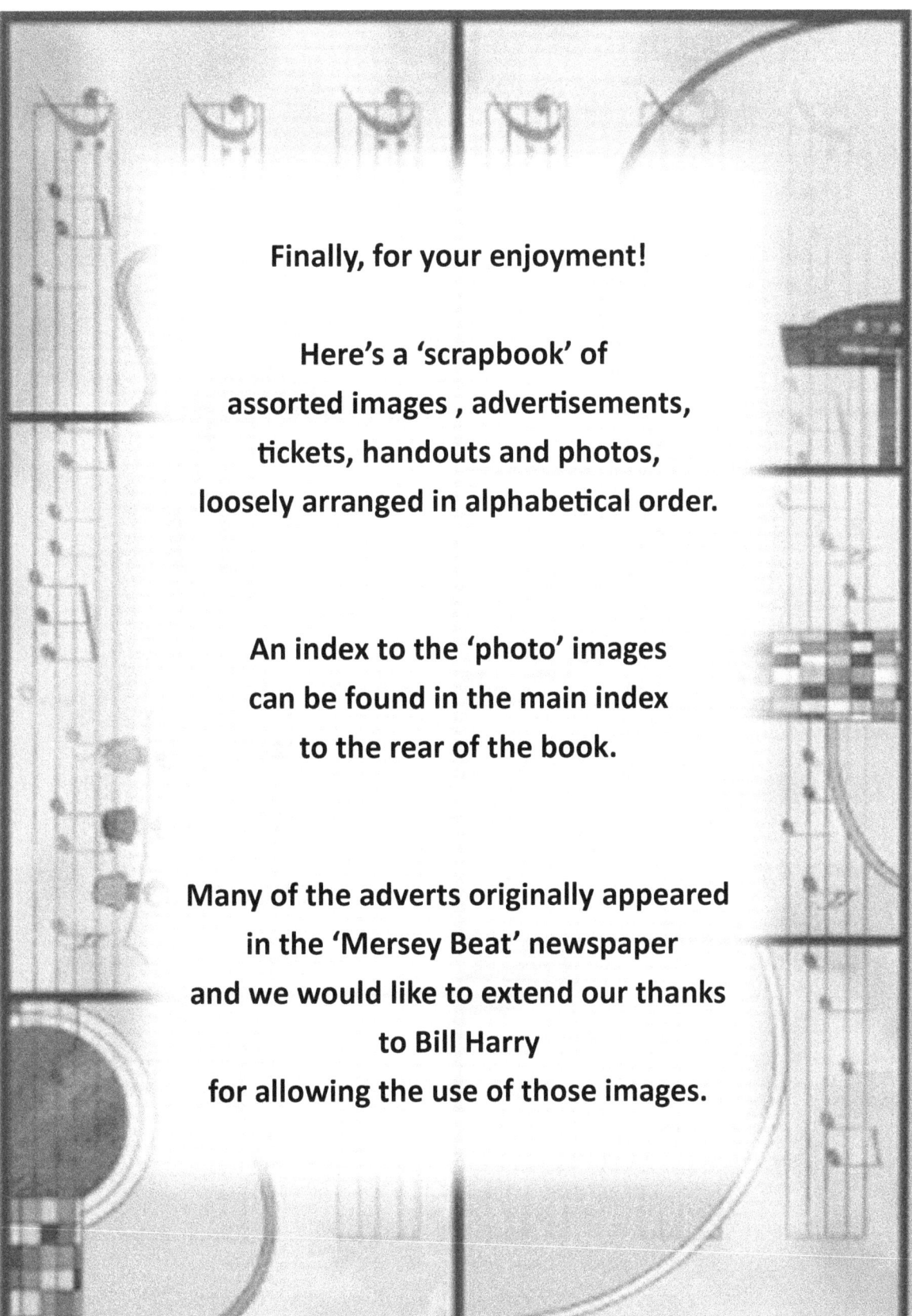

Finally, for your enjoyment!

**Here's a 'scrapbook' of
assorted images, advertisements,
tickets, handouts and photos,
loosely arranged in alphabetical order.**

**An index to the 'photo' images
can be found in the main index
to the rear of the book.**

**Many of the adverts originally appeared
in the 'Mersey Beat' newspaper
and we would like to extend our thanks
to Bill Harry
for allowing the use of those images.**

A.G.C. RECORDING STUDIOS
'DEMO DISCS' — 'MASTER TAPES'

THE FOREMOST AND BEST EQUIPPED SOUND RECORDING STUDIO IN THE NORTH

E.P. DISC 21/-   STUDIO TIME £4/10/- PER HOUR

"TONE-BOOSTING" and "ECHO-REVERB" facilities.
"STEREO TAPES"

For further information, write to:
ALAN G. CHEETHAM, LIMITED,
Fiveways Corner, Hazel Grove, Stockport.
Or phone Poynton 4793.

FOR THE BEST IN ENTERTAINMENT

The Aarons

A3193

Sole Representation   ~~SS Elaine Street,~~
GARRY CLAMPH   Liverpool, 8
JoR Siddall   Lanes.
    ~~ROYal 7342~~

LANE ENTERPRISES
Presents the one and only
ABSTRACTS
Contact: Norman MacFarlen
ANFIELD 4 3 3 6

WEDDINGS . SOCIALS . PARTIES

The Abstracts

20 Brooklands Avenue,
Waterloo,
Liverpool 22.   WATerloo 5609

BIRKENHEAD'S TWO TOP GROUPS!

THE PROWLERS
and   (Free Record Vouchers)
THE ABSTRACTS

at British Legion Hall, Park Rd East, Birkenhead
on Friday October 30th 1964

7.30 p.m. to 11 p.m.   Same price as usual **3/6**

ABSTRACTS
Rhythm and Blues Group

WEDDINGS   10 BIRKETT RD.
21st Birthdays
CLUBS   ROCK FERRY.

WE GUARANTEE A GREAT SHOW
Every FRIDAY and SATURDAY at....   # AINTREE INSTITUTE

Buses 20, 21, 30, 61, 91, 92, 93, 95, 96, 500 to the Black Bull—we're next door

LOOK! This Friday— DOMINOES With their new Kingsize sound
LEE EDDIE 5 Liverpool's Livesome Fivesome

LOOK! LOOK! This Saturday— GREAT BOPPIN' BEATLES!! This Saturday
plus Johnny Sandon and the Searchers

IT'S ALWAYS A1 AT THE AI——YOUR WEEKEND DANCES

Alby & the Sorrals
Original line-up in late 1961

Alby & the Sorrals

Dig This!

5

Great Groups for Your

SATURDAY JIVE DATE

Rock! Rock! Rock! to
1. EARL PRESTON & THE TT'S
2. DALE ROBERTS & THE JAYWALKERS
3. JOHNNY SANDON & THE SEARCHERS
4. KARL TERRY & THE CRUISERS
5. JOHNNY PAUL & THE DEE JAYS

All these for YOU this Saturday at

Aintree Institute (NEAR THE BLACK BULL)

Buses
20, 21, 22, 30, 53, 61, 91, 92, 93, 95, 96, 500.

Come and Jive at Merseyside's Best Jive Dance
AINTREE INSTITUTE
THIS SATURDAY and every Saturday
— CARNIVAL —
Hats, Balloons etc.
FARON AND THE TEMPEST-TORNADOES
THE BEATLES FROM HAMBURG
Your Compere — DYNAMIC BOB WOOLER
7-30 to 11 p.m.   Admission 4/-
THIS FRIDAY, DOMINOES, RAVENS 2/6
NEXT WED. CLIFF ROBERTS, Senior Service Gift Night 2/6

ALBY AND THE SORRALS

FOR ALL ROUND ENTERTAINMENT

TELEPHONE
HUNts cross 2809

LEADING BALLROOMS AND CLUBS ARE NOW BOOKING

THE ALPHAS

ALLerton 3871.

For real swingin' harmony...
THE ALAMO'S
SEFton Park 2966.

For your Entertainment

The Associates

WEDDINGS - DANCES - PARTIES
OUR SPECIALITY

Contact M. McINTOSH
8 BRANCOTE GARDENS
BROMBOROUGH   Telephone
WIRRAL   BROmborough 1027

```
MAY YOU CONTINUE TO
BE A GOOD AMBASSADOR
FOR ROCK 'N' ROLL
FROM

The
Ambassadors

ENQUIRIES
SEFton Park 6135
```

Almost Blues with 'Jerkin' George Paul 1965

```
ARCADE VARIETY AGENCY
New Offices: 49a BOLD ST., L'POOL 1.
Telephones: ROYAL 1409/8895.
Sole Representation:
● THE FEW (Oriole)   ● LEE CASTLE AND THE BARONS
(Parlophone)   ● RHYTHM AND BLUES INC. ● DERRY
WILKIE AND THE OTHERS (Fontana)   ● THE BOYS
● THE EASYBEATS ● THE WHEELS
Also Available:
● IAN AND THE ZODIACS ● MARK PETERS ● RORY
STORM ● THE VALKYRIES ● THE SHAKES ● BUDDY
BRITTEN AND THE REGENTS

LICENSED BY            ALL MAJOR STAR
LIVERPOOL CITY COUNCIL  ARTISTES BOOKED
```

```
          A
          T   Billy    Rhythm Guitar
          O   Don      Instrumental Guitar
          M   Johnny   Singer
The ATOMICS   Jim      Lead Guitar
          C
          S   A Good All Round Group
              with Johnny and 3 Guitars

 ✱ For Enquiries        J. A. TRIGGS,
   or Engagements —     21, Beresford Road,
          Write         Oxton, Birkenhead.
```

```
GRAND RE-OPENING OF
SATURDAY EVENING
DANCES AT

BARNABUS
HALL

PENNY LANE, LIVERPOOL
-on-
SATURDAY
AUGUST 25th

TWO GREAT GROUPS:
WAYNE STEVENS
and THE VIKINGS.
DANNY and THE
ASTEROIDS
```

The Argonauts at the 'Flyin' Dutchman'

The Banshees original line-up
L to R: Dave Walker, Rob Allin,
Rod Flanagan and Roger Cooper

★★★★★★★★★★★★★★★★★
BEST WISHES TO A SWINGIN'
PAPER FROM A ROCKIN' COMBO

THE BANSHEES

Enquiries: BUR 2388
★★★★★★★★★★★★★★★★★

RYTHAM GROUP FOR ALL OCCASIONS

The ATOMICS

Enquiries For
Engagements Write :-

W. VAUGHAN,
67 Vittoria Street,
Birkenhead,
Cheshire.

Pete Best Four

BEATSVILLE
CARLTON
ROC(K)HDALE
THURSDAY, 6th AUGUST
EARL PRESTON'S
REALMS
MR. SMITH AND
SUM PEOPLE
7—11 p.m.   Only 2/6
SATURDAY, 8th AUGUST
THE MERSEY 4
THE PILGRIMS
THE INBEATS
ONLY 5/-   7.15 to 11.45 p.m.
Late buses to Bury & Oldham
GONKS GIVEN AWAY FREE
SUNDAY, 9th AUGUST
THE PAWNS
GERRY DE VILLE &
THE CITY KINGS
7—11   2/-
NEXT THURSDAY
THE MIGHTY AVENGERS
THE DAWNBREAKERS

Dave Bell & the Bell Boys

BOOK THEM NOW

THE BLACK VELVETS

Ring ANF 3172

Manager:
★ Darrel P. Core
7 Holly Road
Liverpool 7

The Black Velvets L to R: John Ryan (dr), Dave O'neill (lg), Stan Alexander (rg voc), Ian Colyer (bg)

THREE MEN WITH A NEW SOUND

★ *The Berry Pickers* ★

CLUBS — DANCES — CABARET

Phone 55741 or 3143

SOLE MANAGEMENT:
R. MALPAS,
5 YORK AVENUE, BIRKDALE,
SOUTHPORT

---

the BORGIA CLUB presents—

Week commencing March 16th

MONDAY — SAVA & THE DEMOCRATS
TUESDAY — THE KORBAS
WEDNESDAY — JUKE BOX NIGHT
THURSDAY — THE ZEROS
FRIDAY — THE SKYERS
SATURDAY — THE RAINCHECKS
SUNDAY — THE SILVER STONES

DANCING 7 p.m. to 11 p.m.

65 CHURCH ROAD, TRANMERE

Telephone: Bir 6913

Have a "Merry" Evening at the

BLACK CAT CLUB Above Sampson & Barlows, Lond'n Rd

FRIDAY: JAMBOREE CLUB
SATURDAY and SUNDAY

Rock with ... Sonny Webb & Cascades ... The Kentuckians ... The Kansas City Five ... The Thunderbirds ... & others

MEMBERS ONLY   LICENSED

THE ★ **T.T.S.** ★ WITH ★ **AMOS BONNY** ★

LIVERPOOL STO. 3141

The Black Cats

GIVE A BIG HAND TO THE RETURN OF MR. SHOWMANSHIP—RORY STORM AND THE HURRICANES FRIDAY, SEPTEMBER 15th

FRIDAY, SEPTEMBER 22nd, THE REMO 4 AT

The Blue Penguin Club

St. John's Hall, Bootle   Opposite Bootle Town Hall

THE BORGIA CLUB

BIRKENHEAD'S LATEST AND GREATEST BEAT CLUB NOW OPEN!

AFTERNOON SESSIONS
from 2 p.m. to 6 p.m.
and
NIGHTLY SESSIONS
from 7 p.m. to 11 p.m.
Entertainment by Juke Box and Groups

65 CHURCH ROAD Tranmere, Birkenhead

(Take No. 60 bus from Woodside Station)

Tel: BIR 6913

The Bo-Weevils at the British Legion, Port Sunlight

TOP GROUP THIS SIDE OF THE MERSEY
THE BLUE DIAMOND COMBO
Phone (DAY) ARR: 4616   (NIGHT) NEW: 5117

BOOK

bo-weevils

GAT 2916

Them Calderstones at the Mardi Gras 1967

The Casuals 'practice room'

CAVERN
BRITAIN'S FOREMOST BEAT MUSIC CENTRE
10 MATHEW ST. (OFF NORTH JOHN ST.) LIVERPOOL CENtral 1591

LUNCHTIME SESSIONS Noon to 2-15 p.m. Monday to Friday
EVENING SESSIONS 7-30 to 11-15 p.m. Sundays, Tuesdays, Wednesdays, Fridays and Saturdays
DJ/Compere: Bob Wooler

EVENING SESSIONS

WEDNESDAY, FEBRUARY 12TH —
THE MERSEYBEATS
THE ESCORTS · THE GEORGIANS · THE VALKYRIES

FRIDAY, FEBRUARY 14th —
THE REMO 4 (On "Saturday Club" tomorrow)
THE LIVERBIRDS
THE RIOT SQUAD
ALBY AND THE SORRALS

SATURDAY, FEBRUARY 15th —
THE ESCORTS
THE PANTHERS
THE MARKFOUR
THE EXECUTIONERS

SUNDAY, FEBRUARY 16th —
THE ESCORTS
THE NOTIONS
BILLY (Spin a Disc) BUTLER AND THE TUXEDOS
BOBBY AND THE BACHELORS

TUESDAY, FEBRUARY 18th —
THE ROADRUNNERS
THE SPIDERMEN · THE IVAN D. JUNIORS · THE VIBRATORS

WEDNESDAY, FEBRUARY 19th —
THE ESCORTS
THE CORVETTES
THE KUBAS
THE CONCORDS

Friday, February 21st —
HERMAN AND THE HERMITS
THE MARK FOUR · THE NOTIONS · BOBBY AND THE BACHELORS

SATURDAY, FEBRUARY 22nd —
THE ROADRUNNERS
THE SPIDERMEN · THE GEORGIANS · THE £5,000 ASTRALS

SUNDAY, FEBRUARY 23rd —
BIG RHYTHM & BLUES SESSION
ALEXIS KORNER
THE REMO 4 · THE GEORGIANS · THE DOMINANT 4

CAVERN
BRITAIN'S FOREMOST BEAT MUSIC CENTRE
10 MATHEW ST. (OFF NORTH JOHN ST.) LIVERPOOL CENtral 2674

LUNCHTIME SESSIONS Noon to 2-15 p.m. Monday to Friday
EVENING SESSIONS 7-30 to 11-15 p.m. Sundays, Tuesdays, Wednesdays, Fridays and Saturdays
DJ/Compere: Bob Wooler

WEDNESDAY, 24th JUNE
THE ESCORTS
THE NOTIONS, HERMAN'S HERMITS, THE MEMPHIS 3

THURSDAY, 25th JUNE
GERRY & THE PACEMAKERS
KRIS RYAN AND THE QUESTIONS, THE PRETENDERS

FRIDAY, 26th JUNE
THE SPIDERMEN
THE RIOT SQUAD, THE PRETENDERS, THE NOCTURNS

SATURDAY, 27th JUNE
THE KINSLEYS
BILLY BUTLER AND THE TUXEDOS, THE TTs, THE DOODLE BUGS

SUNDAY, 28th JUNE
EARL PRESTON'S REALMS
TIFFANY & THE 4 DIMENSIONS, THE GEORGIANS, THE MOONRAKERS

TUESDAY, 30th JUNE
THE REDCAPS
THE ROAD RUNNERS, THE MARK FOUR, THE PILGRIMS THE VIKINGS

WEDNESDAY, 1st JULY
THE ESCORTS
THE NOTIONS, BOBBY AND THE BACHELORS, THE MERSEY FOUR

THURSDAY, 2nd JULY
SPECIAL R & B SHOW
INEZ AND CHARLIE FOXX
SPENCER DAVIES GROUP

BEAT WITH A CLASSIC TONE
THE CHEVRONS
DRUMS   ELECTRIC ORGAN   GUITARS
MANAGER: E. SPENCER,   HUNTS CROSS 3426

THE 🎵 🎵 🎵
CHEQUERS
RING — HUY 3752
or contact Bob Radford,
65 STUART RD., L'POOL 4

THEY'RE NOTED
THEY'RE QUOTED
THEY'RE VOTED
THE TOPS

THE COASTERS
RING:
Daytime ROYal 0033
Evening AINtree 9927

Lee Castle & the Barons

THE CHANTS
JOE NAT EDDIE EDDY ALAN
Sole Representation: Ted Ross Enterprises,
6, Southern Street, Manchester, 1
Tel.: DEAnsgate 5657-2.
Pye Recording Artistes

THE CAZZIE — THE BEAT 'ALL THAT BEATS ALL!

21 AIGBURTH ROAD, NR. LARK LANE.

SHAKE STOMP RATTLE	EVERY FRI., SAT., SUN.: 3/6	7.30 to
	TUES.: 3/-. MEMBERSHIP 1/-	11 p.m.

Featuring Top Liverpool Groups!
THE PATHFINDERS ● THE NASHPOOL ● THE BUMBLIES
LEE EDDIE AND THE CHEVRONS ● BOBBY AND THE HALERS ● JOHNNY TEMPLER AND THE HI-CATS ● THE CASUALS — AND MANY MORE.

New Members Welcome — Be Early! Tel.: LAR 6386

The Chants - 1967

It's always "plain sailing" with
CAROLE AND THE CORVETTES
Phone: SIM 3119

Tel: MAGhull 3079.

The Centaurs

2. PIMBLEY GROVE WEST, MAGHULL.

Eddie Amoo

Joe Ankra

Alan Harding

The Chants

Nat Smeda

PYE Recording Artists

Eddie Ankra

COFFEE CLUBS

BASEMENT. Mount Pleasant.
BLACK ROSE. South Castle Street. For membership apply to the secretary.
CASBAH. Haymans Green, Strictly members only.
EL CABALA. Bold Street.
JACARANDA. Slater Street. Members only.
KON TIKI. Wood Street.
LANTERN, Aigburth Road. Open until 4 a.m.
LA LOCANDA, Duke Street. 10 p.m. until 2 a.m.
MASQUE. Clarence Street.
ODD SPOT, Bold Street. Opening shortly.
SCORPION, Duke Street. Members only.
PHOENIX, Mount Pleasant: New members welcome.

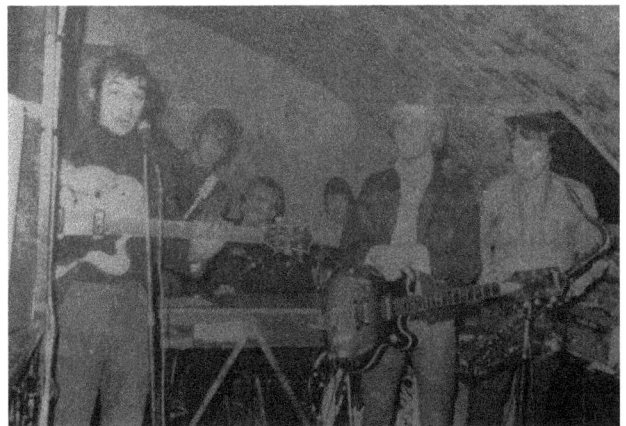
Clayton Squares in Bad Vilbel Germany L to R: Karl Terry, Gordon Loughlin, Chris Hatfield, Tommy Maguire, Lance Railton & Mike Evans - 1966

The Cheetahs with Ronnie Ince

The Chessmen

The Citadels

The Clansmen

OPENING SOON!
THE CONTRAST CLUB
BEAT MUSIC!
SESSIONS EVERY LUNCHTIME AND
MON — TUES — THURS
FRI — SAT EVENINGS
LIMITED MEMBERSHIP
5/- PER ANNUM — FORMS AVAILABLE NOW
WATCH THE EVENING PRESS FOR DETAILS OF BIG OPENING NIGHT
CALL NOW TO JOIN AT
85 LINACRE ROAD
LITHERLAND

Rock Rhythm Swing — ROCK FERRY 6279
Lee Crombie and The Sundowners
weddings, dances, parties, etc.

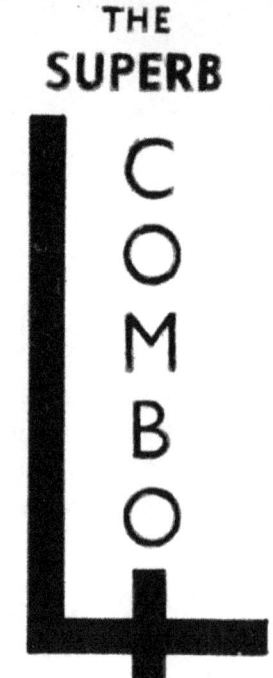
THE SUPERB COMBO 4
Phone B. DEAN
LARk Lane 3948

THE CONTRAST CLUB
85 LINACRE ROAD, LITHERLAND
PRESENTS FOR YOU
BIG BEAT SESSIONS
MON—TUES—THURS
FRI.—SAT. EVENINGS
EVERY TUESDAY ITS THE "TOP 20 SHOW"
JUKE BOX SESSIONS EVERY LUNCHTIME
FOR A CHANGE GO TO THE CONTRAST
Membership only 5/-

Phone THE CORALS NOW!
T. J. Hughes — SEF 3783

CRACKSMEN
ANYTIME — ANYWHERE
TONY VARNEY
ANF 3968 (after 9 p.m.)

Corals

The driving sound of the
CORSAIRS
Manager: J. L. DALE
Telephone: HUY 2450

THE Cordes
DAVE: CHI 4835
CLIVE: HUY 5097

ALWAYS A WINNER
THE GROUPIERS
ROYal 7470

The Croupiers L to R: Bobby Roberts,
Vinny Thomas, Arthur Hurst, Dennis Swale

CORONA BALLROOM
COLLEGE RD. - CROSBY

BIG
BANK HOLIDAY
BEAT NITE!

MONDAY, AUGUST 3rd,
at 7-30 p.m.

Meet...
THE PROWLERS
THE PROWLERS
plus
THE WURLITZER
plus
SPOT PRIZES

Before 8 p.m.   After 8 p.m.
3/-   4/-

Note :- OPENS THURSDAY, AUGUST 6th.
"CORONA COFFEE CLUB"

Also! EVERY FRIDAY, "THE VAMPIRES"
and Other Big Beat Groups.

The Cosmonaughts

AVAILABLE AT LAST!
First-class professional recording
facilities and tape to disc service
CYMBAL RECORDING STUDIOS

(Proprietor: TOM SMITH)

99 MOUNT PLEASANT LIVERPOOL, 3

REASONABLE CHARGES

Phone this number now!
ROYal 3051

THE MERSEYSIDE GROUP
TO WATCH
GERRY-DE-VILLE
and the
CITY KINGS
Tel.: STA 5703

INTRODUCING

The Cyclones

Roy - Tony - Bill - Fred

All Enquiries   STA. 6924

DARVILLE ENTERTAINMENTS   WAL LASEY 1421 AND 2484

PHIL RYAN AND THE CRESCENTS
SEPT. 6—OCT. NO DATES. NOV. NEW DATES AVAILABLE
COLUMBIA RECORD RELEASED DURING NOVEMBER
Radio and TV coverage   BOOK NOW!

DELMONT FOUR
SEPTEMBER—NO DATES
BOOKING OCT. & NOV.

JEANNIE
SEPTEMBER—NO DATES
BOOKING OCT. & NOV.

LOOK OUT FOR THE **REDS** AND **RAINCHECKS**

DAILY HERALD BEAT FESTIVAL 1963

(BY ARRANGEMENT WITH JACARANDA ENTERPRISES)
13 Hours Non-Stop Beat!
10-30 a.m. until 11-30 p.m.
STANLEY STADIUM
Prescot Road, Liverpool
SATURDAY AUGUST 31st.

BILLY J. KRAMER with THE DAKOTAS
JOHN LEYTON — THE SEARCHERS
MIKE SARNE — THE BIG THREE
ALEXIS KORNERS BLUES INC.
THE HOLLIES — RICKY VALANCE

JOHNNY SANDON & THE REMO 4 — THE MERSEY BEATS
CHRIS NAVA COMBO — EARL PRESTON & THE TT's
THE NOMADS — THE UNDERTAKERS
LEE CURTIS & THE ALL STARS — SONNY WEBB & THE CASCADES
PETE McLAIN & THE CLAN — THE ESCORTS
RORY STORM & THE HURRICANES — THE EASY BEATS
MARK PETERS & THE SILHOUETTES — IAN & THE ZODIACS
BERYL MARSDEN & THE RENEGADES — THE PANTHERS
THE YOUNG ONES

COMPERES:
KENNETH COPE (TWTWTW & Coronation Street)
BOB WOOLER (Merseyside's Own D-Jay)

THE DAY BREAKERS
LIVERPOOL'S MOST POLISHED GROUP
Book them now with TONY REUBEN—Bootle 3778

The Curiosity Shoppe (All 3 images)

THE DELEMERES

THE CURIOSITY SHOPPE
Deram Records

PAUL DEAN and the CLANSMEN
Enq.: C. H. WALKER
Tel.: Burscough 2388.

LIVERPOOL'S BIG BEAT GROUP—
THE DEFIANTS
ANFIELD 6851

DAVID FORSHAW
ENTERPRISES
6 DALEY PLACE, BOOTLE, 20.
LANCS. Tel: AIN 9654 Day and Night
Sole management for the following groups.

THE PREMIERS

The TOPSPOTS
STARS OF B.B.C. RADIO AND THE STAR CLUB HAMBURG
TOURS OF LONDON, SCOTLAND AND BRISTOL, etc.

THE MOTIFS

The Defenders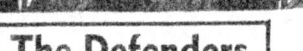

THE JENSONS
MEMPHIS 3 ★

THE RENICKS

FAREWAYS
CAFE - Wrexham

BEAT SESSIONS
EVERY SATURDAY
commencing Tomorrow,
June 20th
Featuring **TWO TOP LIVERPOOL GROUPS** each Saturday

The Rockerfellers
(from The Cavern)
and the
Fabulous Prowlers
Non-Stop 8.00 — 11.30
Admission 5/-   1F19Fx

Agent: MAJOR A. J. MACKENZIE

The Dions

Phone AIN 3804 (Liverpool)

COUNTRY & WESTERN - BALLAD - BEAT

THE DIALS
Vocal and Instrumental Group

Telephone : HUYton 5322

SOCIAL CLUBS &   78 ROBY ROAD
WEDDINGS a SPECIALITY   HUYTON

RECORDING STUDIO Available for **GROUPS, BANDS, SOLOISTS** etc.

Top professional quality. 20 years' experience Tapes & Discs made for Decca/E.M.I. Audition Managers — Many top names started in our Studios. Tapes also transferred to Discs
Phone Hest Bank 2444 for Appointment. S.A.E. for leaflet:
DEROY SOUND SERVICE, 52 Hest Bank Lane, Lancaster

The Defenders

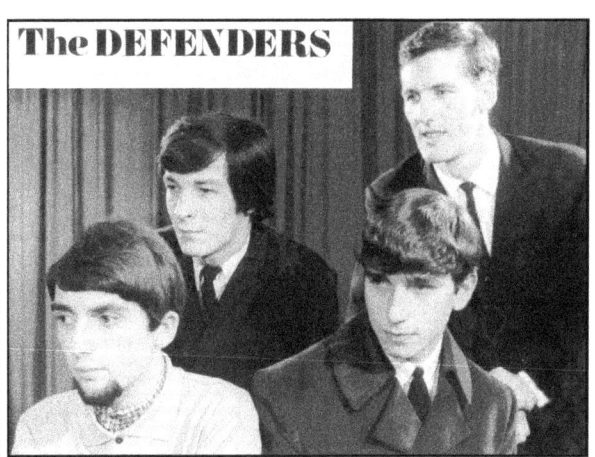

PLEASE BOOK IN ADVANCE   **THE DIPLOMATS**
PARTIES   Vocal & Instrumental Group
DANCES   Write - D. TOLLINS
REASONABLE CHARGES   85, Bath Street, Southport.

Spin-a-long with the
DEE-JAYS
AIN. 7279

Tel : BIR. 6874.
Vince Earl and the Talismen
Manager
LEONARD McCORMICK,
42 Clifton Road,
Birkenhead.

To Coin a *Expression*
Phone : IRBy 1491
★ *The Expressions*
Manager : MR. E. HEWITT

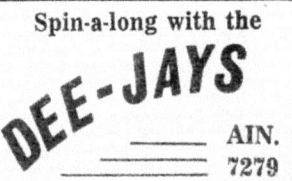
The Delemeres (Both images)

LIVERPOOL'S — DYNAMIC — VOCALIST
LEE EDDIE
&
THE CHEVRONS
Instrumentally Terrific
Sole Management: E. Spencer. Hunts Cross 3426

A Fabulous Group!
A Fabulous Sound!   THE
FABZ
AIN 9145 — ANF 4485

The Fabulous Sobells ★
Frank
Benji
Bernie
Kenny
Eddy
S.A.E.
JOAN & MARIE,
106 PETHERICK RD.,
LIVERPOOL 11.   TEL. STA 4765

Dee Fenton
AND THE ORIGINAL
Silhouettes
SAY
"KEEP UP THE GOOD WORK"

PLEASE NOTE—
BOOKING ENQUIRIES
ROYal 5571

THREE FOR THE TOP / ELEKTRONS

| HUY 6317 | STO 4921 | GAT 1042 |

The Exiles L to R: Phil Williams, Mike Charlton, Paul Lowry & Colin Humphreys

---

THERE'S A NEW SOUND AROUND ST. HELENS IT'S THE FEDERAL 5

LOOK FOR THEM IN LIVERPOOL SOON

UNDER THE MANAGEMENT OF J. R. CHIBBER ★ TELEPHONE GAT 2928

FOUR DIMENSIONS (with Tiffany)

"FIREFLYS"

DANCES — PARTIES — SOCIALS

MR. M. McKAY,
70 RUFFORD ROAD,
SOUTHPORT.   TEL. 88179.

THE 5 TRIBUTES

MODERN BEAT GROUP

CHI 5812   LAR 3220
LIVERPOOL

THE FLINTSTONES

Pure Beat Extract

Telephone: GATeacre 2405

THE FLINTSTONES
Guaranteed Pure Beat Extract
GAT 2405.

The FONTANAS
The NEWTOWNS
MAGhull   1540

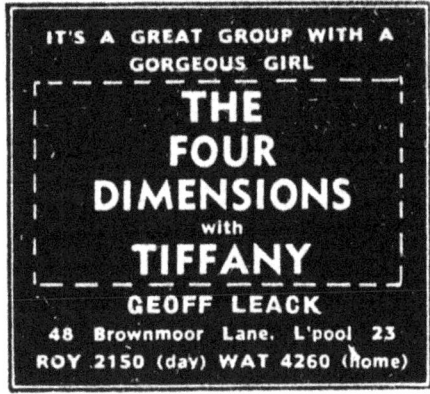

IT'S A GREAT GROUP WITH A GORGEOUS GIRL

THE FOUR DIMENSIONS with TIFFANY

GEOFF LEACK
48 Brownmoor Lane, L'pool 23
ROY 2150 (day) WAT 4260 (home)

The Four Dimensions with Tiffany

```
WE'RE STILL
The Four Jays
(Watch for a new name in
the near future)
BACK FROM A SUCCESSFUL
SEASON at the ISLE OF MAN
BROmborough 3454
```

The Few

Johnny Gentle

```
Mersey Scene Promotions Present:

BEAT CITY '66
      at THE GRAFTON, WEST DERBY ROAD
      on THURSDAY 24th MARCH 1966

Starring ... The Realm  Hard Time Lovin' You Baby (CBS.)

        The Hideaways  ·  The Dark Ages
        The Defenders  ·  The Excerts

Introducing . The Keez    Compere . Billy Butler

Dancing 7.30 - 12.30   Admission 6/-   Bars 7.30 - Midnight
```

```
The public demand only the best
   The Group to
   watch during      THE FOUR JUST MEN      ROYAL
      1963                                   5571
We are supplying this demand!                 ·
                                            PREscot
                                             6827
```

Johnny Gentle

Arnot/Heague presents
SPECIAL BONFIRE NIGHT
Country & Western JAMBOREE
AT THE GRAFTON BALLROOM
7.30 - 12 p.m.
(Licensed Bar 7.30-12 p.m.)

COME AND DANCE TO THE MUSIC OF LIVERPOOL'S TOP COUNTRY AND WESTERN GROUPS

THE RANCHERS
HANK WALTERS
DUSTY ROAD RAMBLERS
JOHNNY GOLDS
COUNTRY COUSINS
FOGGY MOUNTAIN RAMBLERS

TICKETS IN ADVANCE 5/-
FROM GRAFTON
Actu Ltd., 187 County Road, 4
Allen's Music Stores, Lodge Ln.
Wells Fargo Club, Dale Street

PAY AT DOOR 7/6
Don't Forget the 5th

JIM GRETTY
The Versatile Entertainer

Television - Radio - Revue
Cabaret . Variety . Etc.

THEM GRIMBLES

For Bookings Ring:
Liverpool NOR 0471
Liverpool GAT 2404
ORMSKIRK 2200
(Evenings)

THE Ghost Riders
ANF 5628

CHICK GRAHAM
THE SINGING SENSATION with
THE COASTERS
Ted Knibbs AIN 9927

TO THE PAPER WITH
PUNCH ★ PEP ★ PERSONALITY
from
THREE GROUPS IN ONE

GROUP ONE

Telephones:—
EASTHAM 1818 (evening)
ELLESMERE PORT 1951 (day)
ASK FOR DAVE WILLIAMS

DANCES . PARTIES . WEDDINGS, Etc.

GROUP ONE
TOP CLASS TOP POPS

DAVE WILLIAMS
31, Mansfield Road,
Whitby,
Ellesmere Port.   EAS 1818.

WHAT HAS FRANK KNIGHT
GOT UP HIS SLEEVE? . . .
WATCH THIS SPACE FOR NEWS OF GROUPS INC.
with
FRANK KNIGHT

VALUE! A Special Reduced Admission of 2/- only will be allowed on all holders of this advertisement at HAMBLETON HALL on WEDNESDAY, 20th SEPTEMBER
DON'T MISS THIS OFFER — Cut out this advertisement and take it to
HAMBLETON HALL
PAGE MOSS · HUYTON
Bus routes 10, 40a, 92, 12, 12a, 8c, 8d, 97, 97a, 98
GREAT ROCK SHOW DANCES EVERY WEDNESDAY AND SATURDAY
THIS SUNDAY NIGHT'S SPECTACULAR
THE BEATLES — JOHNNY SANDON AND THE SEARCHERS — DEE AND THE DYNAMITES
WATCH OUT FOR THE SENSATIONAL EARL PRESTON AND THE T.T.'s

Rhythm Group
The
HALERS

HALE 3369 | Representation: TED LAMBE. STO. 6957

Don't Miss
THE SENSATIONAL
HUNTERS
Management:
N. J. Littler
14 Barnett Avenue
Newton-le-Willows OR RING

COMEDY — RHYTHM — VOCAL
HOBO RICK AND THE CITY SLICKERS
Wilf Neilson, 37 Venmore St. Liverpool, 5.
For the Best Entertainment at Your Club

HOLE IN THE FLOOR
OPENS FRIDAY 26th JUNE
featuring
THE MINITS
7-0 till 11-45 p.m.
106 BRIGHTON ST., SEACOMBE, WALLASEY

The Hammers

**Danny Havoc & the Ventures
with Barbara Harrison**

The Hideaways 1968

COMING NEXT WEEK

THURSDAY, 23rd JULY
CONNOISSEURS
Members 3/- non-members 3/6

FRIDAY, 24th JULY
DETROITS
Members 3/- non-members 3/6

MONDAY, 27th JULY
GROUP TO BE BOOKED
Members 2/- non-members 2/6

DANCING EVERY NIGHT
7-30—11-30 p.m. except Sunday
Membership 3/6 p.a.

186 Brighton Street, Seacombe
5 minutes from Ferry

Tel. Waterloo 7723.   Tel. Stoneycroft 8115.

For a Sensational Sound ...

The Inmates

Manager: J. SMITH.
Tel.: Aintree 2670.   North 3251 (8—5 p.m.).

FOR RHYTHM, BEAT AND HARMONY

THE HUNTSMEN

TELEPHONE: STONEYCROFT 8182

Sole Representation:
N. GARLAND
21 THE FAIRWAY
LIVERPOOL 12

Join the rebellion with the
JACOBEATS
GRE 2936

IAN WAT 5189 **and the ZODIACS**

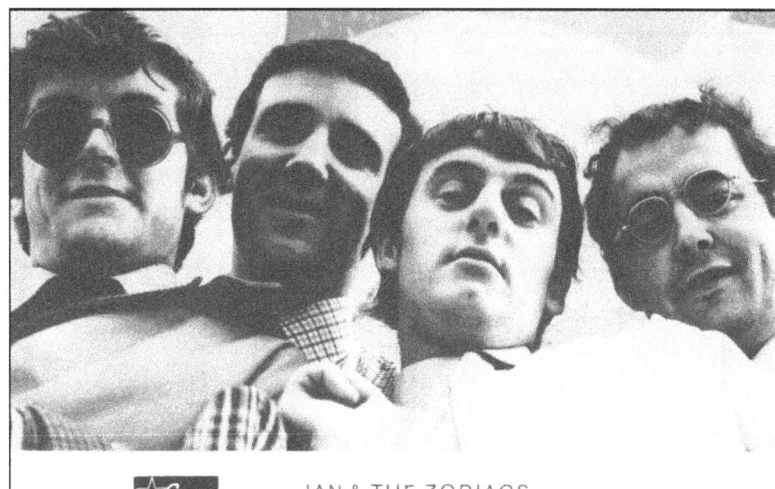

IAN & THE ZODIACS

HOLYOAKE JIVE HALL
Smithdown Road

Grand Easter Monday
ROCK 'N' ROLL
CARNIVAL
MONDAY 30th MARCH
7.30 to 11.20 p.m.

- ★ Big Beat Bands   ★ Guest Singers
- ★ Easter Hit Parade Requests   ★ Prizes
- ★ Gifts   ★ Gaiety   ★ Gimmicks

Special Attraction
The Sensational Teenage Rebels

Come Early – Pay at Door 3/-
Remember!
There's Jivin' at Holyoake Every Saturday Night

"Where the Crowds Roll Up 'N' Rock"

JIVE HALLS

- AINTREE INSTITUTE. Every Friday and Saturday.
- BLAIR HALL. Every Saturday and Sunday.
- BLUE PENGUIN CLUB. St. John's Hall, Bootle. Every Friday.
- COLUMBA HALL, Widnes. Every Thursday and Saturday.
- DAVID LEWIS. Every Friday.
- EMPRESS CLUB.
- GROSVENOR BALLROOM.
- HAMBLETON HALL. Every Wednesday and Sunday.
- JIVE HIVE, St. Luke's Hall, Crosby. Every Wednesday and Saturday.
- LA MYSTERE, Maghull.
- LITHERLAND TOWN HALL. Every Monday and Thursday.
- LA SCALA. Runcorn.
- LATHOM HALL. Every Saturday.
- NESTON INSTITUTE.
- ORRELL PARK BALLROOM.
- QUAINTWAYS Chester.
- ST. JOHN'S HALL, Tuebrook. Every Thursday.
- IVAMAR CLUB, Skelmersdale.
- KNOTTY ASH HALL. Every Friday.
- SPRINGWOOD HALL, Mather Avenue.

JAY-EL and THE EXECUTIVES
Agent L. LOMAX   Tel CLA 5043

BEAT
BLUES
BALLADS   Telephone GRE. 2936

The Jacobeats
12 CAVENDISH ROAD
BLUNDELLSANDS,
LIVERPOOL 23

INTERNS
RHYTHM GROUP
R. Carter,
19 Virginia St.,   Phone, 4960
SOUTHPORT.   (after 6 pm.)

IVAMAR
WHAT DOES IT MEAN?

It means a first class Jive Hall using only first class Groups. It is your guarantee of a

FABULOUS TIME
AT

THE JIVE HIVE
ST. LUKE'S HALL, CROSBY
WED. & SAT.

THE IVAMAR CLUB
SKELMERSDALE
MON. & SAT.

MOSSWAY HALL
CROXTETH
EVERY FRIDAY

You've Heard the Rest —
THE INTRUDERS
— Here's The Best

ARRowebrooke 6210

✴ SWING ALONG SING ALONG ✴
WITH
J J AND THE HI-LITES
★ ★

Sole Management :
DAVID FORSHAW
6 Daley Place
Bootle 20 Lancs.   AINtree 9654

IRON DOOR CLUB

13 TEMPLE STREET,
(off Dale Street)
LIVERPOOL
MEMBERSHIP 2/6 per annum

Thursday, 29th August—
IAN & THE ZODIACS
THE NOMADS

Tuesday, 3rd September—
JOHNNY SANDON & THE REMO FOUR
THE FOUR CLEFS

Sunday, 8th September—
JOHNNY TEMPLER & THE HI-CATS
VIC & THE SPIDERMEN
THE EXCHECKERS

Friday, 30th August—
SONNY WEBB & THE CASCADES
THE EXCHECKERS
GARY B. GOODE & THE HOT RODS

Thursday, 5th September—
IAN & THE ZODIACS
DENNY SEYTON & VINCE EARL & THE TALISMEN

Tuesday, 10th September—
JOHNNY SANDON & THE REMO FOUR
THE SABRES

Saturday, 31st August—
EARL PRESTON & THE T.T.s
SONNY WEBB & THE CASCADES
THE PATHFINDERS

Friday, 6th September—
EARL PRESTON & THE T.T.s
VIC & THE SPIDERMEN
THE PATHFINDERS

Thursday, 12th September
DERRY WILKIE & THE PRESSMEN
THE ALAMOS

Sunday, 1st September—
JOHNNY TEMPLER & THE HI-CATS
VINCE EARL & THE TALISMEN
DERRY WILKIE & THE PRESSMEN

Saturday, 7th September—
DERRY WILKIE & THE PRESSMEN
DANNY & THE ASTEROIDS

SEE YOU AT THE **I.D.C.**

Welcome to the . . .

13 TEMPLE STREET
(off Dale Street)

HAPPY, FRIENDLY
ATMOSPHERE . . .
PLEASANT DECOR . . .
GOOD COMPANY . . .
and TOP LINE
ENTERTAINMENT !
See for yourself on . . .

Thursday, 28th March—
THE MERSEYBEATS;
THE SENSATIONAL SABRES.

Friday, 29th March—
THE SEARCHERS; THE COASTERS; RORY STORM and THE HURRICANES.

Saturday, 30th March—
SONNY WEBB and THE CASCADES; VIC and THE SPIDERMEN; IAN and THE ZODIACS.

Sunday, 31st March—
THE SEARCHERS; THE UNDERTAKERS; THE FOUR CLEFS.

Tuesday, 2nd April—
THE CASCADES; THE REMO FOUR.

Thursday, 4th April—
THE SEARCHERS; THE SENSATIONAL SABRES.

Friday, 5th April—
GARRY B. GOODE and THE HOT RODS; THE DENNISONS; EARL PRESTON and THE T.T.'s.

Saturday, 6th April—
FREDDIE and the DREAMERS
SONNY WEBB and THE CASCADES; The THREE DEUCES.

Sunday, 7th April—
THE COASTERS; VIC and THE SPIDERMEN; FARON and THE FLAMINGOES.

Tuesday, 9th April—
THE SEARCHERS; THE CASCADES

Thursday, 11th April—
SONNY WEBB and THE CASCADES; THE FOUR CLEFS.

Extra Lunchtime Sessions
Wednesday (1-30–4 p.m.) and Friday (12-0–2 p.m.) featuring
THE UNDERTAKERS
Membership only 2/6 p.a.
Note—No admission after 2-30
SEE YOU AT THE
IRON DOOR CLUB

Special thanks to Pamela Beesley for this candid photo

HAVE HEARSE, WILL TRAVEL
THE KARACTERS
Ring **WALLASEY**
2793
Evenings and weekends

The Maggie May
The Colquitt Club, Seel Street, Liverpool
To-night — To-night
The R and B Band
the fans love
The Clayton Squares
and The Master Minds
The Blue Angel Club,
Seel Street, Liverpool 1
Members Please Note
To-night — To-night
Freddie Starr's Flamingoes

To-night at the Cavern:
The Hideaways
The Sheffields
The Excelles
The St. Louis Checks
The Blues System
A Really Fabulous Night Out!
MEMBERS 3/- VISITORS 4/-
TO-NIGHT AT THE CAVERN

Excelling All Others!
The Excelles!
They're Marvellous! They're Great!
They can be booked through:
CAVERN ARTISTES LTD.
Phone Central 2674.

Sink Club
RUMBLIN TUM, 45 HARDMAN ST.
To-night: MEMBERS 1/-. VISITORS 1/6.
Record Session!
FRIDAY: ST. LOUIS CHECKS.

Left Bank Club
TO-NIGHT: Prowlers
FRIDAY: Feelgoods
65 CHURCH ROAD, BIRKENHEAD.

The Footprint Club,
59 WAVERTREE NOOK ROAD.
To-night: Members 2/6. Guests 3/6.
THE PHOTONS
THE TROLLS AND THE HARPOS.

St. John's Hall, Bootle
Opposite Bootle Town Hall. Friday:
JENSONS. Ricky Gleason
THE REBALS. FIRST 50 only 2/6.

Roger James Four

The Katz

Tommy Jordan

RANGIORA ROVER CREW present ...

A Summer Beat Night

with ... JOAN AND THE DEMONS

and ... THE PROWLERS

ON SATURDAY, 8th AUGUST, 1964
AT ST. MARK'S, SLATEY ROAD, BIRKENHEAD

7 p.m. to 11 p.m.   Admission 3/6d. (to be paid at door)

If you are unable to come, please give this ticket to a friend

Kingfisher Combo

Mountwood 4694
220 MOUNT ROAD
BIRKENHEAD

SOUTHPORT'S TOPPERMOST
THE JOKERS
PHONE: SOUTHPORT 55806
Liverpool WAT 1596

GOT A DANCE — BUT NO GROUP?
GET THE
"K - MEN"
BEAT GROUP
(POOREST GROUP IN BRITAIN)

Write to:
S. D. DAVIES,
29, SOMERVILLE CRESCENT,
ELLESMERE PORT,
CHESHIRE.

RANGIORA ROVER CREW present...

Another Big Beat Night

with ... **THE KARACTERS**
(and their 1932 Rolls Royce Hearse)

and ... **THE PROWLERS**
("The Group with the wildest stage act in Birkenhead"—B'head News and Ad)

ON SATURDAY, 6th JUNE, 1964
AT ST. MARK'S, SLATEY ROAD, BIRKENHEAD
7 p.m. to 11 p.m.   Admission 3/6d. (to be paid at door)

If you are unable to come, please give this ticket to a friend

Karl Terry & Lance Railton

The Kinetic

THE KINGS R & B CLUB LITTLE SUTTON

Thursday, 12th March, at 7-30:—
THE CAVERNERS and THE DEKKAS
Plus Top 20 records FREE!

Friday, 13th March at 7-30:—
THE KARACTERS with Moria & Beverley
THE GLOBE TROTTERS
Plus Top 20 records FREE!

Saturday, 14th March at 7-30:—
THE NASHPOOL FOUR & THE CAVE DWELLERS

Sunday, 15th March, 7-30:—
THE DIONS & THE FONTANAS

Tuesday, 17th March,—
St. Patrick's Night, at 7-30:—
SAVVA & THE DEMOCRATS & THE ROCKFELLERS

Thursday, 19th March at 7-30:
THE INTERNS & THE HUSTLERS
Plus Top 20 records FREE!

Friday, 20th March—3 Groups
THE VIBRATORS — THE DEKKAS — THE COUNTDOWNS
Plus Top 20 records FREE!

Saturday, 21st March, at 7-30:
THE PATHFINDERS & GUEST GROUP

Sunday, 22nd March:—
JOAN AND THE DEMONS THE CAVERNERS

THE KIRKBYS
Sole Management:
BERYL ADAMS,
23 CANNING ST.,
LIVERPOOL 8.
TEL. ROYAL 8029.

WILD! WILDER! WILDEST!
IT'S THE
KRUZADS
LIVERPOOL'S LONG-HAIRED
WITCHES OF R&B
BOOK THROUGH
MATHEWS & BROWN
ANF 4370

The Kruzads in Brussels (Belgium) 1966

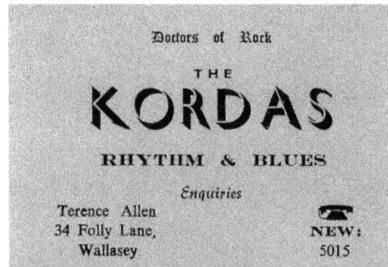

Take note of the new sound of
THE KINGPINS
Enquiries: D. B. Fillis,
15 Palmerston Drive, Litherland

THE BEST IN BEAT! YOU WANNA KNOW, RING FOR
MR. LEE & CO.
THE BEAT GROUP THAT REALLY IS DIFFERENT
Manager: F. Q. SCANES, Witches Cauldron Club NEW 5849

DO YOU BOOK GROUPS OR BANDS?
... IF SO
... CONTACT

THE L. E. AGENCY
6 CROSS STREET
HINDLEY, WIGAN

Tel.: Wigan 55500. Ext. 3

for any professional name group or for some of our groups listed below:—

Fabulous Adders/L'Ringo's
Roy Marsden Five/Checkers
David John & The Mood
/Vulcans
Northlanders/Hawaiian Eyes
The Boys/Bill Culshaw Band
Hammers/Overlanders
Beat Boys/Hobo's (C & W)
Daltons/Ray Malcolm and
The Sunsets
Madmen/Kev Kurtis and
Four Escorts
Falcons/The Paramounts
Zodiacs/Viceroys
Brokers/Vigilantes

and over 70 other groups

The L.S.D.

'Swinging Lunch Time Rock Sessions'
AT THE
LIVERPOOL JAZZ SOCIETY,
13, TEMPLE STREET (off Dale Street and Victoria Street),
EVERY LUNCH TIME, 12-00 to 2-30
RESIDENT BANDS:
Gerry and the Pacemakers,
Rory Storm and the Wild Ones,
The Big Three.

Next Wednesday Afternoon, March 15th
12-00 to 5-00 Special
STARRING—
The Beatles,
Gerry and the Pacemakers
Rory Storm and the Wild Ones.

Admission—Members 1/-, Visitors 1/6
"Rocking at the L. J. S."

The Victor Printing Co. 210, West Derby Road, Liverpool, 6

Mr LEE & Co.

For a Different Line in Beat...
The Only Group that GUARANTEES SATISFACTION

MANAGER: F. G. SCANES,
WITCH'S CAULDRON CLUB,
62 ALBION ST., NEW BRIGHTON

NEW 5849

'LEFT BANK CLUB'
— ★ —
Thursday:
THE FABULOUS
'PROWLERS'
— ★ —
Friday:
'MEMPHIS R & B COMBO'
— ★ —
Sunday:
DON'T MISS
The 'KREEPS'
65 Church Road, Tranmere
(W)

SEE THE STAR SHOW
with recording artistes

TOWN HALL LITHERLAND

Brian Poole and the Tremilos
★ ★ ★
Ian and the Zodiacs
★ ★ ★
The Spidermen

on THURSDAY
SEPTEMBER 6th

MECCA DANCING
LOCARNO
●
THURSDAY, FEB. 27
WAYNE GIBSON AND
THE DYNAMIC SOUNDS
AND
RHYTHM & BLUES INC.
●
FRIDAY, FEB. 28
HERMAN & THE HERMITS
and THE ZEROS
●
COMING
THE DENNISONS,
THE MERSEYBEATS,
DAVE BERRY & THE CRUISERS,
MANFRED MANN,
JOHNNY KIDD & THE PIRATES,
AND THE PARAMOUNTS.

RESIDENTS ALL SESSIONS:
THE DELEMERES

SOUND EQUIPMENT

HIGH-QUALITY AMPLIFIERS TAILOR-MADE TO SUIT YOUR REQUIREMENTS

SOUND VALUE FOR MONEY

HIGH-QUALITY SOUND SYSTEMS FOR HALLS AND CLUBS
Cash, or Contract hire with full maintenance

LAMBDA RECORD COMPANY LTD.
95 Liverpool Road, Crosby, Liverpool, 23
Telephone: GREAT CROSBY 4012

THE BEST IN BEAT YOU WANNA KNOW RING FOR
MR. LEE & CO.
MANAGER F G SCANES
WITCH'S CAULDRON CLUB
62 ALBION STREET NEW
BRIGHTON Tel. NEW 5849

The Beat Group that Really is Different

LIVERPOOL NEW BEAT CENTRE
LOCARNO
WEST DERBY ROAD
General Manager: JOHN MORGAN

2/6 THURSDAY, 2nd JULY — THE BOYS / The Censors

2/6 FRIDAY, 3rd JULY — HERMAN'S HERMITS / THE SPINNING TOPS

5/- SATURDAY, 4th JULY — ST. LOUIS CHECKS

2/6 SUNDAY, 5th JULY — THE WHEELS / BERNADETTE AND THE 4 GENTS

2/- MONDAY AND WEDNESDAY — GEAR OFF THE RECORD SESSION

BIG, BIG, NEWS!
GERRY AND THE PACEMAKERS
CILLA BLACK — FOURMOST
Appearing at the Locarno Ballroom for 5 days from 5th JULY
FURTHER DETAILS NEXT WEEK!

MAGGIE MAY
COLQUITT CLUB
71a SEEL STREET
ROY 1229

"FOR THE BEST IN POP"

OPEN SIX NIGHTS A WEEK 7.30
UNTIL 11.30 · CLOSED TUESDAY
NO ADMITTANCE AFTER 10 P.M.

THE MAGGIE MAY
Colquitt Club   Seel Street
Top Groups Every Night ● 7—12 ● Licensed Bars
"To-night, To-night . . ." (Thursday):
RORY STORM & THE HURRICANES
"America" — Parlophone R 5197
Also ADRIAN LORD'S FACES

Sat., Nov. 21st: EARL PRESTON ● Fontana
Mon., Nov. 23rd: THEM GRIMBLES ●
Thurs. Nov. 26th: THE HILLSIDERS ● Decca

LATEST RECORDS PLAYED EVERY NIGHT ● FOOD SERVICE

TOP RANK

THE TOPS IN ENTERTAINMENT WISH EVERY CONTINUED SUCCESS TO THE TOP PROVINCIAL ENTERTAINMENTS PAPER

— ★ — ★ — ★ —

JIVE TO THE BEST
MERSEYSIDES ROCK GROUPS
7-30 p.m. EVERY
SUNDAY & MONDAY
Groups to be presented include
Gerry and The Pacemakers
Group One
Faron and The Flamingoes
Clay Ellis and The Raiders

★

DON'T FORGET WE PRESENT
THE BEATLES
ON THURSDAY NIGHTS

★

Top Rank Dancing
MAJESTIC BALLROOM
Conway Street, Birkenhead

Manager Bill Marsden says:
We at the Top Rank

MAJESTIC
BALLROOM CONWAY ST.
BIRKENHEAD (Tel. 6320)
Are proud to be associated with MERSEY BEAT in connection with our
FABULOUS SATURDAY NIGHT "MERSEY BEAT BALLS"
Variety with a Beat
STARRING
The Bluegenes
Billy Kramer
with The Coasters
Lee Curtiss
with The All Stars
The Spidermen
YOUR SATURDAY NIGHT OUT
7-30 to 11-30 p.m.

Lynette Cawood - The Bo-Weevils

MAJESTIC BALLROOM
TOP RANK DANCING
CONWAY STREET, BIRKENHEAD

DATES TO REMEMBER

THURSDAY, 16th JANUARY—THE FABULOUS HOLLIES

Thurs., 23rd January
JIMMY CRAWFORD & the Shantells
plus
The Original ALL STARS with Pete Best

Thurs., 30th January
FRANK KELLY & THE HUNTERS

Sunday 26th January
THE BIG THREE

RAY MALCOLM AND THE SUNSETS
CONGRATULATE THE PAPER THAT IS GOING PLACES

★ ★ ★

Manager: TED GLOVER
119 MILL LANE, ST. HELENS
St. Helens 8137

A Great Sound . . . A Great Group
★ ★ ★ THE ★ ★ ★
MANAGERS
DAVE – JIMMY – PHIL – DAVE
Telephone: WAT 3517

THE MAGGIE MAY
Colquitt Club Seel Street
Open every night 7.30—12 Licensed Bars

RESIDENT GROUP   THE BLUES SYSTEM

EARL PRESTON: "THE BEST GROUP IN LIVERPOOL"
JOHN BANKS (MERSEYBEATS): 'A MUSICIANS' GROUP'
MIKE GREGORY (ESCORTS): 'FANTASTIC'

Also Liverpool's top groups : Thurs : Fri : Sat : Sun

NOTE: TONIGHT, NOVEMBER 5 ★ ★
THE CLAYTON SQUARES

LATEST RECORDS PLAYED EVERY NIGHT ● FOOD SERVICE

TOP CLASS MODERN MUSIC
PRESENTING
Ray Malcolm AND THE SUNSETS

'Phone ST Helens 8173

T. Glover [Manager]
119 Mill Lane, St. Helens.

LIVERPOOL'S NEWEST AND GREATEST VENUE
MAGGIE MAY
(The Colquitt Club)
SEEL STREET, LIVERPOOL.

TOP GROUPS SEVEN NIGHTS PER WEEK
RESIDENT GROUP: THE BLUES SYSTEM

GRAND OPENING NEXT MONTH

BLUESTEMPOMUSIK
Maraccas
MANAGER: Jim Pemberton
Phone Liverpool STAnley 2449

MAGHULL PROMOTIONS
- THE ROADRUNNERS
- THE NASHPOOL
- EDDIE AND THE SHEVRONS
- THE APPROACHERS
- THE AARONS
- THE FORGERS

Groups supplied at 24 hours notice

MAG 4620   MAG 4620   MAG 4620

CONGRATULATIONS TO THE LEADING SHOW BIZ PAPER IN THE NORTH from
THE M.I.5
ENQUIRIES
CRESSINGTON 2354

BERYL MARSDEN

The Manchester Playboys

A POLISHED PRESENTATION
Johnny Marlowe and The Whipchords
STO. 6793
HUY. 2133

SOUTHPORT'S LARGEST DANCE CLUB
MARINE CLUB
KINGSWAY, SOUTHPORT, Tel. 56566

TOP GROUPS EVERY
FRIDAY, SATURDAY & SUNDAY

★ ★

Licensed Bars : Luxurious Lounge
New Members Welcome
(OVER 18's ONLY)

Annual Membership Only 2/6d
YES — FABULOUS NATIONAL AND MERSEYSIDE RECORDING ARTISTES APPEAR REGULARLY AT THE

MARINE CLUB

COMING—
FRIDAY
SEPTEMBER
20th—
EARL PRESTON AND THE T.T.s

THE GROUP WITH A STRIKING DIFFERENCE!!
THE MATCHBOX 5
Manager: M. J. OWEN,
151 LIVERPOOL RD.,
SOUTHPORT.
Tel.: 65039

MARKFOUR ★
Phone
PRE
5536

The Marracas

L to R: Dave Rhodes, Brian "Slack" Donovan, Fred Seddon, Frank Baker and Tommy Cunningham.

THE MEDALLIONS

Mr. Macdonald, Manager
10 St. John Street
Birkenhead
BIR 7755

FOR YOUR ENJOYMENT **The Manhattan Club** Mount Pleasant, Liverpool

---

TOP PRESENTATION
R & B and Blue-Beat
MERSEY BLUEBEATS
Enquiries: ANF 3142

The Mersey Monsters

MERSEY MONSTERS
INVITE BOOKINGS FROM SEPTEMBER —ONWARDS—

TONY REUBEN
POP INN LTD.
361 363, STANLEY ROAD,
Liverpool, 20   BOO 3778

THE MELODIBEATS
The Group with the New Sound - catering for all age groups
Featuring Peter & Alan Wall
B.B.C. Broadcasters
Phone Southport 68973

The Masterminds

..it's all BEAT a real TREAT (with apologies to JOCK) !
the master minds
ASSOCIATED ENTERTAINMENTS   ★   BOOTLE 6209

```
MIRABEL CLUB
(BEACHCOMBER)
56-58 SEEL STREET, LIVERPOOL 1
SATURDAY:
THE EXPRESSIONS
and
JIM CRAIG TRIO
SUNDAY:
WASHINGTON SOUL BAND
and
JIM CRAIG TRIO
8 P.M. START
WINING — DINING — GAMING
BLACKJACK — ROULETTE
and Dancing To-night
MEMBERS' NOTICE
```

The Movement

```
MIRABEL CLUB
(BEACHCOMBER)
56-58 SEEL ST., LIVERPOOL 1.
SATURDAY
CHAPTER SIX
LOCOMOTIVE SOUL
BAND
SUNDAY
The NUCLEAR MAGENCA
WASHINGTON SOUL
BAND
RESTAURANT :: CASINO
DANCING TO-NIGHT
8 p.m. Start
MEMBERS' NOTICE
```

```
ORGAN
RHYTHM          BASS
LEAD    The
        MUSIC
        STUDENTS     DRUMS
        RHYTHM & BLUES
        G. HORNBY
        Formby 5164
        VOCALIST
```

```
AUTHENTIC R & B
THE
NASHPOOL
CRE 1603

THE MOROCKANS
RHYTHM GROUP
Tel.: HOYlake 7040
```

```
WINNERS OF THE
SOUTHPORT
ROUND TABLE
BEAT CONTEST

THE
MOTIFS

SOLE
MANAGEMENT:
DAVE FORSHAW
'Phone: AIN 9654
```

```
TERRY              TOMMY
      THE MYSTERY
           4
           Manager 'ERIC BOWNESS
           Tel. ANfield 3640
BRIAN                TONY
```

The Nashpool Four

Modern Blues Quartet

The Merseybeats

408

SHAKE ! SHAKE ! SHAKE
AT
THE NASHVILLE TENNESSEE CLUB
RHYTHM AND BLUES

4 MERCER COURT, OF RED CROSS STREET, LIVERPOOL 1

Swinging Sessions EVERY NIGHT including Sunday

8 P.M. - 2 A.M.

ALSO LUNCH TIME SESSIONS DAILY

12 P.M. - 2-15 P.M.

LUNCH TIME SESSIONS 1/-   COFFEE AND SNACKS etc.

YOUR BEST GROUPS IN THE NORTH

□ □ □ □

WHERE IS THE NASHVILLE TENNESSEE CLUB ?

Find Victoria Monument, go down Red Cross Street, turn left into Mercer Court.

THIS IS YOUR STOMPING GROUND

STOMP !   STOMP !   STOMP !

The Nashpool at the Star Club Cologne

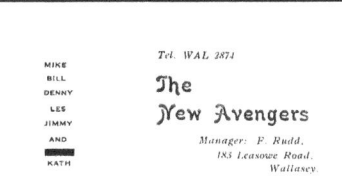

The Nashpool Four at the Paladin Club

THE NEONS
BEAT GROUP
Dances Weddings Etc.
MANAGER
W.H.BALMER
TEL SIM 2367   9 WINGATE ROAD
NORTHWOOD
KIRKBY

THE NEW PRESSMEN..
ring' NEW 1503..

409

THIS SPACE IS RESERVED FOR THE O.P.B.
WHICH PRESENTS ONLY TOP GROUPS Every FRIDAY SATURDAY SUNDAY and MONDAY

The Nocturns

The N-Signs

You don't have to be in the desert to see——

THE NOMADS
★
THE NOMADS
★
THE NOMADS

THEY'RE COMING YOUR WAY
★
Messages only
ROYal 0033
ASK FOR PAT DELANEY

N. V. A.

Representing the "cream" of MERSEYSIDE groups

FREDDIE STARR AND THE MIDNIGHTERS	SONNY WEBB AND THE CASCADES
CHICK GRAHAM AND THE COASTERS	THE EXCHECKERS
IAN AND THE ZODIACS	MARK PETERS AND THE SILHOUETTES
RORY STORM AND THE HURRICANES	THE FOUR CLEFS

| THE FOUR DIMENSIONS | THE CENTREMEN | DOMINANT FOUR |
| TALISMEN | PATHFINDERS | CONNOISSEURS |

ANY NATIONAL ARTISTE BOOKED
TELEPHONE OR CALL NOW

NORTHERN VARIETY AGENCIES
LIMITED

86a BOLD ST., LIVERPOOL 1   Tel: ROYal 1795 & 4382

THE BUCCANEERS OF THE LIVERPOOL SCENE...

THE PATHFINDERS

PULLING IN CAPACITY HOUSES WHEREVER THEY PLAY

SOME JUNE DATES ARE STILL AVAILABLE

A shrewd promoter will book them now   **ARR 7112**

THE NOTIONS
F. E. DELANEY
WAT. 6023

THE PANTHERS
Phone: A. POWER
SIMonswood 2344

THE PAGE-BOYS
Rhythm & Blues Group
Manager: George H. Parker
146a Bedford Rd., Rock Ferry

parties ★ dances ★ clubs

★★★ *The* Page - Boys

Manager: Mr. G. H. Parker
146a, Bedford Road . Rock Ferry

ARTISTES! MUSICIANS! CONCERT SECS!
and EVERYONE CONNECTED WITH CLUBLAND AND SHOWBIZ are all cordially invited to the artistes night at

THE PARKSIDE CLUB
(THE WIRRAL ARTISTES AND CONCERT SECRETARIES SOCIAL CLUB)
55 HILLSIDE ROAD, BIRKENHEAD
THE ONLY SHOP WINDOW SHOW AND ARTISTES NIGHT OUT ON THE CHESHIRE SIDE OF THE RIVER
EVERY WEDNESDAY
MEMBERS AND VISITORS — ADMISSION FREE
FABULOUS BACKING! FABULOUS MIKES! FABULOUS CLUB! ALL WELCOME!

MAKE PROGRESS WITH:

THE PILGRIMS

KEN ELLIS
ARRowebrook 5944
ARRowebrook 4648

Phillips Recording Studio

PARK HIGH SCHOOL (BOYS)

VIth Form

Summer Dance

FRIDAY, 25th JUNE, 1965

7-30 to 11-0 p.m.

★ The Pathfinders

  ★ The Cordes

    ★ Steve Day and The Drifters

Admission 4/6   No Stiletto's please
(By ticket only)   — New Floor —

PAWNS
NORTHERN VARIETY AGENCY
ROYAL 4382

DANCES   SOCIALS   ETC.

Pharoh and the Exiles
A New Rock Group

phone   phone
Claughton 1779   or   Rock Ferry 2658

TELFORD HALL SHAKEDOWN

with the

"PATHFINDERS"

Saturday, February 8th, 1964

7-45 — 12-0

GENT 4/-   BAR

★ FOR MUSIC WITH A BEAT

The
P.A.T.H.F.I.N.D.E.R.S

Manager:
G. POOLE   Enquiries:
IRBy 2605   MOUntwood 2838

THE PEPPERMINT LOUNGE
FRASER STREET, LONDON ROAD
Presents
Christmas and New Year Entertainments
FOR MEMBERS ONLY

CHRISTMAS EVE., TUES., DEC. 24
7-30 p.m. TILL 1 a.m.
1. THE BLACK VELVETS
2. THE FOUR DIMENSIONS
3. THE DETONATORS
4. MIKE AND THE EXPLORERS

Fully Licensed Bar until 12-45 a.m. Admission by Ticket only 11/6d

BOXING DAY AT THE PEP!
THURSDAY, DECEMBER 26th. — 7-30 p.m. TILL 12-30 a.m.
1. EARL ROYCE AND THE OLYMPICS
2. THE DETONATORS
3. THE DETOURS

Fully Licensed Bar till 12-15 a.m. Admission by Ticket only, price 9/6d

HOGMANAY HOP TUES., DEC. 31
7-30 p.m. — 2 a.m. AT THE PEP!
BEAT IN THE NEW YEAR!
1. THE BLACK VELVETS
2. THE CONNOISSEURS
3. THE NOCTURNES
4. THE INVADERS
5. LEE AND THE BARONS

Fully Licensed Bar till 1-15 a.m. Admission by ticket only, price 13/6d

All the above prices include Snacks and Chicken and Turkey Sandwiches. Tickets are now On Sale at: Sampson & Barlow, London Road; Rushworth & Dreaper, Whitechapel; The Peppermint Lounge Fraser Street. When purchasing a ticket — your membership card must be produced

---

THE PEPPERMINT LOUNGE
LIVERPOOL'S MOST SELECT RHYTHM AND BLUES VENUE
TOP CLASS GROUPS EVERY NIGHT

OPEN 7.30 P.M. TILL 11.45 TUES., THURS., FRI., SUN., AND

ON SATURDAY

OPEN 7.30 P.M.

IF YOU ARE LOOKING FOR THE BEST IN BEAT IN THE BEST OF SURROUNDINGS

TILL 1 A.M.

IT MUST BE **The Peppermint Lounge**
FRASER STREET, LIVERPOOL

TWO FULLY LICENSED BARS OPEN UNTIL 11.30 P.M. AND 12.30 A.M. ON SATURDAY

PEPPERMINT PROMOTIONS
PROUDLY PRESENT

2 OF LIVERPOOL'S TOP PROFESSIONAL BEAT GROUPS

THE SENSATIONAL EARL ROYCE and the OLYMPICS

THE FABULOUS "BLONDE" BOMBSHELLS THE BLACKWELLS

BOOK YOUR DATE BEFORE IT'S TOO LATE!
(THERE ARE A FEW STILL AVAILABLE)

PHONE NOR 0753 — STO 1704

BOOKING AGENT FOR VIC AND THE TT's

Peppermint Promotions, Fraser Street (off London Rd.), Liverpool 3.

PHONE NOR 0753 OR STO 1704

Peppermint Lounge Sign

'Tunnel Only' traffic would be on London Road Fraser Street would be to the right

---

Peppermint Promotions
FRASER STREET, LIVERPOOL

EARL ROYCE & THE OLYMPICS

THE BLACKWELLS

Two of Liverpool's Fourmost Professional Beat Groups currently Resident at the famous "Peppermint Lounge," have a limited number of evenings when they will be available for Bookings

IF YOU WANT TO FILL YOUR DANCE HALL OR CLUB RING STO 1704

THE PEPPERMINT LOUNGE
FRASER STREET (OFF LONDON ROAD)

★ LIVERPOOL'S MOST SELECT RHYTHM AND BLUES
TWISTING AND SHAKING TO TOP CLASS GROUPS
EVERY TUESDAY, THURSDAY, FRIDAY, SATURDAY AND SUNDAY
MEMBERSHIP INQUIRIES NOR 0753

PEPPERMINT PROMOTIONS
TWO OF LIVERPOOL'S TOP BEAT GROUPS
EARL ROYCE AND THE OLYMPICS and THE BLACKWELLS
RING NOR 0753, STO 1704

Johnny President & the Senators

```
THE BIG BEAT GROUP

JOHNNY PRESIDENT
AND
THE SENATORS

PARTIES    DANCES    SOCIAL FUNCTIONS
                  M.R.
TELEPHONE              153 WALTON HALL AVENUE
GRE 1973                          LIVERPOOL 4
```

The Profiles

The Prowlers - L to R: Mally, Phil, Ian, Alan & Dave

PLAZA | DUKE STREET ST. HELENS | Telephone: St. Helens 23822

Friday, 20th December—
THE SHONDELLS
IAN & THE ZODIACS
THE STEREOS

Friday, 27th December—
ALBY & THE SORRALS
THE BEATHOVENS
THE DETOURS

Saturday, 21st December—
THE PILGRIMS
THE RIOT SQUAD

Saturday, 28th December—
UNIT FOUR
THE STEREOS

Sunday, 22nd December—
FOUR CLEFS
UNIT FOUR
GERRY DE VILLE &
THE CITY KINGS

Sunday, 29th December—
THE DOMINANT FOUR
THE RIOT SQUAD
THE INCAS

Monday, 23rd December—
THE SHONDELLS
THE PILGRIMS
THE INCAS

Monday, 30th December—
MARK PETERS AND
THE SILHOUETTES
THE SHONDELLS
THE KARACTERS

Christmas Eve and New Year's Eve
SPECIAL BEAT NIGHTS

PLAZA | DUKE STREET ST. HELENS | Telephone: St. Helens 23822

A leading venue for leading groups

Friday, 13th March:—
RICKY GLEASON AND
THE TOPSPOTS
Four Dimensions. Stereos.

Friday, 20th March:—
RORY STORM AND THE
HURRICANES,
THE DEFIANTS
THE BLACKWELLS

Saturday, 14th March:—
BLACK KNIGHTS, THE
KARACTERS, THE
HUSTLERS

Saturday, 21st March:—
SAVVA WITH THE
DEMOCRATS
THE PILGRIMS
THE STEREOS

Sunday, 15th March:—
THE DETOURS, THE
DELMONT 4, THE
NIGHTWALKERS

Sunday, 22nd March:—
THE DOMINANT 4, THE
RIOT SQUAD,
THE CHALLENGERS

Monday, 16th March:—
THE RATTLES, THE
NASHPOOL 4, THE RIOT
SQUAD

Monday, 23rd March:—
THE UNDERTAKERS,
THE KARACTERS,
THE HAMMERS

ROCK AND ROLL GROUPS

Birkenhead's Own Group
Socials, Dances, etc. For
TONY AND THE QUANDROS
you ring CLA 1779   Ferry 2658

Contact the Group who are going places
KEN DALLAS AND THE SILHOUETTES
BOOtle 5362

No 'Strangers' to large audiences—
THE STRANGERS, Harry Hutchings,
Tel.: AINtree 5659.

BIRKENHEAD'S TWO TOP GROUPS!

THE PROWLERS
and   (Free Record Vouchers)
THE ABSTRACTS

at British Legion Hall, Park Rd East, Birkenhead
on Friday October 30th 1964

7.30 p.m. to 11 p.m.   Same price as usual **3/6**

BIG 6 SOUND
THE **REASONS**
PETER G. DENTON
LARk Lane 3320

CONGRATULATIONS AND BEST WISHES FOR THE FUTURE FROM THE
PONTIACS
ORMskirk 2047

★ Best in R and B ★

THE PROWLERS

Mr. McDonald, Manager   Tel:
10, St. John Street   Birkenhead
Birkenhead   7755.

Ray and the Del-Renas

R. WALKER
24 HEATH ROAD
ALLERTON   Tel. GARSTON 1927

ANNOUNCING
GRAND OPENING NIGHT
at
THE RAVE'L CLUB
MEMBERS ONLY

Have pleasure in presenting 3 great groups—Non stop Rock 'n' Twist to the
TEEN-BEATS
SANDGROUNDERS
TOLEDOS

WHIT MONDAY NIGHT
(June 3rd) 8 p.m. to Midnight

NOTICE.—To facilitate convenience to prospective members the Club Secretary will be in attendance, 7 p.m. to 9 p.m., on Mon., Tues., Wed., Thurs., Fri., 27th to 31st May, to register applicants in person. Apply at the Club, over the New Esso Station, Eastbank Street, Southport. Join Now! Closing date for applications is Friday, May 31st, 1963.

Exclusive Membership, no admittance to non-members

Coming Shortly: Terrific Group
"**THE DOMINATORS**"

Sessions on THURSDAY, SATURDAY, SUNDAY NIGHTS
ALSO SUNDAY AFTERNOONS

RAVE'L CLUB
EASTBANK STREET
(over New Esso Service Station)

MEMBERS' NOTICE
THURSDAY, JUNE 6th—Special Request Group
THE DOMINATORS

Membership re-opened, join now for grand opening Whit Monday, with three terrific Groups . . .

TEEN-BEATS ★ **SANDGROUNDERS**
★ **TOLEDO FOUR** ★

8 till midnight   Admission **5/-**

The Remo Quartet (1960)

Top Class Modern Music
The
Remo Quartet
All Enquiries to: Donald M. Andrew,
6, Davidson Road,
Liverpool, 13.

The Remo Four - L to R: Don Andrew, Harry Prytherch, Keith Stokes & Colin Manley

---

THE RHYTHMICS
Welcome the new beat page
THE RHYTHMICS
Are available for future bookings
ENQUIRIES
THE RHYTHMICS
Telephone: MOUNTWOOD 3618

RING RIGHT NOW FOR THE
REMBRANTS
'phone SYD   A. Gibb, 2
STO 4224   Barbara Avenue, Fazakerley, 10

BALLAD   WESTERN   POP   ROCK

The Reece Alan Five

Available for   75 Hamilton Road
Parties, Socials, Clubs   Liverpool, 5

ANNIVERSARY GREETINGS TO "MERSEY BEAT" FROM THE GROUP WITH THE 'BERRY' SOUND . . .
THE RENEGADES
ENQUIRIES: G. PECKHAM
41 BYRON ROAD, WALLASEY
Daytime: BIRkenhead 3087

RICKY GLEASON
is
back again !!
WITH THE
REBELS
Phone J. Cropper
Ormskirk 2317

The Roadrunners - L to R: John Peacock, Pete McKay, Mike Byrne, Mike Kontzle & Terry McCusker (1965)

DANCES - WEDDINGS - SOCIALS

RIKKI
AND HIS
REDSTREAKS

Manager
WATerloo 2269

Rikki
WATerloo 3026

The Riot Squad - L to R: Bob Reece, Alan Noone, Bill Ennis & Pete Ritson (1963)

INTRODUCING
4'6 WIRRALS BIGGEST BEAT NIGHT 4'6
RIVERSIDE

KING'S PARADE,   NEW BRIGHTON

Opening Night   March 16th
and each following Monday
7-45 to 10-45

T.V. Personalities:
☆☆☆   THE CONCORDS
☆☆☆   DERRY WILKIE & THE PRESSMEN
☆☆   THE INTERNS
☆☆   OLIVE CONWAY

Personally autographed photographs distributed during the evening.

Ricky & The Dominant Four

Rita and the Vogue

Manager C. GLOVER
175 Doulton Street, St. Helens, Lancs.

GEOFF TAGGART
Phone St. Helens 28137

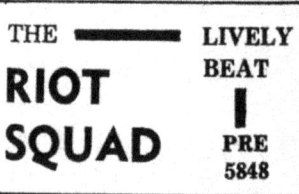

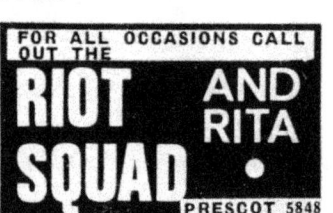

FOR ALL OCCASIONS
JOHNNY RINGO
AND
THE COLTS
HOT ROCK SPECIALISTS
(Manager A. Holt)
Early Bookings Available
PHONE ROYal 9393

Rangiora Rover Crew — Claughton

Present . . . .

★ *The Prowlers*

and

★ *The Rockefellers*

on SATURDAY, 5th DECEMBER, 1964

at ST. MARK'S, SLATEY ROAD . BIRKENHEAD

7-0 p.m. to 11-0 p.m.

Admission 3/6d. — *to be paid at door*

Bring your friends and meet new ones as well.

The Best for Beat in Birkenhead!

FAB! FAB! FAB!
NEW YEAR'S EVE BEAT CRUISE
ABOARD THE 'ROYAL IRIS'
DOWN THE MERSEY
8-30 p.m. from Liverpool Landing Stage
(Coaches leave from Manchester at 7 p.m.)
Non-stop dancing until 2-30 p.m. to
The Black Velvets
THE INFORMERS and
THREE DOTS AND A DASH others
REFRESHMENTS ● LICENSED BAR
HURRY! HURRY! HURRY! **15/-**
GET YOUR TICKETS NOW FROM
SIVEWRIGHT, BACON & CO.
SHIP CANAL HOUSE, KING STREET, MANCHESTER.
9 TITHEBARN STREET, LIVERPOOL
8 CAMBRIDGE STREET, ELLESMERE PORT,
or at LEWIS'S MANCHESTER OR LIVERPOOL TICKET BUREAU

Rory Storm & The Hurricanes

**Rory Storm & The Hurricanes
With a Butlins Redcoat**

Rumblin' Tum - Sink Club

ENJOY YOUR BIG BEAT SESSION ON T.S.M.V. 'ROYAL IRIS'

THREE HOUR MERSEY CRUISE. Sailing from Liverpool 8 p.m. each Saturday.

'THE GALVANISERS' and 'ROYAL MURISIANS' ORCHESTRA

Fully Licensed Bars Fare 5/- Refreshment Buffet

SHIP AVAILABLE FOR PRIVATE CHARTER Accommodation for 950 passengers
Enquiries to: Passenger Transport Manager, Seaview Road, Wallasey
Tel: NEW Brighton 6047

Dances — Parties — Social Functions

THE SANDGROUNDERS RHYTHM GROUP *with* **Tony Sands**

CONTACT:
MR. J. DEAN,
63 WINDSOR ROAD,
SOUTHPORT. TEL. 5563

FOR THE BEST IN BEAT..
THE SARACENS
Phone: J. ARCHER .. BOO 3942

The Sandgrounders at the Birkdale Labour Club

FOR THE BEST IN BEAT
THE
SCHATZ
TEL: SIM 3422
KIR 3116

The Saints (Liverpool)

JOHNNIE SANDON with THE REMO FOUR
Available 24 hours a day
Enquiries: Don Andrew,
6 Davidson Road, Liverpool 13

PEAK PROMOTIONS
Telephone: SEFton Park 3398
'SAVVA'
and the
DemoCrats
Agents for several Top Liverpool Combos

SECRETS
VIC GRACE
SEF 3962

MR. F. HOWARD   SEF. 7985
                EVENING
THE
"SETT"
FOR
DANCES.   CLUBS.   WEDDINGS.   ETC.

SOME OTHER GUYS
Gerry, Mick, Jim, Ray & Mike
Manager: R. O. Lamb.   22 Beech Ave., Upton
First Record Release Soon

FOR THAT MERSEY R & B—
THE SENATORS
ANF^{IELD} 6851 & 7697

The Senators

The Seftons

The Senators at the Pier Bar, New Brighton

Denny Seyton

CONGRATULATIONS TO "MERSEY BEAT" from LEE SHONDELL and the CAPITOLS

ENQUIRIES TO—
HARRY KEHOE — LARK LANE 6014
BE WISE — CAPITOLISE

Lee Shondell & The Capitols

ICE SKATING

SILVER BLADES, PRESCOT ROAD.

No MEMBERSHIP FEES. SESSIONS 2.15 & 7.15 DAILY. SATURDAYS 10.0, 2.15 AND 7.15. SUNDAYS AT 7.0. SUNDAY SKATING CLUB 10.0 AND 2.30. SKATE HIRE 1/3. TELEPHONE ANFIELD 1990.

FRIDAY: VIKKY LANE AND THE MOONLIGHTERS.

SATURDAY: THE (MANCHESTER) FEDERALS.

Shake at the Shakey

EVERY EVENING AT 7.30 p.m.
ALL NIGHT SESSIONS
EVERY SATURDAY NIGHT
AFTERNOONS FROM 12 noon
CLOSED ALL DAY TUESDAY
THE SHAKING AROUND CLUB
26 SLATER STREET (Off Bold St.)

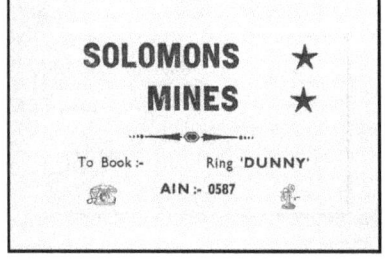

SOLOMONS ★
MINES ★

To Book :— Ring 'DUNNY'
AIN :- 0587

TO ALL BEAT GROUPS ON MERSEYSIDE SUNDAY, MARCH 22nd 12 noon ST. GEORGE'S HALL

Don't miss this fabulous chance to appear in the historic photograph of Liverpool's Beat!

THE FIRST 200 MEMBERS OF GROUPS WILL BE PAID £1 EACH

This is to be a photograph of all Merseyside Beat Groups

The German magazine "STERN", of Hamburg (the largest selling picture magazine in Continental Europe) invites all groups to appear on this unique photograph with their guitars and drums.

ONLY ENTIRE GROUPS WITH THEIR INSTRUMENTS ARE WANTED FOR THIS PICTURE.

The sitting will last about an hour.

EVERY GROUP ON THIS PHOTOGRAPH WILL RECEIVE ONE COPY FREE OF CHARGE AFTER PUBLICATION IN STERN MAGAZINE

Don't Forget Your Instruments

THANK YOU, "MERSEY BEAT," FOR PUBLISHING THE BEST MUSICAL PAPER WE HAVE EVER READ

from

THE SORRALS

THE GROUP WITH THE "SAXY" SOUND

Telephone: HUNts Cross 2809

THE SOUL SEEKERS R & B
WAT. 7554

The Sink Club

SONNY GROSS AGENCY

SOLE REPRESENTATION — **THE KIRKBYS**

THE X—L's ● ● ● ● ● THE SNEAKERS

453 BARLOW MOOR ROAD, CHORLTON-CUM-HARDY
MANCHESTER 21 — Tel: CHORLTON 4708

"S.O.S" NORTH WEST COAST BEAT CHAMPIONS 1967
Manager: Mr. S. Woods, 37 Lime Avenue, Weaverham, Nr. Northwich, Cheshire or phone Frodsham 3477

The S.O.S.

Dean Stacey
and the Dynamic
DETONATORS
TEL. STO. 2538

The Spectacular
SPECTRES
Book them now
MIKE
STO 4681

SPIDERMEN
LIVER
ENTERTAINMENTS
2 RICHMOND WAY
HESWALL

HESWALL 4638
BIR 7442 (day)

STORYVILLE
★
13 TEMPLE STREET
(off DALE STREET)
LIVERPOOL

The Slightly Sensational
ST. LOUIS CHECKS
Phone AUG 2692

SOUL MUSIC
TABS
SAXOPHONE — GUITAR
DRUMS — VOCALIST — BASS
RAY — GATacre 2406

The Stereos

KEEP UP THE GOOD WORK, MERSEY BEAT, FROM
WAYNE STEPHENS AND THE VIKINGS
ELLESMERE PORT 1439
ROCK FERRY 5280

THE STARLIGHT ★ ☆ ★
MERSEYSIDE'S MOST EXCITING BEAT CLUB
THIS WEEK'S ATTRACTIONS
THURSDAY: SOUTHBANK 4 & THE STRETTONS
FRIDAY: THE EXCERTS — SATURDAY: THE PRESSMEN
SUNDAY: THE CITY BEATS   LIMITED FREE MEMBERSHIP
MINIMUM AGE 17
96b WAVERTREE ROAD, LIVERPOOL 7 (Entrance in Juno Street)

SUPREME BEAT SCENE
THE
TEENBEAT
CLUB
Corona Ballroom,
College Road,
Crosby.
FRIDAYS
SATURDAYS
SUNDAYS

Congratulations to Mersey Beat on First Anniversary
GEOFF STACEY AND THE WANDERERS
Merseyside's Most Musically Perfect Group
Manager: John George, jr.
Telephone: Widnes 3571

```
* * * * * * * * * * * * * * * *
*                              *
*    THE THREE                 *
*      DEUCES                  *
*  MUSIC WITH RHYTHM AND       *
*          BEAT                *
*     Available for Weddings   *
*       Parties, Dances, etc.  *
*          Manager:            *
*       MR. A. J. RANKIN       *
*          The Melodisc        *
*  102 West Derby Road, L'pool 6 *
*       Day: ANF. 5815         *
*       Night: HALE 2329       *
* * * * * * * * * * * * * * * *
```

ROY W. COCKEN
105, Stamforden Drive.
Liverpool, 19.

GAR 4740

Johnny Templer AND THE Hi-Cats

Karl Terry & The Crusiers
At the Chateau Roux - France
L to R: Geoff Caddick,
Gordon Templeton, Karl Terry
& Nicolete Moran (1962)

For The Best in Rock Groups Ring
STUART ENTERPRISES
50 STUART RD., WATERLOO, LIVERPOOL, 22

Mersey 4	The Inbeats
The Connoisseurs	The Orbit 5
The Chessmen	Toledo 4
The Motifs	The Marchions
The Big 4	The Berry Pickers
The Invaders	The Jensons.

Business: WAT 7554   Night: Ormskirk 2868
                              WAT 7587

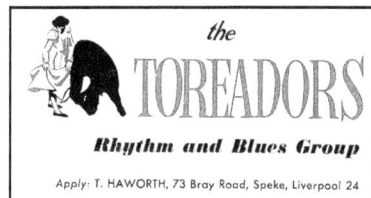

the **TOREADORS**
Rhythm and Blues Group
Apply: T. HAWORTH, 73 Bray Road, Speke, Liverpool 24
or Phone HUNts Cross 2389 (Between 5 and 7-30)

THE **THUNDERBIRDS**
"Music with a Beat"
FOR YOUR
Dance - Club - Private Party - Barbecue
All enquiries to:—
MIKE BYRNE,   Telephone:
169, Whitehedge Road,   CENtral 0298
Liverpool, 19.   (9-30 a.m—5-0 p.m.)

TOKENS
TOKENS
TOKENS
SOLE   MANAGEMENT
Mike Chamberlain
WIGAN 83424
ROYAL 8897

TOMORROWS P E O P L E
beat group
Dances ★ Weddings ★ Clubs ★ Functions
Presented by:

Tillie with the Talismen

Ticket Price 5/- for The Rhythm & Blues Spectacular

'Thank Your Lucky Stars'

Staged in the TOWER BALLROOM New Brighton
Thursday 17th May, 1962. 7-30 p.m. to Midnight
Late Transport — Licensed Bars & Buffet

Starring "Mr. Rock 'N' Roll" Himself

The Fabulous **JERRY LEE LEWIS** and the Echoes

Plus a Galaxy of Ten Star Groups

The Big Three	Billy Kramer with The Coasters
The Pressmen	Lee Castle & The Barons
The Undertakers	Kingsize Taylor & The Dominoes
The Strangers	Steve Day & The Drifters
Vincent Earl & The Zeros	Rip Van Winkle & The Rip It Ups

Britain's Mightiest Ever Non-Stop Big Beat Show Dance!
A Bob Wooler Rockerscope '62 Presentation
Read all about it in "Mersey Beat" — Out 2nd May

ALL THE LEADING VENUES ON MERSEYSIDE YOU WILL FIND

GUS TRAVIS AND THE MIDNIGHTERS

LEADING THE WAY WITH
RHYTHM & BLUES NUMBERS
COUNTRY & WESTERN NUMBERS
COMEDY NUMBERS
FRENCH TWIST NUMBERS

Representatives:
G.B. Entertainments Inc.
Enquiries:
A. G. Watts,
3 Monks Way,
West Kirby,
Wirral.

THE TOWER BALLROOM
(NEW BRIGHTON TOWER CO.)
PRESENTS

ON AUGUST BANK HOLIDAY
3rd AUGUST FROM 1 p.m.—11-30 p.m.

8 Stupendous Groups — For Only **5/-!!**

THE BIGGEST BEAT SHOW FOR MILES AROUND!

THE BLACKWELLS — THE DETOURS
THE NIGHTWALKERS — THE ZEROS
THE BREAKDOWNS — THE TRIUMPHS
THE MODES — THE MEMPHIS COMBO

PLUS YOUR ACE COMPERES:
GERRY NORTON AND MIKE LEE

DON'T MISS THIS MAMMOTH SHOW!

ELEVEN GREAT RECORDING GROUPS ARE FEATURED IN THE GREAT SPECTACULAR EVENT YOU CANNOT MISS.

NORTHERN SOUNDS 1963
AT NEW BRIGHTON TOWER
FRIDAY, JULY 26. 7.30 to 1 a.m.

STARRING
BILLY J. KRAMER
WITH THE DAKOTAS.
FREDDIE AND THE DREAMERS
THE BIG THREE

AND (In alphabetical order)
THIS FABULOUS LINE-UP:
THE DENNISONS
Plus
THE FOURMOST
Plus
MARK PETERS & THE SILHOUETTES
Plus
EARL PRESTON & THE T.T.s
Plus
JOHNNY SANDON & THE REMO FOUR
Plus
FREDDIE STARR & THE MIDNIGHTERS
Plus
SONNY WEBB & THE CASCADES.
and, just returning from Hamburg,
THE UNDERTAKERS

WOW! What a Night! Make sure of your Tickets NOW. 6/- (in advance) 7/- (on night) for this magnificent, mammoth BOB WOOLER Production.

BEAT-AN-BLUES

THE TROLLS

Weddings, Dances, Etc.

Phone:— Steve STO 1315 — Phone:— John STO 4674

BEAT-AN-BLUES

THE TROLLS

WEDDINGS · DANCES · ETC

Phone - Steve STO 1315 — Phone - John STO 4674

The Tudors

The Tudors

The Tudors- L to R: Terry Tasker, Stuart Gaukroger, Les Pinch & Keith Dutton

The Tributes

The Tropics at Fisher & Ludlow, Kirkby (1963)

The Trolls at the Highfield Tenants Club

THE T.T.'s WITH AMOS BONNY

35 MOSCOW DRIVE, LIVERPOOL 13   TEL: STOneycroft 3141

IT'S NEW   PARAMOUNT'S   **IT'S NEW**

TWIST-O-BEAT CLUB
AT THE WALLASEY
GROSVENOR BALLROOM
EVERY FRIDAY commencing 29th MARCH

★ 2 All-Star Groups every Friday ★

OPENING NIGHT — TO-MORROW FRIDAY

JOHNNY TEMPLER AND THE HI-CATS

PLUS

SONNY WEBB AND THE CASCADES

FRIDAY 5th APRIL

THE SEARCHERS and THE CITY KINGS

MEMBERS 4/-   NON-MEMBERS 5/-   8 to 11 p.m.   JOIN NOW
MEMBERSHIP FEE FOR SEASON 1/- APPLICATION FORMS FROM
Grosvenor Ballroom or 67 Seabank Road or ring NEW Brighton 1232

The Undertakers in Berlin

BALLAD   WESTERN   POP   ROCK

THE VALIANTS
Vocal and Instrumental Group

Available for   62 St Domingo Vale,
Parties, Dances, Clubs   Liverpool, 5

The Undertakers (both images)

WHAT'S YOUR NAME
Words and Music by IAN HUNTER

Recorded by **THE VALKYRIES** on PARLOPHONE

2/6

THE VAMPIRES
and London R & B Group
THE AUTHENTICS
Dick Wilson. WAT 6786.

FOR ALL ROUND ENTERTAINMENT

Dances
Parties
Clubs
Etc.

THE VANDUNES

R & B's Group

Will Travel

Ring
AIntree 7549

MANAGER: N. FLAYE
MOSTYN AVE.,
AINTREE,
LIVERPOOL.

CARL VINCENT
and the
FABULOUS COUNTS
★ Rock and Roll Entertainment ★

Booking Manager:
Harold Hill.   Phone Bootle 3815

VICTORIANA

77 VICTORIA ST., LIVERPOOL 1.
Central 2396
(Strictly Members Only)
TO-NIGHT:
THE DETOURS
Plus THE VIX (Our Resident Group)
To-morrow:
THE WASHINGTON SOUL BAND
with THE VIX
Sunday:
THE BEECHWOODS
and THE VIX (Our Resident Group)
* * Wednesday next * *
(January 10th, 1968)
P. P. ARNOLD
Watch 'ALL SYSTEMS FREEMAN'
To-night BBC 1 at 6.40 p.m. for
preview on which she sings her
latest record:
(If you think you're)
GROOVY.

Sandy Dean ★ Mark Peters
& the **VEETONES**

MAYOR OF WALLASEY'S CHARITY FUND
AND NEW BRIGHTON A.F.C.

7.0 p.m. to midnight   300 SWINGING MINUTES   7.0 p.m. to midnight

MARATHON FLOODLIT BEAT FESTIVAL

with the

SEARCHERS

and the

MERSEYBEATS

also including

CHICK GRAHAM with the **COASTERS**
THE CONCORDS   **THE KARACTERS**

BOB WOOLER

DJ/Compere of The Cavern and Radio Luxembourg

OPPORTUNITY OF WINNING   FOR ADVANCED TICKET HOLDERS ONLY
AUTOGRAPHED L.P. RECORDS

THURSDAY, MAY 14th

NEW BRIGHTON FOOTBALL GROUND, MOLYNEUX DRIVE
LARGE CAR PARK
Refreshments available   Late Transport

Tickets 10/6   At Door 12/6
From STROTHERS, LEWIS'S, RUSHWORTHS, CRANES, USHERS AND
VENTRIS ARDEN

THERE'S **BIG BEAT BREWIN'** AT THE NEW

WITCH'S CAULDRON CLUB

GRAND RE-OPENING NIGHT

THIS SAT!
**BLACK KNIGHTS
THE DENIMS**

THE WIRRAL'S TOP BEAT CLUB
Now under new management

TOP GROUPS
every
THURS.—FRI.
SAT.—SUN.

RECORDS & AUDITION GROUPS EVERY MON.—TUES.—WED.

COME AND ENJOY THE UNIQUE ATMOSPHERE OF THE CAULDRON at

62 ALBION ST
NEW BRIGHTON
(BACK OF VICTORIA HOTEL)
2 minutes from Station.

NEW 5849

THE WARRIORS
Decca Records

FOR THE AMBITIOUS GROUP——
HAVE YOU CUT YOUR FIRST DISC YET ?
CONSULT
WELSBY SOUND RECORDINGS
RECORDING and PUBLIC ADDRESS ENGINEERS
About Recording, Production and Publication of Your Records whether 1, 100 or 1,000 Copies

RAINHILL **LIVERPOOL** **RAINHILL 143**

THERE'S BIG BEAT BREWIN'
AT THE NEW
WITCH'S CAULDRON CLUB
WIRRAL'S TOP BEAT CLUB

THURSDAY COUNTDOWNS   ★   FRIDAY GALVANISERS
SATURDAY MYSTERIES   SUNDAY ALPHAS

MONDAY, TUESDAY, WEDNESDAY BIG RECORD SESSION, PLUS AUDITION GROUPS
62 ALBION STREET, NEW BRIGHTON

THERE'S BIG BEAT BREWIN'
AT THE NEW
WITCH'S CAULDRON CLUB

The re-opening of The Wirral's Top Beat Club has resulted in packed houses. For YOU we present:

Thursday, August 6th: **THE SUBTERANES**
Friday, August 7th: **THE NEW PRESSMEN**
Saturday, August 8th: **BOBBY AND THE BACHELORS**
Sunday, August 9th: **THE VIBRATORS**

62 ALBION STREET, NEW BRIGHTON
(Back of Victoria Hotel)
Free admission offered to girls wearing Topless Dresses!

BOILING HOT BEAT
AT THE NEW
WITCH'S CAULDRON CLUB
Wirral's Top Beat Centre

THURSDAY — **POETS**
FRIDAY — **DEANS**
SAT. AFTERNOON & UNDER 15s — **PRESSMEN**
SAT. EVENING — **DRESDENS**
SUN. AFTERNOON — **MR. LEE & CO.**
SUN. EVENING — **KINGFISHERS**

62 ALBION STREET, NEW BRIGHTON
(Back of Victoria Hotel)

The Young Britains
L to R: Jimmy Cross, Colin Prescot, Gerry Norton, Ray Lee & Colin Lee

The Zeniths (1964)

THE ZEPHYRS
ROCK GROUP

Manager: B. MORRIS
56, Leach Lane, Sutton, St. Helens

The Zephyrs
L to R:
Johnny Olive
Ray Malcolm
Geoff Taggart
Gordon Marsh
& Les Stocks

Finally - here's 3 groups that I believe were 'Liverpool' based but I was unable to find any information on them - can anyone help identify them?

If you can help, please email the information to: www.VelocePress.com

INDEX

GROUP STORIES (110 GROUPS)

KEY: Page numbers in **BOLD** type are the main story. Page numbers in REGULAR type have an association to the main story.

ABSTRACTS: 5, **16-19**, 81, 280
STEVE ALDO: **20-23, 150-151,** 238, 319, 342
APPROACHERS: **24-25,** 81, 82, 83
AZTECS: **26-27,** 118, 153

GERRY BACH & THE BEATHOVENS: 15, **28-30,** 113
BANSHEES: **31-33,** 69, 245, 322, 366, 381
BLUE SOUNDS: **34-35,** 245
BOBBY & THE BACHELORS: **36-37,** 373
BO-WEEVILS: **38-40,** 245
BROTHERS GRIMM: **41-42**

CADILLAC & THE PLAYBOYS: **43-48,** 63, 73, 98, 99, 406
WAYNE CALVERT & THE CIMARRONS: **49-50,** 289
CAREFREES: **51-53**
TONY CARLTON & THE MERSEYBOYS: **54-56**
CASUALS: 8, **57-59**
CENSORS: **60-62**
CHRIS & THE AUTOCRATS: **63-64,** 373
CITY BEATS: **65-68**
CLANSMEN: 33, **69-71,** 387
CLASSICS: 44, 45, **72-73,** 97, 195
CORSAIRS: **74-75,** 249, 250
COUNTDOWNS: **76-77**

DALEKS: **78**
DEANS: 18, 24, 25, **79-81,** 280
DEFIANTS: 25, **82-84**
DELEMERES: **85-87,** 392
DETROITS: **88-89,** 235
DIPLOMATS: 8, **90-92**
DOMINANT FOUR: **93-95,** 285, 316, 374, 416
DOWNBEATS: 45, 73, **96-99**
DUKE DUVAL'S ROCKERS: **100-105**

EASY THREE: **106-107**

FAIRYTALE: **108-109**
FIRECRESTS: **110-112,** 126, 288
5 A.M. EVENT: 29, **113-115,** 204, 295, 319
FIVE TRIBUTES: **116-119**
FOCAL POINT: **120-121**
FOUR GENTS & BERNADETTE: **122-123**
FOUR MUSKETEERS: 8, **124-125**
FOUR ORIGINALS: 111, **126-127**

GEORGIANS: 76, **128-131,** 374
GIBSON JAMES BAND: **132-133**
GLOBETROTTERS: **134-135,** 207, 276, 315

431

HARLEMS: 33, **136-139,** 319, 320
HERALDS: 140-141
HUNTSMEN: 142-143

IAN & THE REBELS: 42, 58, **144-145,** 244
INFORMERS: 146-148
IN CROWD: 149-151

'J' & THE JUNIORS: 26, **152-153**
JACOBEATS: 154-156
ROGER JAMES FOUR: 157-161, 400
JENSONS: 76, **162-163**

KARACTERS: 164-165
KESTRALS – SABRES: 166-167
KONDA GROUP: 168-171

L.S.D. 172-173, 402
RAY LEWIS & THE TREKKERS: 174-176
LIVERPOOL RAIDERS: 177-179

MAFIA GROUP: 39, 65, **180-183**
MAGGOTS: 184-188
MAGIC LANTERNS: 189-193
RAY MALCOLM & THE SUNSETS: 63, 72, **194-199,** 339, 429
MEDALLIONS: 200-201, 276
MIKE & THE THUNDERBIRDS: 115, **202-204,** 261
MINITS: 135, **205-208,** 315
MOONRAKERS: 209-210
MOROCKANS: 36, **211-213**
MOTOWNS: 204, **214-216**
MYSTERY FOUR: 217-218

OGI & THE FLINTSTONES: 202, **219-222,** 264

PERFUMED GARDEN: 223-225
PIKKINS: 226-228, 301
PILGRIMS: 229-231
PROWLERS: 13, 89, 200, **232-236,** 267, 413

TOMMY QUICKLY: 20, **237-239,** 260, 297
QUINTONES: 240-241

RENICKS: 8, 58, 145, **242-244**
RIGG: 35, 39, **245-247**
RIOT SQUAD: 74, 75, 197, **248-251,** 416
ROCKING VICKERS: 8, **252-255**
PAUL ROGERS: 256-258

JOHNNY SANDON: 13, 238, **259-262**
SANTONES (ANZAKS): 263-265
SARACENS: 234, **266-268**
SASSENACHS: 184, 259, **269-271**
SAVVA & THE DEMOCRATS: 272-275
SHAKE-SPEARS: 135, 201, **276-278**
SOLOMON'S MINES: 18, 25, 81, **279-281,** 295
SOME OTHER GUYS: 282-283
GEOFF STACEY & THE WANDERERS: 94, **284-286,** 332

TEENAGE REBELS: 287-289
THUNDERBEATS: 8, **290-292**
TIMEBEATS: 115, **293-295**
TIMEBOX: 54, 230, **296-300**
TOKENS: 227, **301-302**
TOMMY & THE METRONOMES: 303-305
TRIBUTES (ROBBIE GRAY SOUL BAND): **306-309**, 425
TROPICS: **310-312,** 425

VAMPIRES: 135, 207, **313-315,** 370
VIC TAKES FOUR: 93, **316-317**
VINCE & THE VOLCANOES: 114, 115, 136, 204, 222, **318-320,** 328
CARL VINCENT & THE COUNTS: 321-323
VOCALS: 324

WARRIORS: 325-328
CLIFF WARWICK & THE DOLLYBEATS: 329-330
DERRY WILKIE: 12, 30, 103, 181, 285, **331-334**
WITNESSES: 335-336

DEE YOUNG & THE PONTIACS: 195, 196, **337-340**

ZEROS: 341-344

LINE-UPS (133 ADDITIONAL GROUPS)

AARONS: 345
ADAM & THE SINNERS: 345
ADDS: 345
ADMINS: 346
ALAMOS: 346
ALIBIS: 346
ALPHABEATS: 346
ARGONAUTS: 346

BEATWOODS: 346
BECKET'S KIN: 347
BLACK DIAMONDS: 347
BLUE BOYS: 347
BLUE DIAMONDS: 347
BLUE PRINTS: 347
BLUES ANGELS: 347
BOBBY & THE CADILLACS: 348
BONES OF MEN: 348
BONNEVILLES: 348
BREAKDOWNS: 348
BROKERS: 348
BUFFALOES: 348

CASUALS: 349
CAVEMEN: 349
CENTAURS: 349
CHEETAHS: 349
CHRIS & THE QUIET ONES: 350
CLIMAKS: 350
COLUMBIANS: 350
CORDELLES: 350
CROSBYS: 350

DAWNBREAKERS: 351
GENE DAY & THE DJANGO-BEATS: 351
DEACONS: 352
BUDDY DEAN & THE TEACHERS: 352
PETE DEMOS & THE DEMONS: 352
DENIMS: 352
DIABLOS: 352
D.J. & THE FOUR JETS: 353
DRESDENS: 353
DRIFTING SANDS: 353
DRUMBEATS: 353
DU-FAY: 354

ELEKTONES: 354
EXIT: 354
EXPRESSIONS: 354

FABZ: 354
FIREFLYS: 354
FLAMES: 355
FUTURISTS: 355

GERRY OWEN FOUR: 355
GOOD TIMES: 355
GRADUATES: 355

HANK & THE DRIFTERS: 355
BRUCE HARRIS & THE CAVALIERS: 355
HUNGRY I's: 355

ICE BLUES: 356
IMPACT: 356
INBEATS: 356
INMATES (1): 356
INMATES (2): 356
INTERNS: 356

JAY-ELS: 357
JERRY & THE JUVENILES: 357
JOKERS: 357

KEGMEN: 357
KEITH'S KIND: 357
KEYSTONE COMBO: 358
KINGFISHERS: 358
KINGPINS: 358
KNIGHTS: 358
KORDAS: 358
KWANS: 359

LAWRENCE JAMES FEDERATION: 359
LAY-BYS 359
LEGENDS (1): 359
LEGENDS (2): 359

MARESCAS: 359
MARINERS: 359
MATADORS: 360
MEMPHIS R&B COMBO: 360
MERSEY BLUEBEATS: 360
M.I.5: 360
MOONSTONES: 360
MOVEMENT: 361
MUSTANGS (1): 361
MUSTANGS (2): 361

NUTROCKERS: 361

OTTERS: 362

PALADINS: 362
JOHNNY PAUL & THE DEE JAYS: 362
PHAROH & THE EXILES: 363
PHASE FOUR: 363
JOHNNY PRESIDENT & THE SENATORS: 363
PRESSURE POINTS: 363
PRINCIPALS: 364
PULSATORS: 364
PYRAMIDS: 364

REBEL ROUSERS: 364
RHYTHM AMALGAMATED: 364
RHYTMICS: 364
RICKY & THE RESTLESS FOUR: 365
RONDELS: 365

SANDGROUNDERS: 365
SCORPIONS: 365
SCRIBES: 366
SINCLAIRS: 366
SMOKESTACKS: 366
SOUL SEARCHERS: 366
SOUL SEEKERS: 366
SOUNDS PLUS ONE: 367
SPEKEASYS: 367
St. JAMES INFIRMARY: 367
STROLLERS (1): 367
STROLLERS (2): 367

TAGG: 368
TEENBEATS: 368
TEMPOS: 368
TENABEATS: 368
T.J's: 369
TOMMY & THE SATELLITES: 369
TOMBSTONES: 369
TOREADORS: 369
TREK: 369
TRIDENTS: 370
TRIFFIDS: 370
TUDORS: 370

VANDUNES: 370
VAQUEROS: 371
VARASOUNDS: 371
VIBRATORS: 371
VULCANS: 371

WISHBONES: 371

ZENITHS: 371

SCRAPBOOK PHOTO INDEX: 377-429

ALBY & THE SORRALS: 379
ALMOST BLUES: 380
ARGONAUTS: 380
BANSHEES: 381
PETE BEST FOUR: 381
DAVE BELL & THE BELL BOYS: 381
BLACK CATS: 382
BLACK VELVETS: 382
BO-WEEVILS: 383
CADILLAC & THE PLAYBOYS: 384
THEM CALDERSTONES: 384
CASUALS: 384
LEE CASTLE & THE BARONS: 385
CHANTS: 386
CHEETAHS & RONNIE INCE: 387
CHESSMEN: 387
CITADELS: 387
CLANSMEN: 387
CLAYTON SQUARES: 387
COLONEL BAGSHOTS BUCKET BAND: 387
CORALS: 388
COSMONAUGHTS: 389
CROUPIERS: 389
CURIOSITY SHOPPE: 390
DEFENDERS: 391
DELEMERES: 390, 392
EXILES: 393
FOUR DIMENSIONS & TIFFANY: 393, 394
FEW: 394
JOHNNY GENTLE: 394, 395
JIM GRETTY: 395
HAMMERS: 396
DANNY HAVOC & THE VENTURES: 396
HIDEAWAYS: 397
IAN & THE ZODIACS: 397
IRON DOOR CLUB: 399
ROGER JAMES FOUR: 400
TOMMY JORDAN: 400
KATZ: 400
KARL TERRY & LANCE RAILTON: 401
KINETIC: 401
KRUZADS: 402
MR. LEE & CO. 402, 403
L.S.D. 402
LYNETTE CAWOOD (Bo-Weevils): 404
MANCHESTER PLAYBOYS: 406
MARRACAS: 406

BERYL MARSDEN: 406
MASTERMINDS: 407
MERSEYBEATS: 408
MERSEY MONSTERS: 407
MODERN BLUES QUARTET: 408
MOVEMENT: 408
N-SIGNS: 410
NASHPOOL FOUR: 408, 409
NOCTURNS: 410
PHILLIPS RECORDING STUDIO: 411
PEPPERMINT LOUNGE: 412
JOHNNY PRESIDENT & THE SENATORS: 413
PROFILES: 413
PROWLERS: 413
REMO QUARTET: 415
REMO FOUR: 415
ROADRUNNERS: 416
RIOT SQUAD: 416
RICKY & THE DOMINANT FOUR: 416
EARL ROYCE & THE OLYMPICS: 417
RUMBLIN' TUM – SINK CLUB: 417, 421
RORY STORM: 417
ROYAL IRIS: 418
SAINTS: 418
SANDGROUNDERS: 418
SEFTONS: 419
SENATORS: 419
DENNY SEYTON: 420
LEE SHONDELL & THE CAPITOLS: 420
S.O.S. 421
SOUL SEEKERS: 421
STEREOS: 422
KARL TERRY & THE CRUSIERS: 423
TILLIE & THE TALISMEN: 423
TOWER BALLROOM: 424
GUS TRAVIS: 424
TRIBUTES: 425
TROLLS: 425
TROPICS: 425
TUDORS: 425
UNDERTAKERS: 426
VALKYRIES: 426
VEETONES (Mark Peters & Sandy Dean): 427
WARRIORS: 428
YOUNG BRITAINS: 429
ZENITHS: 429
ZEPHYRS: 429

NOW THAT YOU HAVE READ THE BOOK ~ WOULD YOU LIKE TO HEAR THE MUSIC?

CD Insert (rear)

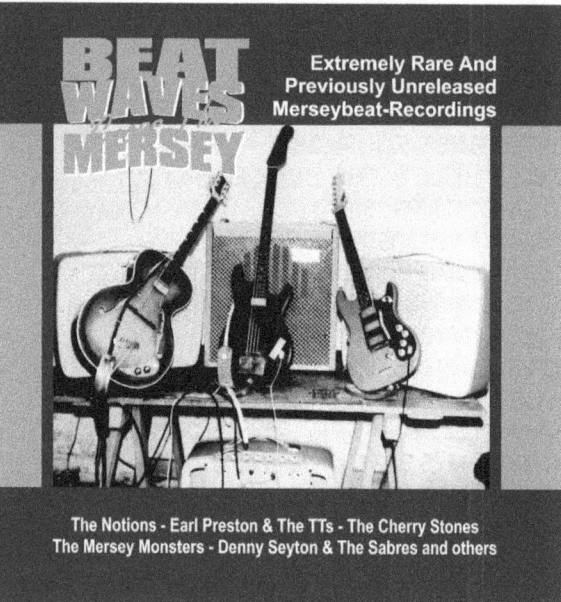

CD Insert (front)

A series of CD's that compliment the stories in this book. All original recordings from the 1960's, many of them never previously released.
Plus some live recordings from the famous Liverpool clubs, all digitally re-mastered.

For additional details, pricing and online purchasing information please visit our web-site:
www.velocepress.com/books/arts/

As a 'thank you' to everyone that purchased a copy of this book please enter the code MBWSOG in the coupon box in order to receive your special discounted pricing.

Here's just a sample of the groups (and the songs) that you will find on these CD's:

The Undertakers - Hold On I'm Coming; the Notions - Another Time; Gus Travis - My Babe; the Prowlers - I'm A King Bee; the Rebels - Little Queenie; the Black Knights - That Feeling; the Defenders - Mr. Soul; Alby & the Sorrals - Why; Johnny Ringo & the Colts - Mean Woman; Clay Ellis & the Raiders - Put The Blame On Me; J.J. & the Hi-Lites - Yes Tonight Josephine; Mike Mulloy & the Mountwoods - Parchment Farm; the Kirkbys - Friends And Relations; L.S.D. - Oh Carol; the Mersey Monsters - Wait A Minute; the Original All-Stars - Hide And Seek; Them Calderstones - Children And Flowers; the Profiles - I Can Tell; the Victims - I'd Never Find Another You; the Tabs - Don't You Hear Me Calling; Sounds Plus One - Girl Of My Dreams; the Runaways - Back Again

ALSO NUMBERS BY: Ricky Gleason & the Topspots; the Topspots; the Premiers; the Blackhawks; the Newtowns; a 1966 live-tape of the Kruzads; the Cordes; the Panthers; the Motifs; the Deans; two recordings of Perfumed Garden; the complete Connoisseurs recordings; a terrific live-recording of Ogi & the Flintstones; as well as Earl Preston & the TTs; Denny Seyton & the Sabres; the Clayton Squares; Cy Tucker; Almost Blues; Terry Hines Sextet; T.L.s Bluesicians

THE REVISED EDITION OF 'THE SOUND WITH THE POUND' ~ 'BEAT WAVES 'CROSS THE MERSEY'

Featuring the complete stories of 164 Merseyside groups of the 1960's.
NONE of these stories are included in "Some Other Guys".
Also includes an additional 100 line-ups, PLUS an additional list of 344 group names
for a total of 607 groups!

Once my first book, "The Sound With The Pound", was published, I began to receive communications from many of the musicians mentioned in the book that, for one reason or another, I had previously been unable to contact. Some of them had lost touch with their fellow group members and some no longer lived in Liverpool or even in the UK. These new contacts were able to provide me with additional information such that I felt a revised version of "The Sound With The Pound" was necessary. Ultimately, this resulted in the publication of a completely updated edition titled, "Beat Waves 'Cross The Mersey", which contains significant additions to my original publication.

The information I received through these new, direct contacts with the musicians, also led me to make the decision to write this follow-up book. Leaving all those interesting stories and line-ups behind, or ignoring them because they were not included in "Beat Waves 'Cross The Mersey" would, in my opinion, have been a historical sin. And then all these wonderful photos, these alone were worth a book . . . .

"Beat Waves 'Cross The Mersey" is possibly the most comprehensive anthology of the 'Merseybeat' era. The book chronicles the complete stories of 164 groups, that either recorded, or played a substantial role in creating the Mersey Sound and the Merseybeat era and it is a fitting companion to this publication. 547 Pages, 482 black & white illustrations, 7.4 x 9.7 inches (18.8 x 24.6 cm). The revised and updated edition includes an additional 142 illustrations and 112 additional pages.

Publication date: July 2012 ~ ISBN 9781588502018 or ISBN 1588502015
For additional details, pricing and online purchasing information please visit our web-site:
www.velocepress.com/books/arts/

ANOTHER 'MERSEYBEAT' BOOK FROM: www.VelocePress.com

THIS BOOK MAY BE PURCHASED ONLINE AT www.velocepress.com/books/arts/ PAYMENT BY PAYPAL AND SHIPPED DIRECTLY TO YOU, FROM OUR DISTRIBUTION CENTERS IN THE USA, UK & AUSTRALIA

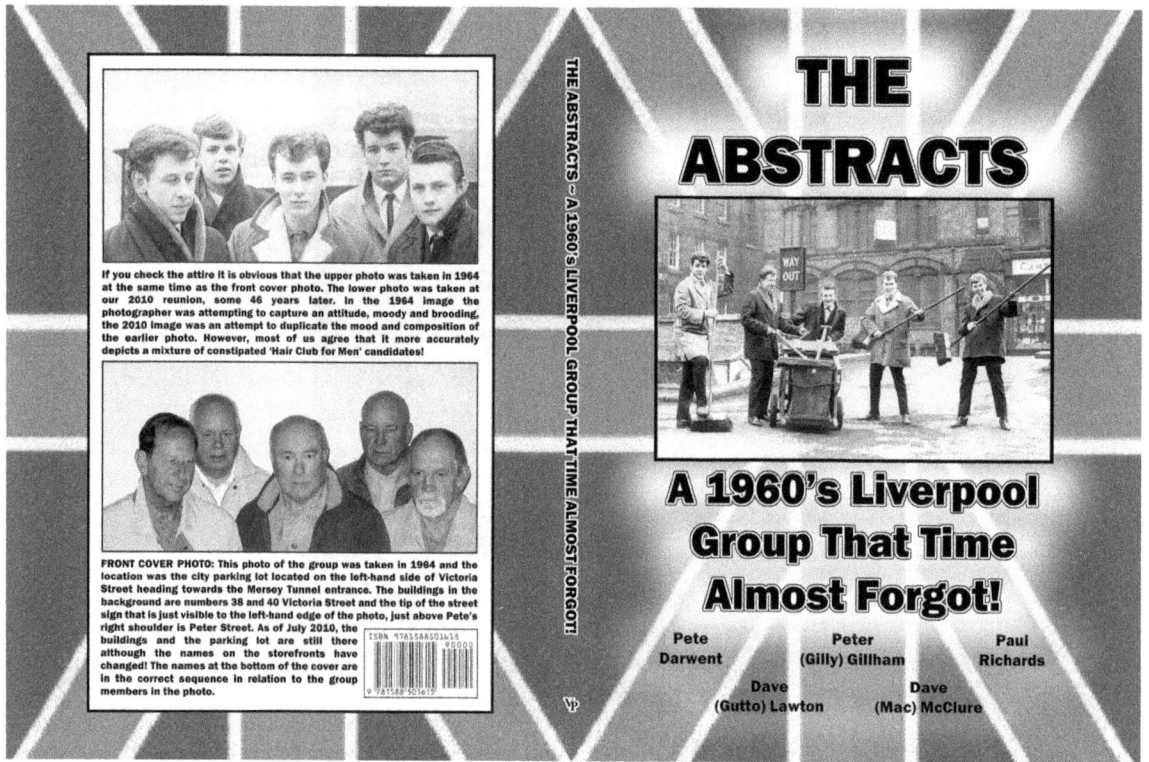

Rear Cover | Front Cover

148 pages, 162 illustrations, size 8.5 x 11 inches. The 1960's were a time of change and uncertainty. In 1961 the Berlin wall was built, in 1962 the Cuban Missile Crisis erupted, in 1963 JFK was assassinated, and on February 7, 1964 the Beatles arrived in New York to be welcomed by 10,000 screaming fans and music, as the world knew it, would never be the same again.

While the Beatles are by far the most famous Liverpool group of the era, they did not create the 'Mersey Sound', it created them. Unfortunately, it's sad that a great era of musical history will only be documented for future generations by the multitude of books that have been written about them. Liverpool in the 60's was a wondrous place, it was alive with music and the sheer number of local musicians and the depth of the talent pool was mind numbing.

Depending on your method of research, you will find that there were between 750 to 950 Liverpool based groups performing at any one time during the early to mid 1960's. So here's a story of one of the not-so-famous groups that's part of that total. While their story will always be overshadowed by those that made the 'big time', it is an honest and down to earth tale and a fairly typical representation of the many hundreds of other groups that created the 'Mersey Sound' and the real Merseybeat era.

Colour Edition: ISBN 9781588501615 or 1588501612
Black & White Edition: ISBN 9781588501646 or ISBN 1588501647

ADDITIONAL COPIES OF THIS BOOK (and other VelocePress books) MAY BE PURCHASED ONLINE AT

www.VelocePress.com

PAYMENT BY PayPal AND SHIPPED DIRECTLY TO YOU, FROM OUR DISTRIBUTION CENTERS IN THE USA, UK & AUSTRALIA

ALSO AVAILABLE THROUGH THE FOLLOWING UK, USA & AUSTRALIAN SUPPLIERS:

Available in the UK from:

Adlibris.com
Amazon.co.uk
Bertrams
Blackwell
Book Depository
Coutts
Gardners
Mallory International
Paperback Shop
Eden Interactive Ltd.
Aphrohead
I.B.S – STL U.K

Available in the USA from:

Ingram
Amazon.com
Baker & Taylor
Barnes & Noble
NACSCORP
Espresso Book Machine

Available in Australia from:

TheNile.com.au
RainbowBooks.com.au
DA Information Services
ALS Library Services
Dennis Jones & Associates
Emporium Books Online
James Bennett
PeterPal.com.au

If for any reason you are experiencing difficulty in purchasing a copy of this book, please contact us by email at: info@VelocePress.com and we will be happy to assist you.

© 2012 Veloce Enterprises Inc., San Antonio, TX 78230, USA

All rights reserved. This work may not be reproduced or transmitted in any form without the express written consent of the publisher.

Lightning Source UK Ltd.
Milton Keynes UK
UKHW030628280721
387905UK00007B/520